Dying on the Job

Dying on the Job

Murder and Mayhem in the American Workplace

Ronald D. Brown

ROWMAN & LITTLEFIELD PUBLISHERS, INC.
Lanham • Boulder • New York • Toronto • Plymouth, UK

Published by Rowman & Littlefield Publishers, Inc.
A wholly owned subsidary of The Rowman & Littlefield Publishing Group, Inc.
4501 Forbes Boulevard, Suite 200, Lanham, Maryland 20706
www.rowman.com

10 Thornbury Road, Plymouth PL6 7PP, United Kingdom

British Library Cataloguing in Publication Information Available

Library of Congress Cataloging-in-Publication Data

Brown, Ronald D., 1949– .
Dying on the job : murder and mayhem in the American workplace / Ronald D. Brown.
p. cm.
Includes bibliographical references and index.
ISBN 978-1-4422-1843-7 (cloth : alk. paper) — ISBN 978-1-4422-1845-1 (ebook)
1. Violence in the workplace—United States. 2. Murder—United States. 3. Mass murder—United
States. I. Title.
HF5549.5.E43B76 2012
364.152'30973—dc23
2012032268

Printed in the United States of America

For Patricia,
Ronald Jr.,
and Sherin

Murder, though it have no tongue,
will speak with most miraculous organ.
　　　　　　　　　　—Shakespeare, Hamlet, act II

Contents

Acknowledgments

To those whose friendships are still valued, even though they have passed this mortal way: Thomas Brown Wilbur, Arnold McKinnon, Ron Stone, Vance Jordan, and Elizabeth F. Stier; to a great teacher at Arts High who genuinely cared, Louis Spindler; to the college professors who became role models and friends: Alan Stone, Nancy Topping Bazin, and E. Theodore Stier; to the law professors who not only taught but truly inspired: Carol Bohmer, Stanislaw Pomorski, George Ginsburgs, Milner S. Ball, Roger Clark, Samuel Estreicher, and Cynthia Estlund; to my favorite law school classmates for whom I always enjoyed cutting class: Linda Boentgen, Paulette Sapp, and Rebecca Wendy Bass; and to that human miscellany of co-horts, co-conspirators, colleagues and friends whose lives have enriched mine so generously over the years: Kenneth Schnall, Maxine Harvard, Isiah Rubin Scott, Suzanne Ochse, Janet Hope Greenlee, Andrew E. Ingram Jr., Benilde Little, Clara Little, Kenneth Hanko, Militza Iliana Mizray and Sammy Lowell, Marlena and Barnaby Grzaslewicz, Carol Federighi, and cousin Wesley Brown. Also a grateful thanks to those recent acquaintances whose support was appreciated, including Anesta R. Vannoy , Margaret Weems, and James Geppner; to my technical expert Carlton Prescott who fixed every laptop malfunction and computer glitch; and to "Buddie" and Kaye Behney, the proprietors of the Bank SQ Coffeehouse and its staff (Alex, Doreen, Niko, etc.) whose great coffee fueled those long hours at my favorite little table in the rear of the cafe (where much of the final manuscript was typed). And, finally, to those in the book business: my long-time literary agent, the late Nancy Love, and to the folks at Rowman & Littlefield Publishers, Inc., including assistant editor Kathryn M. F. Knigge, and particularly editors Suzanne I. Staszak-Silva and Karen Ackermann, who labored so indefatigably on my behalf.

Introduction

On February, 12, 2010, Professor Amy Bishop rose from her chair in a crowded faculty meeting at the University of Alabama and pulled a nine-millimeter semiautomatic handgun from her sensible plaid blazer. She shot three colleagues in the head at point-blank range, killing all three, and wounded three others, one critically.

A Harvard PhD, neurobiologist, inventor, author, wife, and busy mother of four, Bishop had no criminal record and no history of mental illness. But she had recently been denied tenure and knew she would soon lose her job. She was promptly arrested and later charged with several felony counts, including one count of capital murder.

Every year, nearly eight hundred employees are killed in the American workplace. They aren't killed in factory accidents or industrial mishaps. They're not electricians who mistakenly touch the wrong wires, zookeepers being mauled by frisky lions, or welders falling from ten-story construction sites. No, these employees are intentionally killed by *other people*, brutally murdered in acts of homicide. Where once the murderers were disgruntled postal employees or angry blue-collar factory workers on the assembly line, increasingly they now include engineers, teachers, doctors, scientists, and other professionals who kill coworkers, supervisors, and onlookers in corporate conference rooms, faculty lounges, and plush executive suites.

Why does an employee murder the boss? When does an employee decide *how* to murder the boss? In October 1991, Joseph Harris decided to murder his supervisor, Carol Ott, for what he felt was a history of unfair treatment on the job. Armed with a nine-millimeter Uzi handgun, a .22-caliber machine gun with a silencer, and several hand grenades and bombs, he forcibly entered her suburban New Jersey home. But once inside, finding her half-nude and wearing only a skimpy T-shirt, he tossed his high-tech weapons aside and killed her with repeated thrusts of a faux eighteenth-century samurai sword. What provokes one worker to kill another worker? In October 1999, Jeffrey White shot and killed a coworker, leaving the bullet-riddled body near the Elkins, West Virginia, lumberyard where they worked, after a heated argument over Beanie Babies. How much favoritism should a manager avoid showing one worker to prevent a jealous, murderous rage in another? In April 2000, two young striptease dancers in El Paso, Texas, Vivian Prince and Marlene Dunan, strangled a coworker because they were angry at the club manager who always let her dance on the "good" pole.

According to FBI data, in 1982 there were only fifteen workplace homicides; six years later, in 1988, the number had doubled to thirty.[1] Current data and statistics are difficult to come by, but in 2007 alone there were 864 fatal occupational injuries in the American workplace due to assaults and violent acts, including 628 workplace homicides.[2] On-the-job murders now average between 750 and 800 per year, which makes homicide the fastest-growing category of death in the workplace and the "leading cause of death for women on the job."[3] The US Department of Justice, the American Federation of State, County and Municipal Employees (AFSCME), and the Centers for Disease Control (CDC) have declared workplace violence an "epidemic,"[4] while others see a "workplace violence epidemic,"[5] and still others see a "postalization" of corporate America[6] which has gone "largely unnoticed" by the public at large.[7]

The general public is familiar with "domestic violence" disputes and how they often spill over into a work site. In February 2010, Alissa Blanton, 23, a central Florida woman who had been stalked for two years, was shot and killed on her new job by a sixty-one-year-old stalker. The murder occurred just days after a local judge denied her seventy-two-page petition for an emergency order of protection.[8] In July 2010, an Albuquerque woman, Adrienne Basciano, recently separated from boyfriend Robert Reza, 37, found herself in a bitter custody battle over their five-year-old twins. Reza confronted her on her job, shot and killed two female employees, critically wounded her, and then killed himself, ending the worst mass murder/suicide in New Mexico history.[9]

A domestic- violence dispute that spills over into a work site, however, is very different from a "workplace murder." And this book is about workplace murder. What is a workplace murder? A workplace murder is one that occurs within an "employment" relationship by someone whose motive is a "term or condition" of employment. And what exactly is a "term or condition" of employment? The most common include wages; hours; benefits; promotions; bonuses; vacations; performance ratings; pensions; reasons for getting fired, terminated, or laid off; garnishment; withholding wages to pay alimony, child support, back taxes, defaulted loans, and so on. You get the idea.

As the public is less familiar with workplace murder, it's also less sympathetic to the perpetrators of the crime. This perpetrator is more readily dismissed by the public as a paranoid, psychopathic killer, a "crazy" who's genetically predisposed to murder—somebody, somewhere, sometime. The general public believes that these perpetrators and their workplace murders simply cannot be prevented, and that the number of these psychopathic killers is on the rise. Here the public is both right *and* wrong: half wrong because, as we shall see, a surprisingly large number of workplace murderers are *not* psychopathic killers; and half right because the number of workplace murders and their perpetrators *are* dramatically on the rise.

An employee who suddenly "snaps" and kills a supervisor or boss is automatically, almost by definition, considered a psychopathic killer. But given the dramatic rise in workplace murders, and every indication that their numbers will only grow, experts like San Francisco, California, attorney Gary Mathiason now argue that the analysis may not be that simple anymore. "The idea of a normal person snapping is absolutely wrong," he states, but "it's also wrong to view them [all] as a criminal type."[10] "Some show anger and suspicion that border on criminal paranoia," argues John Hamrock, head of Amoco Corp.'s employee assistance program, but "many . . . are people whose unanswered resumes and unpaid medical bills mount until . . . they become so overwhelmed with feelings of futility that they just explode."[11]

The general public knows very little about workplace murder, and what little knowledge it *does* have, unfortunately, is usually outdated, skewed, and distorted by misconception, myth, and half-truth. Even the number of workplace murders thought to be committed every year is grossly underestimated. The number is actually higher—much higher—than official government data and statistics indicate. And as alarming as these statistics are, they still don't include the hundreds of bystanders, nonemployees, and passersby who are also killed or wounded only because they happen to be at the wrong place at the wrong time.

Most of the public, even sophisticated professionals in the labor/employment field, have little or no idea that the problem has grown dramatically, and has already reached crisis proportions. In a recent survey of more than three hundred human resource professionals, it was found that "nearly 60 percent of the 162 respondents either thought there were fewer than 500 workplace homicides in 1992, or had no idea of the number. Combined with the increasing trend of homicides, and the gravity of each incident, it's no wonder [that] many . . . are alarmed and believe there is a 'workplace crisis.'"[12]

As the economy flounders, unemployment and job security become twin topics that dominate much of what people think, if not what they say out loud. In the wake of the tragic 9/11 attacks, fears of rising workplace violence, along with easy access to firearms, place job security near the top of everyone's list of concerns. As a result, growing numbers of American workers are as fearful *for* their jobs as they are *on* the job.

Despite the rising rate of workplace murders, little has been published that addresses the crisis or focuses on that specific topic alone. Of the fifty-odd books published in the last two decades on workplace violence, for example, none focuses on workplace murder. Not a single book. These authors include many top scholars and experts in the field, yet they either squeamishly avoid the topic altogether, or refer only briefly to one or two of the bloodiest, tabloid massacres before they focus on other, less violent workforce behavior.

These authors consistently regard workplace murder as just one of many behaviors on a wide spectrum of workplace violence in general. And they automatically assume, without discussion or analysis, that all the perpetrators were criminally insane. Brief references to three or four of the most sensational, tabloid massacres easily support the blanket assumption of criminal insanity. But when *all* the murders are analyzed and discussed (even those that occurred at the local deli, gas station, or convenience store, or never made the TV news), the assumption does not hold up, certainly not as sturdily.[13]

The number of workplace murderers who were probably "normal" will be left for the reader to ponder. That determination is, in any event, outside the focus of this book. Yet the facts suggest that an astonishingly large (and growing) number of workplace murderers were not "crazy" at all. Which raises the question: How many were just regular employees—much like you and me—who were simply pushed to the limit before they finally "snapped" and went berserk in a homicidal rage?

As a result, and with few exceptions, the literature on workplace violence focuses on workplace violence in general. This broad category of behavior includes almost everything—from exchanging surly glances at the watercooler to bullying, "mobbing," and other acts of aggression, even simple assault. Although these books were instructive, something more was needed. Something obviously was missing. Missing from the bookshelves was a book that focused exclusively on the most extreme form of workplace violence: workplace *murder*. Why murder?

Every day of the week, companies and firms confront problems of sexual harassment, insubordination, and other misbehavior that occurs in a diverse workplace. This includes aggression and some forms of physical violence, as where one worker shoves another against a file cabinet, or pushes a coworker against the watercooler. The list of acts that constitute workplace violence is endless. But it's not the end of the world. After proper counseling, reprimands, disciplinary measures, and maybe the mandatory viewing of a training DVD, everybody returns to work and dutifully moves on—to avoid the messy business of arbitrations, grievances, hearings before the Equal Employment Opportunity Commission (EEOC), and litigation in federal court.

But murder is different.

After a workplace murder, even large companies can fold, slowly go under, and never bounce back. Most survive, but it's never the same again. Disruptions in productivity; loss of customers, contractors, and clients; some workers return but they rarely perform as well as before; some never come back at all; and attending funerals and wakes is never good for office morale. All add up to irreparable damage and irrecoverable loss. CEOs and senior management often face the choice of changing sites, outsourcing, downsizing, or closing the doors for good.

And then the lawsuits begin.

The bookshelves were filled with dozens of books on workplace violence—all drily academic handbooks, manuals, and guides written expressly for chief executive officers (CEOs), executive vice presidents, and middle management. Of the books that briefly discussed workplace murder, the murders were always either domestic violence disputes which had spilled over into the workplace, or murders by intruders during the commission of a crime—for example, assaults against the police, taxicab robberies, late-night stickups at a convenience store. Missing from the bookshelves, what was sorely needed, was a book that not only focused on workplace murder, but focused on murder exclusively between employee and employer—people who usually knew each other beforehand and who had worked together for years, and whose motives were issues that related to the job.

That book had never been written.

Also, the book that was missing from the shelves not only focused on these types of murders, but did so in a reader-friendly, accessible way. This book would not only educate and inform the CEO and upper management, but also engage everybody else, including the support staff, the security guards, even the temps on the factory floor. After all, workplace safety—how to spot a homicidal coworker, how to assess/diffuse a volatile office situation, or how to interpret the behavioral clues of a colleague bent on homicide—is valuable, potentially life-saving information that should be widely shared, not hoarded by a small management elite.

Finally, the book missing from the shelves would not only focus on these types of murder in a reader-friendly way, it would also be accessible in the presentation and structure of the text. It would avoid the traditional format of listing a series of rigid "rules," to be followed or ignored at one's own peril. That book would rely instead on more than *three hundred and fifty real-life, actual cases of workplace homicide.* The unprecedented use of hundreds of real-life cases of workplace murder would not only provide a valuable statistical framework, it would also afford a glimpse into the lives and circumstances—the "narratives"—of the people described on the page. This structural format would also contextualize the knowledge, and facilitate the retention and application of that knowledge to real-life situations long after the book was read and reluctantly returned to the shelf.

In November 1999, a supply technician named Bryan Uyesugi, who feared he would be fired, shot and killed eight coworkers at a Xerox plant in Honolulu, Hawaii. In the days following the tragedy, general manager Glenn Sexton heroically rose to the task and successfully handled the company's response. These measures included emergency tutorials with management, on-site shock/trauma treatment for eyewitnesses, therapy for coworkers, grief counseling for survivors, and so on. Sexton later reflected on the massacre and admitted that it was one of the greatest challenges of his life. "What's clear," he said, "is that there's no book on how to handle this." [14]

Cases like Uyesugi's have grown in the last two decades, both in frequency and gravity, and they have altered the American workplace. Yet they are rarely mentioned in the classroom, seldom cited in the journals, and almost never discussed in the textbooks. And Sexton was correct: no book has ever focused on murder exclusively between employee and employer, over issues that relate to the workplace and define the employment relationship. These employees—their passions, pathos, their grievances, and the violence and bloodshed that ensued—have been largely neglected, squeamishly ignored, and never looked at again.

That is, until now.

This study grew out of a review of more than three thousand cases of workplace violence. The cases spanned almost a century, from Julian Carlton's slaughter of his boss's dinner guests in a Wisconsin mansion in 1914 to Jeffrey Johnson's murder of his former boss in front of the Empire State Building on August 24, 2012. The cases included capital murder, first-degree murder, manslaughter, attempted murder, and aggravated and simple assault. As we will see, the act of "homicide" has many different faces. They include the murder of young children (infanticide), the murder of siblings (fratricide), the murder of mothers (matricide), fathers (patricide), kings and queens (regicide), whole groups of people (genocide), and the act of murdering oneself (suicide). Of those thousands of cases, more than three hundred and fifty (368 to be exact) ultimately qualified for this study, and each involved at least one form of homicide.

But as so few cases qualified for this study, and so many more were systematically eliminated, it's only appropriate that a brief note on methodology be provided at this point. The criteria were deceptively simple and easy to state. Each case had to present: (1) at least two adults in an "employment" relationship, in which one worked for (or with) the other; (2) a negative action against an employee, relating to a "term or condition" of employment; and (3) an employee who sought to exact revenge, to retaliate in response; (4)

which resulted in at least one intentional death; (5) with all the above occurring within the United States.

Under these criteria, hundreds of on-the-job murders were excluded because the victims were first responders, for example, police officers, emergency medical services personnel, and so on. These victims, as they were acting within the normal course of their employment when they were murdered, were excluded because they had assumed the risk. But application of the criteria was not always that cut-and-dried. Ted Maher, for instance, was a brilliant registered nurse (and ex–Green Beret) who lived most of his life in New York. He later worked as a nurse for Edmond Safra, the billionaire banker and founder of the Republic National Bank, who owned elegant residences in New York, London, Geneva, Monaco, and France. In early December 1999, Safra died in a fire which, ironically, had been set by Maher to curry his favor. But as Maher later pled guilty to arson, was sentenced, and later served his jail term in Monaco, his case was excluded from this study as having occurred outside the United States.

In September 2009, Raymond Clark III, 26, a Yale University lab technician, killed his lab partner, pharmacology student Annie Le, just days before her scheduled wedding date. The case was included (despite speculation of a star-crossed romance) because Clark's principal motive was actually his resentment of how the lab was run. [15] Of course, the "locus" of a murder wasn't always where the perpetrator physically worked or punched a time clock. One especially horrific workplace massacre was included even though the murders began in the cramped cockpit of a USAir passenger jet cruising 22,000 feet above the central California coast. [16] Hundreds of other cases were excluded because they weren't really workplace murders at all, but domestic violence disputes which had "spilled over" into a job site, like the Blanton and Basciano cases cited earlier. A handful of cases (and thankfully *only* a handful) were excluded even though they qualified technically, as when John Gotti orchestrated the murder of his boss Paul Castellano outside a popular Manhattan steakhouse for promoting a coworker and colleague consigliere (Tommy Bilotti), and then took control of the Gambino enterprise after the hit.

The exclusion of some cases seemed arbitrary because it turned on a single, easily overlooked fact. These cases included most postgraduate or doctoral candidates who, because they often taught undergraduate courses as well, were both students *and* employees. In November 1991, Gang Lu, 28, a graduate student at the University of Iowa, killed several professors and administrators for their lack of enthusiasm for his dissertation. In July 2002, Peter Odighizuwa, 42, a student at the Appalachian School of Law, opened fire on the Grundy, Virginia, campus, killing several faculty members and students after he was dismissed. Neither gentleman was included in the study as neither was involved in an employment relationship. Both Wayne

Williams, the infamous Atlanta serial killer, and Chicago's John Wayne Gacy, the Killer Clown, were excluded from the study. Despite the dozens of brutal murders they committed during the late 1970s, their status as "employers" was questionable, and their "employees" were, in any event, virtually all juveniles or older boys, not adults.[17]

Yet, paradoxically, a few cases were included even though no murder occurred and nobody was actually killed. These cases typically involved a disgruntled worker who finally snapped, pulled a gun, and opened fire at point-blank range—and *missed*. Or a suicidal worker who lodged a .357 Magnum in his mouth, shut his eyes and squeezed the trigger, but nothing happened . . . just the sound of a metallic click—the gun having chosen that moment to run out of bullets or jam. In June 1968, radical feminist drifter Valerie Solanas fired several shots at contemporary pop artist Andy Warhol at nearly point-blank range, injuring Warhol and a bystander, but causing no deaths.[18] In April 1998, Lenda Glass Spencer, who worked for a Windsor, Connecticut, engraving firm, finally responded to her boss's ongoing sexual harassment when she brought a nine-millimeter Smith and Wesson to work. She confronted him with the gun, chased him around the warehouse, and fired at least seven shots from a seventeen-round magazine, but never once hit her mark.[19] These cases were included in the study anyway, not because no one was killed, but for the simple reason that—by all the laws of nature, ballistics, Newtonian physics, and the known universe—somebody *should* have been.

The blanket exclusion of so many cases was meant only to ensure that this study had the full benefit of only the clearest examples of workplace murder available in the public record. Based on more than three hundred and fifty actual cases of workplace murder, this is the first and only study of its kind. And this must be repeated: this is *the first and only study that focuses on murder exclusively between employees, over issues that were job-related, and that relies statistically on more than three hundred and fifty real-life cases of workplace murder.* As both the topic analyzed and the methodological approach were without precedent, the cases ultimately chosen had to be factually pristine. The cases couldn't be influenced, even in the slightest degree, by other cases that shared a surface similarity but were factually entangled with other issues, or colored by motives or agendas deemed more fashionable, in vogue, or politically correct.

For those few cases that qualified but were lost in the shuffle, or fell between the cracks, be reminded that the definitions were permeable and highly porous, the criteria always more easily declared than applied. This wasn't an attempt at formal scholarship, but a meditation on murder—an informal look at how and why folks kill each other on the job. The observations, findings, and insights shared on the following pages hold value, then, not only because they are exhaustive or definitive in some way. They hold value also because they consciously seek to inform and engage the reader—to challenge and question the prevailing orthodoxy—in ways that are both original and new.

The attempt here was to compile and study as many of these neglected cases as possible, however violent and bloody, without squeamish reservation or a lot of complicated graphs and charts; to describe these murders and explain their motives without the jargon of tenured PhD-speak or the need to master the mysteries of the M'Naughten rule. The goal was to analyze the cases as a separate and discrete phenomenon, against which new ways to prevent and survive workplace murder may be tested, from which new answers and clues may be teased.

Chapter One

Murder in the Workplace

Nature, Scope, and Origins

The whole nation was stunned and outraged by a January 2011 shooting rampage in an Arizona shopping mall that left six dead and sixteen wounded, including congresswoman Gabrielle Giffords (Democrat, Arizona).

Giffords, 42, was shot in the head at point-blank range, was hospitalized for months, and miraculously survived. The six dead included a senior federal judge, three of Giffords's congressional aides, and a nine-year-old girl. The gunman, Jared L. Loughner, 22, had worked his way through the crowd concealing a pistol, having specifically targeted Giffords for her views on health care legislation. He continued to shoot until he ran out of bullets and was finally subdued by members of the crowd, who wrestled him to the ground.

The public was relieved to learn that the gunman wasn't a foreign terrorist or part of a larger group, and had also acted alone, even though political assassination is still very rare on American soil. The media coverage of the shooting was extensive not only because it was newsworthy with prominent victims, but also because Giffords was young, bright, attractive, and articulate, and even married to an astronaut. All of which explained why the news media covered the story as intensely, as thoroughly, and for as long as it did.

Six months after the attack, during the summer of 2011, most TV news outlets routinely reported on four unrelated shooting incidents: Mark Geisenheyner, 51, a vindictive neighbor who murdered Manhattan, New York, art professor Monica Shay and three members of her family at their rural Pennsylvania retreat; Jeremy "Billy" Davis, 51, a employee at the Louisville, Kentucky, Gas and Electric Co. who killed his longtime foreman and then committed suicide; Robert Shonte Dantzler, 34, of Grand Rapids, Michigan, who murdered seven, including two former girlfriends and a teenage daughter; and Everett Conant, a thirty-something Wyoming man who murdered three sons and a brother, and also wounded his wife, before he surrendered to the police. Almost as disturbing as the seventeen murders, however, was the fact that all had occurred, not over the whole summer, but between July first and the sixth—within *less than a week.*

What linked the Tucson attack to a series of murders that occurred over a six-day period six months later? The high-profile, nationally televised shootings obscured the fact that local, individual shooting incidents—those without prominent victims—occur literally every day of the week but go unnoticed (and mostly ignored) nationally. Nor was it coincidental that two of the four assailants were unemployed and the other two had murdered over terms and conditions that govern the workplace.

THE NATURE AND SCOPE OF WORKPLACE MURDER

As already noted, according to FBI data, in 1982 there were only fifteen on-the-job homicides; six years later, in 1988, the number had doubled to thirty. Today the number averages between 750 and 800 per year. Why are the numbers on the rise? As manufacturing and other sectors struggle to compete in a highly globalized twenty-first-century economy, the most "profitable" strategies more frequently include downsizing, outsourcing, mass layoffs, plant closings, and so on. But as these strategies also result in more home foreclosures, evictions, bankruptcies, union give backs, and unpaid medical bills at home, not only does workplace civility decline, the rate of workplace anger and violence soars, which contributes to the rising rate of workplace murder.

The nature and scope of workplace murder may also be assessed in terms other than human life. These losses are often regarded as the hidden costs, not always apparent to the untrained eye or at first glance. The company that suffers a workplace murder almost always faces an array of hidden costs and expenses, such as higher legal fees and insurance premiums, negligent hiring/retention claims; sabotage; vandalism; disruption of productivity; building repair, replacement, and cleanup; increased security costs; public relations; and diminished employee morale.

These losses also usually include the costs of employee/survivors' claims, disability, psychological care and counseling for posttraumatic stress disorder (PTSD), and other forms of "closure." The dollar figures vary widely, depending on the accounting methods used and what figures are included. One source placed the cost of workplace violence to US companies in 1992 at $4.2 billion,[1] while the Workplace Violence Institute estimated the cost at $36 billion per year.[2]

The cold, hard statistical data on workplace murder take on flesh and blood with the case of Robert Earl Mack. On January 24, 1992, Mack was fired by his boss at the General Dynamics plant in San Diego, California. Enraged, Mack pulled a handgun and went on a shooting rampage, killing the company's labor negotiator, Michael Konz, and also wounding a company supervisor, James English. The incident ultimately cost General Dynamics more than $1.2 million in legal fees and lost business.[3]

In a similar case, on December 28, 1988, John Rosh fired a temporary employee, Tung Hgo Hua, who had arrived at his San Jose, California, job site four hours late. Hua had been late on several previous occasions, and had received warnings that he faced termination if he was late again. Rosh fired Hua for chronic tardiness, and had him escorted to the front security desk. Rosh advised the guards that Hua was no longer an employee and wasn't permitted on company property again. Despite these instructions, Hua returned later that day, was allowed to enter the plant, then produced a gun and shot Rosh in the back as he tried to flee. The shooting caused Rosh severe, permanent spinal injuries. He sued the company, and a jury awarded him $3.9 million in damages. The award was upheld on appeal.[4]

Despite the rapidly rising number of workplace murders, little has been published that focuses on the issue or adequately addresses the problem. That so little of the available "literature" focuses on workplace murder only underscores the need to review many of the tenets of labor/employment law that have become obsolete, distorted, and skewed by myths and half-truths. There's very little on the bookshelves to clarify the misconceptions and half-truths, and virtually nothing to explain how, for example, worker frustration and anger slowly (almost imperceptibly) escalate to murder and hate. There is, in short, not a single book on the shelves that provides answers to critical questions so often asked only after a workplace murder has already occurred:

1. Why do single white males in their early forties commit almost 75 percent of the workplace homicides?
2. What behavioral clues do virtually all workplace killers give just before they embark upon their murder sprees?
3. How much of the recent rise in workplace murder is explained by the fact that American workers usually don't realize how *few* legal rights they actually have against employers, especially in right-to-work states?
4. Why are labor unions typically ineffective as valves to protect management against angry employees who eventually snap and kill their bosses?
5. On average, how long after being fired does it take a homicidal employee to return to the job site with a weapon to get even or exact revenge?

6. Why do so few future workplace killers have the support of the union leadership and/or members of the bargaining unit in their escalating battles with management?
7. Why are preemployment screening systems virtually useless as a means of weeding out potentially homicidal employees?
8. Why do HR offices and personnel departments, even in the largest *Fortune* 500 companies, still use these ineffective preemployment screening systems?
9. Under what circumstances does a supervisor or boss (in a reversal of the traditional analytical model) murder a subordinate employee?

The proliferation of federal laws, statutes, and other measures during the 1980s and 1990s transformed the modern workplace into a more democratic, more racially and culturally diverse work environment than ever before. Yet some of those statutory measures still don't reflect an awareness of workplace violence, let alone the crisis of workplace homicide. As a result, the problems that arise in today's ("politically correct") workplace usually require not only a knowledge of workplace murder, but a knowledge also sufficient to answer questions that are not always asked on the record—or out loud:

1. What percentage of workplace murder is committed by women? African Americans? Hispanics? Asians?
2. What percentage of workplace murder victims are women? African Americans? Hispanics? Asians?
3. Is there a uniquely "male" or "female" management style? If so, which is more likely to provoke a disgruntled employee to pick up a weapon and kill?
4. Why do women workplace murderers seem to kill mostly *other* women? (Females make up about 14 percent of the workplace murderers, but kill almost 40 percent of the women.)
5. Why have workplace suicides skyrocketed in the last decade? Are Asian workers more likely to commit suicide? Are African American employees less likely to commit suicide?
6. Are female supervisors and managers more likely to become victims of workplace murder than their male counterparts?
7. Which angry, single white male in his early forties is more likely to show up tomorrow with a nine-millimeter handgun and blow your brains out? The one who's been with the company ten months? Or the one who's been with the company twenty years?
8. Why is a supervisor or boss in the private sector far more likely to have an adulterous relationship with a (female) subordinate—and then murder her—than his public-sector counterpart?

9. Which American city seems to breed twice as many workplace killers as all the other cities combined? (Hint: It's not New York City or Los Angeles.)

The complexity and scope of the crisis of workplace murder may also be appreciated by how easily the crisis may be mislabeled or resemble another societal ill. Once mislabeled, of course, it more easily falls within another agency's jurisdiction or someone else's technical expertise. The problem is thus minimized and ultimately becomes less of a problem to worry about. Three highly publicized, so-called school massacres aptly illustrate the point.

The first so-called school massacre occurred on August 1, 1966, when Charles Whitman, 25, a student at the University of Texas at Austin and an ex-marine, shot and killed fourteen people and wounded thirty others during a shooting rampage on and around the Austin campus. He killed three people inside the university tower before he took an elevator up the tower and killed ten more victims from the twenty-ninth floor of the observation deck. Just hours earlier, he had murdered both his wife and his mother. Disillusioned with the marines, which withdrew his scholarship due to poor grades, he held a series of menial jobs. And during the days and weeks before he snapped, he was physically dependent on amphetamines, suffering the pain of an undiagnosed brain tumor, and financially dependent on his authoritarian, abusive father, whom he despised.[5]

The second school massacre occurred on April 20, 1999, when two seniors at Columbine High School in Colorado, Eric Harris, 18, and Dylan Klebold, 17, murdered twelve students, wounded dozens more, and also killed a teacher before they committed suicide. Both had been raised in comfortably suburban white middle-class families and homes, and they shared an interest in explosives and automatic weaponry. According to FBI experts, Klebold was a depressive, and Harris was a clinical psychopath who orchestrated the massacre because he had a messianic-level superiority complex and needed to demonstrate his massive superiority to the world.[6]

The third so-called school massacre took place eight years later, on April 16, 2007, on the campus of Virginia Tech in Blacksburg, Virginia. In two separate attacks, about two hours apart, senior English major Seung Hui Cho, 23, shot and killed thirty-two people and wounded twenty-five more before he shot and killed himself. This was the deadliest peacetime shooting massacre by a single gunman in American history, on or off a school site. Cho had been diagnosed with a severe anxiety disorder, and had received therapy and medical educational support since grade school. Records of his diagnoses and treatment history had not been made available to Virginia college administrators, however, because the documents were covered by federal privacy laws.[7]

These three so-called school massacres left a total of fifty-nine murdered and eighty-one wounded and are often cited as the three bloodiest school massacres by shooters in US history. But only the Columbine case was a true school massacre. The others were actually workplace murders whose victims were professors, teachers, administrators, clerks, and postgraduate and doctoral candidates, in addition to many onlookers and passersby. The list of Virginia Tech's dead, for example, included several middle-aged, even elderly, professors and nine postgraduate and doctoral candidates, all in their twenties and thirties, and didn't include a single child or juvenile. To label all three tragedies school massacres is not only descriptively misleading, it also minimizes—even trivializes—the actual gravity of the problem as it existed then, and the crisis society still confronts today.

The problem of workplace murder has also been characterized as part of the Midwest farming crisis or the "rural ghetto" phenomenon that first drew national attention in the mid-1980s. Two compelling works, one by Kathryn Marie Dudley[8] and the other by Osha Davidson,[9] lament that dairy farmers, as self-employed workers, may not toil claustrophobically inside stuffy offices or suffer the daily indignities of a boss on the assembly line.

Yet many remain subject to the same stresses that afflict the urban chronically unemployed, and many also suffer the same angry frustration and rage in dealing with loan officers and the often callous bureaucracy of local lending banks. As a result, they daily face problems of farm foreclosure and repossessed farm equipment that stands idle in fallow fields or sits rusting in abandoned barns. In losing their land, their houses, their farms, and even their will to live, increasing numbers of Midwest farmers committed murder, even suicide.

Joseph Amato poignantly describes the life of James Jenkins, 46, a Minnesota farmer whose farm machinery had been repossessed more than a dozen times in the last twenty years. On September 29, 1983, he shot and killed Rudy Blythe, 42, president of the Buffalo Ridge State Bank, and also killed Deems "Toby" Thurlin, 37, the bank's chief loan officer. Thurlin was shot once in the throat. Blythe was shot in the shoulder, then chased into a ditch where he was shot three more times by Jenkins and his 18-year-old son. Jenkins killed the two men after Blythe told other local bankers in the area that he was a bad credit risk.[10]

Another rural, midwestern farming case was that of Dale Burr, 63, an Iowa farmer whose financial problems had claimed his farm machinery, his stored grains, and his beloved quarter horses. On December 9, 1985, Burr shot and killed his wife of forty years before he drove to the Hills Bank and Trust Company of Hills, Iowa (population 550), at which his checking account had long since been overdrawn. After he arrived at the bank, he aimed a twelve-gauge shotgun and killed bank president John Hughes, 46, shooting him in the head as he looked up from his tufted chair. Burr also shot and

killed a neighbor before he turned the gun on himself and committed suicide.[11] Whether part of a looming farm crisis or a "rural ghetto" phenomenon, Burr's financial problems were hardly unique. The tragedies only continued, and in 1987, the adult suicide rate in Iowa had reached its highest
level since the Great Depression.[12]

By far the most complex "model" of a workplace murderer was the perpetrator who was the most chameleonlike and therefor the most difficult to
discern. This was a male perpetrator who was universally—and justifiably—
regarded as a paranoid, psychopathic killer, and whose utterly "senseless"
murders were rarely even associated in the public mind with the workplace.
The complexity of this "workplace" killer owed mostly to the fact that,
paradoxically, he was chronically unemployed and didn't have a job.

This model of workplace murder was seen in two very different men
whose murders were committed in two different types of attacks. One attack
occurred in a single flash of gunfire, on a suburban commuter train; the other
occurred in a series of individual strikes, spread over a period of two
decades, and designed not only to kill but also to maim, taunt, intimidate, and
terrorize. These two different attacks resulted in nine dead and forty-nine
wounded, and everyone agreed the men were paranoid, psychopathic criminals whose killings lent new meaning to the words senseless and vile.

The first perpetrator was Colin Ferguson, 35, an African Jamaican who
couldn't keep a job. On December 7, 1993, he bought a ticket at New York
City's Penn Station and then sat quietly on a commuter train scheduled to
pull into the Merillon Avenue Station, Garden City, Long Island, New York,
at exactly 5:33 p.m. In the months before the attack, he had moved to California looking for a job, including at a car wash whose manager laughed in his
face. He returned to New York the next month complaining that he didn't
like "competing with immigrants and Hispanics for jobs."[13] On that day, he
sat on the train with a bag that held a handgun and 160 rounds of ammunition. The six passengers he killed included an office manager, a corporate
interior designer, and an account executive, all from Mineola; a Roslyn
Heights college student, 24; and a 30-year-old lawyer from Westbury, New
York.[14]

The second perpetrator was Ted Kaczynski, a.k.a. the Unabomber, a former child prodigy in mathematics who was accepted to Harvard at sixteen
and later earned a PhD in mathematics from the University of Michigan. He
became an assistant professor at the University of California–Berkeley at age
25, the youngest in the school's history. However, he abruptly resigned a
year later without explanation, after numerous complaints and low ratings
from undergraduate students. "Many students noted . . . he seemed uncomfortable teaching, often stuttering and mumbling during lectures, becoming
excessively nervous in front of a class and ignoring students during designated office hours."[15] Unemployed and unable to interact with people in social

situations, Kaczynski in effect left academia, and most of the civilized world, to live in the woods of Kansas, never to return. Then, beginning in 1978, people across the country started to receive handmade bombs that exploded in the mail.[16] And the victims were not random choices. They comprised a carefully selected group of science professors, mathematicians, and engineers. They were, to a man, brilliant, scholarly, and dedicated white men, just like Ted Kaczynski, men who would have been worthy, admired cohorts and colleagues, fellow faculty and friends; that is, had Ted been able to hold a job.

Ferguson and Kaczynski came from very different worlds, yet what joined them, ultimately, was the extent to which they had invested themselves in securing employment that forever exceeded their grasp, in finding a job that was always just beyond their reach. In both cases, their victims were discrete, demographically exclusive groups for whom they held the deepest hatred and jealousy—but simultaneously wanted desperately to join as coworkers and colleagues. Ferguson deliberately sat among white, upwardly mobile middle-class professionals during rush hour, on a train whose route traversed Long Island's affluent lily-white suburbs. For almost two decades Kaczynski threatened, taunted, and terrorized only those white men who—by education, age, background, alma maters, and academic posts—would have also been his cohorts, colleagues, chess partners, and fellow faculty in a major university's graduate program.

Neither Ferguson nor Kaczynski was included in this study for the simple reason that neither was employed when he committed his crimes. Yet, ironically, sadly, few people included in this study identified more deeply with the workplace; few wanted more desperately to be counted among the gainfully employed. So pervasive is the crisis of workplace murder, so difficult the task of defining the scope and breadth of the problem, that Ferguson and Kaczynski stand virtually alone in their rage against the workplace, despite the fact that—or solely because—neither could hold a steady job.

THE ORIGINS OF WORKPLACE MURDER

The origins of murder in the American workplace are murky at best, and it's impossible to determine with any biographical accuracy the identity of the first American employee to murder his or her boss. Though it's not implausible to assume that he or she was an angry indentured servant or perhaps even a slave, his or her identity and motive, along with other facts of the crime, have long been lost in the colonial past.

Arguably one of the first documented cases of workplace murder occurred in August 1831, and was conceived and organized by Nat Turner. Of course, Turner is a figure already notable in US history for having also led the first and only effective slave revolt in the annals of American slavery. A literate black slave and a preacher, Turner lived in a remote region of southeastern Virginia, and was later immortalized in fiction by William Styron's Pulitzer Prize–winning novel.[17] Turner's revolt was put down in a few days, though he survived in hiding for several months. The state executed fifty-six slaves for their part in the rebellion, and Turner, as the admitted leader, was executed by hanging on November 11, 1831. His body was delivered to the doctors, who skinned it and made grease of the flesh. According to records, a local family owned a money purse made of his "hide," and his skeleton was owned for many years by a local physician but was eventually misplaced.[18]

Perhaps the first "modern" workplace massacre occurred on April 15, 1914, on a wealthy Wisconsin estate. Julian Carlton, 30, a Caribbean servant, killed his employer's seven dinner guests by setting the stately mansion on fire while his employer was out of town, convinced that his employer would fire him as soon as he returned.

The homicidal rage that drove early cases of workplace murder, of course, wasn't limited demographically to deranged Caribbean servants and literate black slaves. Nearly eighty years before Professor Amy Bishop snapped in that faculty meeting and murdered three colleagues, another highly educated professor shot and killed the dean he felt was responsible for his firing.

On April 2, 1921, Professor Holmes Beckwith, 37, shot and killed his boss, Dean J. Herman Wharton, in the latter's private office at Syracuse University. Though Beckwith held a PhD from Columbia and an LLD from what is now UCLA, in the previous decade he had been dismissed from nine different positions. He was brooding over his career misfortunes when he shot Wharton five times at point-blank range with a large army revolver and then shot and killed himself, falling premeditatedly next to Wharton's body on the thickly carpeted floor.[19]

The amount of information available on these first modern cases of workplace murder clearly suggests how unusual and newsworthy they were at the time. As already noted, according to FBI records, as recently as 1982 there were only fifteen cases of workplace murder, and six years later, in 1988, the number had doubled to thirty. Examples of workplace murder were still so rare and infrequent that, prior to 1982, apparently no organization or group even bothered to keep formal count. The question that must be asked is, if only *fifteen* workplace murders occurred in 1982, what happened—what social, economic, and political forces came into play—to explain why the number grew so quickly and so steadily and now averages almost e*ight hundred* a year?

If the origins of workplace murder as a crisis cannot be fully explained in a page or two, they might be at least better understood by the convergence of four events—events that occurred over little more than a decade. The first event was passage of the Postal Reorganization Act of 1970.[20] This law addressed a long history of labor/management strife and a host of fiscal and organizational problems which had plagued the United States Postal Service (USPS) for decades. Under the act, the position of postmaster general, as an example, no longer held cabinet status (as it had since 1829); more than 750,000 workers could now collectively bargain; and 1982 was mandated as the year the public-service subsidy would end—a critical step toward privatizing the USPS and deregulating the industry as a whole.

The second event was the election of Ronald Reagan to the US presidency in a resounding victory over incumbent Jimmy Carter. According to recent research, Reagan was not only a conservative, he was the very embodiment of the corporate mentality, namely General Electric.[21] Though he started out politically as a Democrat (even serving briefly as president of the liberal Screen Actors Guild), even then he was promanagement. His switch to the Republicans was like that of the proverbial convert, and he preached the conservative gospel of antiunionism with twice the passion and zeal.

And Reagan was different from his GOP predecessors. They dealt with labor unions only begrudgingly, as an opportunistic act of political expedience, or viewed them as a necessary evil in a shrewdly cold game of realpolitik. But Reagan sincerely questioned labor unions' very *legitimacy*. His was a principled opposition, and he waged an almost continuous battle with organized labor his entire public life. He truly believed, as an example, that labor unions were morally reprehensible if not illegal in their inhibition of competition, and that they were antithetical to the tenets of free-market capitalism.

The third event, which occurred on the heels of the second, was Reagan's impressive 1981 victory over the leaders of the Professional Air Traffic Controllers Organization (PATCO) strike. This victory sent a clearly antiunion, promanagement message to all of corporate America. *And corporate America was listening.* In the wake of his PATCO victory and firing the strikers, for example, private union activity nationwide plummeted, and concessionary bargaining by labor unions increased dramatically, even in industries that were far removed from the federal government and air transportation.[22] The firing of the PATCO workers in 1981 had a chilling effect on major strike activity in particular. Professor Christopher R. Martin writes: "Each year since the late 1940s, there were regularly more than 100 major stoppages, as labor organizations flexed their muscles to jump-start contract bargaining impasses. Since 1981, however, major strikes in the United States have numbered far less than 100 each year."[23]

Reagan thus set a new, highly negative tone for public discourse, and helped to create an environment that was amenable—even receptive—to hatefully virulent, often violent opposition to organized labor. No longer was it considered mean-spirited, narrow-minded, or irresponsible to blame the poor or criticize the disadvantaged. No longer was it deemed tacky, déclassé, or gauche to boast about wealth and riches, to live lavishly, consume conspicuously, and wine and dine with extravagance. Nor was it shameful to enjoy it all—vicariously—by watching Robin Leach host *Lifestyles of the Rich and Famous*, which became a phenomenally successful TV show.

Few noticed at the time, but the average annual CEO salary also started to rise much faster than that of the average American employee. In 1978, for example, "CEOs of the large US corporations made on average 30 times their workers' salaries; by 2001 CEOs made 571 times their average workers' salaries."[24] Moreover, management had deliberately started to instill fear and stress in the workforce in order to maximize productivity on shrinking operational budgets, to squeeze more and more for less.[25]

The fourth event was actually the cumulative effect of a series of innovations in the daily operation of the USPS. These included the new zip code plus four, the introduction of computerized code-routing systems, competition from new companies (like Federal Express), and new technologies like faxing, email, and bill-paying services, which the post office couldn't provide. And all of these innovations occurred at the same time the Act phased out the general public-service subsidy. This withdrawal of funding was critical, since even *with* the subsidy the USPS had operated at a loss 131 of its 160 years of operation. The push for local postmasters and their supervisors to increase productivity on rapidly shrinking operational budgets inevitably led to abuse.

Perry Smith, as an example, had worked for the USPS in Johnston, South Carolina, for decades when his son committed suicide, which naturally affected the quality of his work. He lost weight, stopped grooming himself, and generally looked and behaved like a man in a downward spiral. His supervisors responded not by showing sympathy or attempting to reasonably accommodate him, but by reprimanding him for every minor violation they could find. And no infraction was too petty, including leaving his mailbag unattended for a few minutes, for which he was suspended. His supervisor rode him hard if he exceeded his lunch break or delivered a letter to the wrong address. In the end, miserable and constantly harassed, Smith resigned from the USPS in 1983, after decades on the job.[26]

A few months later, another postal worker, James Brooks, 53, of Anniston, Alabama, filed a grievance with his union because he was forced to work overtime without receiving commensurate pay, as required under the Fair Labor Standards Act (FLSA). When his union failed to help, he filed a complaint with the National Labor Relations Board (NLRB) whose proposed final settlement required him to drop his complaint. Still another case of abuse involved Steven Brownlee, 30, an African American with twelve years at the Atlanta, Georgia, post office. He had been forced to work seventy- to eighty-hour workweeks in order to keep up with his supervisor's demands.

One day in particular, the mail load was so heavy that he was ordered to come to work two hours earlier just to finish the job.[27]

As local postmasters and supervisors tried to meet impossible goals, they inevitably committed more abuse. Given the USPS's long history of acrimony and strife between labor and management, the workers' response had a tragically predictable, almost inevitable result. Employee frustration, resentment and anger had slowly festered, and then escalated to rank-and-file vengeance, violence, and homicidal hate.

Three months after his retirement, Smith returned to the Johnston post office with a shotgun, wounded two workers, and then shot and killed the local postmaster.[28] In December 1983, Brooks returned to the Anniston post office with a .38-caliber handgun. He shot his immediate supervisor twice, once in the abdomen and once in the arm, then shot and killed the local postmaster with multiple gunshots to the head.[29] And in March 1985, Brownlee reported for work at the Atlanta post office with a .22-caliber pistol. He opened fire, wounding a coworker and killing two others, one his supervisor.[30]

If the murders by Smith, Brooks, and Brownlee didn't attract much attention, the whole nation suddenly took notice of events in a small Oklahoma town the following year. On August, 20, 1986, Patrick Sherrill, a mail carrier who had been repeatedly harassed and abused by supervisors and coworkers, arrived at the Edmond post office with two .45-caliber pistols in his satchel. He shot and killed fourteen employees and wounded six others before he turned a gun on himself and committed suicide.[31]

The workplace carnage had just begun. And while many observers were still confused, scratching their collective head, the bloodshed they thought was somehow unique to the post office and the public sector had already spread to the private sector as well.

In February 1988, Richard Farley, 40, a former employee of Electromagnetic Systems Labs (ESL) in Sunnyvale, California, shot and killed seven people and wounded four others at ESL, including the woman he had stalked for several years.[32] That June, Dominic LuPoli, 40, of Chelsea, Massachusetts, shot and killed coworker Lisa Bruni in a postal parking lot before he fled the site and committed suicide.[33] Six months later, in December 1988, Warren Murphy entered a New Orleans postal facility with a twelve-gauge shotgun under his clothes, shot and wounded two coworkers, and fatally shot his supervisor in the face be before he surrendered to the police.[34]

Just months later, in May 1989, Alfred J. Hunter III of Boston, Massachusetts, killed his wife before he commandeered a light plane and used his AK-47 automatic rifle to spray bullets at the post office in which he worked.[35] That August, John Taylor, 52, of Escondido, California, shot and killed his wife and two coworkers and then wounded a fourth at an Orange Glen post office before committing suicide.[36] And the following month, in September

1989, Joseph T. Wesbecker, 47, an angry ex-employee on disability leave from a Louisville, Kentucky, print manufacturer, shot and killed eight former coworkers and wounded twelve more before he committed suicide.[37]

The term "going postal" had entered the English lexicon, and its meaning was no longer confined to the post office. The modern American workplace had dramatically changed, for the worse, and would never be the same again. An explanation of what happened and why will be explored in later chapters. For now, the critical questions to be addressed are: Why does the general public know so little about the crisis? Why hasn't more been done to publicize and then address this critical workplace issue? And how has this silence on the issue been maintained for so long?

Chapter Two

Why So Little Is Known about the Problem

In little more than two generations, the American workplace has come to occupy a unique position in American society. The workplace has achieved a unique reversal, holding a position of dominance in the social fabric that was inconceivable to those entering the labor pool for the first time in the mid-1960s, little more than fifty years ago.

Those workers consisted principally of teenagers and young adults eager to start their first full-time jobs, acquire a marketable skill, enroll in college, find a career, or evade the draft. They now make up the senior workforce, the aging employees, senior management, and the recent retirees of today.

THE DOMINANCE OF THE WORKPLACE

Exactly how much has the position of the workplace changed?

Any list of popular TV sitcoms of the mid-1960s would surely include such weekly network offerings as *My Three Sons*, *The Donna Reed Show*, *Leave it to Beaver*, *The Adventures of Ozzie and Harriet*, and *Father Knows Best*. The sole breadwinner in these sitcom families was always the father, and the story line or plot usually centered around the home. But even the best TV trivia experts today, who easily recall the fathers' real-life names (Fred McMurray, Carl Betz, Hugh Beaumont, Ozzie Nelson, and Robert Young, respectively), would be hard pressed to recall their TV jobs, where they worked, how they supported their TV families and earned a TV livelihood. Back in the mid-1960s, the workplace, both on TV and in society in general, was not only a strictly male preserve, it was also largely *invisible*.

The situation could not be more different today. Now, widely syndicated comic strips like *Dilbert* focus on the workplace in a way that only reflects the perennial popularity of TV sitcoms, starting with those like *NewsRadio*, which begat later successes like *The West Wing*, *The Office*, and then *Scrubs*. These led to current smash hits like *30 Rock*, scores of crime whodunits that include *CSI: Crime Scene Investigation*, and highly rated, critically acclaimed dramas like *Mad Men*, all of which reflect how influential, important, even dominant, the workplace has become in contemporary life.

Jill Andresky Fraser has aptly chronicled how the booming 1990s decade of the "miracle economy" led to many dot-com disasters, massive layoffs, and explosions in every sector of the economy. For those who have not gone postal and still hold meaningful jobs, their employment has almost imperceptibly become a nightmare of a seven-days-a-week workload, reduced salaries, and a pervasive fear and anxiety that compels many to work ever-increasing hours on the job. Fraser writes: "Few people possess the valuable ability to shut work out of their personal lives, at least for a long enough period to unwind from the intensive job schedules they must cope with seven days a week."[1] She adds that since "weekends scarcely provide relief for many overloaded men and women, vacations and holidays loom ever more important as an opportunity to restore balance. Yet these too are under siege in the white-collar sweatshop both from cost-cutting corporations and from the ever present job-spill."[2]

In this regard, several startling discoveries have been made by Arlie Russell Hochschild, who spent three years studying a *Fortune* 500 company, interviewing everyone, from top-level executives to factory hands. Hochschild concludes that none of the working parents took advantage of the company's invitation to use flex time, paternity leave, or other "family-friendly" programs.[3] Instead, they were fleeing homes invaded by the pressure of work, while the workplace seemed transformed into a strange kind of surrogate home. In her study, Hochschild also exposes the rifts in the crunch-time world and reveals how the way employees work and live doesn't work as well anymore because the home increasingly takes on the time pressures and efficiencies of the job, and the job, for many parents, has been transformed into a strange kind of "surrogate" home.[4]

In fact, the workplace for many has become so dominant a part of their lives that professor Cynthia Estlund advances an astonishing thought: since the workplace has eclipsed schools, churches, civic organizations, and neighborhoods as the place where most Americans are regularly nudged to work together and to achieve shared goals and try to get along, perhaps the workplace might also offer valuable lessons on the realization of democratic possibilities in the larger society as well.[5]

Of course, remaining competitive and profitable in an increasingly globalized economy often demands management strategies that include downsizing, outsourcing, plant closings, massive layoffs, and so on. And the continuing need for these strategies may not support Estlund's optimistic view. In fact, the rising incidence of employee violence has more often turned the traditional workplace into a "sweatshop" of anxiety, stress, and nine-to-five rage. As Charles C. Heckscher argues, many workplaces have become so toxic and inimical to the cultivation of friendships that even talk of possible layoffs, firings, or other personnel changes is forbidden—in both the carpeted boardrooms and executive suites as well as the aisles of the factory floor.[6]

For better or for worse, the workplace now dominates as it never has before, and if more people are now "bowling alone,"[7] it's only because more people are working more overtime. As the economy worsens, and both job security and physical safety become associated with the quaint past, workplace incivility grows into workplace violence, and workplace violence only fuels the growth of workplace murders. Given the slow but inexorable rise in workplace murders, where is the bipartisan groundswell of public outrage? Where is the outcry for government intervention and relief? Why haven't civic leaders, organizations, and nonprofits from both sides of the political aisle accepted the challenge? If, as many suspect, most of the American public does not even know there *is* a workplace crisis, the next question becomes why not? Why the silence? Why is the subject all but invisible? How can a crisis be so pervasive, yet simultaneously so invisible to so many? And how has this silence been maintained?

This duality in perception is much like the appearance of the woman who is three months pregnant: it's obvious she's pregnant, but only to those who *already know*. To everybody else, to those who *don't* know she's pregnant, it looks like she's just gained a little weight. The silence may also be explained as a government strategy not to exacerbate a problem by giving it official recognition. This is especially true where the tabloid news media in particular often reward even "copycat" murder wannabes with their fifteen minutes of fame, and the biggest real-life distinction between fame and infamy may often be found in a prefix alone.

The pervasiveness of the problem, however, now justifies the discontinuation of the silence. The point at which the silence no longer confers a public benefit has long since passed. The ignorance fostered by the silence now only endangers the safety and welfare of the public as a whole. The silence is clearly noticeable in mainstream culture, including plays, movies, nonfiction books, academic literature, and even TV talk shows. And the resultant ignorance is reinforced and perpetuated by the society at large—the criminal justice system, the civil courts, journalistic and authorial bias, the realities of broadcasting the network news, the publishing industry, and the unique features of the topic itself. Even the perpetrators of workplace murder, incarcerated as they are behind bars, contribute to the silence.

THE GENERAL CULTURE: PLAYS, MOVIES, AND FILM

Some of the factors that ensure the silence are structural, and cannot realistically be changed or even modified. However critical the need for the media to broadcast national events, the *over*broadcast of some stories does little to convey truly "new" news, and only obscures local news as the stories break from locale to locale and coast to coast.

As already noted, the media attention that was lavished on the shooting of Representative Giffords also obscured the equally tragic fact that similar shootings occur literally every day of the week, but go unnoticed (and ignored) nationally. When Joseph Harris murdered four people in October 1991, including his supervisor, whom he gored with a faux eighteenth-century samurai sword, only one major US newspaper carried the story. Of course, the story sparked little interest in TV newsrooms across the country on a day when the nation's headlines blared the nomination of Judge Clarence Thomas to the US Supreme Court.

The inevitable result is a public whose awareness of the world is celebrity-focused, with little room to appreciate actual, real-life news events that don't carry a high "human interest" value or feature a well-known face. It's also a public that's wholly ignorant of a growing crisis in the workplace. Network news thus resembles just another sitcom, just another business partnering with the ever-widening entertainment industry,[8] which itself has long avoided acknowledgment of the problem, let alone addressing it head-on.

Broadway plays and movies, for example, rarely depict an employee being fired. Rarely is a supervisor's ineptitude sufficient to justify violence, let alone homicide. And a fired employee is never outraged or angered enough to inflict physical harm on a boss. Almost never. In those instances where the employee *is* actually let go, the harshness of the event is typically lessened in different ways: injecting an element of humor to make it funny, depicting the employee as a despicably lazy oaf who deserved the axe, portraying the boss more sympathetically than the worker, or having the erstwhile employee quickly realize that getting canned was ultimately fortuitous or a blessing in disguise.

In Arthur Miller's play *Death of a Salesman* (1949), Willy Loman confesses to his sons that "The woods are burning, boys, you understand? There's a big blaze going on all around. I was fired today." This sad realization triggers both his descent and his ultimate suicide near the play's end. Yet the audience (like his sons) no doubt realizes that the firing was Loman's own fault.

In David Mamet's *Glengarry Glen Ross* (1984), few sympathize with the Shelly Levene character, and fewer regret the inevitable criminal consequences (despite his disabled daughter at home). Why? Because the audience knows who burglarized the office to steal the list of profitable real estate deals. If efforts to avoid dealing frankly with getting fired, or responding violently to an abusive boss, are evident on the Broadway stage, the efforts are even more evident in stories written for Hollywood movie stars on the silver screen.

In *Falling Down* (1993), Michael Douglas portrays a man very recently fired from his well-paying job in the defense industry. Suddenly out of work, he now faces the fact that, after many years of hard work and a steady paycheck, he's unnecessary and irrelevant. The conveniently nameless employer, the nameless character Douglas portrays, and the absence of a scene depicting him actually getting fired (which is backstory the audience must infer) make it unnecessary for director Joel Schumacher to depict the actual source of the Douglas character's anger and rage: the workplace. Schumacher dutifully acknowledges and even validates the anger and rage that may follow sudden termination from a job, but by starting the story *after* the Douglas character has already been fired, he shrewdly shifts the source of the man's anger and rage away from the employer and toward the blacks, Latinos, and Asians he meets on the road.

In *Which Way Is Up?* (1977), Richard Pryor plays three different roles. The principal character is Leroy Jones, an orange picker who accidentally joins a labor union before he's fired, run out of town, and lands in another city where he meets a beautiful union organizer and begins a romance. Based loosely on the Italian filmmaker Lina Wertmuller's *The Seduction of Mimi* (1972), whatever social commentary and "bite" the original held is all but lost in the translation. Leroy's termination and his union involvement are also lost in Pryor's hilarious take on the three different roles, especially since he ends up working for the same employer who fired him in the first place. And in a world where the employer is beyond retribution and scorn, it follows that the employee will do whatever management asks, if the employee is loyal and wants to keep his job. In Alberto Lattuada's forgotten little masterpiece, *Mafioso* (1962), Alberto Sordi plays an efficient foreman in a Fiat factory, Antonio "Nino" Badalamenti, whose boss asks him to do the unthinkable. And he *does* it—while vacationing with his beloved wife and two young daughters, spending time with his family and old friends in Sicily—then matter-of-factly returns to his duties in the Fiat factory.

A boss's decision to fire an employee often turns out to be a blessing in disguise. In *Jerry Maguire* (1996), the firing of the main character (Tom Cruise) forces him to value the truly important things in life, like settling down with his wife, played by Renee Zellweger. In the taut thriller *The Fan* (1997), director Tony Scott explores the fanatical admiration of salesman Gil Renard (Robert De Niro) for his favorite baseball player, Bobby Rayburn (Wesley Snipes). As the De Niro character's passion for the game (and his idol) interferes increasingly with company sales—and his behavior becomes more creepy and bizarre—De Niro's character is finally fired. By this point, however, audience sympathy has long since shifted, and the only question is why the firing took so long!

In *Thirteen Conversations About One Thing* (2001), the office supervisor (Alan Arkin) is required to fire one employee but decides to base his decision not on merit but on his dislike for the one employee whose chipper optimism infuriates him. Of course, the central joke is that even the firing can't dampen the employee's optimism ("You know, maybe I should look at the upside of this: I can take that vacation I've always wanted."). In *Boogie Nights* (1997), porn star Dirk Diggler (Mark Wahlberg) is fired by his boss when his cocaine addiction prevents him from performing before the camera. Though he lashes out at his boss (played very sympathetically by Burt Reynolds), the boss has always treated him like a son. And in *What Happens in Vegas* (2008), the Ashton Kutcher character is fired from his construction job by the boss (Treat Williams), who *is* his father.

Perhaps the silliest attempt to avoid showing anything unpleasant about being fired is the movie *Larry Crowne* (2011). The central character is Larry (Tom Hanks), who's suddenly fired after working twenty-odd years for a giant retail store called U-Mart. Though he's been named employee of the month nine times, he lacks the college degree required for further advancement. Changing his lifestyle, he trades in his giant, gas-guzzling Suburban for a small motor scooter, gets a cool haircut, and starts to hang out with a group of motor scooter bikers as he attends classes at the local community college to earn his associate's degree. While a student he also befriends and becomes romantically involved with one of his teachers, Mercedes Tainot, played by Julia Roberts.

But *Larry Crowne* is so afraid to depict anything negative about losing one's job that some scenes don't seem "real" or even make any sense. When Larry is fired, as an example, there's no mention of a severance package. After all those years of devoted service to U-Mart, was Larry given a generous sendoff? Or was he screwed? In real life, suddenly being fired may also mean an abrupt loss of office friends and acquaintances that were cultivated over the years. As questions of self-worth and lowered self-esteem tug at the ego, as feelings of isolation and futility quickly settle in, they often start to feed on each other. This leads to depression, sometimes even suicide, especially with men.

Not with Larry they don't. Larry seems oblivious, even impervious, to these human pitfalls. Indeed, it's at this point in his life that he happily befriends members of a motor-scooter gang of environmentalists, though it's not clear why any of its younger, presumably "cooler" members would even want to know—let alone associate with—someone like Larry. (Since the group also remains largely faceless and nameless, its sole cinematic function seems to be that of a cheering section for Larry.) And even more baffling than Larry's pursuit of Ms. Tainot is her attraction and response to him. After all, it's not every semester that a tall, beautiful, fortyish PhD English professor with gorgeous legs and a passion for Shakespeare falls in love with a dorky high school grad who's pushing 60, virtually penniless with no car and a drowning mortgage, and has at least another year of classes before he lands a menial job and earns an associate's degree.

Even movies that are more honest and empathetic in this regard ultimately pull a few cinematic punches in the end. This is especially true if all it requires is a little jiggling of the camera and some creativity in the editing room. In *Up in the Air* (2009), George Clooney plays Ryan Bingham, who earns a living by visiting different companies for the sole purpose of firing employees. His is a vital and expanding function for companies that need to downsize quickly but fear the unpredictable reactions of people abruptly kicked out the door after twenty or thirty years on the job.

Film critic Roger Ebert calls *Up in the Air* "a film for this time," and he couldn't be more correct. Director Jason Reitman reportedly cast people who had been fired from jobs in real life to play some of the people fired in the movie, a casting option that certainly would have helped the *Larry Crowne* script. In fact, one of the first questions a fired worker asks Bingham concerns the severance package. What makes the Bingham character hard to hate (and easy to respect) is Reitman's deft juxtaposition of his compassionate firing "style" with that of his younger colleague (Anna Kendrick), whose impersonal, brutally quick method makes Bingham's the preferred approach.[9]

Reitman's movies tend to be honest, but with "edge," and he deserves kudos here for the rare film that basically gets it right. (The script even allows a fired employee to commit suicide by jumping off a local bridge!) But even Reitman must pull punches in the end. In his depiction of the Galifianakis character's response to getting fired, Reitman deploys a shaky, handheld camera and speeds up the reel's twenty-four frames per second to obscure the footage of what the employee actually does in revenge—what many might feel are the funniest two seconds (and the fastest forty-eight frames) in the whole movie.[10]

BOOKS: NONFICTION, JOURNALISM, AND TRUE CRIME

Of course, the pervasive silence about workplace murder cannot be blamed on the network newsroom and Hollywood alone. Some part of the silence is also attributable to the conduct of business in the far-flung reaches of the publishing industry—from the top echelons of a half-dozen global media conglomerates down to the local bookstore at the mall. And though much has recently been written about workplace violence in general, almost nothing focuses exclusively on the narrower topic of workplace homicide.

The critical word here, of course, is "exclusively," especially as the last decade alone has witnessed the publication of a laudably high number of titles on workplace violence in general. Most have been written by highly regarded experts and scholars whose knowledge and expertise have been widely recognized and, indeed, they will be cited and acknowledged on these pages as well.

Yet, as already noted, these books never treat workplace homicide as a separate and discrete topic, divorced from other manifestations of workplace violence. Workplace "violence" obviously includes a much broader range of conduct, such as assault, verbal abuse, mobbing, and so on, and even different forms and degrees of workplace "aggression." And workplace "aggression" is broader still, as it includes 1) hostile speech (making nasty remarks to a coworker or engaging in hateful gossip), 2) hostile gestures (giving a colleague the "finger"), and 3) "gestured" speech, which includes elements of both speech *and* conduct, as where a male voice announces on a store's loudspeaker system, "Attention Wal-Mart customers: all black people leave the store now."[11]

The titles of many of these books include some combination of the words workplace, violence, aggression, and prevention. But as book titles are not subject to the laws of copyright, at least a half dozen share the identical title *Workplace Violence* and can be distinguished from each other by subtitle alone.[12] Nor is it always clear what the book is offering to be read. For example, in *Stalking, Harassment, and Murder in the Workplace—Guidelines for Protection and Prevention*, the authors discuss only a few case studies of stalking, and not a single case of murder. Despite the title's seductive reference to murder, not a single homicide or murder is discussed or even described in the text, nor do the words "murder" and "homicide" ever appear in the index.[13]

Generally, the literature in this area of the law consists almost entirely of books that assume one of three different structural formats. The first format includes those that mention the narrower topic of workplace murder, but ultimately devote their pages and discussion to other, less extreme behaviors on a broader spectrum of prohibited workplace conduct.[14] The second format consists of books that often provide references to the most publicized, sensational cases of occupational homicide, but lack any extended discussion of the issue. These books refer to murder only to frame or contextualize elements of a much broader discussion, to serve as a pedagogical bookend, or to preface or introduce the heading of the next chapter.[15] The third format consists of books that are either biographical or autobiographical in that they actually discuss workplace murder, but lack a comparative perspective, as they focus at length on a single example of workplace murder.[16]

Another reason the public knows so little about workplace murder is attributable to the element of individual journalistic choice, which reflects an authorial bias in the publishing industry. For millions of readers, few books are more enjoyable than a good true-crime story, or even a good murder mystery yarn. Writers like Scott Turow, Steve Martini, Patricia Cornwell, and John Grisham have forged lucrative careers out of their considerable talents in this area. But however many might love to *read* about murder and mass killings, to spend many months, even years, researching and writing on the topic can adversely affect *anybody*'s mental state.

Workplace murder, in other words, can be a depressing topic, to be avoided by researchers, scholars, and journalists alike. And the resultant scarcity of books on the topic is just another reason why the public's knowledge in the area is so scant. It's not difficult to understand a writer's aversion to the topic, whether the writer is a serious "literary" author, a journalist, or a writer of genre westerns, romance, chick lit, or sci-fi. Even the most commonplace, boring example of workplace homicide (if such a case ever exists) may take a devastating toll and wreak havoc on entire families, friends, neighbors, and colleagues. And this devastating toll often lasts not just for weeks or months but often years, even the rest of their lives. Their frequently touted claims of professional objectivity notwithstanding, even the most seasoned, the most hardened veteran writers are not immune.

In the mid-1960s Truman Capote won instant literary wealth and fame with the publication of *In Cold Blood*, a journalistic account of the 1962 murders of a prominent Kansas family by two psychotic drifters. Capote spent four years researching and writing the book, including interviews with the killers, who were executed by hanging in 1965. For years afterwards, Capote remained in the media spotlight as a popular celebrity. He frequently appeared on the TV talk-show circuit as a regular on NBC's *Johnny Carson Show*, and a member of the glitterati whose friends included the rich and famous both in and outside fashionable literary circles. What went virtually unnoticed over the years was that Capote—a prolific writer of dozens of novels, short stories, and movie scripts—after the 1966 publication of *In Cold Blood* until he died eighteen years later in 1984 never wrote another book.

And the stakes can often be tragically higher. Two-time Pulitzer winner J. Anthony Lukas spent several years completing the first draft of his last book, *Big Trouble*. The book was a towering 875-page historical study of America at the tumultuous start of the twentieth century through the spectacular trial of a labor leader and the assassination of a former Idaho governor.[17] Sadly, before completing the final draft, Lukas sank deeper into a depression, and in June 1977 tied a bathrobe sash around his neck and committed suicide.[18] A similar fate befell Iris Chang, whose masterful historical exposé, *The Rape of Nanking*,[19] recounts the unspeakable atrocities committed by the Imperial Japanese Army after it captured the city during the Second Sino-Japanese War. The book had already won Chang international acclaim, awards, and other recognition when she finally succumbed to years of depression, purchased a revolver in November 2007, and killed herself.[20]

THE SILENCING EFFECT OF THE CRIMINAL JUSTICE SYSTEM

Still another reason so little is known about workplace murder, and why the silence is so stubbornly pervasive, may be found in the workings of the criminal justice system. The silence is attained through the administrative efficiency with which it effectively silences the perpetrators and makes them all but inaccessible to both the media and the public at large.

As crimes go, workplace murders are never mysterious whodunits. The facts that constitute the elements of the offense are, almost by definition, *public*. As a result, the prosecutor or district attorney preparing the case rarely has a difficult time rounding up cooperative eyewitnesses, presenting evidence to a grand jury to return an indictment, and convincing a trial jury of the defendant's guilt beyond a reasonable doubt. Even after trial and conviction, the procedural cakewalk continues. The district attorney usually requests (and is granted) the harshest, longest sentences on multiple counts, and these are often served consecutively rather than concurrently, in order to maximize the time the perpetrator actually spends behind bars. Promptly locked away and made inaccessible to the public. The convicted perpetrators are silenced, and whatever might have been learned from their lips, whatever they could have taught the public, is forever lost behind bars or taken with them, after execution, to the grave.

The cold statistics eloquently recount the same facts. Of the 350-plus murderers included in this study, more than 35 percent committed suicide rather than surrender to the police. They typically shot themselves in the head just minutes before (or after) the police showed up. (Eerily, the frequency of this scenario suggests that the perpetrator quietly chose to be his or her own judge and jury, quickly considered the evidence, arrived at a guilty verdict, and then imposed the ultimate sentence—graciously saving the district attorney, the state, and the taxpayers the time and expense.)

Of the more than 58 percent who pled not guilty, picked a jury, and proceeded to trial, a full 94.5 percent were promptly convicted on all counts. At least 85 percent of those who were convicted received a sentence of life imprisonment without parole; about 30 percent of those sentenced to life were sentenced with stipulations of parole ineligibility for periods that ranged from ten to eighty years; and about 18 percent of those who were convicted on all courts received the death penalty, dying ceremoniously at the state's behest or from natural causes as they languished on death row, waiting for the appellate process to run its course.

How successfully were the perpetrators of workplace murder prosecuted, tried, and convicted in the courts? The statistics are startling. Not a single workplace murderer who elected to go to trial was ever found not guilty or acquitted on all counts. In no other category of criminal proceedings were the conviction rates on all counts nearly as high as those routinely returned in cases of workplace homicide. Of the almost two hundred perpetrators in this study who pled not guilty and went to trial, the conviction rate was more than 94 percent, and the total number of perpetrators who went to trial and were found "not guilty by reason of insanity" amounted to less than 2 percent. Of the almost two hundred workplace murderers who entered pleas of "not guilty," picked a jury, and went to trial, not one ever "got off," "beat the rap," or "went free," not a single male perpetrator walked out of the courthouse on his or her own, without being handcuffed, dressed in really loud orange fatigues, or assisted by a sheriff's officer or court marshal on either side.

And that's not all. Not a single workplace murderer on death row was ever granted a new trial by an appellate court, or the opportunity to file another appeal. Although there was a single case found in which a governor granted a (very temporary, pro forma) stay of execution, not a single perpetrator on death row ever received a telephone call from the governor's office granting a reprieve. Not one. And while the efficiency of the prosecutorial process is always a commendable governmental goal, in these cases, unfortunately, it also hides the crisis of workplace murder from public view, and only maintains and perpetuates the silence that much more effectively.

The criminal justice system not only determines the guilt of the perpetrators with amazing consistency and efficiency. Once the perpetrators are imprisoned, the system all but guarantees their imprisonment—with the perpetrators made inaccessible to everybody—for the maximum period permitted by law. For these perpetrators there will be no guest appearance on *The Oprah Winfrey Show*, no request by a *60 Minutes* producer for an interview from jail. These inmates will never be paroled or pardoned by a liberal governor, nor will poets pen sonnets about them, put the words to music, and sing their praise in quaint, overpriced coffee shops. These inmates will never receive a call from a literary agent to review a screenplay, approve foreign subsidy rights, or be offered a lucrative book deal.

Of course, the criminal justice system isn't alone in ensuring that perpetrators convicted of workplace murder receive the harshest sentences prescribed by law, and that they also remain behind bars for as long as the law allows. Through application of mandatory sentencing statutes, enacted in all the states, these longer sentences, often served consecutively, also ensure that the convicted are silenced for the longest periods behind bars, their cases buried deep in the computer system or nationwide database. In silencing the perpetrators, and ensuring that nobody learns about their cases, however, here the criminal court system is assisted by the civil court system, which lends a helping hand.

THE SILENCING EFFECT OF THE CIVIL COURT SYSTEM

Whenever a corporation or business suffers an incident of workplace murder, as already noted, it usually also suffers other hidden costs—costs that usually go unnoticed by the general public. These costs typically include those incurred for property cleanup, replacement, or repair, and increased billings for insurance coverage, security, and public relations. These costs are astronomically higher, however, if the corporation or business is sued in civil court, the defendant wins the case, and the company must pay even greater legal fees as well as damages—actual, compensatory, and punitive.

The damage awards against a losing company in civil court are often substantial, and sometimes total in the millions of dollars, even for a single litigant who prevails at trial, either by verdict or by the company electing to settle out of court. Recall John Rosh, who was shot by a fired employee, sued his company and the security firm, and was awarded $3.9 million, which was upheld on appeal? Why is so little known about those cases? Where are the David and Goliaths of the civil courts? Where are the "little" folks who bravely take on the big multinational corporations and *win*? Win, not just the important moral battles based on principles or "conscience," like those of Erin Brockovich[21] or the family of Karen Silkwood,[22] but win as private litigants who were motivated mostly by lucre as well?

These cases are won against big corporations and *Fortune* 500 companies in courtrooms across the country almost every day. Yet few people ever learn about them, few are ever provided the news. This news " blackout" is no accident, nor does it have anything to do with airwave reception, FCC jurisdiction, electronics, or technology. In-depth reportorial news on these cases is rarely done, if at all, even on the most morally lopsided trials that result in the highest damage awards by outraged juries and even an occasional judge or two. If the blackout is no accident, but the result of deliberate human agency, *how* is it achieved? And again, why?

This silence is legitimized and perpetuated by a legal document called the "confidentiality agreement" or "secrecy order." The widespread use of confidentiality agreements in civil litigation has been called one of the least discussed and most fundamental problems with the American civil court system. Unique to the civil courts, it functions essentially like an indefinite gag order. The document, duly signed by all the parties, ensures that neither party (the plaintiff or the defendant) speaks to the press or to the public to disclose or reveal any terms of the damage award, verdict, or settlement of the case. [23]

On the one hand, it protects the interests of the losing corporation by minimizing the effects of any adverse publicity that accompanies an unfavorable jury verdict or the company's decision to settle the matter out of court. The agreement also ostensibly protects the collective interests of the corporate stockholders, the value of whose shares in the corporation may drop as a result of, and in response to, the adverse publicity. And this adverse publicity may also negatively affect the corporate "goodwill" the company might've spent years building and cultivating in both the business community as well as the public eye.

On the other hand, these agreements also function to keep the public in the dark about the critical facts of the case, the parties, and the court system in general.[24] The general public thus never learns how to use the civil courts to protect its own interests. Nor does the public ever fully appreciates the extent to which large corporations, even *Fortune* 500, multinational corporations, are subject to the authority of the courts and the law of the land, and must ultimately abide by the rules as interpreted by a duly appointed judge and a jury in a court of law. All of which an employee, or any citizen for that matter, would be well advised to know, but which is rarely in the best interest of the corporation to disclose or publicize.

The greatest dangers to the public interest, however, are most evident not in cases brought by typical survivors of a workplace murder victim. The greatest dangers are most evident in cases in which the plaintiff who sues a large corporation for causing significant harm, say, to the local environment, also gains access to other dangerous information. If the parties settle the case, all the information acquired by the plaintiff that implicates the corporate defendant in some massive wrongdoing will have to be kept secret. This is because the agreement prohibits the plaintiff from sharing any information that's likely to incriminate other corporate defendants who are sued by other small individual plaintiffs.[25] All future plaintiffs must therefore sue and go to court *on their own* before they too can gain access to the damaging or incriminating information that can be used against other large corporate defendants.[26]

THE SILENCE OF THE WORKPLACE MURDERERS THEMSELVES

The public's lack of knowledge about workplace murder may also be explained, truth be told, by the perpetrators themselves. Typically only moderately educated, angry white men in their early forties with few friends and large gun collections at home, convicted workplace murderers aren't generally a very likeable (or even photogenic) group. And theirs is a milieu that taints even their law-abiding womenfolk who seek a day in court. This may explain why public intellectuals like Betty Friedan, Gloria Steinem, and Camille Paglia all rushed to the nearest podium to support the Yale-educated law professor Anita Hill in her largely unsubstantiated claim of sexual harassment against Clarence Thomas, but chose to remain silent on claims of actual sexual assault by Bill Clinton brought by Paula Jones, an Arkansas rube. (It may also explain why another Yale-educated female lawyer ventured far beyond fair criticism of Jones's legal strategy for the sole purpose of gratuitously poking fun at her "cheap," "trashy" look, her clothes and hair, her "elongated nose" and shiny skin, and her desperate need for a haircut, a facial massage, and some custom-mixed powder for her face.)[27]

In short, most male workplace murderers have a lot of ideological axes to grind. They generally share a vague but mounting fear of bossy, modern women with advanced degrees, immigrants of any hue, society's acceptance of lesbians and gays, one too many "foreign-born" blacks in the Oval Office, and far too many Jews on the Supreme Court.

For two generations the writing of Studs Terkel exalted and praised the strength, ingenuity, and industry of American labor, whose individual worker always spoke collectively to something grand and noble in the human spirit.[28] In an era of the globalized economy, however, that labor force has lost its strength and ingenuity, and the workers have lost their will to inspire. As the forces behind the global economy also raise the tensions and anxieties that fuel workplace violence, the typical American worker is now too easily imagined storming the boss's office angrily loading a clip in the AK-47 tucked under his arm. Convinced that workplace murderers are psychopathic, paranoid criminals whose conduct is inevitable and beyond prevention, the public is less inclined to enter the discussion or even listen to the necessary dialogue and debate.

Note has already been made of how easily the crisis of workplace murder may be mislabeled or mistaken for some other problem or societal ill. But just as it looks different within the context of a Midwest farm recession or a rural ghetto phenomenon, it also becomes less recognizable when the victims lead lives that are different from those we commonly associate with the crime. For reasons not readily apparent, the general public seldom recognizes cases of workplace murder, somehow becomes even more blinded to the problem, when the victims are "celebrities"—prominent artists, business leaders, well-known entertainers, and athletes.

Few would still recall the name Valerie Solanas, for example, until reminded that one afternoon in July 1968 the lone drifter waited patiently for the iconic artist Andy Warhol to arrive at his Manhattan office/studio, The Factory, while carrying a concealed handgun. When Warhol finally arrived, Solanas pulled the gun and fired three times at near-point-blank range. Incredibly, she missed him twice, striking art critic Mario Amayo nearby before trying to shoot Warhol's manager, Fred Hughes, and then fleeing on an elevator just after the gun jammed. Also likely forgotten over the years was that the incident grew out of an argument over "terms and conditions" of employment. For months Solanas had been asking Warhol to return a movie script she had written entitled *Up Your Ass*, which he had promised to read.[29] But Warhol had lost the script, unread, and for months avoided her calls demanding either the script or financial payment.[30]

Another case of "celebrity" workplace murder unfolded in November 1978, when former San Francisco supervisor Dan White shot and killed San Francisco mayor George Moscone, and only minutes later shot and killed San Francisco supervisor Harvey Milk. The double assassination made national headlines, as Milk was also one of the nation's first openly gay politicians and an iconoclastic, pioneering leader in the burgeoning gay rights movement of the 1970s. Long since forgotten over the years was the fact that the tragedy actually grew out of an "employment" relationship. Dan White was destitute and desperately needed Milk to give him his old job back, a position from which he had just recently resigned because the salary was so meager. And Milk had refused.[31]

On March 31, 1995, Yolanda Saldívar, 34, fatally shot her boss in the back. Few realized from the first news reports, however, that her boss was Selena Quintanilla-Perez—or "Selena"—the Mexican American singing sensation who was on the cusp of international superstardom. Later that same day Selena was pronounced dead from the loss of blood, two weeks before her twenty-fourth birthday. This tragedy also grew out of an employment relationship. Saldívar, the president of the local Selena fan club as well as the manager of her boutiques, had been caught embezzling money, had had an argument with Selena's father, and knew Selena had already decided to fire her.

Also included in this study was the suicide of Mark Madoff, 46, who hanged himself in his Manhattan, New York, SoHo apartment on December 11, 2010, which was also the second anniversary of the arrest of his father, Bernard Madoff. Mark Madoff reportedly felt victimized by the far-reaching ramifications of his father's crimes, which consisted of cheating clients and investors out of $18 billion, and for which his father had been sentenced to 150 years in jail. The son, who had been employed by Madoff Investments, LLC, as a codirector in the securities trading division, denied any wrongdoing in his father's massive Ponzi scheme. Though never charged with any wrongdoing, he had grown increasingly distraught over his father/employer's crimes, which drove him to commit suicide.[32]

THE DENIAL OF THE CRISIS BY SCHOLARS AND EXPERTS

Much of the blame for why so few realize the magnitude of the crisis may also be attributed to how differently scholars and experts in the field interpret the available data and research. An often-quoted, highly regarded Boston criminology professor, for example, recently pointed out that the vast majority of workplace murders occur during commission of violent crimes—like taxicab stickups, convenience store robberies, police assaults, and so on. The criminology professor then pointed out that "the least common form of workplace homicide . . . are the murderous acts of disgruntled employees and ex-employees seeking revenge over work-related issues. *The term 'epidemic,' which has been used to describe the problem of workplace violence and murder, is more hyperbole than reality*."[33]

It cannot be denied that the number of workplace homicides has dropped significantly from what it was twenty years ago, and that the likelihood of a workplace murder is substantially less than what it was in the mid-1990s.[34] This is likely part of a trend that reflects a well-documented leveling off of the nation's rising homicide rate.[35] Even a highly regarded insurance publication states that "contrary to popular belief . . . the majority of [workplace murders] are not crimes of passion committed by disgruntled workers and spouses, but . . . result from robberies."[36]

But this, quite simply, is no longer the case. There is, as several major governmental organizations have recognized, an epidemic in workplace violence. With all due respect to the criminology professor, using that term to describe the crisis is hardly an example of "hyperbole." The rising incidence of workplace murder is in fact, and quite literally, a workplace "epidemic."

In a disturbing new trend, workers are now killing other workers much more frequently than they were just a decade ago. "Increasingly," according to the *National Law Review*, citing a report by the National Council on Compensation Insurance (NCCI), "the highest share of workplace homicides is still due to the category of robbers and other perpetrators, but that share has fallen from 85% to 69% from 1997 to 2009."[37] "Over that same period, the share due to work associates has grown from 9% to 21%," or more than doubled.[38] The rapidly rising rate of murders committed exclusively between employees and employers, coworkers, or "associates" on the job is therefore sufficient to justify official governmental designation of the crisis as a workplace "epidemic."

The opinion of the criminology professor that using the word epidemic to describe workplace violence is "more hyperbole than reality" also fails to consider a critical factor that's increasingly common in true cases of workplace homicide. In the vast majority of murders committed in the workplace by robbers or other intruders during the commission of a crime, even in the worst-case scenario, the intruder kills a single victim and then flees the scene of the crime. In domestic violence disputes that spill over into a job site, the victim is usually a woman who rejected the advances of a male perpetrator, or a female employee who won a custody battle against an ex-spouse, and so on. The murder victim of a robbery or other serious crime is often only a single individual, like a single security guard, a taxicab driver, or a convenience store clerk.

What the criminology professor fails to realize is that the situation is very different, and the dynamic is much deadlier, in cases of true workplace homicide. In cases where an intruder enters a workplace and kills an employee during the commission of a crime, the intruder rarely knows his victim, never commits mass murder, and also quickly flees the scene. In almost half the cases where the murder is committed by a disgruntled employee against a boss or coworker, however, the killer and the victim knew each other, and familiarity *does* breed contempt. The disgruntled employee shoots and kills *multiple* coworkers and colleagues, even onlookers and innocent bystanders who just happened to be nearby.

Nor do these disgruntled employees flee the scene after they commit the crime. Indeed, as the body count grows, the likelihood also grows that the disgruntled employee, having already committed multiple murders, will not only *not* flee the scene like the intruder, but will raise the murder toll still higher, avoid arrest and prosecution, and save the last bullet to commit suicide. Hyperbole, indeed.

THE CHANGING FACE OF WORKPLACE MURDER

The myths and half-truths that quickly surface in any discussion of workplace violence—and workplace murder in particular—quickly reveal how ingrained and deeply rooted they have become in the public's thinking and in the public discourse. They've become so ingrained that they now function as a kind of orthodoxy whose tenets are accepted as universal truths. In few areas are the myths and half-truths more comforting and deeply entrenched, however, than those that inform our notions of who among us in the workplace has the greatest potential to kill.

The "science" of phrenology has long since been discredited, and the shape and contours of the skull are no longer acceptable signifiers of personality and psychological traits. Yet vestigial traces of this thinking remain, and many (consciously or unconsciously) still ascribe personality traits to physical features or characteristics. The subliminal association of a black mustache and/or beard with villainy and evil is still with us, still thrives in the collective imagination, even though it runs counter to the well-established fact that virtually all serial killers and rapists on record are actually clean shaven with no facial hair.

Given how little the public knows about workplace murder, must it continue to rely on a kind of "profiling" to protect itself? One need only ponder the face of Michael McDermott to see what much of the American public *still* regards as the twentieth-century face of workplace homicide. McDer-

mott was an angry software technician who had worked for the Massachusetts firm Edgewater Technologies only a few months when he was told he
would be laid off, just days before the Christmas holidays. He was also angry
at the company's compliance with an order to withhold a substantial portion
of his salary each pay period to pay installments on back taxes he owed the
IRS.[39]

A strapping six-foot-two giant of a man, McDermott was fully bearded
and beer-bellied, reminiscent of TV's popular Grizzly Adams character—
only on PCP or crack cocaine! In response to his employer's scheduled
layoffs and its willingness to deduct money from his paycheck to pay the
IRS, McDermott loaded an AK-47, a rifle, a shotgun, and a semiautomatic
handgun, and then entered the company's administrative complex. Only minutes later he had shot and killed his supervisor, as well as six fellow employees. He then politely surrendered to the police.[40]

If the face of Michael McDermott was the face of workplace murder for
the twentieth century, what does that face for the twenty-first century look
like? The faces, names, gender, religions, and even motives of today's workplace murderers are very different from those of just twenty years ago. Is the
face of twenty-first-century workplace murder a foreign-born face, newly
arrived from some distant Mediterranean shore? Is it the deranged, psychopathic face of a home-grown terrorist like Ted "Unabomber" Kaczynski,
Colin Ferguson, or Timothy McVeigh, or some other pseudopatriot waving a
flag in each hand?

Or is it the more familiar, more reassuring face of someone we see every
day but never notice—like the quiet man who walks his cocker spaniel across
the street, or the average girl who lives next door?

Chapter Three

Definitely Not Your Average Girl Next Door

She probably tugged at the sleeve of her red V-neck sweater to adjust the extra weight of the bulge under her sensible plaid blazer. She had already taught her anatomy and neuroscience class earlier that day and was now on her way to another faculty meeting. These faculty meetings were routine, held every month, and fortunately had nothing to do with tenure anymore. She also probably knew that some of her colleagues who had voted against her tenure months ago would be at this meeting as well.

This was supposed to be just another faculty meeting, a routine gathering of the members of the biology department. At least, that's what *they* thought. But she knew better. This meeting would be *very* different. The meeting was already underway, in a faculty conference room on the third floor of the Shelby Center. The Shelby Center was a modern, multimillion-dollar structure that housed the mathematics and biology departments of the University of Alabama's sprawling Huntsville campus, or the UAH. And she knew this meeting would end like no other meeting ever held in the building before, which is why her blazer felt heavier as she approached the conference room on the third floor.

THE HARVARD-TRAINED ECCENTRIC YANKEE

"Dr. Amy Bishop, Harvard-trained" was how she often introduced herself to people she didn't know. But her biology students called her simply "Professor Bishop." A Harvard-educated neurobiologist and busy mother of four, Amy Bishop lived with her husband, James Anderson, also a scientist, and their four children on the UAH campus. She was hired in 2005 as an assistant professor in biology after earning a biology degree from Northeastern University in 1988 and a PhD in genetics from Harvard in 1993.[1]

The only daughter of Samuel Bishop, a full professor in the art department at Northeastern, and a second cousin to the novelist John Irving, Amy Bishop had also written three unpublished novels, and her 1993 thesis was entitled "The Role of Methoxatin (PQQ) in the Respiratory Burst of Phagocytes," and was 137 pages long. Her research interests included the induction of adaptive resistance to nitric oxide in the central nervous system, and the utilization of motor neurons for the development of neural circuits grown on biological computer chips. She had also published several articles in scientific journals as either a lead or coauthor.[2] Not by any stretch of the imagination was Amy Bishop to be considered just your average girl next door.

Despite her academic achievements, eleven months earlier, in March 2009, Bishop had been denied tenure by the faculty. Her teaching contract wouldn't be renewed. In a few weeks she would be unemployed, and now she needed to find another job. She had already appealed the faculty's adverse tenure decision to the Equal Employment Opportunity Commission (EEOC),[3] and she knew that at least one of her colleagues who had voted against her tenure would also be at this meeting on the third floor.

She arrived at the meeting at 3:20 p.m. and joined about a dozen other faculty and administrative staff, taking a chair at the cramped oval-shaped table. The others included professors Gopik Podila, the department chair, and professors Maria Davis and Adriel Johnson, both black, who also taught biology. Also seated were professors Leahy and Luis Cruz-Vera, along with a senior staff member, Stephanie Monticciolo. Whether it also occurred to Bishop that chairman Podila was a light, olive-skinned Southeast Asian, and that both Davis and Johnson were black, is not known.

What everyone later recalled was that Bishop sat mute at the table for about thirty minutes. Then, just before 4:00 p.m., she slowly rose from her chair as if she wanted to address the group, but said nothing. Then she pulled a nine-millimeter semiautomatic Ruger handgun from inside her blazer.

According to eyewitnesses, what followed during the next five minutes seemed to take only a few seconds, as if time had compressed every minute into a second, and every second into a few nanoseconds. Joseph Ng, a biology professor who was sitting in the conference room, recalled that Bishop "got up suddenly, pulled a gun and started shooting at each of us. She started with the one closest to her, and went down the row shooting her targets in the head."[4] Another eyewitness, Debra Moriarity, dean of UAH's graduate program and also a biochemistry professor, observed: "This wasn't random shooting around the room; this was execution-style."[5]

After Bishop fired several shots, according to Moriarity, she pointed the gun at her (Moriarity), at near-point-blank range, and then pulled the trigger. But nothing happened. All they heard was a metallic sound of a click. At this,

Moriarity recalls, Bishop seemed initially "angry" and then, following this apparent mechanical malfunction, seemed "perplexed" as the gun had either jammed or run out of ammunition.[6] As a half-dozen professors slumped dying or dead, bleeding in their chairs or on the floor, Moriarity quickly joined several others who had gang-rushed Bishop, slowly forcing her from the conference room and into the hallway.

As the surviving professors and staff barricaded themselves inside the conference room, Bishop evidently discarded her blood-splattered blazer and tossed the Ruger nine-millimeter handgun as she left the building. She was arrested just minutes later, in front of the building, where a small crowd had already started to gather. Minutes later the police recovered the nine-millimeter Ruger from a second-floor restroom. Bishop had just killed three professors, each shot in the head at point-blank range, and wounded three others, one critically. As the police led her away in handcuffs into a waiting vehicle, she mumbled to no one in particular, "It didn't happen. There's no way. They're still alive."[7]

Bishop's triple murder made national and international news, and dominated the regional news for weeks. She was charged with several felonies, including one count of capital murder. County district attorney Robert Broussard confirmed that he would seek the death penalty. Bishop later pleaded guilty to the murder charges, and on September 24, 2012, was sentenced to life in prison without parole. Still, however compelling the details of the massacre, however tragic the particulars of the deaths, by far the most compelling aspect of the case was that the perpetrator was a brilliant Ivy League–educated female.[8]

THE GRISLY SAN MARCO PRECEDENTS

Of the 350-plus individuals who qualified for this study, almost 14 percent were women. Analyses of their cases show that in a majority of instances, the behavior of female workplace murderers differed significantly from that of their male counterparts, and was often so different that it defied belief. Still, the question of whether women are just as violent, just as cold-blooded as men, will be left to the individual reader to ponder. Suffice to say that, as brutal and cold-blooded as the Amy Bishop case was, it was not the bloodiest workplace massacre by a woman. That gruesome distinction, that grisly (dis)honor, is held by another woman, whose rampage occurred almost three thousand miles away, in California, two years before Bishop was hired by UAH and taught her first biology class.

Jennifer San Marco, 44, of Goleta, California, had worked as a dispatcher for the Santa Barbara police department before she worked briefly for the USPS as a postal clerk. After six years on the job, however, she was removed from her post office position in 2003 and placed on "medical disability," more for her own safety than for that of others, according to a postal inspector.[9] She moved to her native New Mexico, where she tried unsuccessfully to start a publication, *The Racist Press*,[10] and also exhibited other bizarre behaviors that suggested mental problems. She often mumbled to herself as if she were two people engaged in an argument, she once showed up at a local gas station naked, and she made no effort to hide her hatred for minorities, especially Asians.[11]

San Marco soon left New Mexico and returned to California angry, frustrated, and bent on revenge. On the evening of January 30, 2006, she passed through a heavily guarded security station at a mail processing plant and distribution center in Goleta, and entered the building in which she had worked two years ago.[12] Just hours earlier she had killed a former neighbor at an apartment complex, and no one at the Goleta facility knew she was armed with a fifteen-round, nine-millimeter Smith and Wesson pistol and more than a hundred rounds of ammunition.[13] At gunpoint, she took an employee's badge, entered the building, and then opened fire—shooting and killing two postal workers in the parking lot and shooting and killing four more once inside the plant. Minutes later, she turned the gun on herself and committed suicide. (Five of her victims died at the site, and a sixth died two days later at a local hospital.)[14]

San Marco's massacre was a statistical oddity, first, because she never targeted a single supervisor or boss, and focused instead on a former neighbor and the coworkers she believed had been responsible for her earlier termination as a clerk. The case also set three grisly precedents. If we define "massacre" as the murder of three or more people, as part of a single, continuing event, the San Marco case was the first (and, until the Amy Bishop case, the only) workplace massacre in the United States ever committed by a woman.

According to criminologist James Alan Fox, female perpetrators of massacres of any kind are unusual. "In the string of postal shootings in the 80s, there were no female offenders . . . When the term 'going postal' got coined, it was all men."[15] In this study, only two cases of workplace murder by women qualified as "massacres"—those by Jennifer San Marco and Amy Bishop.

The second precedent set by the San Marco case was in her motives. Although the Bishop massacre had a racial aspect, the element of race was an obvious factor in the formulation of San Marco's motives. Her victims included three blacks, one Asian, one Filipino, and one Hispanic. San Marco herself was Caucasian, and her coworkers reported that she often made racially inflammatory remarks, and had once even tried to start a newsletter called *The Racist Press*.[16] The third precedent set by the San Marco massacre was that it also suggested an oddly misogynistic element. All but one of her victims were other women. Although a handful of cases present facts that suggest a misogynistic element, the San Marco massacre is the only case where misogyny played a prominent part in the decision of who to kill. Finally, the San Marco massacre was the first (and only) workplace massacre by a female that also ended with the female committing suicide. [17]

The San Marco case was (and remains) such an oddity primarily because so many grisly precedents were established by the facts of a single case. Armed with a single nine-millimeter handgun, she shot and killed six women, one man, and then killed herself, ending what remains the worst workplace massacre in the United States ever committed by a female. As the case included so many elements—racism, misogyny, elitism, mass murder, suicide, mental illness, and so on—it raised more issues and posed more questions than any three other cases of female workplace murder combined.

THE FEMALE WEAPON OF CHOICE

Since the San Marco case set so many factual precedents, it's hardly a surprise that one behavioral feature in the case was repeated in every case of an armed female workplace murder that followed—every case without exception. Even in cases that occurred years *before* the San Marco case, the fact stood out—from the 1982 case of Mary Barbara Austin (who murdered her frugal boss, the managing attorney in a prestigious Fifth Avenue law firm, after she received a paltry annual bonus), the case of Mozella Dansby (who murdered her supervisor at a Georgia power company in 1987 after she was denied a promotion), and the case of Roxanna Ullery (who murdered her boss in 1987 after repeated acts of sexual harassment), to the more recent female killers like Arunya Rouch, who murdered a coworker in 2010, Yvonne Hiller, who murdered two coworkers in 2010, and, of course, Amy Bishop, who murdered three coworkers in 2011. And what was that single behavioral feature?

As already noted, San Marco and Bishop committed their workplace massacres with handguns; Jacquelyn Ferguson shot and killed her supervisor in a doctor's office before she went home and killed herself with a handgun. Yolanda Saldívar shot and killed Selena with a handgun. Elizabeth Teague shot and killed her boss at the Eveready Battery Company with a handgun. Cathline Repunte shot and killed a fellow bus driver with a handgun. Kerri Faye Brown, Faedra Rhondelle Satchel, to name just a few, they all killed their bosses, coworkers, or colleagues while armed with a single handgun. The single most consistent behavioral pattern in the entire study was that women who used a firearm always—and without a single exception—used a handgun, and only *one* handgun.

Not surprisingly, men typically assessed the need for the appropriate fire-power very differently. Joseph Harris, we recall, decided to kill his supervis-or, and drove to her house armed with a nine-millimeter Uzi handgun, a .22-caliber machine gun with a silencer, several hand grenades, a few bombs, and a faux eighteenth-century samurai sword. Dr. Nidal Malik Hasan, the American-born Muslim psychiatrist who in November 2009 shot and killed thirteen and wounded thirty more at Fort Hood, Texas, was armed with two handguns, an FN Five-seven semiautomatic pistol and a .357 Magnum revol-ver, and his fatigue pockets were heavy with several pistol magazines.

Others who reinforced this behavioral difference between men and wom-en included Michael McDermott, who was armed with an AK-47 rifle, a shotgun, and a semiautomatic handgun. William Baker had armed himself with an AK-47, a .38-caliber revolver, a Remington shotgun, a .30-caliber hunting rifle equipped with a telescopic lens, and a box of bullets and maga-zine clips. James E. Pough was armed with a .38-caliber revolver and a Universal M1 Carbine rifle. Richard Wade Farley, who had stalked a co-worker and was later fired from his job, returned to the company armed with a Benelli semiautomatic shotgun, a .22-250 rifle with a scope, a pump-action shotgun, a Sentinel .22 Winchester Magnum Rimfire revolver, a Smith and Wesson .357 Magnum revolver, a Browning .380 Automatic Colt Pistol, and a Smith and Wesson nine-millimeter pistol, along with a foot-long buck knife, a smoke bomb, an ammunition vest, earplugs, and a leather glove—*and Farley wasn't even sure which supervisor was responsible for his termi-nation, or even if he should shoot anyone at all.*

Of course, not every woman in the study used a gun. Some used make-shift weapons; some used landscaping rocks; others used poisons, such as horse tranquilizers, chemicals, and arsenic; and a couple used their bare hands. But of those women who *did* use a firearm, they all used only a single handgun. Not a single rifle, carbine, AK-47, or shotgun was ever used by any women who murdered in the workplace. This was more than an understand-able female aversion to toting heavy, metal objects. And the practical ramifi-cations of this one behavioral difference, this single difference in "choice" between men and women, were nothing short of profound. Profound because it influenced several other behaviors as well, like the timing of the response, the logistics of implementation, focus, the degree of violence, the level of lethality, the number of collateral victims, and even the nature and extent of the property loss that often accompanied the loss of human life.

THE OTHER FEMALE WEAPONS OF CHOICE

In a handful of cases of workplace murder by women (e.g., Yolanda Saldi-var), the facts suggest a motive that also included jealousy—of wealth, celebrity, talent, or good looks. This was never the case with men. Nor was motive the only area in which male and female murderers differed.

Another area of behavioral difference was in how the murder was accomplished, or what type of weapon was found most appropriate for the job. As the handgun was the exclusive weapon among women who used a firearm, the second-most-popular weapon wasn't another type of gun, but poison. The act of poisoning a despised boss or a hated supervisor occurred in more than 20 percent of the cases of workplace murder where the perpetrator was a woman. And this figure is even more astonishing when one considers that men did not use poison as a weapon in the workplace. Indeed, of the 350-plus cases of workplace murder included in this study, not a single case was found in which a male perpetrator sought to exact revenge by using poison.[18]

We recall Judith Coffin who, faced with the daily taunts and harassment by both male superiors and subordinates, committed suicide with an insulin overdose. In October of 2004, Debra Baker, a bookkeeper for Texas millionaire entrepreneur Jerry Sternadel, poisoned him with a lethal dose of arsenic. On September 11, 2001, Sarah Dutra, 21, was working as a part-time legal secretary in the Sacramento, California, law office of Larry McNabney when she (along with McNabney's wife) used a horse tranquilizer to poison the attorney, whose body was found months later buried in a Joaquin County vineyard.

Even female *attempts* to murder the boss often included the use of poison. In late February 2011, two Norwood, North Carolina, high school cafeteria workers, Angela Johnson, 38, and Eileen Hallamore, 64, were arrested after attempting to poison their supervisor by adding a cleaning solution to her tea. They were later charged with distributing a poisoned food, a charge which had been reduced from that of attempted murder. And in January 2000, a Pembroke Pines Wal-Mart employee, Femesha Foster, 32, of Miami, Florida, was arrested for placing rat poison in her boss's can of Dr. Pepper, unaware that she had been taped on a surveillance camera her boss had installed in the store.

THE FEMALE NONPROCRASTINATOR, ETC.

Patience was not a virtue with women, certainly not when it came to workplace revenge. Still another area in which women differed significantly from men was in their perception of how urgently the situation required a deadly response. Although there were a few notable exceptions, women tended to be far more impatient and less likely to procrastinate after they decided to seek revenge.

Typical of the women in this respect were cases like Erika Ray, the Chicago waitress who, in June 2006, killed her boss the day after she was fired; Cathline Repunte, the Los Angeles school bus driver who shot and killed one of her coworkers and wounded three others just minutes after she was provoked by a union activist; and Arunya Rouch, 41, the Publix worker in Tarpon Springs, Florida, who shot and killed a coworker, Gregory Janowski, 40, as he sat smoking a cigarette in his car within minutes after he threatened and taunted her for being a neurotic "perfectionist" on the job.

There was also the Bethesda, Maryland, store clerk Brittany Norwood, who stabbed and beat her coworker to death on March 11, 2011, only minutes after she realized the coworker knew she was stealing from the store. Kraft Foods worker Yvonne Hille, ran to her vehicle parked in an adjacent lot, retrieved her .357 Magnum, and killed two taunting female coworkers and wounded a third on September 9, 2010, only "ten minutes" after she was suspended from her job. Indeed, it could even be argued that Amy Bishop, who shot and killed three of her professor colleagues when she was denied tenure, had avenged the denial months *before* she actually received a pink slip.

This sense of urgency and impatience, this unwillingness, refusal, or inability to wait, with few exceptions, runs through all the cases of female workplace murder, as well as those to which we have already been introduced, like Femesha Foster, Natavia Lowery, Yolanda Saldívar, and Elizabeth Teague. All of these cases show a female perpetrator who couldn't or wouldn't wait; these were women who, confronted with some perceived indignity or insult, snapped in a sudden act of homicidal anger and rage.

Men usually handled this aspect of their revenge very differently. With few exceptions, men took their time and were far more likely to wait for weeks, months, even years before they finally struck back in revenge. Of course, it's impossible to determine from outward conduct alone the precise moment at which someone arrives at a decision to perform a physical act. An employee fired from a job on Tuesday, as an example, might be upset, but not upset enough to justify revenge immediately, and might then wait until Friday. And even if the employee decided to exact revenge that Friday, the vagaries of chance and opportunity might force a further delay until Monday, when the factory gates or the office doors opened again.

Despite the difficulty in interpreting outward conduct, the cases clearly showed men to be more patient, to be more likely to procrastinate or wait, and to not need to exact revenge immediately or even the same day. On June 1, 2011, Keith Little, 49, who worked in a Bethesda, Maryland, hospital, murdered his boss by stabbing him more than seventy times—several weeks after a poor performance review. On June 13, 1997, Soon Byung Park, 36, of Santa Fe Springs, California, shot and wounded his boss, killed his boss's sister, and then committed suicide—a month after he was fired. On February 9, 1996, Clifton McCree, 41, opened fire in a Fort Lauderdale, Florida, trailer, killing five former colleagues and wounding another, then turned the gun on himself to commit suicide—fourteen months after he was fired. On February 5, 2010, Socorro Hurtado-Garcia of Grand Rapids, Michigan, murdered his boss two months after losing his job. On June 19, 1999, Denis Czajkowski, 43, a psychiatric nurse at Norristown State Hospital in Pennsylvania, shot and killed his supervisor almost two months after being fired.

Other men took much longer before they exacted revenge. On July 20, 2005, Levi Andre White, an employee of a Baltimore, Maryland, juice company, shot and killed his supervisor two months after being fired. On September 15, 1997, Arthur Hastings Wise, 43, of North Augusta, South Carolina, shot seven people, killing four, two months after being fired. On June 4, 1991, Larry Hansel, 41, a technician with Elgar, a San Francisco–based electronics firm, shot and killed two of his supervisors with a twelve-gauge shotgun more than three months after he was laid off. On August 19, 1983, Perry Smith of Johnston, South Carolina, shot and killed the local postmaster, and wounded two others, three months after he had resigned. On June 29, 2000, Dr. Jian Chen, a University of Washington resident, shot and killed his boss, and then committed suicide, almost three months after he learned his contract wouldn't be renewed.

In August 2008, Robert Diamond, an employee of a Simon and Schuster book distribution center in suburban Philadelphia, Pennsylvania, shot and killed two former coworkers four months after he was fired. On February 27, 2004, New York City transit worker Darryl Dinkins, 39, shot and killed two supervisors four months after he was fired. On April 3, 1995, metallurgist James Simpson shot and killed six coworkers before shooting himself in the head, apparently depressed, seven months after he quit the job. In January 1993, Paul Calden of Tampa, Florida, shot and killed three of his former supervisors and injured two others, eight months after losing his job. On April 13, 1994, fiber-optic-cable inspector Ladislav Antilak shot and killed two former coworkers and wounded two others before committing suicide, eight months after he was fired. On August 27, 2003, auto parts worker Salvatore Tapia, 36, shot and killed six former coworkers on Chicago's South Side before he was killed by the police in a shoot-out that occurred six months after he was fired.

In many cases, the male perpetrator waited even longer. In some cases, however, the greater patience wasn't attributable to personality or temperament, but owed instead to necessity. These perpetrators were not sufficiently provoked or finally prodded into action until they received adverse appellate decisions or unfavorable judicial or administrative rulings, or were denied permissions by governmental agencies or bureaucracy—or until they were released from jail. On November 14, 1991, postal clerk Thomas McIlvane, 31, having lost his appeal for reinstatement, shot and killed three former coworkers and wounded six others in a Royal Oaks, Michigan, postal facility almost a year after he was fired. On September 26, 2005, Victor M. Piazza,

55, of Warwick, New York, returned to his former workplace, shot and wounded three former supervisors, and then committed suicide, nineteen months after being fired.

Incredibly, some men took *years*—planning, scheming, burning with a private hatred—before they took the law into their own hands. In the infamous Bath Massacre, one of the bloodiest cases of workplace violence in US history, Andrew Kehoe, 55, set fires and detonated two bombs, killing forty-five (including thirty-eight children between the ages of seven and twelve) and injuring fifty-eight. As rescuers gathered at the burning remains of the first bomb, Kehoe calmly detonated the second, thereby committing suicide and killing several more bystanders as well. Kehoe's careful planning and preparations took the better part of a year. On May 9, 2005,Gregory Gray returned to his former workplace, a mental health center in San Francisco, and shot and killed a former coworker a year after he had been fired. On December 9, 1995, Iowa farmer Dale Burr, 63, shot and killed three people before killing himself almost two years after he learned he was losing his farm to the banks. On November 6, 2003, former Cincinnati, Ohio, truck driver Tom West, 50, shot and fatally wounded two, and injured two more, two years after he resigned.

On April 26, 2010, Dr. Lishan Wang, 44, who had a pending discrimination suit against his employer, shot and killed a Yale University colleague two years after he had been dismissed. On August 30, 2007, Manhattan janitor Paulino Valenzuela, 54, shot and killed his former boss and wounded two others after losing a wrongful termination case, more than two years after he was fired. On July 7, 2011, vindictive neighbor Mark Geisenheyner shot and killed a Manhattan professor and three members of her family in their rural Pennsylvania retreat, after seething with vengeance for five years. And on February 5, 2001, William D. Baker, 66, scheduled to go to jail for stealing from his employer, returned to the company, shot and killed four workers, and wounded four more—almost six years after he was fired. And the list goes on and on. As far as could be determined from the cases in the study, the average response time for women was less than an hour; the average response time for men was more than a month.

THE "THELMA AND LOUISE" PHENOMENON

The Prince/Dunan case was significant to the study because it was one of only three cases (or about 0.75 percent) in which a workplace murder was perpetrated without a weapon—makeshift or otherwise—and the killer(s) killed with bare hands. The case, it will be recalled, involved two El Paso, Texas, striptease dancers in their early twenties who, angry at the club manager, killed a coworker because the manager always let her dance on the "good" pole. The case was significant statistically, however, not only because the perpetrators were women who strangled a coworker with their bare hands, but because they also introduced another gender-based behavioral trend—the "Thelma and Louise" phenomenon.

This phenomenon was far more common than initially assumed. And each case presented a "team" killing—where the female perpetrator recruited coworkers, relatives, or girlfriends to join her in attaining the homicidal goal. More than a search for an accomplice, it was more often a grasp for companionship, support, and communal trust by someone plotting a serious crime. More than a third of the forty-odd women in the study formed some kind of "Thelma and Louise" bond before they committed the workplace homicide. And the bond was especially pronounced among younger, presumably more impressionable women who were in their twenties at the time they murdered on the job.

Jessica Dayton, 19, was a waitress in a Belle Plaine, Iowa, restaurant, the Lincoln Café, which was managed by her boss, Curtis Bailey, 33, of Marengo. On July 18, 2009, Dayton and two associates put into motion a plan they had devised to kill Bailey in his Marengo home. Dayton's two accomplices were Denise Frei, 44, Bailey's live-in girlfriend, and Frei's 19-year-old son, Jacob Hildgendorf.

The plan was to kill Bailey by getting him drunk on whiskey with the promise of three-way sex, and when he was incapacitated or had passed out from the alcohol, they would crush his skull with repeated blows to the head. But the plan went wrong. Instead of passing out, Bailey woke up and started to struggle with the two women and the teenager. In the confusion, Dayton deliberately dropped a large landscaping rock on Bailey's head several times, killing him on the spot. All three were later tried and convicted, and Dayton was found guilty of first-degree murder.[19]

Erika Ray, 27, a former waitress at Leona's restaurant in the Hyde Park section of Chicago, was fired by her boss, Corey Ebenezer, the restaurant manager, the day before. Hours later she went back to her old neighborhood and rounded up Lorenzo Wilson, 19; a juvenile cousin, Paris Gosha, 14; and two others to help her get revenge. Knowing that the restaurant's back door would be unlocked, and that Ebenezer would be inside alone, Ray drove the group to the restaurant where Wilson shot and killed Ebenezer as he counted the day's receipts, while the others took off with 1,700 dollars in cash. Ray, who had been waiting outside in a car, drove them away after the robbery-homicide. She was later tried, convicted, and then sentenced concurrently to forty-two years for the murder and twenty-two for the armed robbery.[20]

Roxanna Ullery, 23, of Orlando, Florida, was a bookkeeper at an Orange County construction company when she shot and killed the company owner, Wayne Evans, 30, after a dispute over embezzled money. On February 16, 1987, Ullery had a close female friend drive her to Evans's home, where

Ullery and Evans reportedly argued over sixty thousand dollars he claimed she had embezzled during her five-month stay at the firm. During the argument, Ullery withdrew a .22-caliber pistol she had purchased earlier that day and shot Evans in the chest, abdomen, and face. Evans died four days later, after he gave a full statement to the police.

Ullery was charged with second-degree murder, but the jury acquitted her of the murder charge and convicted her on the weapons charges instead. The lenient verdict (one of the most lenient in the study) owed in significant degree to Ullery's female friend, whose corroborative testimony also helped to persuade the jury to accept Ullery's (less than convincing) version of the events that occurred that night.[21]

On January 27, 2010, a Pinellas County, Florida, woman, Samantha Estelle Brownlee, 21, murdered her boss by driving over him with his own Toyota van. Hired as housekeeper at a Budget Inn on US 19, Brownlee got into an argument with her boss, Bhupendrakumar Patel, 49, who managed the hotel, and later ran over him with the van, which was registered under his name, and then set the vehicle on fire. Her "accomplice" in planning the murder and the arson was her teenage boyfriend, who was a juvenile.[22]

Sometimes the women formed a Thelma and Louise bond with a woman who wasn't at all what she seemed. Sarah Dutra, 21, was a Sacramento State College coed, and a former high school senior-class president, when she started part-time employment as a legal secretary in the law office of prominent local attorney Larry McNabney, who was also a horse enthusiast. It was during this period that Dutra met and became close friends (and lesbian lovers) with McNabney's wife, Elisa, who was also known as Laren Jordan. They soon hatched a plan to kill McNabney and steal money from his law practice account.

During a horse show, on the fateful day of September 11, 2001, Dutra and Elisa injected the lawyer with the horse tranquilizer drug acepromazine at a nearby Los Angeles hotel. For the next few hours, the two women drove around Yosemite National Park searching for a place to bury Larry McNabney, who lay conscious but dying on the backseat.[23] While almost everybody else in the United States sat in speechless horror, watching the TV image of the World Trade Center crumbling in flames after two terrorists' attacks, Dutra and her lesbian lover were driving around searching for a suitable place to bury a warm corpse. When they couldn't find a suitable spot (the soil was too rocky), they returned, wrapped the body in plastic, and stored it in the garage refrigerator for several months.

The body was discovered five months later, on February 5, 2002, on the grounds of a San Joaquin County vineyard.[24] A jury convicted Dutra of voluntary manslaughter, and the judge imposed the maximum sentence of eleven years in jail. Her partner in crime, Larry McNabney's wife, Elisa, it turned out, was a career criminal and ex-convict from Florida who had used thirty aliases and had a rap sheet 113 pages long. She never stood trial, but killed herself while awaiting extradition to California.[25] Dutra was released from jail on August 26, 2012, after having served most of her jail term.[26]

Another example of a Thelma and Louise bond was seen in the case of Angela Johnson, 38, of Norwood, North Carolina, who recruited cafeteria coworker Eileen Hallamore, 64, to poison their supervisor by adding a chemical cleaning solution to her tea. Both women could've faced charges of attempted murder, according to a Stanly County sheriff's officer, but were released on five-thousand-dollar bonds and will face charges of distributing a food containing poison instead, a considerably less serious charge.[27]

And still another Thelma and Louise case was that of Debra Baker, a bookkeeper and business manager who poisoned her boss, the Texas millionaire entrepreneur Jerry Sternadel, with the help of Lou Ann, Sternadel's wife. In facts eerily similar to those in the Sarah Dutra case, while working in the husband's office Baker became a close friend and confidant of Lou Ann's. They were so close, in fact, that Sternadel (like McNabney) also correctly suspected that they had conspired to poison him. He died soon afterwards, having ingested a lethal dose of arsenic, which was traced to Baker's custody.

A jury later found Baker guilty of murder, but sentenced her to only ten years' probation and a fine. If Sternadel's family and survivors were disappointed in the leniency of the sentence imposed, they were likely reassured a few years later when Baker was arrested for parole violations in 2003, and in a proceeding that often results in incarceration for a period of days and months, she was sentenced to ten years in jail.

The Thelma and Louise phenomenon that formed so easily and so often among women, however, was noticeably absent among similarly situated men. This kind of personal bonding between two male individuals occurred only once.[28]

Of the 350-plus cases of workplace murder that qualified for this study, few findings were established as conclusively—or based as much on gender—as these findings of fact. Women who used firearms to exact revenge always used just a single handgun, they rarely procrastinated or postponed what had to be done, and they preferred the company of a colleague or girlfriend to assist them in the deed. Men usually armed themselves with all the guns and weaponry they could physically carry; they waited weeks, months, and even years before they finally did the deed; and whether they wanted to kill a group of twenty people or a single individual, they always murdered alone.

MENTAL ILLNESS/DEPRESSION AND SUICIDE

As already noted, women comprised almost 14 percent of the cases in the study. The records suggest that approximately half (between 45 and 55 percent) suffered from some kind of depression or had undergone psychological or psychiatric treatment of some kind before they committed the crime. This contrasted sharply with the men, only about 12 to 15 percent of whom were depressed or had undergone similar treatment of some kind. This wide disparity is attributable at least in part to the fact that women were far more likely to recognize, admit, discuss, and seek help for mental illness or other disorders.[29] These women included Valerie Solanas, Jennifer San Marco, Elizabeth Teague, Yolanda Saldívar, Kim Harris, Jacquelyn Ferguson, and Judith Coffin, among others.

The extent to which Ferguson's murder-suicide owed solely to mental depression, a full-blown mental disorder, or the fact that she was taking at least two over-the-counter antidepressant medications, will never be known. Yet her situation was hardly unique. Kim Harris, 27, of Louisville, Kentucky, had been working as a nursing assistant at the Jefferson Place nursing home for eighteen months when she was fired.[30] Two months later, on April 29, 1991, she returned to the nursing home and shot and killed both Deborah Bell, 46, the executive director of the nursing home, and Patty Eitel, 43, the director of nursing. At the time of her firing, she had been evaluated by a psychiatrist who later testified at trial that she was severely depressed, even "delusional."[31] Another psychiatrist, Dr. Sherif El-Asyouty, testified at trial that on a scale of one to a hundred, he rated Harris's level of functioning at fifteen.[32]

Another case, also involving a female nursing home employee, was that of Renita Williams Dozier of Fayetteville, North Carolina. On October 15, 2005, Dozier took two hostages as part of an attempt to renegotiate her job, from which she had resigned several weeks before. She held the hostages for four hours, in a standoff with the police and a police negotiator, before she released the two hostages unharmed and then turned the gun on herself to commit suicide.[33]

Further exploration will be given to the issue of workplace suicide later in this discussion. But it should be noted here that of the women included in the study, less than 8 percent committed suicide, either as a solo act or as part of a murder-suicide. Men, on the other hand, committed suicide almost 30 percent of the time—either as solo conduct or as part of a murder-suicide—almost four times more often than their female counterparts. Although the percentage of male workplace murderers who had a history of mental illness was significantly lower than that of females, the lower number needn't be accepted at face value. Men were also statistically far less inclined to acknowledge mental illness, to seek professional help, or to discuss the issue with someone else. Also, if men were in fact less prone to mental illness and depression, less susceptible to job pressure, anxiety, and stress, it would be logically inconsistent with (and even contradict) the fact that they also commit 75 percent of the workplace suicides across the board. As Allison Pearson aptly observes: women are exceedingly good at depression, but they're hopelessly inept at committing suicide; men, on the other hand, are hopelessly inept at depression or even talking about it, but they're exceedingly good at committing suicide.[34]

Another reason women commit suicide far less frequently than men (even though they threaten or consider suicide more often) is their greater willingness to discuss their depression with another person, accept medication, and participate in group counseling or a treatment plan. Still another reason women commit suicide less often owes to the methods they use to accomplish the deed. Their methods tend to be unreliable, messy, time-consuming, easily interrupted, or require too much work beforehand, and their attempts (wisely) leave room for reflection, second thoughts, intervention, or even timely rescue.[35] No, men are not good at depression, but they're very adept at suicide, which can be seen in the methods they choose to accomplish the deadly deed. Unlike those of the women, men's methods tend to be quick, efficient, virtually foolproof, solitary, and final—like hanging with a belt or a quick, self-inflicted bullet to the head.

Another indication that mental illness among men in the study was much greater than statistics indicate (or than men care to admit) is that the men often embarked upon bloody murder sprees even *before* they walked out the front door. These perpetrators included those who first murdered neighbors or coworkers at their homes or as they raked leaves in the backyard, even before they drove to the work site proper, where they commenced to kill supervisors, coworkers, and colleagues. Jennifer San Marco, for example, shot and killed a former neighbor before she drove to the mail warehouse and killed several coworkers at the distribution plant. But as we know, the San Marco case was a statistical rarity in several respects, because killing someone before they drove to the workplace never occurred with women. Murdering neighbors or coworkers even before the disgruntled employee arrived at the workplace was more typical of men, like Frank Garcia, a nursing supervisor who first gunned down two former coworkers at their home before he drove to the hospital and shot and killed two more.

But the true measure of serious mental illness was seen in those perpetrators (all men), who killed *family*—wives, girlfriends, children, and other close relatives (even Fido the dog!)—just before they drove to their jobs and resumed their murder sprees. In May 1927, the perpetrator of the infamous Bath Massacre, Andrew Kehoe, set fires and detonated bombs that killed forty-three people (most elementary-school children), wounded fifty-eight others, and then committed suicide—just hours after he bludgeoned his sickly wife to death as she lay in bed.[36] In August 1966, Charles J. Whitman shot and killed twelve people and wounded thirty-two others during a shooting rampage on and around the Austin campus of the University of Texas—just hours after he had murdered his mother and then murdered his wife in their respective homes.[37] In August 1989, John M. Taylor, 52, a letter carrier for twenty-five years, shot and killed two coworkers and wounded a third—just hours after he first shot and killed his wife at home.[38]

In March 2000, Frederick Williams, 41, an off-duty Memphis fireman, opened fire on fellow firemen as they arrived to extinguish the flames from his home—after he shot and killed his wife and left her body in the burning garage.[39] In July 1999, Mark Barton shot and killed ten coworkers and injured thirteen more in two separate murder rampages in two Atlanta, Georgia, office complexes where he worked as a day trader—a day after he bludgeoned to death his wife and two adolescent children as they slept in their beds.[40] And Kenneth Tornes, 32, a Jackson, Mississippi, fireman, hunted down and then shot and killed four supervisors in the fire department—only hours after he shot and killed his estranged wife in her home.[41]

This bizarre twist on an already brutal factual scenario was a pattern that also included perpetrators like the Iowa farmer Dale Burr; the Sonoma, California, wine worker Ramon Salcido; Tracey Moss; Michael McLendon; R. Gene Simmons; Alfred J. Hunter III; and several others as well. These cases were by far the bloodiest in the study, and almost 90 percent of the perpetrators not surprisingly ended the slaughter by committing suicide. As these cases involved the highest body counts, they also begged the question: Which set of victims did the perpetrator want to destroy more? Did this particular perpetrator (perhaps unconsciously) actually want to kill members of his own family—the wife, kids, parents, and in-laws—and the folks he hated at the job were mere homicidal afterthoughts? Or was the murder of his family and loved ones itself an act of "compassion"—to spare them the embarrassment, ridicule, and shame that would surely follow the mass murders he intended to commit an hour later at the job—so it didn't really matter if he killed them first?

How and why these men established a deadly link between their domestic lives and individuals they supposedly loved, and their workplace and people they supposedly hated, is not readily apparent. It's a behavioral connection, of course, that lends itself to any number of theories, explanations, and analyses. And almost as baffling as the deadly link these men established between their domestic and employment lives was the fact that the distinction, this further indication of mental illness, was never a factor in a single case in which the perpetrator was a female.

The final indicator of how much more the disease of mental illness afflicted the male perpetrators than their female counterparts was the morbid postmortem rituals men performed with the corpses before the police arrived.

Before Michael McLendon left his home and drove to his workplace to kill his former bosses and coworkers, he first shot and killed—execution-style— his mother, his grandmother, his girlfriend, and his mother's four pet dogs. Then he carefully, respectfully placed the bodies of the four dogs at the feet of his mother's corpse before he set them all on fire, much the same way ancient civilizations buried their leaders on a funeral pyre.[42] In December 1987, a former Arkansas convenience-store clerk, R. Gene Simmons, shot, strangled, drowned, and bludgeoned to death sixteen people, including fourteen members of his immediate family. His first victim was his wife, whom he shot with a gun before he shot and killed his adult children and drowned or strangled his younger children and grandchildren. The killings were spread over a weekend, during which he drank beer, watched TV, and then positioned several of the corpses at a dining room table, in what seemed a bizarre, drunken attempt to reconstruct the biblical scene of the Last Supper. That Monday, of course, he drove to his former place of employment to wound and kill all those he felt had mistreated him on the job. Then he meekly surrendered to the local police.[43]

The point to be emphasized here is not that these men were especially violent or that they represented about 15 percent of the male murderers included in the study. Again, what makes them so rare and statistically exceptional is not only their macabre, gruesome conduct with the corpses— dead men, women, children, and even small animals—but that not a single case was found in which similar conduct was exhibited by a perpetrator who was female.

In the days and weeks following Amy Bishop's arrest for triple murder, the news media learned much more about her background, including several previous brushes with law enforcement—one of which implicated her in the shooting death of her younger brother while he was a freshman at Northeastern University more than twenty years before.

Amid the uproar, students, faculty, families and friends of the victims, and even members of the general public had begun to ask questions. How could someone like Bishop, who was obviously dangerous, with a violent, mercurial temper, be hired in the first place? What went wrong? Had the university's department of human resources failed? Should the preemployment screening system be scrapped?

Many wondered what could prevent this horrible tragedy from happening again. As a young nursing student, Caitlin Phillips, asked, "Do they not do background checks on teachers? How did all this slip through the cracks?"[44]

Chapter Four

The Limits of the Human Resources Function

The young UAH nursing student Caitlin Phillips summed up the fears and frustrations that many on the UAH campus felt in the wake of the tragedy when she asked if they still did background checks on teachers, and wondered how a triple murderer like Amy Bishop could slip through the hiring cracks. There was an understandable need to have it explained and, truth be told, a corresponding need to place some of the blame. Although the questions were rhetorical, they still seemed directed at the UAH's department of human resources, and they demanded a clear, prompt reply.

The questions were based largely on trust in the human resources (HR) function, and the collective assumption that the HR office was involved in the hiring of Amy Bishop when she applied for the teaching job. As three brilliant scholars and pillars of the academic community lay dead, it seemed to many that the UAH human resources system had obviously failed. The sentiment and the confusion were understandable. Given the magnitude of the tragedy, what was easier to conclude than that somebody had failed or that the HR office in particular hadn't done its job? Although the underlying sentiments were understandable, the questions only begged other, more difficult questions whose answers were not always what the public could readily understand or wanted to hear.

Why did the nursing student have such faith and trust in the HR function and the preventative role it could have played anyway? Why did she automatically assume that the tragedy reflected poorly on the HR office because it hadn't prevented the tragedy by rejecting Bishop's job application back in 2005? More specifically, why did she feel the HR office should have done more—and was *able* to do more—to prevent the tragedy in the first place?

This faith in the HR function, and its supposed role in preventing the murders, was unfounded and without a basis in historical fact. Nor should it be assumed that HR personnel or the UAH "system" had somehow failed because they hadn't eliminated Bishop's application when she first applied for the job in 2005. Both the expectation and the assumption were rooted deep in the institutional origins of the HR office, its history, the rapid expansion of traditional HR functions, and how both the office and the functions evolved over the decades.

THE ORIGINS AND GROWTH OF THE HUMAN RESOURCES DEPARTMENT

The earliest recognizable HR functions emerged shortly after the turn of the century, along with the rapid rise of industrialization of the post–Civil War boom. According to Alan Downs's history of the HR office, "The period between 1910 and World War I saw the beginnings of the first real personnel functions. Due largely to the popularity of Frederick Taylor's scientific management approach and its emphasis on the proper selection of employees, the field of employment management evolved. The employment manager's job was to assist in hiring employees who were capable of meeting very specific requirements for the jobs. This gave the personnel function its first real contribution to the organization: hiring employees who could perform jobs efficiently and safety."[1] Downs adds: "With the passage of workers' compensation laws, safety became an increasingly important (and expensive) issue. In fact, legislation regarding worker safety led to the creation of much of the personnel, [HR] department as we now know it."[2]

With the crash of 1929 and the Great Depression that followed, however, most Americans lost their jobs as well as their faith and hope in the business community. They turned away from the business sector, and toward the federal government as the new source of hope and support. And the federal government quickly intervened. This unprecedented intervention by the government created additional HR functions, like unemployment compensation, social security, and minimum wages, and, with passage of the Wagner Act (1947), provided the federally protected right of millions of workers to join a union and to collectively bargain with their employers/management for the first time.

Almost all of these programs required that the company make contributions, exercise a monitoring function, and engage in extensive record-keeping activities. Downs writes: "Coupled with an exponentially growing tide of unionization, companies raced to beef up personnel departments with clerks to administer programs designed to comply with the law and deter unionization. Labor relations positions were created in the department to deal with negotiating labor contracts. Compensation clerks were hired to conduct surveys to make sure that the labor contract wages were comparable to those of other companies. By the 1950s, the personnel department [was] one of the largest staff functions in the corporation."[3] A generation later, the traditional HR functions had expanded, particularly during the recessions of the 1970s and 1980s, as management relied increasingly on HR staffs to do more than merely ensure technical legal compliance with the law, but to serve as a buffer between capital and labor as well.

With increased pressure on companies, management began to delegate to personnel staffs the responsibility for streamlining the workforce. As a result, hordes of behavioral experts joined hands with HR offices, and since the mid-1980s, "senior management has continually looked to HR for assistance in choosing the names for a layoff."[4] With the personnel department given such a broad mandate, modern managers no longer had to address the potentially volatile issues of salary, wages, bonuses, and promotions, which only reinforced the personnel department's role as an institutional "buffer" between capital and labor.[5] As a result, nowadays the HR office's information-gathering function confers broad organizational power, and its staffs routinely determine how much to pay employees; which employees should be promoted, transferred, granted leaves of absence, or offered early retirement; and who should be fired. Along with being responsible for a host of other decisions, the HR office was, in short, soon regarded by many in the company as virtually all-powerful.[6]

This history of the HR office, and the expansion of its largely information-gathering functions over the decades, only confirm the modern notion that the office should also be held responsible—and ultimately liable—for hiring employees who later kill their colleagues. Given the scope and breadth of HR authority, covering as it did so much administrative territory, it was perhaps only inevitable that a tragedy like the Amy Bishop case fall first within its jurisdiction and then promptly fall "between the cracks," exactly as the young nursing student supposed. But the practical, administrative, day-to-day reality could not have been more different. Not only was the modern HR office unable to fulfill the broad functions of its widely perceived authority, it also lost sight of its original, narrower mission, and the cases that fell between the cracks included even those that fit perfectly within its traditional role. The MIT case illustrates the point.

CRACKS IN THE HR SYSTEM—FALLING BETWEEN THE CRACKS

As the dean of admissions at the Massachusetts Institute of Technology (MIT), Marilee Jones, 55, was an unusually popular, widely admired administrator on campus. Indeed, many regarded her as the chief advocate of a new way of thinking about college admissions by college administrators nationwide.

Her popularity owed in significant degree to her belief that students should not allow themselves to become unduly stressed or anxious over the competition to gain entry into the nation's elite colleges and universities. Originally from Albany, New York, her philosophy provided what many welcomed as a much-needed corrective, an alternative to the view, popular among high school seniors, that they had to earn perfect aptitude scores. Dean Jones argued that not getting perfect scores was not the end of the world, and that the flame of college-entrance competition definitely needed to be turned down. Though she was well known for these views, she nevertheless did much to enhance the prestige and reputation of MIT, like recruiting women to MIT, where the enrollment percentage of women had been about 17 percent, but rose during her tenure to about 49 percent today.[7]

Jones was a popular speaker across the country, and had also received MIT's highest honor for administrators, the MIT Excellence Award for Leading Change. She had also written a book, entitled *Less Stress, More Success: A New Approach to Guiding Your Teen through College Admissions and Beyond*, which she had coauthored with Boston pediatrician Dr. Kenneth R. Ginsburg, which only enhanced her reputation as a kind of guru in the frenzied field of college admissions.[8] Given her stellar professional achievements, no one was surprised that her resume listed degrees from several prestigious institutions, like Albany Medical College and Rensselaer Polytechnic Institute. That is, until it was discovered, in April 2007, that Jones had actually fabricated and lied about her educational credentials years ago. In fact, MIT's Dean Marilee Jones had never earned a single college degree.[9]

Nor was the MIT case an isolated incident. Instances in which HR personnel fell short, dropped the ball, or had not thoroughly checked and verified resumes are not uncommon. And the high-profile examples of HR blunders and mishaps in this regard remain in the headlines. In February 2006, RadioShack CEO David Edmonson resigned after it was learned that his resume listed two nonexistent degrees.[10] Bausch and Lomb CEO Ronald Zarrella resigned when it was revealed that he falsely claimed a New York University MBA.[11] And Notre Dame football coach George O'Leary lost his job after admitting in December 2001 that he lied about his academic and athletic achievements. He claimed a master's degree and a varsity letter in football, neither of which was true.[12] CFO of Veritas software Kenneth Lonchar resigned in October 2002 after it was revealed that he lied about his education, claiming an MBA from Stanford, which was not true.[13] And the Lotus Corporation's CEO Jeff Papows resigned his post after the *Wall Street Journal* reported that he exaggerated his military record (he'd been a lieutenant, not a captain), lied about his education (he didn't have a doctorate from Pepperdine University), and even falsely claimed he was an orphan (both parents were alive and well). [14]

Understandably reluctant to hire or promote "executive Pinocchios," employers have increased efforts to detect and weed them out. [15] In the field of industrial and organizational psychology, the analysis of how and why job applicants fabricate their qualifications and credentials is a popular research area, and new studies warn companies of the legal risks and liabilities of hiring a liar. As a result, 96 percent of businesses now conduct some sort of background check on job applicants, according to the Society for Human Resource Management (SHRM), a trade group. [16]

The mistakes and errors committed by in-house HR departments, even those larger and better staffed than the HR department at MIT, are both commonplace and pervasive, in both the public and private sectors. As a result, the ranks of third-party screeners have exploded in the last decade, and now comprise a two-billion-dollar industry. [17] But this increased reliance on outsourcing this aspect of the HR function may not only *not* solve the problem, it may just make it worse. According to a 2008 study commissioned by SHRM, the first and most commonly outsourced HR functions are background checks and employee assistance programs. [18]

If, as the same report indicates, the biggest disadvantage of outsourcing is the loss of interaction with a much-needed "face," the problem of workplace violence will only grow worse. Calling an 800 number is rarely as effective an exchange as one that's face-to-face. In this atmosphere, not only will the potential Amy Bishop red flags become even more difficult to detect and weed out through the HR process, the number of "puffed" resumes submitted to employers every year may only increase.

FURTHER LIMITS OF THE HR FUNCTION

Bishop's case, of course, was different. Unlike the case of the former dean at MIT, who had clearly fabricated material facts on her resume and then continued the deception over the years by not coming forward to correct the data, Bishop's resume contained no falsifications or fabrications of any kind. Bishop hadn't lied on her resume about her educational or professional background, and in the absence of a formal criminal conviction sheet, her record was clean and raised no red flags that would have invited further inquiry.

The nursing student's questions about background checks and slipping through the cracks, though understandable, were based on an erroneous assumption and expectations that were wholly unrealistic. The expectation was that the HR office would have reviewed Bishop's application when she first applied for the job, detected some red flag that inevitably led to homicidal behavior, and then eliminated her application from consideration, thereby preventing the triple murder that occurred five years later. Unfortunately, the HR office was not prescient, couldn't have foreseen the tragedy, and never had the authority—or the clairvoyant capacity—to do so.

The nursing student's questions also hinted, alternatively, that if no identifiable person was to blame, then the UAH "system" had obviously failed. How else could such a terrible tragedy have occurred? To suggest otherwise was to accept the brutal murders as part of the normal course of an average day on the campus. And they clearly were not. But the assumption, like the expectation, was without a historical factual basis, and wasn't supported by a careful review of the available facts.

Amy Bishop's arrest on February 12, 2010, resulted in three charges of felony murder and one count of capital murder, by which she was eligible for Alabama's electric chair (if convicted of the charge). Unfortunately, that wasn't the total number of criminal charges she would face in the criminal courts. The tragedy of the triple murder charges, along with the death penalty count, were virtually eclipsed by disclosures about her family background and the atmosphere of entitlement that was part of her privileged private life. These disclosures, widely reported in the local and regional news media, only lent credence to the view that, Harvard PhD in genetics notwithstanding, this was indeed a volatile, extremely violent woman who was more than capable of committing three cold-blooded homicides.

What had been viewed initially by everyone as an unlikely tragedy to befall an upper-middle-class white New England family would soon be exposed as something very different, even bizarre. Bishop was charged with the murder of three prominent citizens, and thus became a most unlikely candidate for Alabama's electric chair. Still, she found herself in a situation that was even worse than she imagined. For members of law enforcement, the media, and the public at large, the situations invited a reassessment of both the function and the scope of the preemployment screening process, as well as a questioning of the HR function in screening out potentially violent, homicidal job applicants.

Among the damaging disclosures was that Bishop was charged with assault and battery and disorderly conduct back in 2002 following a public tirade with another parent at an International House of Pancakes (IHOP) restaurant in Peabody, Massachusetts. As Peabody police captain Dennis Bonaivto recalled the incident, Bishop became "incensed" when told another woman in the restaurant had been given the last available booster seat. Bishop apparently hit the woman, punching her in the head while yelling, "I'm Dr. Bishop." The woman, identified as one Michelle Gjika, later declined comment, saying, "It's not something I want to relive." Bishop admitted the assault charges in open court, but the case was never "adjudicated," she was never convicted, and the charge was in effect dismissed.[19]

Another disclosure was that Bishop and her husband had been suspects in a 1993 letter-bomb probe. Paul Rosenberg, a Harvard Medical School professor and a physician at Children's Hospital Boston, had received a package containing two pipe bombs that failed to explode. It happened that Rosenberg had also been Bishop's immediate supervisor at a Children's Hospital neurobiology laboratory. She had allegedly been anxious after receiving a negative evaluation from Rosenberg, had argued with him, and then resigned from her position because her superior felt she "could not meet the standards" required for the work. According to witness interviews, Bishop had been extremely upset and on the verge of a nervous breakdown, and her husband had reportedly told witnesses prior to the bomb attempt that he wanted at various times to "strangle," "stab," and "shoot" Rosenberg as a result. FBI agents questioned Bishop and her husband about the incident; both consistently denied any involvement while simultaneously refusing to cooperate. The FBI later decided not to pursue the investigation any further, however, due to the lack of credible evidence.

Still another discovery, by far the most damaging, was that Bishop, more than two decades earlier in 1987, had been implicated in the shooting death of her younger brother, Seth. An accomplished eighteen-year-old pianist and violinist, Seth Bishop was in his freshman year at Northeastern when he died of a single shotgun wound to the chest. And that single gunshot was only one of several shots fired by Amy during a heated family argument. According to the 1987 police report, their father told the Braintree, Massachusetts, police that his son and daughter had had a disagreement and she had tried unsuccessfully to unload the weapon during the argument. Massachusetts authorities, weighing the evidence twenty-two years later, were not persuaded. More than three months after Amy Bishop was arrested and charged in Alabama with triple murder, and more than twenty years after Seth Bishop's death, Massachusetts indicted Amy Bishop, in June 2010, for the 1987 shooting death of her kid brother, Seth.[20]

Whatever one thought of the letter-bomb investigation, or the IHOP incident, or even the shooting death of her kid brother, few could deny how bizarre it seemed that Bishop had also written three oddly incriminating, unpublished novels. One of the novels featured a female scientist struggling to defeat a potential pandemic virus while fighting thoughts of suicide if she failed to earn tenure at a university. Another novel included a female protagonist who felt guilty for having murdered her younger brother, and whose quest in life was to become a brilliant scientist—to atone for her sins.

In addition, and perhaps unbeknownst to Amy Bishop's husband, she had acquired an unlicensed nine-millimeter semiautomatic Ruger handgun.[21] And despite Bishop's seemingly disoriented, incoherent ramblings at the time of her arrest, during the two or three weeks before the shooting, her neighbors reportedly saw her on several occasions going to the local indoor shooting range for target practice, presumably with the gun.

Finally, as if Bishop's situation wasn't already a public relations nightmare, as photographs, obituaries, and biographies of the victims appeared in the news, it slowly dawned on members of various ethnic and racial groups in the diverse college community that most of Bishop's half dozen shooting victims were *nonwhite*. She had shot almost every nonwhite member of UAH's biology department. (She also shot and wounded two white victims, a professor and a staff member.) She had killed the department chairman (Podila), who was Southeast Asian, and two black professors (Davis and Johnson), one of whom was too junior in departmental seniority to have had any influence on the earlier negative tenure vote. She had also shot and wounded a Latino faculty member. There were only two other nonwhite or minority faculty members in the department. Amy Bishop, whatever her intentions, had single-handedly effected a "racial purge" of UAH's entire biology department.

These revelations focused on Amy Bishop, her family, and her background. But more importantly, they also demonstrated the ineffectiveness of HR screening procedures in detecting and interpreting certain types of information and data. If, as the MIT and CEO cases showed, the ineffectiveness was evident in detecting fabrications and falsehoods made sometimes years in the past, the procedures could hardly be expected to function prospectively—to detect personality traits and temperaments that might lead to violent conduct at some point in the distant future.

University of Alabama president David B. Williams defended the 2005 decision to hire Bishop, explaining that when her personnel file was reviewed, none of the contents raised any red flags. Indeed, he pointed out that a criminal background check was made that very Monday, after Bishop had been formally charged with three counts of murder and one charge of capital murder, and even then, "nothing came up."[22]

Williams, of course, was correct that computers do not always pick up on the filing of a criminal charge, much less an arrest, and that they typically track only complete dispositions and criminal convictions. He was also correct that even the most rigorous background check in Bishop's case would not have revealed any red flags. Whatever her prior brushes with law enforcement, not a single red flag appeared. Though she had committed minor offenses in the IHOP restaurant, was questioned by the FBI in the letter-bomb inquiry, and was also implicated in the death of her kid brother, according to all available court records—and as a matter of fact—she had never been convicted of a crime.

The HR preemployment screening system at the UAH, like the systems virtually everywhere, was not designed or intended to detect and then weed out violent, potentially homicidal job applicants. That task is impossible without a tangible, verifiable document of conviction of a violent act or some other document from which the tendency may be reasonably inferred. Of the 350-plus cases included in this study, only about 2 percent included something in their personnel files that documented or suggested the likelihood of violent behavior in the future. Rare examples included Mark Barton, who, at the time he killed and wounded his coworkers at the day-trading companies in Atlanta in July 1999, had been the principal suspect in (but was never formally charged with) the bludgeoning death of his first wife and mother-in-law a decade earlier.[23] And six years before former boxing promoter Don King murdered Ron Garrett in the street by stomping him to death, he had shot and killed a rival gambler in his early days as an Ohio gambler and racketeer.[24]

Of course, Bishop never *volunteered* that she had had several brushes with law enforcement, or that she had been implicated in the shooting death of her kid brother almost twenty years before. But she wasn't legally *required* to do so. The system at UAH was designed and intended to detect criminal convictions or documented behavior from which a violent disposition could reasonably be inferred. At the time Bishop was hired for the professorship in 2005, she had never been convicted of a crime, and no such record existed.

PREEMPLOYMENT SCREENING: WHAT DOES HR *REALLY* NEED TO KNOW?

In today's economy, employers have access to a greater number of applicants as unemployment rates climb and the unemployed continue to seek jobs. With increased choice comes the opportunity to develop ways to improve and streamline procedures for recruiting and hiring employees. And preemployment screening is one of the best ways to ensure that a company hires the right person for the right job.

Such screening allows an employer to "screen in" applicants who are a good fit for the organization, and can also help to "screen out" potential employees who do not meet the requirements of the job. Screening procedures can also reduce an employer's exposure to a later negligent hiring claim, which is why certain screening procedures are statutorily required. As an example, all employers are required to verify the identity of their employees and whether they are allowed to work legally in the United States.[25] Also, background checks are required for employees who will work in an environment with children or vulnerable adults, or to qualify for certain Department of Motor Vehicles driving licenses to transport hazardous materials in interstate commerce.

But there are drawbacks. Some prescreening techniques can be time-consuming and/or expensive. If the screening procedures are too numerous, time-consuming, or invasive, qualified applicants may decide, out of frustration or anger, or both, not to go through the process. Employers can also open themselves up to legal liability, depending on how the procedures are performed.[26] The different types of preemployment screening tests, and the most frequently used, include those that measure different aptitudes and abilities or discern and test for personality traits. Other preemployment screening procedures include polygraph tests, and seek information on the applicant's medical, credit/financial, and personal background, including criminal records and other court documents, like repossessions, child support orders, bankruptcies, and so on. If few preemployment screening procedures can guarantee specific, objectively measurable results, even fewer can be expected to weed out those job applicants most likely to commit a violent act, including workplace homicide. In neither the Bishop case, nor in any of the hundreds of other cases in this study, was a test successful in this regard. Nor should any screening procedure be expected to accomplish this impossible feat. As already noted, in not a single case included in this study was there any indication that a perpetrator was given such an examination or test. The preemployment screening procedure that was in place at UAH when the murders were committed was not designed or intended to detect potentially violent job applicants. And no one was justified in expecting it to perform such a feat.

These inescapable facts, however, only pose two critical questions. If the university's HR system functioned exactly the way it was supposed to function, was the cold-blooded murder of three brilliant scientists still preventable? Should the three brutal, execution-style murders still be considered within the bounds of prevention or other human agency?

The answer to both questions is yes, of course. *Absolutely.* Workplace murders like those in the Bishop case can be easily prevented perhaps 80 to 90 percent of the time, and that's a conservative estimate. These murders are preventable by two different means. The first is through technology, a practical, non-labor-intensive, environmentally responsible, visually unobtrusive mechanism or device that's also surprisingly inexpensive. The second means is not a tangible object or thing but more a process—a process that quickly fosters an attitude. And this attitude requires that management establish three policies that must be implemented, routinely practiced, and vigorously enforced.

The technological means will be explained later in the discussion. And of the three policies that must be implemented, the first must be implemented at the earliest recruitment stage. This necessity places it within the HR function, and thus requires that it be mentioned here. That practice is to seek, detect, measure, and assess a single personality trait. This trait is the single most important trait in the prevention of workplace violence, particularly workplace homicide. What, you may ask, is this one, all-important trait?

THE GENERAL QUEST FOR CHARACTER

For the purpose of confirming honesty, trustworthiness, and so on, preemployment screening tests are truly indispensable. As already noted, these tests run the gamut in exploring a job applicant's background, and allow access to much of a person's private life. And therein lies the potential for abuse, and the basis for civil liability in court. An HR assistant may go too far, may pry a tad too deeply. Even the most well-intentioned HR assistant may find him or herself on that morally slippery slope where the investigation—though meant ostensibly to ensure that the best person is ultimately hired for the job—is actually motivated by the same mildly erotic impulse that shapes the actions of chronic eavesdroppers, voyeurs, and Peeping Toms.

Many modern HR offices are now equipped with prescreening software that can crunch a thousand resumes in an hour. Though perhaps unavoidable, it's still unfortunate. And rather than developing more and more prescreening tests to discern an ever-increasing number of traits, characteristics, and personality flaws, a more feasible goal would be to devise more tests to detect, assess, and measure different expressions of a single general, all-encompassing trait.

In his series of books on the underbelly of the restaurant industry, between his astute observations and his recollection of the years spent in the business, he's also drawn a group portrait of a vast subeconomy that steadily transforms illegal immigrants and others, especially from Central America, into solid citizens who soon hold steady jobs, pay taxes, and maintain bank accounts, with car notes and mortgages and children who are fluent in English and thinking about college, a career, or graduate school.

Few people have done more to help minorities and recent immigrants arrive in this country—help them find homes, adjust, earn gainful employment, earn legal immigrant status, learn how to save money, open bank accounts, build credit, purchase homes, finance cars, and even put children through college—than one individual. Few Americans have directly helped as many of these workers become productive American citizens, and few have better and more insightfully observed how people work in job slots, in different positions, in pursuit of a common goal. That individual is not the head of a federal agency, not a prominent tenured law professor, not an expert on employment law, not a labor theoretician or employment scholar. That individual is a wise-cracking, streetwise but intellectually sharp former restaurant chef.

In Anthony Bourdain's first best-selling book, he expresses his heartfelt personal gratitude to an early professional inspiration and source of admiration in his early food career. The man forever impressed upon Bourdain that "*character* is far more important than skills or employment history. And he recognized character—good and bad—brilliantly. He understood, and taught me, that a guy who shows up every day on time, never calls in sick and does what he said he was going to do is less likely to fuck you in the end than a guy who has an incredible resume but is less than reliable about arrival time. Skills can be taught. Character you either have or don't have."[27]

Bourdain's philosophy finds strong support in a recent Google survey—Project Oxygen—whose results showed that "skills" were not the most important factor in workplace success. Attitude beat technical skills, and what was more important than strategy? *Character!*[28] At least a dozen other recent studies and surveys support the view that managerial skills are not uppermost in importance. Far more important, the results uniformly show, are traits like "attitude," "commitment," and "honesty" in achieving a collaborative goal.[29] This view was best articulated by Carol Smith, senior vice president and chief brand officer for the Elle Group, one of the nation's leading media companies. And it's not coincidental that a determination of the existence of character, and the assessment of a person's character, revolves around the preparation and consumption of food.

During an interview by Adam Bryant, Smith shared some of her views on hiring and firing, and Bryant specifically asked about her recruitment philosophy, what she looked for, and how she found and hired specific people to do a specific job. The gist of the interview went, in relevant part, as follows.

> Q. *Let's talk about hiring.*

> 1. You've got to meet someone three times and one of them better be over a meal.

> *You learn so much in a meal.* It's like a little microcosm of life. How they order, what they order. How are they going to give instructions to a waiter? Are they sending back the meal eight times? Can they keep the conversation going, especially if you're hiring someone who is in sales? Are they asking smart questions?
>
> Throughout a meal, the personality comes out, I think. Are you going to connect with us? Are you going to be part of the team, or are you going to be one of these independent players who wants to take all the credit? Are you good with assistants? Those are things you can find out in some subtle ways when you eat with someone.
>
> Q. *Any other tips on hiring?*
>
> A. Don't hire somebody you don't like. There is always a strong internal pressure to give a job to a person who has all the right credentials and says all the right things, even if something about her sends up little signals of alarm.

They may be slight, but in my experience it is a great mistake to ignore them. Every time I went against my instincts and gave a job to someone who, though clearly capable, made me feel uneasy during the interview, it has ended badly.[30]

Much like Anthony Bourdain, Smith places a high value on the recognition and assessment of personal "character." Of course, Smith never used the word "character," and emphasizes instead the importance of relying on her own "intuition" and "instincts" in the hiring process. Yet both clearly agree (and endorse the results of the Google survey) that general character is by far the single most important element, the single most critical personal trait, and a criterion that remains as viable and promising as any test yet devised.

The question that may be asked at this point is: if the quest for "character" is so all- important—if "character" might even be an effective tool in detecting a potentially violent job applicant—how did Amy Bishop fall through the cracks?

And the answer is: Amy Bishop *didn't* fall through the cracks.

It should be recalled that, in all of the hullabaloo, in all the hue and cry, Amy Bishop *failed* to receive tenure. William Setzer, the chairman of UAH's chemistry department, acknowledged an inescapable truth about the tenure process when he lamented that "politics and personalities" always play a role. He added that "in a close department it's more so. If you have any lone wolves or bizarre personalities, it's a problem and I'm thinking that certainly came into play here."[31]

It's impossible to know exactly what documents served as a basis for the faculty's denial of tenure in Bishop's case. Nor is it known how thoroughly (or cursorily) University of Alabama president Williams reviewed the tenure file, or on what basis he approved and concurred with the committee's negative vote.[32] For that reason, Setzer's words could not be more apt. Factors that were not strictly academic inevitably came into play. And whatever Bishop's obvious talents and strengths as a second-generation academic with a brilliant mind, she was not greatly endowed with people skills, and clearly was not socially adept in her day-to-day dealings with teachers, students, and colleagues. Few found it difficult to conclude that she was acutely eccentric and potentially violent, if not homicidal. Indeed, some knew, even then, that she was an oddity, and they were willing to dismiss her as "crazy."[33]

Bishop was known to interrupt meetings with "bizarre tangents . . . left field kind of stuff," and was regarded by students and colleagues alike as "strange," "crazy," and as a person who "did things that weren't normal" as if she was "out of touch with reality."[34] One colleague in the science department (who also voted on Bishop's tenure) had openly referred to her as "crazy."[35] When Bishop heard about the comment, she filed a complaint with the EEOC, alleging gender discrimination, with the professor's comment to be used as evidence to support her charge. But the professor didn't back down, retract the characterization, or claim it was just a flippant remark. "I said she was crazy multiple times and I stand by that," the professor said. "She has a pattern of erratic behavior. She did things that weren't normal . . . She was out of touch with reality."[36]

Of course, it can only be speculated how many times members of the faculty had the opportunity to lunch or dine with Bishop, either at her home, in a restaurant, or even at the local IHOP. But if Carol Smith is correct in her belief that much can be learned about a job applicant over dinner, it seems unlikely that Bishop would have won friends or helped her cause by having lunch or dinner with colleagues.

Bishop had also impressed many students unfavorably, both as she lectured in front of the classroom and in how she performed or explained experiments in the lab. In 2009, several UAH students had complained to administrators on at least three occasions that Bishop was "ineffective in the classroom and had odd, unsettling ways." Indeed, "dozens of students" had even signed a petition, which was sent to the department chairman, but the complaints did not result in any classroom changes. Other students described her as "smart but someone who often had difficulty explaining complicated concepts."[37]

Nor did Bishop feel the need to allay fears that she was "consumed" with the negative tenure vote. After she learned of the faculty's negative vote on her tenure, she took the rare, if not unprecedented step of pursuing a *counter-*attack. After she was denied tenure, she promptly filed a complaint with the EEOC, and was very "vocal among colleagues about her displeasure over being forced to look for work elsewhere after the semester."[38] In some quarters, of course, the student response wasn't all negative; it was mixed. "Some saw a strange woman who had difficulty relating to students, while others described a witty, intelligent teacher."[39] Bishop's students, coworkers, colleagues, and the people around her either sensed or picked up on the same eccentricities that the tenure committee translated into unfitness for tenure. And some were convinced she was an oddity, even in how she reacted and responded to the faculty's negative tenure vote. What, if anything, could her students, associates, and colleagues have done to thwart or even prevent the tragedy, given the conclusions they had already drawn about her? There is no indication in the record that any formal action was taken in response, though it's hard to see much that would have justified a formal, official university response to Bishop's behavior after the unfavorable tenure vote.

It can only be assumed that those who feared Bishop, who thought she was mentally unbalanced or crazy, did exactly what the hospital staff at the University of Washington did in June 2000, when their troubled colleague Dr. Jian Chen threatened to kill his mentor and talked openly about buying a gun: they simply avoided him, reduced their interaction with the brilliant scientist, politely shut their office doors whenever he was in the building, and just stayed out of his way. [40] That is, until he showed up at the hospital a few weeks later, withdrew a handgun, murdered his mentor, and then committed suicide. [41]

Would it be fair to conclude that Bishop's denial of tenure, confirmed on appeal, only demonstrated that the university's HR system ultimately *worked*? Many of the facts that supported the faculty's unfavorable tenure vote were, after all, the same facts observed and reluctantly noted by her incredulous students and colleagues. These were the same facts that suggested a brilliant but behaviorally erratic, impulsive individual who was indeed capable of extreme violence, even homicide. And it bears repeating that, given her failure to win tenure, if her three murders demonstrated the failure of the university's HR system, they also suggest that she murdered her three colleagues *because* the system worked.

Among the 350-plus perpetrators who qualified for this study—young and old, male and female, black, yellow, brown, and white—Amy Bishop (like Jennifer San Marco) was truly unique. Unique not only as a Harvard-trained geneticist, second-generation academic, inventor, wife, and busy mother of four, but also in the genesis of her capacity to kill. Her capacity to murder in the workplace took root, it seems, long before she was hired for what would be her last job; for almost everybody else, the capacity to kill came afterwards.

CONGENITAL MURDERERS NEED NOT APPLY

Virtually all organizations attempt to prevent violence, and certainly homicide, through the preemployment screening process. In fact, it was this thinking that prompted the UAH nursing student to ask, "Don't they do background checks on teachers?" Yet, these same organizations usually pay little or no attention to the job applicants and how they are treated after they are hired and become fully pedigreed employees on the job.

Research in this area is scant, but according to one study, by Professor Julian Barling, organizations rarely pay sufficient attention to how new employees are treated after they have been hired. After all, few applicants are demonstrably homicidal, or even have serious criminal records, when they initially apply for the position. Very few have criminal records or histories of mental illness, the former of which would have precluded employment in the first instance. Yet under enough pressure and management mistreatment and abuse, in case after case, they seem to turn homicidal *after* they have been hired.

In his article on how employees form aggressive behavior, and the causes of that aggression, Barling demonstrates that many workplace murderers were not killers when they applied for the jobs. The murderous violence and rage that later exploded in the workplace were not caused by juvenile delinquency, a broken home, or having been raised by a single lesbian parent who nursed a cocaine jones or an addiction to some other drug. The true source of the rage and violence was outside the home; it was their job. They became murderers and killers only after extended employer abuse or systematic mistreatment on the job.[42] And the only thing more surprising than how often and pervasively employee abuse takes place, especially in low-paying or menial jobs, is how little is known about the problem by the public and even the experts in the field.[43]

The same message is conveyed and confirmed in less technical, more popularly mainstream venues as well. In Jonathan Demme's classic movie thriller, *The Silence of the Lambs*, FBI Special Agent Clarice Starling (played by Jodie Foster) meets with Dr. Hannibal Lector (played by Anthony Hopkins) on several occasions in her attempt to find serial killer Buffalo Bill. In the third meeting, Lector advises her that Buffalo Bill mistakenly thinks he's a transsexual and had probably applied to the three major medical institutions that performed sexual reassignment, but had been rejected by all three. When Starling asks, "On what basis would they reject him?" Lector's words do much to explain the dynamic of the workplace murderer as well; he tells her: "Look for severe childhood disturbances associated with violence. *Our Billy wasn't born a criminal, Clarice. He was made one through years of systematic abuse*" (emphasis added). Much like the Tom Harris fictional serial killer Buffalo Bill, workplace murderers are *made*—and they are made after *years of abuse*.

Since the traditional preemployment screening process is appropriately ineffective in screening out the violent/homicidal job applicant, what this means, in practical terms, is that the job applicants who suffered bouts of alcoholism, kleptomania, spousal abuse, repeated convictions for driving under the influence, and so on, were likely never hired in the first place, as this data and background information was readily accessed by HR technologies. But the employee most likely to arrive at work tomorrow morning with a nine-millimeter handgun and kill the supervisor—or wipe out the whole accounting department—has already been hired; that employee is *already* working at the company, *already* in the office, *already* sipping coffee and munching chocolate glazed donuts in the company cafeteria.

What makes this truth so difficult to accept is the fact that it's so counterintuitive. The employee most likely to snap and kill his coworkers is—simultaneously—usually among the most pathetic, socially stunted, teased, taunted, and ridiculed workers in the whole building. If these employees were popular, socially skilled, articulate, and adept at modulating their anger and rage—and they never are—those same traits would obviate the need to address a serious workplace problem by retrieving a gun.

That the office idiot could—in the sixty seconds it takes to retrieve a gun from a lunch box or a locker room—become the most powerful man in the firm is a thought that's difficult to reconcile with everyday experience. And this makes it that much more difficult to accept. More than either the nursing student or the general public can comfortably admit, the modern HR office, even with its many functions, is ill equipped to detect, let alone weed out, the potentially violent or homicidal employee.

However broad the differences between those employees who murdered on the job and those who didn't, almost as broad were the differences that surfaced among the murderers themselves. As different as Amy Bishop was from any man in the study, as an example, few were more different from each other than Amy Bishop and Jennifer San Marco. And this was the case even though both were 44-year-old angry white women whose murder victims were almost exclusively nonwhite.

Yet among the many similarities shared by the 350-plus murderers who qualified for this study, none killed under identical circumstances, as virtually every case was different from all the rest. Rarely were any two remotely the same. Of course, every individual who qualified for this study was obviously a murderer (or had at least attempted to kill) and this alone, in the eyes of many, made them pathological murderers, or crazy as a loon from the start.

Still, in every group of workplace murderers that was summarily dismissed by the public as "crazy" or acutely "disturbed," the face of at least one always stood out from the crowd. Just behind the blank, childlike stare, or the impassive police mug shot, just beneath a will and determination borne of cunning and deceit, at least one perpetrator always stood out from the rest. These were not the victims of employer harassment or management abuse, and the public's perception of them wasn't wrong—just descriptively incomplete. These perpetrators were, after all, much more than just "crazy." They were, ultimately, "crazy like a fox."

Chapter Five

Some Were Crazy, Some Not So Crazy

Among the 350-plus murderers whose cases form the statistical basis for this study, it wasn't always difficult to recognize and distinguish between those who were acutely psychotic and those who were just mildly affected, or more or less still in touch with reality, and didn't need intense, ongoing psychiatric treatment or care.

Nor was it always difficult to appreciate, even as a layperson with no formal expertise in psychology, the degrees of mental illness, to realize that mental illness is a broad spectrum of behaviors with progressive steps toward conduct and acts commonly recognizable as "insane." Still, in the absence of scientifically objective diagnostic criteria, "insanity" may often look much like "obscenity," which a jurist once famously confessed he couldn't define, but he definitely "knew it when he saw it."[1]

A review of the cases gradually suggested two broad categories in this respect. The first category consisted of cases in which the employee's act of vengeance quickly disintegrated into a haphazard mission of random violence, a wholesale massacre of anonymous victims in a blind orgy of apocalyptic slaughter, wanton bloodshed, and massive human destruction and property loss. As the body count rose, and the corpses were stacked ever higher, these cases increasingly became cases of workplace "massacre" (i.e., the killing of at least three people), and the cases of workplace massacre soon became instances of "mass murder" on the job.

The second category of cases, however, presented a marked contrast. These cases were carefully focused responses to a particular individual for specific conduct that occurred at a certain time, executed by an employee with an efficient use of manpower, organization, and available resources, with little wasted effort, no unnecessary bloodshed, a minimum of human casualties, and no collateral property damage or loss.

SOME WERE WILD AND CRAZY

Jennifer San Marco, 44, of Goleta, California, we recall, on January 30, 2006, drove to her former condominium complex in Santa Barbara and shot and killed a former neighbor who had once complained about her behavior. Then she drove her red pickup truck to the sprawling distribution center at 400 Storke Road and took another employee's identification badge at gunpoint to gain entry. Once inside the facility, she withdrew a nine-millimeter semiautomatic pistol and opened fire, reloading her weapon at least once, and killed six more.[2]

San Marco, who was a Caucasian female, had not fired her weapon randomly: all but one of her victims were women, and all of her victims at the work site were nonwhite. After she killed her last coworker, she turned the gun on herself and committed suicide, ending what was (and remains) the most deadly workplace shooting in the United States ever perpetrated by a woman. There was a long history of bizarre behavior and conduct which had made her coworkers anxious or uneasy, and in 2003 she was placed on psychological disability before she was fired from the job.[3]

If it's common knowledge that San Marco was the perpetrator of the deadliest workplace shooting ever committed by a woman, it's not as well known that she also was (and remains) the first and only woman to end a workplace massacre by committing suicide. In this respect, she instantly joined the ranks of dozens of men who had committed even deadlier workplace massacres before they killed themselves. And where she was focused and deliberate in picking her targets, many of the men shot and killed indiscriminately, whoever they saw after they loaded the clip and opened fire. Such was the case of another post office employee, whose killing spree occurred in a small town few outside Oklahoma had ever heard of.

Patrick Henry Sherrill, 44, was a former wrestling scholarship recipient at the University of Oklahoma who left during his first year due to poor grades. He joined the marines and was honorably discharged two years later, seeking employment in the civilian world. Still living with his mother, he held several odd jobs unsuccessfully, as he was innately uncooperative and rude in his behavior, which made it difficult to work with coworkers and other employees. "He was a man who did not take direction well and preferred to work alone without any hindrance or supervision."[4]

In 1985 Sherrill landed a job with the post office, working as a full-time letter carrier, but he was incompetent, often making delivery errors and delivering mail late. He was reprimanded on August 19, 1986, by two superiors in a glass-enclosed office and reportedly warned that he would soon be fired. "On the afternoon before the killings, he approached a female clerk who had been kind to him (while most people ignored or hassled him) and asked her if she was coming to work the next day. She replied, 'Of course.' He told her she should stay at home."[5] The next day, August 20, 1986, Sherrill came to work with his postal satchel, which contained a loaded .45-caliber semiautomatic and a .22-caliber pistol, along with two hundred extra rounds of ammunition.

Moments after entering the rear entrance to the Edmond post office, Sherrill shot the first supervisor dead at point-blank range. (The second supervisor, for the first time ever, had overslept that morning and was an hour late for work, by which time the massacre was already underway.) The second victim was Mike Rockne (grandson of Notre Dame football coach Knute Rockne). Sherrill then proceeded through the building, shooting at random. "He didn't have any preference . . . Women and men, black and white. He shot anything that moved. People were scrambling everywhere, and he was shooting at everyone who was moving."[6]

As Sherrill walked through the building, he closed and locked doors behind him, ensuring that no one would escape. He only stopped temporarily—to reload—and then resumed shooting his guns. The rampage took approximately fifteen minutes and fifty rounds of ammunition, after which he turned the gun on himself and committed suicide. When the police arrived at the scene, they saw that Sherrill had killed a total of fourteen men and women coworkers and wounded seven other employees in what was for years the worst mass murder committed by a single gunman in US history.

On March 10, 2009, Michael McLendon, 28, went on a shooting spree that spanned three towns in southern Alabama, killing eleven people, including several members of his own family, and wounding six others, before he returned to his former job site and committed suicide during a shoot-out with the police. He had quit his job at a family-owned meat-processing firm the previous week; had been fired from a job at a processing plant for Pilgrim's Pride, the nation's largest poultry producer; and had also been fired from his job at Reliable Metal Products, a producer of air conditioner parts.

He first shot and killed his girlfriend and his mother and her four dogs in the home he shared with them before he burned the house down. After he killed his mother he placed the dead dogs at the feet of his mother's corpse, much like the ancient civilizations buried their royalty, and then set their bodies on fire, as if they were on a funeral pyre. Heavily armed, his weapons included an automatic rifle and a shotgun.

McLendon then drove his Mitsubishi Eclipse east, to the town of Samson, Geneva County, where he shot and killed his grandmother and grandfather and an aunt and uncle. After these murders, he didn't discriminate, and anybody was fair game. Minutes later he shot and killed a tenant on his grandparents' property; then killed a woman, the wife of a deputy sheriff, and her toddler daughter. After an exchange of gunfire with a pursuing sheriff, he shot and killed two strangers before speeding down Highway 52 toward the town of Geneva and Reliable Metal Products, his former place of employment. Holed up inside the Reliable plant, and surrounded by the police, McLendon fired more than thirty rounds in the shoot-out before he shot and killed himself.[7]

The day before he murdered his coworkers, Mark Barton, 44, murdered his second wife and his two adolescent children by repeated hammer blows to the head as they slept in bed. The next day, July 29, 1999, he drove to the two Atlanta, Georgia, offices at which he was a day trader and had suffered trading losses in excess of $105,000 in the previous two months. First he drove to Momentum Securities, where he shot and killed four coworkers. Then he strolled across the busy street, a gun in each hand, to the All-Tech Investment Group, where he shot and killed five more. Barton had also been the principal suspect, but was never charged, in the deaths of his first wife and her mother in Alabama six years earlier in 1993 (also by bludgeoning with a blunt, hammer-like object). Hours after the 1999 massacre, the police spotted Barton in his vehicle at a gas station, but he shot and killed himself before they could approach the vehicle and effect an arrest.[8]

An early case of workplace murder, as already noted, involved Julian Carlton, 35, a Barbados immigrant, servant, and handyman who worked on a famous Wisconsin estate with his wife, who worked as the cook. On the afternoon of August 15, 1914, Carlton, afraid of being fired, served dinner to his boss's common-law wife, her two young children, and six other guests. As they ate, he methodically bolted the windows of the mansion's main dining room, locked the exits, and then poured buckets of gasoline under the doors before he set the mansion on fire. As the mansion burned, he waited outside with an axe and hacked to death those who managed to jump from the windows to escape the flames.

Carlton murdered seven people and left the world-famous estate—called Taliesin—a smoldering mass of rubble and ashes. He was soon caught, narrowly escaping the wrath of a local lynch mob, and two months later committed suicide with poison while awaiting trial. His motive? He was afraid of being fired by his boss, then America's most influential and prominent architect, Frank Lloyd Wright.[9]

On February 16, 1988, a former employee of Electromagnetic Systems Labs (ESL) in Sunnyvale, California, Richard W. Farley, 40, shot and killed seven people and wounded four, including a female coworker he had been stalking for years. Farley first met the woman at an ESL function in 1984, and doggedly pursued her for the next four years—through stalking, telephone calls, and hundreds of letters—despite her lack of interest. By 1986 Farley was also threatening coworkers, which, when coupled with his poor work performance, got him fired. In 1988, the female coworker got a temporary restraining order against Farley, and a court date was set to determine if it should be made permanent.

The day before the court hearing, Farley drove his motor home to the ESL parking lot, ostensibly to convince the woman to rescind the order, but also armed with several firearms, including two shotguns, two revolvers, a couple of pistols, a knife, and a smoke bomb. He also wore an ammunition vest, earplugs, and a single leather glove. He entered the building through a side door, shooting as he approached her office, and shot and wounded her before he moved on, from room to room, until he had killed seven and wounded four, having fired a total of ninety-eight rounds. [10]

Not all the cases resulted in multiple murders and a high body count. A few of the cases were likely just as sad and tragic in the private suffering and grief they caused as those that involved multiple deaths, even though no high-tech weaponry was used and there was only a single death.

Sarah Dutra, 21, was an art student at California State University in Sacramento, California, when she and a friend, on September 11, 2001, murdered her boss, attorney Larry McNabney, by poisoning him with a horse tranquilizer. It was while working as a part-time legal secretary for McNabney that she and McNabney's wife, Elisa, hatched the scheme. As part of the scheme, they stole money from the law firm and during a five-month period spent McNabney's money on shopping sprees, clothes, cosmetics, vacations, and fancy cars. [11]

The poisoning took place at an American Quarter Horse show in Los Angeles County, and as the nation reeled from two terroristic attacks at the World Trade Center in Manhattan and the Pentagon in Washington, D.C., Dutra and Elisa were driving through Yosemite National Park searching for a spot to bury McNabney, who was still alive but dying on the backseat. [12] When they found the ground too rocky for digging, they brought him back to his Woodbridge home, by which time he had died. They wrapped the body in plastic, then stuffed it in a garage refrigerator. Prosecutors discovered the body five months later, in February 2002, buried in a San Joaquin County vineyard.

Dutra was initially charged with capital murder. A jury ultimately convicted her of the lesser crimes of voluntary manslaughter and being an accessory to murder. [13] Her accomplice, McNabney's wife, who had an extensive criminal record, hung herself in a Florida jail while awaiting extradition to California. [14] The judge sentenced Dutra to the maximum eleven-year term, and she was released in August 2011, and placed on active parole for three years. [15]

Valerie Solanas was a lone drifter who had traveled the country as an itinerant, supporting herself by begging and prostitution. In 1966, she landed in New York's trendy Greenwich Village, where she met artist Andy Warhol outside his office/studio, The Factory. She asked him to look at a play she had written, entitled *Up Your Ass*, about a man-hating prostitute and a panhandler. Intrigued by the title, Warhol agreed. Warhol was reportedly distrustful since his "films were often shut down by the police for obscenity [and he thought] the script was so pornographic that it must be a police trap."[16] He never returned the script, having lost it, unread.

Later that year, Solanas began calling him, demanding that he return the script. When he admitted that he'd lost it, she demanded payment, convinced he was trying to rip her off. Warhol never returned her calls. Solanas finally decided to confront him face-to-face, and she clearly had murder on her mind when she arrived at his studio, The Factory, on June 3, 1968, and waited for him to arrive.

When Warhol finally arrived, with two friends, Solanas pulled a handgun and shot at him three times at near-point-blank range. Incredibly, she missed him twice, striking the art critic Mario Amayo, who was standing nearby, before she tried to shoot Warhol's manager, Fred Hughes, and then realized the gun had jammed. The next instant, the elevator arrived, and she jumped inside, leaving Warhol and Amayo bleeding on the floor. (Warhol survived the shooting but never fully recovered, and for the rest of his life wore a corset to prevent the injuries from getting worse.)[17]

Gian Luigi Ferri, 55, was a well-dressed, middle-aged businessman who looked like he was just paying a routine visit to his attorney's office. On Thursday, July 1, 1993, just minutes before 3:00 p.m., he stepped into an office building on San Francisco's California Street and made his way to the thirty-fourth floor—to the law firm of Pettit and Martin. The firm had represented Ferri in business matters a decade earlier, but he held a grudge against the office for several years, especially the attorney who had handled the case. Stepping from the elevator, he ominously placed a set of ear protectors over his head. Next he withdrew a pair of TEC-9 handguns and a MI911 pistol, and then opened fire.

After roaming around on the thirty-fourth floor, he descended through an internal staircase where he continued to shoot indiscriminately whoever crossed his path. The carnage continued on several floors, resulting in eight murders and six wounded. The dead included three attorneys, a law student, and a young mother. Ferri fatally shot himself, committing suicide, as the San Francisco police moved in.[18]

Convinced his supervisor had mistreated him for years, in October 1991, Joseph Harris, a night clerk with the USPS, decided to kill his supervisor, Carol Ott. Armed with a nine-millimeter Uzi handgun, a .22-caliber machine gun with a silencer, three hand grenades, several homemade ether bombs, and a samurai sword, Harris drove to her suburban New Jersey home. After forcing entry, he found her clad in only a T-shirt. "Swinging his sword in a great arc," he deeply slashed her left shoulder and continued to thrust as she staggered backwards. Stepping over her lifeless, nearly nude body, he crept downstairs to the basement and shot her live-in boyfriend as he sat watching TV.[19]

Early the next morning, October 10, 1991, Harris entered the rear of the Ridgewood, New Jersey, post office and shot and killed two mail handlers. After a four-hour standoff with the Bergen County SWAT team, Harris finally surrendered to the police.[20] He was later charged and convicted of first-degree murder and sentenced to death, but died of natural causes in 1966 while awaiting execution on New Jersey's death row.[21]

On the morning of June 21, 2000, successful businessman, entrepreneur, and one-time mayoral candidate Stuart Alexander, 39, was the owner of Santos Linguisa Sausage factory in Leandro, California. He was the self-proclaimed Sausage King whose success owed largely to the manufacture of a popular Portuguese sausage product made from an original recipe handed down from his father, from whom he inherited the business in 1993. Twelve hours later, that very evening, Alexander was also known as a mass murderer, after he shot and killed two US Department of Agriculture (USDA) agents and a state meat inspector during a confrontation at his meat plant.[22]

The three inspectors had expected some difficulty when they arrived at the plant, as they had previously clashed with him several times before. After these confrontations with the inspectors about entering the plant to inspect the meat, Alexander decided he had had enough.[23] When the meat inspectors arrived on June 21, an angry but calm-looking Alexander quietly retrieved one of the guns he kept in his office drawer. He returned to the inspectors, and then shot and killed all three: two federal inspectors from the federal USDA and one from a state agency. A fourth inspector managed to escape the hail of bullets, although the video cameras Alexander had installed in the factory captured Alexander chasing the fourth inspector down the block, pursuing him with the gun still in his hand. The local police soon arrived at the plant, where Alexander was standing, ready to surrender and be taken into custody.[24]

Alexander was later tried and convicted on three counts of first-degree murder, and on February 15, 2005, was sentenced to die by lethal injection. While awaiting execution he gained almost a hundred pounds, and also began to experience health problems. On December 27, 2005, he died of a pulmonary embolism. The sausage factory was soon sold and later converted into a nightclub.[25]

On April 15, 1989, Ramon Salcido, 28, killed seven people, including his boss at the Grand Cru Winery in Sonoma, California, his wife, and two of his three young daughters, whose bodies he tossed in a nearby dump. He then drove to his mother-in-law's house, clubbed her to death, and also killed her two young daughters before he drove off, drinking champagne. He was later convicted on seven counts of murder and sentenced to death.[26]

Few cases of workplace murder matched the insanity and lurid brutality of the massacre by R. Gene Simmons, 46, a Russellville, Arkansas, resident who on December 22, 1987, killed fourteen people and wounded four others—including his wife and children—after losing his job at local convenience store. Beginning on December 22, Simmons, dubbed by the media as the "hillbilly from hell," murdered fourteen members of his immediate family and two former coworkers, and then wounded four others before he politely surrendered to the local police. He'd held several low-paying jobs, including a clerical position at a motor freight company, from which he was fired for making improper sexual remarks to women coworkers. And he later worked at a Sinclair Mini Mart before being fired (or quitting) on December 18, 1987, a few days before he started his string of ghastly homicides. [27]

Simmons first bludgeoned and shot his wife to death, bludgeoned and shot his visiting son, and strangled his three-year-old granddaughter, tossing all three bodies in a shallow pit which also served as the family's makeshift outhouse. Later that day, he drowned or strangled his four younger children (ages 8 to 17) after they got off the school bus, also tossing their bodies into the outhouse. The next day, he shot and killed another adult son, the son's wife, and their 20-month-old daughter, whose bodies were later found propped on the dining room table and covered with their bedding and their coats. Next to arrive for the Christmas holiday was another of his adult daughters, her husband, and their two children (one of whom Simmons himself was alleged to have fathered). All four were either shot or strangled, and their bodies laid on the dining room table and covered with a tablecloth. With his family members murdered, he spent the weekend drinking beer and watching TV, oblivious to the corpses propped about him in the dining room. [28]

That Monday morning, Simmons drove to a local office and killed the young receptionist with whom he had been infatuated but who had rejected him. Next he drove to an oil company, shot and killed one man and wounded another, then drove to the mini-mart where he had previously worked, shooting and wounding two more. Finally he drove to the office of the motor freight company, where he had worked until the week before. He shot and wounded a woman, reportedly telling her, "I've come to do what I wanted to do. It's all over now. I've gotten everybody who wanted to hurt me," before he quietly surrendered to the police. [29]

Leo Held, 39, of Lock Haven, Pennsylvania, was upset with his supervisors on the job, and also annoyed with the members of his carpool and one of his neighbors. On the morning of October 23, 1967, Held decided to solve all of these problems. Before the day was over, he had killed six people and wounded seven, three critically. [30] Known as a devout Christian, Held was also recalled by friends and neighbors as a faithful husband and a "quiet, peaceful man devoted to his family." [31] On that fateful morning, Held drove his kids to school, dropped his wife off at her job, and then arrived at his job at the Hammerhill Paper Company plant, at which he had worked for twenty years. Armed with a .38-caliber Smith and Wesson revolver and a .44-caliber

Magnum, Held was an avid hunter and a damn good shot. He burst into the plant with both guns blazing, and he knew his targets. With icy calm, he methodically shot and killed each and every one of his five supervisors as more than fifty employees and coworkers watched in silent shock.[32]

Leaving his five supervisors dead and others critically wounded, Held then left the plant and drove to a nearby airport, where he shot and wounded the airport switchboard operator, who was also a member of his carpool. Then he drove back to town, where he shot two neighbors, the Quiggles couple, one of whom was killed. The other survived the wounds.[33] When Held returned home, the police had surrounded his house, and they fatally shot him during an exchange of gunfire after he refused to surrender to the police.[34]

SOME WERE WILD BUT NOT SO CRAZY

Of course, not every workplace murderer lacked focus, or shot and killed as indiscriminately as Patrick Sherrill, Mark Barton, Julian Carlton, Richard Farley, Gian Ferri, or Joseph Harris. A number of cases presented perpetrators whose conduct suggested not "crazy" but diabolical cunning as they paid meticulous attention to detail both before and after their crimes to cover their tracks. They showed their innate talents, gifts, and personality traits in how efficiently they went about their deadly tasks, how promptly they achieved their murderous goals, how little extra blood was spilled, and how few lives were lost as they finally vented their anger and private vengeance with maximum focus, organization, and design. These killers aimed their weapons with the precision of a marksman. They wasted little time and spent few bullets. They caused minimal "collateral" damage, and they shot or killed only those within a discrete, carefully defined group (their own family household or specific individuals), in ways that were businesslike in their cold efficiency and aplomb.

We have already seen some of these traits in the triple-murder case of Amy Bishop, the Ivy League biology professor who went berserk at the University of Alabama–Huntsville faculty conference room. Yet Bishop's cool intensity and focus paled next to those of other workplace killers. These killers showed much greater patience and deceived a much larger number of people and over a much longer period of time, which permitted them to commit acts of even greater violence and bloodshed.

On June 4, 1991, three months after he was fired, Larry Hansel, 41, returned to the Elgar Corporation, a San Diego–based electronics firm in Los Angeles, riding a bicycle with a twelve-gauge shotgun slung over his back. He had been fired for improper office behavior, including the espousal of right-wing extremist politics and religious views and quoting extensively from the Old Testament prophets of doom and gloom. Much of this behavior, however, was dismissed by his coworkers and colleagues as mere eccentricities because "that's Larry. Sure, he's a little strange, but basically he's all right."[35]

Even his outside-the-office conduct was cause for concern, as his marriage had deteriorated and he was convinced that UFOs were using his backyard as a strategic landing site. Angrily claiming that his supervisors had inhibited his rights to free speech, among other injustices, he returned to the plant with the shotgun looking for the executives on his hit list. After detonating several homemade bombs, which he had set as diversionary distractions, Hansel methodically searched the second-floor hallways of the building, searching for the executives on his hit list. He found some of his victims, and shot and killed a vice president and a sales manager. Then, as stunned employees and coworkers looked on, he calmly mounted his bicycle and pedaled away.[36]

Michael McDermott, 42, armed with an AK-47 rifle, a shotgun, and a semiautomatic handgun, on December 26, 2000, shot and killed seven coworkers on their first day back to work after the Christmas holidays. A software technician with Edgewater Technologies, an Internet consulting company about ten miles north of Boston, McDermott had worked for the company since March, or for almost nine months before he went berserk.

He had entered the building carrying a bag and three weapons, and then strolled through several offices firing at different coworkers in different areas of the building. He reportedly was upset over the company's plan to implement layoffs just before the Christmas holidays and infuriated by the company's decision to comply with a court order to withhold a substantial part of his pay checks to pay back taxes he owed the IRS.[37]

According to prosecutors, McDermott had planned the killings, having test-fired his shotgun two days before the rampage, and he also took the guns to work on Christmas Day, the day before the rampage, when he knew nobody would be around. Also, for all of his claims of delusional, crazy afflictions during the trial, it was odd that he walked through several offices during his rampage, bypassing several employees, on his way to the accounting and personnel departments, where all of his victims were assigned. McDermott was later convicted of all seven counts of first-degree murder.[38]

On November 9, 1971, John E. List, 46, a devout Lutheran who taught Sunday school, methodically killed his entire family—his wife, his mother, and all three of his children—in their large Westfield, New Jersey, home. Embarrassed at having been fired from his job at an accounting firm, he left the house every morning but sat in the local train station all day as if he were holding down a job.[39] Using his father's nine-millimeter Steyr automatic handgun and his own .22-caliber revolver, he first shot his wife in the head, then shot his mother above the left eye. As each of his three children returned from school, he shot them in the head. [40] His oldest son, John Jr., had a soccer game that afternoon. List made himself lunch, drove to watch his son play, and then drove the boy home, where he also shot him in the back of the head.

Not a detail was overlooked. He dragged his dead wife and children, on sleeping bags, into the ballroom of the huge nineteen-room Victorian home after each kill, cleaned up the crime scene, and turned on the radio and all the lights. He sent notes to the kids' schools and part-time jobs that the family would be in North Carolina for several weeks. He stopped delivery of the family's mail, newspapers, and milk. "He had planned the murders so meticulously that nearly a month passed before anyone noticed anything was amiss,"[41] and the bodies weren't discovered for a month. With money taken from his mother's bank account, he fled to Colorado, where he settled down, assumed a new identity, and in 1985 married a local divorcee. [42]

Suffering from financial problems even before he lost his job, List owed at least eleven thousand dollars on his mortgage, and was also dealing with his wife's dementia, brought on by advanced syphilis which she had contracted from her first husband and had hidden from List for eighteen years. According to a psychiatrist who later testified at his trial, List saw only two solutions to his financial problems: either go on welfare, or kill his family and send their souls to heaven.

Fifteen years after he fled, he was found in Virginia, arrested, and returned to New Jersey where he stood trial and was promptly convicted of murder. In March 2008 he died of pneumonia at age 82, while in a New Jersey jail. A year after the murders, the List home in Westfield, New Jersey, was destroyed by arson. What List never knew, and the arsonist never guessed, was that the ballroom stained-glass skylight in the oversized house was a signed Louis Comfort Tiffany worth more than $100,000. [43]

On July 8, 2003, Doug Williams, 48, shot and killed five coworkers and wounded nine others at the Lockheed Martin defense plant in Meridian, Mississippi, before he turned a gun on himself and committed suicide. Williams, who was white, was known to both coworkers and management for his hatred of blacks. Though a few white coworkers tried to downplay the racial motivation for the killings, the glaring facts substantiated the conclusion that Williams had deliberately focused his attack on coworkers who were black. Of his five murdered victims, four were black. [44]

On the morning of September 14, 1989, Joseph T. Wesbecker drove his red Chevrolet Monza hatchback to his former place of employment, the Standard Gravure building in downtown Louisville, Kentucky. He was angry at the company, and was engaged in a protracted labor dispute with management over his job duties and the hours he was supposed to work. He never left the Standard Gravure plant alive. He shot and killed seven and wounded twenty more before he shot and killed himself.

He arrived at the plant armed with an AK-47 semiautomatic and a SIG-Sauer nine-millimeter in his pants. In his shoulder bag were two Military Armament Corporation Model 11 semiautomatic pistols, a .38-caliber Smith and Wesson revolver, and several rounds of ammunition, including five full clips for reloading the AK-47. According to witnesses, he never ran, but walked very slowly. He strolled down the corridor, firing deliberately, and reportedly showed "extreme shooting discipline,"[45] firing directly at his human targets and taking few random shots. He then moved from the white-collar executive suite down a hall into the third-floor bindery, where he shot and killed one, and wounded two more. From the bindery he went downstairs, where he shot and wounded two more men and then shot and killed another.

Next he crossed the tunnel to the pressroom basement, where he encountered a buddy who said "Hi." Wesbecker, who had always been friendly with the man, said, "Hi . . . told them I'd be back. Get away from me."[46] The friend said, "What are you doing?" and started to approach. But Wesbecker answered more firmly this time, telling his friend to "get the fuck away."[47] The friend obeyed and motioned to others nearby to move away. Farther down a hallway, Wesbecker evidently shot and killed someone by mistake and, according to eyewitnesses, actually walked back to the prone body, apologized, and then turned around and continued his murder spree.[48]

Finally, at the far end of the pressroom, he pushed open a door, saw a group of workers, and sprayed the group with bullets, emptying his clip, killing two and wounding five more. Then, according to eyewitnesses, he ejected an empty clip from his AK-47, loaded a fresh one, and then fired into the group again. As bleeding bodies lay strewn in offices and hallways, he withdrew his SIG-Sauer nine-millimeter semiautomatic, placed the barrel at his face, squeezed the trigger, and killed himself, thus ending what was arguably America's first workplace massacre in the private sector.[49]

In January 1993, Paul Calden, 33, dressed in a conservative business suit, calmly walked into the crowded cafeteria of the Fireman's Fund Insurance Company in Tampa, Florida. He had been fired from the company eight months before. He didn't show any sign of anxiety or stress, or of what he intended to do. After he entered the cafeteria, he bought a soda and sat down at a table, then, minutes later, walked over to a group seated at another table, pulled a gun from under his suit jacket, and then opened fire. He shot five people, killing three, and all five were supervisors, managers, or executives with the Fund.

According to a police officer on the scene, "It was not just a matter of him going into the cafeteria and just spraying in every direction. He picked his targets."[50] The local police initially assumed Calden was still somewhere in the twelve-story building, and they made a room-by-room sweep of the premises, shouting for workers to stay in their offices with the doors closed.

Calden was later found in Clearwater Park, however, about fifteen miles away, dead from a self-inflicted gunshot wound to the head.[51]

On November 27, 1978, former San Francisco supervisor Dan White, 32, shot and killed San Francisco mayor George Moscone, and minutes later shot and killed San Francisco supervisor Harvey Milk. The double assassination made national headlines, as Milk was also one of the nation's first openly gay politicians and an iconoclastic, pioneering leader in the burgeoning gay rights movement of the 1970s. Disappointed with the workings of city politics, and the paltry $9,600 annual salary from his government position, White resigned from the board. After he realized that the resignation was politically unwise, as it tipped the balance of power on the board, however, he asked Moscone to reappoint him. Moscone refused.

On the day Moscone was to appoint a more politically liberal replacement, White packed his service revolver along with extra rounds of ammunition into his coat pocket and entered the San Francisco City Hall building through a basement window, avoiding the security alarms. He waited until the mayor finished a conference with assemblyman Willie Brown,[52] and then confronted the mayor, asking again to be reappointed to the board. Again Moscone refused, and the conversation turned into a heated argument. Trying to avoid a public scene, Moscone suggested they retire to a private lounge next to the mayor's office, so they would not be overheard by those waiting outside.

As Moscone lit a cigarette and poured two drinks, White pulled out his revolver and fired shots at the mayor, who fell to the floor as White approached, poised his gun six inches from the mayor's head, and fired two more bullets into his earlobes, killing him instantly.[53] Standing over the slain mayor, White removed the four empty cartridges from his gun. Then he carefully reloaded the gun with hollow-point bullets—specially designed to kill instantly as they mushroom out and explode when they exit the body, often entering the body as a pinpoint, but leaving an exit wound the size of a grapefruit—which he was saving especially for Harvey Milk, whose office was down the hall.

Dianne Feinstein, then president of the board, saw White as he jogged from the mayor's office from a side door and called after him. White sharply responded, "I have something to do first."[54] He quickly met Milk in the latter's office. Once the door was closed, White shrewdly positioned himself between the doorway and Milk, pulled out his revolver, and fired. The first bullet hit Milk's right wrist as he tried to protect himself. White continued to fire, hitting Milk twice more in the chest, fired a fourth bullet directly at Milk's head, killing him instantly, and then fired a fifth bullet at close range.

White escaped from the building, but later turned himself in to be arrested for the homicides.[55] After a controversial jury verdict, he served five years of a seven-year sentence, was paroled in 1984, and two years later, in 1986, committed suicide in his ex-wife's garage.[56]

An American-born Muslim of Palestinian descent, Dr. Nidal Malik Hasan, 39, was an army psychiatrist at Ford Hood, Texas, the most populous US military base in the world. He held several radical Islamic views and had grown increasingly radical in his opposition to all American military involvement in Afghanistan and Iraq. He was especially upset that his superiors didn't process his requests that some of his patients be prosecuted for war crimes based on admissions they had made during psychiatric sessions, despite the fact that such prosecutions would violate doctor-patient confidentiality. He was also upset that he was scheduled for deployment to Afghanistan later that month.[57]

On November 5, 2009, Hasan entered the readiness center, where personnel received routine medical treatment immediately prior to and on returning from foreign deployment. Hidden in his fatigues were two guns, an FN Five-seven semiautomatic pistol and a .357 Magnum revolver, and his pockets were stuffed with pistol magazines. At approximately 1:34 p.m., he took a seat at an empty table, bowed his head for a second, then stood up and yelled "Allahu Akbar!"[58] as he fired more than a hundred rounds.[59]

Almost ten minutes later, he had shot and killed thirteen people and injured thirty more. According to eyewitnesses, he went out of his way to shoot military personnel, and even chased and ran down at least one man in uniform who tried to escape. He knew exactly who he wanted to kill, and his shots were anything but random: of the thirteen killed, twelve were in uniform, and more than half of the thirty wounded were service members. Of the thirteen killed, eleven died at the site, and two died later at area hospitals.[60]

Hasan himself was also wounded, struck at least four times, and remains paralyzed from the waist down. Under the Uniform Code of Military Justice, he faces thirteen counts of premeditated murder and thirty-two counts of attempted murder, and also faces additional charges at court-martial.

Few perpetrators were as focused and patient as Andrew P. Kehoe, 52, a Bath Township school board member known in the small Michigan community for his industry, thrift, and tireless battles against new taxes. He was the perpetrator of the now infamous Bath Massacre on May 18, 1927, in which thirty-eight children (ages 7 through 12) and seven adults were killed, and fifty-eight others injured.

Kehoe was infuriated by the levy of a property tax to fund construction of a new school building, which led to the foreclosure of his farm. In revenge, he first murdered his sickly wife, who had become chronically ill with tuberculosis, and then set his farm buildings on fire—carefully tying up his farm horses and other animals to ensure that they perished in the flames and didn't escape.[61]

As firefighters arrived at the site, Kehoe set off a bomb that destroyed the north wing of the school building, killing most of the people inside. (He used a detonator to ignite dynamite and hundreds of pounds of pyrotol he had secretly stored in the school over the course of many months.) As rescuers gathered at the burning school, he stopped his vehicle in the crowd, then detonated a second bomb inside his shrapnel-filled car, killing himself and several others as well. With thirty-eight dead and fifty-eight injured, the Bath Massacre was and remains the deadliest act of school mass murder in US history.[62]

R. "Bud" Dwyer, 48, was the treasurer of the state of Pennsylvania, and had served in the state legislature for more than twenty years. The previous month he had been convicted in federal court for receiving a bribe, and his sentencing date was scheduled for the next morning. He had consistently maintained throughout the trial and after his conviction, along with many others, that he was completely innocent and had been framed. He even wrote President Reagan, trying unsuccessfully to win a pardon. Because of a loophole in Pennsylvania state law, Dwyer was permitted to serve in his position until the day of his sentencing, which was scheduled for January 23, 1987.[63]

On the morning of January 22, 1987, the day before his sentencing, he held a news conference. Appearing anxious and distracted, he said he wanted to "provide an update on the situation." Again he professed his innocence, and then read from a prepared statement criticizing the trial proceedings which had resulted in his conviction. Then he stopped reading, called three staffers, and gave each an envelope. One contained a suicide note for his wife, the second held an organ donor card, and the third was a note to the newly elected governor. Then he pulled a .357 Magnum from another envelope, warning the crowd, "Please leave . . . if this will offend you."[64] Some in the audience gasped, others begged him not to do it; still others ran for help. To those who tried to approach him, he warned "Don't, don't, this will hurt someone."[65] He then placed the barrel of the .357 Magnum in his mouth and pulled the trigger—in front of five news cameras that were broadcasting live.

Dwyer's sense of fiscal organization and financial planning, however, was still intact until the very end. What few at the press conference knew was how shrewdly he had planned even the timing of his suicide. Because he killed himself while technically still in office—on the day before he would've been sentenced and thus automatically removed from the high-level post—his widow, Joanne, was still eligible to collect the state-provided pension for his household, which totaled more than 1.28 million dollars.

Chapter Six

The Influence of Gender and Race

So pervasive is the influence of gender in our lives that Sigmund Freud famously observed that "sex is destiny."[1] The cases amply support Freud's popular dictum. With few exceptions, they showed that gender—whether one is born male or female—not only influenced the course of one's life, but also influenced how and why employees murdered their coworkers and supervisors on the job.

THE INFLUENCE OF GENDER ON WORKPLACE MURDER

In almost every case of workplace homicide, the issue of gender influenced how the facts came into being, how they unfolded, and how they were concluded. These facts included virtually every step in the typical case of workplace murder—how the initial insult or indignity was perceived, the formulation of motive, choice of weapons, the nature and timing of the responsive attack, the participation of an accomplice, the amount of violence—the "lethality" level—of the attack, the number of collateral human casualties, attendant property loss, and the perpetrator's apprehension, surrender, or suicide.

As already noted, in every instance of female workplace murder where the woman used a firearm, in every case without exception, she used *only* a handgun. Nothing else. Not a single female, however angry or provoked, used a rifle, a carbine, an AK-47, or a shotgun. The two most violent female workplace killers in US history—Jennifer San Marco and Amy Bishop (the only two women to commit workplace massacres, the killing of at least three people)—had armed themselves with a single handgun.[2]

While this unique feature reduced the firepower of each female attack, the lethality level of each attack was simultaneously increased. The ramifications of this choice by women were both far-reaching and profound, and influenced virtually every other aspect, every other step of female workplace behavior that followed.

On September 9, 2010, Kraft Food employee Yvonne Hiller, 43, got into an argument with three coworkers (a man and two other women) in the third-floor employee lounge of the Kraft baking plant in northeast Philadelphia, Pennsylvania. Hiller was a fifteen-year employee at the plant, where Kraft baked Ritz crackers and Lorna Doone cookies. She had argued with these coworkers several times over the years, and had accused them of waging a "war of words" by talking behind her back and spraying her with chemicals. As a result of the altercation, Hiller was summoned to her supervisor's office, immediately suspended, and then escorted from the building.[3]

Instead of driving home, however, Hiller called a (male) friend from her car to confess that she had had "enough." About ten minutes later, brandishing her .357 Magnum, she drove through the security gate and then forced her way back into the plant, looking for the three coworkers in the employee lounge on the third floor. When she reached the lounge, she saw four coworkers—the three she was looking for, plus a fourth with whom she had no quarrel. She waved the fourth employee away, ordering him to leave the room. As soon as he left, Hiller shot the three others, critically wounding the man and killing the two women.[4] After she shot the three coworkers, she found her supervisor and shot at him, but missed. Then she made several telephone calls, including a 911 call, to explain what she did and why. When the SWAT team arrived at the plant, they found Hiller remorseful and contrite, lying in a fetal position on the floor, with her .357 Magnum empty, even though she was carrying more ammunition on her person.[5]

Unlike the cases of Jennifer San Marco and Amy Bishop, the Hiller case didn't establish any gruesome precedents or represent any grisly "firsts" in the annals of female homicide. But the facts are still significant because they dramatically illustrate, within the parameters of a single incident, just how differently men and women conceived, planned, and carried out murder in the workplace. In virtually every respect, Hiller's behavior—broken down step by step—typified that of women, which generally differed markedly from that of men.

First, Hiller was armed with a single handgun, a .357 Magnum, as was the case with every woman in the study who used a firearm. Second, although Hiller's anger and frustration had likely simmered for months, she was not one to procrastinate in committing the actual act. Her decision to actually murder the coworkers was made ten minutes after she was escorted from the plant. Hiller also had a close friend or confidant with whom she had shared her frustration and rage, much like the Thelma and Louise phenomenon seen so often in the other cases. Hiller also knew beforehand exactly who she wanted to kill, and accordingly ordered the fourth employee to leave the lounge before she opened fire. Fifth, as a result of the greater decisiveness and focus on her part, there were no collateral deaths of coworkers she didn't know or didn't mean to harm, and no significant property loss suffered by Kraft.

At the time of Hiller's arrest, her duly licensed .357 Magnum lay at her side, empty. Even though she had more ammunition in her pockets, to her way of thinking, the unspent shells were unnecessary, bullets for which there was no need. Why not? Because she had just accomplished exactly—and *only*—what she set out to do. Nothing more; nothing less. Having decided beforehand that the .357 Magnum alone was sufficient to accomplish the task, she had also calculated how much ammunition was needed for the firearm, and once the job was completed, there was no need to do anything more; no need for any more bullets, no need to fire another shot—or reload. (By contrast, her male counterpart would've returned to the plant—months later—weighted down with rifles, shotguns, and bombs, intending to kill everybody on the board of directors, a half-dozen supervisors, and whoever tried to stop him. This open-ended, apocalyptic vision of wanton death and bloodshed would have only foreshadowed or anticipated his own self-inflicted doom.)

Given the efficient, relative precision with which Hiller completed her task, it's no surprise that she didn't save the last bullet for herself. She politely surrendered to the police, and didn't commit suicide as men so often did. Men committed suicide (either as a solo behavior or as part of a murder-suicide) almost 35 percent of the time; women less than 8 percent. The total number of suicides-only was sixteen (females committing two; men committing fourteen) and the total number of murder-suicides was seventy-four (females committing four; men committing seventy).

As women were generally disinclined to commit suicide, they were also disinclined to commit workplace massacres—that is, the murder of at least three people in a single scenario (including suicide as self-murder). Only two women committed workplace massacres: Jennifer San Marco, who killed six (including herself), and Amy Bishop, who killed three and wounded three. The total number of workplace massacres was seventy-nine; women committed two, and men committed seventy-seven. The total number of deaths that resulted from workplace massacres was 517. The total number of deaths that resulted from female massacres was ten; the total number resulting from male massacres was 507.

Of course, the influence of gender cut both ways. It figured in the murder and suicide data for both men and women, and just as gender influenced the lethality level of female workplace attacks, it influenced the lethality level of attacks *against* women as well.

On February 2, 1993, Jonathan Daniel D'Arcy, 30, stopped at a local gas station and purchased about a dollar's worth of gasoline. He was headed to a

janitorial contracting firm, and he was angry at the bookkeeper, Karen Laborde, 42, for the late payment of a 150-dollar check. After he poured the
gasoline in a bottle, a coworker drove him to the offices of Quintessence, the
janitorial contracting firm where Laborde worked. Once he arrived at the
office, he angrily doused Laborde's face, arms, and dress with the gasoline,
shouting, "This is what you get when you hold up my [expletive deleted]
money," and then set her on fire with a cigarette lighter. As the flames
spread, he shoved her to the ground and then ran, leaving her engulfed in
flames, screaming and writhing in excruciating pain.[6]

D'Arcy was arrested minutes later in a nearby parking lot, smoking a
cigarette as he waited for the police. He reportedly told one of the officers,
"I'm the one you're here to arrest."[7] Laborde, a 42-year-old mother of two
teenage girls, suffered third-degree burns over 95 percent of her body, and
died nine hours later. Before she died, she gave a deathbed statement that she
had D'Arcy's check, and would have given it to him had he asked.[8] The
police later found D'Arcy's 159-dollar check sitting on Laborde's desk.[9]

The D'Arcy case was unusual in some respects, but very commonplace in
others. Male-on-female workplace murder didn't occur often, but it was
hardly unusual. What made the D'Arcy case truly unusual was *how* the
female victim died. Workplace murders were committed with a gun or other
firearm almost 85 percent of the time. But male-on-female workplace murder
occurred only about 12 percent of the time. And no other case presented a
male who murdered a female coworker by setting her on fire with a cigarette
lighter and gasoline.[10]

In still other ways, however, the D'Arcy case was not unusual at all, just
one in a series of cases in which the issue of gender clearly influenced how
the facts unfolded. As far as can be determined, when a female was either the
perpetrator or the victim of workplace murder, there were fewer collateral
human casualties, and significantly less property damage and loss. Yet—and
despite the apparent contradiction—the lethality level of each attack was
simultaneously increased. This interplay between murder and gender in the
workplace presented itself in many different ways. And even in cases where
the interplay could be identified, as where five of San Marco's six murder
victims were other women, the interplay couldn't always be assessed, as
where the seven coworkers shot and killed by Xerox technician Byran Uyesugi were inexplicably all men.

The influence of gender on lethality not only influenced the perpetrator's
choice of weapon, the choice of the weapon itself often suggested a kind of
homicide "hierarchy" in which guns were used for males, and knives, makeshift weapons, and bare hands were more often used to murder females. In
cases where a male murdered a male coworker, the murder weapon was a
gun about 94 percent of the time. When a male murdered a female coworker,
the murder weapon was a gun almost 45 percent of the time. And when a

male murdered a female who was a supervisor or a boss, the murder weapon was a gun only about 15 percent of the time. In almost 70 percent of the cases in which a female was murdered on the job, the murder method was not a gun or other firearm, but a knife, a makeshift weapon, strangulation/suffocation, or the killer's bare hands.

Did this constitute some kind of homicide hierarchy? Did men use guns far more often on men than they did on women? Raymond Clark III, the Yale lab technician, murdered Annie Le on September 8, 2009, by strangulation/suffocation with his bare hands.[11] Yogurt shop owner Robert Yachen Lee bound and gagged his female employee, dressed her in a diaper, and then prepared to rape and murder her when she blacked out after he attacked her without a weapon.[12] Christopher Shumway, 20, murdered his female supervisor in a Caribou, Minnesota, fast food restaurant by kicking and beating her to death and continued to serve patrons while she was left to die in the employee bathroom.[13]

Former Kentucky Fried Chicken assistant manager Ronnie Rice, 29, killed his supervisor, Maxine Urbanczyk, 61, by beating her with a chair.[14] Joseph Harris killed his female supervisor by repeatedly stabbing her with a faux eighteenth-century samurai sword.[15] On June 19, 2010, post-office mail sorter David Barnett, 55, attacked his female supervisor Doris Lloyd, 65, stabbing her seven times with a pair of scissors before a coworker at the John F. Kennedy airport facility in New York jumped on his back and held him down until the police arrived.[16]

On November 14, 1984, Henry Earl Duncan, 20, who worked as a cashier at the International Host Restaurant at Los Angeles International Airport, killed his female supervisor Josephine Eileen DeBaun, 28, by repeated stabbings before he stole 2,100 dollars from the office safe.[17] In September 2011, Ruben Orlando Benitez, a high-level Transportation Security Administration official, killed a female subordinate employee, Stacey Wright, 43, in her ransacked Mississippi apartment by repeatedly stabbing her with a knife.[18]

In July 2006, Ryan Jones, 32, in Fall River, Massachusetts, beat to death his restaurant supervisor, Valerie Oranski, 39, with his bare hands and a small metal pipe. And on April 29, 2012, Jose R. Rojas of Coral Gables, Florida, beat to death his female boss Frances Venezia (along with a colleague) with a wooden mop handle. These cases support the finding that men rarely killed women with guns, which were used almost exclusively to kill other men; men seldom used strangulation/suffocation to murder other men, and almost never killed another man with bare hands.[19]

Of course, men didn't always kill only men with guns. There were exceptions. Men did occasionally kill male coworkers with other weapons as well, from knives, lead pipes, and pairs of scissors to heavy blunt objects and even the crushing impact of a 96,000-pound front-end bulldozer.[20] And just as men occasionally killed other men without the use of a gun, men occasional-

ly killed females by shooting them with guns. But both scenarios were behavioral exceptions. By far the most common scenario, the behavioral "rule,"
was that men killed other men with guns; men killed women with knives,
makeshift weapons, or their bare hands.[21] Only one case was found in which
a man murdered a male supervisor with his bare hands.[22] In short, of the men
who murdered females in the workplace, more than 80 percent used means
that were used by only about 10 percent of the men when the victim was
another man.

Did these men regard the use of guns in those situations as inappropriate?
A violation of some twisted, macabre chivalry? Why was it somehow more
common for a man to murder a female coworker by beatings, by assault with
a pair of scissors, by strangulation/suffocation, or with his bare hands? Did
these men, in their demented, sexually convoluted reasoning, prefer the up-
close, personal "intimacy" of a physical beating over the detached distance of
a coldly metallic gun?

A psychiatric assessment of this murder dynamic is beyond the scope of
this discussion. The answers to the questions, though open to titillating speculation, are not readily apparent. But this interplay between murder and
gender insinuated itself in other cases as well. Why did so many men who
murdered other men in the workplace use guns, while so many female victims were killed with knives, makeshift weapons, or bare hands? Was a gun
used to kill only men—and women they especially hated or despised? A look
at three of the most violent cases in the study may suggest an answer.

The first case was that of Ramon Salcido, 28, who worked at the Grand
Cru winery in Sonoma, California. Convinced his wife was having an affair
with his boss, on April 15, 1989, Salcido loaded his car with their three
young daughters (ages 4, 3, and 1) and went looking for her. High on cocaine
and drunk on alcohol, he couldn't find her, and drove to a junkyard in
Petaluma where he slit his daughters' throats with his fishing knife and left
them in a Dumpster for dead. (The middle girl, age 3, miraculously survived
by playing dead.)[23] He then decided to kill his wife's entire family. He drove
to their house, clubbed and stabbed his mother-in-law to death, and then
stabbed her two younger daughters (Angela's young sisters, ages 8 and 12),
killing them as well. His last two victims, his male boss and his allegedly
unfaithful wife, whom he found later that night, not surprisingly, he killed
with bullets to the head.[24]

The second case was that of R. Gene Simmons, 46, who lost his job at a
convenience store in Russellville, Arkansas. In December 1987, he killed
fourteen people, including his wife, children, and grandchildren.[25] And perhaps as revealing as how many he murdered was *how* he murdered them. All
the adults, without exception—his wife, two adult sons, a grown daughter,
and a son-in-law—he shot and killed/bludgeoned to death. But all the children, without exception—his four youngest (ages 17, 14, 8, and 3), a 3-year-

old granddaughter, a 20-month-old grandson, a 21-month-old grandson, and a 7-year-old (incestuous) daughter—he strangled or drowned in a rain barrel. Given the level of violence associated with the first method of murder, and the relative passivity of the second, it's easy to guess the family members for whom he felt some belated compassion.[26]

The third case was that of Mark Barton, 44, who on July 28, 1999, murdered his wife and two adolescent children by repeated blows to the head as they slept in bed. The next day, July 29, 1999, he drove to the two Atlanta, Georgia, offices where he worked as a day trader and had suffered trading losses in excess of 105,000 dollars in two months. First he drove to Momentum Securities, where he shot and killed four coworkers. Then he crossed the street, to the All-Tech Investment Group, where he shot and killed five more.[27] Hours after his massacre/suicide, investigators found his wife and children, who had been bludgeoned to death. They had been carefully laid side by side and wrapped in blankets, completely covered except for their faces, which were perfectly framed by a comforter. On the daughter's body lay her teddy bear, and on the son's body lay his favorite video game. Barton also left a note in which he explained that he placed both kids facedown in the bathtub after he bludgeoned them, to make sure they didn't wake up in pain. Investigators also found another note in which Barton directed them to his wife's body, which was also wrapped in a blanket, but placed in the bedroom, on the closet floor.[28]

These cases strongly suggest that knives, makeshift weapons, or the man's bare hands were used to murder women far more often than guns. The cases also suggest that the element of gender did in fact influence a man's choice of weapons, and hence the lethality level of the murder spree. Salcido stabbed and clubbed his mother-in-law to death, and used his knife against his two young sisters-in-law and his three young daughters. Of all his victims, he shot only another male—and his estranged wife. By contrast, Simmons shot to death every adult member of his family who crossed his path, but felt the act of strangulation/suffocation more appropriate for each child and grandchild. Barton, on the other hand, bludgeoned everybody to death, including former wives and mothers-in-law, but saved his tender, caring moments for the remains of his two adolescent kids. And whatever differences Barton and Simmons held on the broader issues of Christian theology, both obviously felt enough for their young children to justify acts—drowning them in a rain barrel, and placing them in a bathtub to keep them from waking up in pain—that were eerily symbolic of "baptisms" for an afterlife.[29]

Gender influenced the number of collateral human casualties as well. In those cases where the murder weapon was not a gun, there were also fewer collateral human casualties and little (if any) significant property loss. In neither the D'Arcy nor the Hiller case were there any collateral human casualties, which were far more common in cases where the perpetrator was a male. Indeed, scores of cases were found in which a male had embarked upon a plan to murder a certain supervisor, coworker, or boss in particular, but then changed his mind, was distracted, provoked, or demonically inspired, and ended up killing many more. And they usually continued to shoot until they ran out of bullets, were subdued by someone in the crowd, or were killed in a final shoot-out with the police. In these cases, the perpetrator's path was always strewn with the bodies of nameless coworkers, bystanders, and other anonymous corpses the perpetrator never knew. Though a common occurrence with men, this was never the case with women.

Patrick Sherrill's infamous spree in August 1986, as an example, was reportedly provoked by two supervisors in particular who had publicly reprimanded him the previous day. His rampage resulted in fifteen deaths and six wounded. (Ironically, one of the two targeted supervisors had overslept that particular morning—for the first time ever—and arrived at the site an hour after the massacre ended.) [30] The cases that involved unforeseen or "collateral" killings, not surprisingly, tended to be among the bloodiest, with the highest body counts. These cases included the massacres by Salvatore Tapia, Gian Ferri, Dale Burr, Ronald Davis, Richard Farley, Joseph Ferguson, Frank Garcia, Robert Wayne Harris, Robert Hawkins, Clifton McCree, and Omar Thornton, to name just a few.

Significant collateral human casualties rarely occurred, however, in cases where the murder weapon was a knife, makeshift weapon, or the perpetrator's bare hands. And in cases (like D'Arcy's) where the victim was a female, not only were the odds greater that the perpetrator didn't use a gun, it was also more likely that the deadly encounter was a one-on-one affair with the female victim being the only target. Nobody else. These cases rarely included collateral deaths—onlookers, passersby, or those unlucky enough to be at the wrong place at the wrong time—which was often the case when both the perpetrator and the victim were male.

It's impossible to measure lethality accurately, let alone scientifically, without additional data, like the number of rounds fired, the number spent, misfired, and so on. Still, the cases in this study provided some statistical perspective and ballistic insight. They showed, for example, that of 350-plus individuals who qualified for this study, more than 250 were men. These 250-plus men were armed with more than 410 handguns, rifles, AK-47s, carbines, and shotguns, from which they fired rounds that struck 1,273 people, which resulted in 771 murdered and 502 wounded.

The same cases showed that of the thirty-two women in the study who used a firearm, they fired rounds that struck fifty-three people. These gunshots resulted in thirty-nine people murdered and fourteen wounded. In other words, although women had an aversion to suicide and almost never committed massacres, they still shot and killed more than *three times* as many coworkers as they shot and wounded. Inasmuch as women always carried just a single handgun and rarely reloaded, whereas men often carried multiple handguns in addition to rifles and assault weapons and often reloaded, it can be said that women were, individually, far more lethal in the workplace than men.[31]

As these cases presented significantly fewer collateral human casualties, they also presented little (if any) property damage and loss. Given how heavily men typically armed themselves—and the fact that the women, without exception, never armed themselves with more than a single handgun—men not only left trails strewn with the bodies of nameless, anonymous victims, they also caused more property loss and damage—to office equipment, physical plants, structural facilities, and product inventory.

In most cases of workplace murder, property damage and destruction were minimal and insubstantial, an incidental, almost inevitable result of the violence inherent in the workplace response. This included shattered glass and windowpanes in the face of gunfire, or broken furniture and bloodied carpets left by wounded coworkers and fleeing personnel. But almost 20 percent of the cases showed deliberate acts of vandalism and property damage, even sabotage, by employees for whom shooting and killing human targets wasn't enough. After the human bloodshed was accomplished, these individuals also "attacked" the computers and office equipment, or set fires to company inventory in an attempt to abolish or kill the corporate entity itself, or to somehow destroy so-called intangible property like the company's integrity in the business community or corporate goodwill that might have accrued over the years.

Deliberate property destruction by disgruntled employees who had already murdered someone was not uncommon. John Gardner set fires in the workplace building before he committed suicide.[32] Larry Hansel shot out the switchboard with electronically detonated bombs before he pedaled from the scene on his bicycle with his shotgun strapped over his arm.[33] On September 15, 1997, Arthur Hastings, 43, tore out the telephone lines of the guard station before he entered upon the work site of his former employer, the R. E. Phelon Company in Aikens County, South Carolina, where he killed four coworkers and injured three others, including a security guard.[34]

On August 9, 1982, John Parish, 49, recently fired from his job at the Western Transfer Company in Grand Prairie, Texas, armed himself with an M1 carbine, a .25-caliber pistol, and a .38 revolver. Armed to the teeth, he hijacked an eighteen-wheel rig and led the police on a wild, speeding chase through downtown Grand Prairie, indiscriminately firing hundreds of rounds into two large warehouses, causing significant property damage as well as six deaths.[35] On April 13, 1994, after Ladislav Antilak left his job, he shot his way through the front gate of the Sumitomo Electric Light Wave Corporation in North Carolina, and shot through walls and ceilings before he found a few human targets, killing three and wounding two others before he killed himself with a bullet to the head.[36]

On February 5, 2001, William Baker, 66, returned to his old job at Navistar International Corporation in Chicago's Melrose Park, armed with an AK-47 assault rifle, a .38-caliber revolver, a pump shotgun, and a hunting rifle. In addition to killing four coworkers and wounding four, he also "walked through the center of a large room, where diesel engines undergo tests, and sprayed gunfire" from his AK-47 rifle.[37] He also "began randomly shooting as he walked through office areas," according to several eyewitnesses and officials at the site.[38]

On August 15, 1914, Frank Lloyd Wright's black Caribbean servant Julian Carlton, 30, murdered seven of the architect's dinner guests, but also set fire to Wright's beloved Taliesin, destroying the elegant mansion, its contents, and the entire estate.[39] And the infamous Mark Barton, who had murdered and wounded dozens during his July 1999 rampage in Atlanta, also included the destruction of property at his former work sites. According to one eyewitness account, Barton "was rushing around the trading room floor firing . . . at anyone he could find. He was shooting with a gun in each hand, as if he was a cowboy in a movie. One by one, loud shots rang from both barrels. The air began to smell of sulfur and smoke. Some people hid behind desks, others managed to make it to the exits. Barton took aim at those who were lying on the floor and those who darted away . . . As he walked back through the room looking to finish off his victims, he paused for a moment to shoot out what had been his computer terminal."[40]

Property destruction also motivated other men who had recently been fired, including Paul Calden,[41] Pelayo Errasti,[42] and Michael Julius Ford.[43] Upon learning that he was fired, Frank Lemos climbed inside a company's 96,000-pound front-loading bulldozer, killed his supervisor by crushing him to death, then drove about the property crushing vehicles, buildings, and other company equipment before he was finally shot and killed by the police.[44]

Again, the critical point here is not that 20 percent of the male murderers deliberately destroyed employer property, but that this response was never seen in women. Even in the most violent cases of female workplace murder, such as those by Jennifer San Marco or Amy Bishop (the only two women in US history to commit workplace massacres), there's no indication of deliberate significant property damage suffered by the employer. It's almost as if there is a uniquely female or maternal instinct to keep everything tidy, neat, and clean, or a "good housekeeping gene" that kicks in even during a homicidal rage in which a woman has just committed murder.

THE INFLUENCE OF RACE ON WORKPLACE MURDER

Another significant influence on workplace murder was the factor of race. The influence of race, however, wasn't nearly as strong or pervasive as the influence of gender. Many behaviors in workplace murder that were easily attributable to gender—choice of weapons, planning an attack, using an accomplice, and so on—bore no discernible relationship to race. But the element of race did influence other aspects of workplace murder, particularly in the form of racism, which bolstered the motive for revenge and often determined the extent of violence—the lethality level—of the subsequent attacks.

Cases in which the racism was clear and overt were rare. On July 8, 2003, Doug Williams, 48, a white worker at the Lockheed Martin defense plant in Meridian, Mississippi, shot and killed five coworkers and wounded nine others before he committed suicide. Four of his five murder victims were black.[45] Few were surprised. Williams was known locally as a racist hothead who hated all blacks. Over the years, both management and coworkers had learned of his desire to kill black people. In fact, he had a long history of threatening black coworkers, and only weeks before the shootings he had paraded around the plant wearing a head garment that resembled a Ku Klux Klan hood.[46] When told to remove the hood, rather than complying, he left the factory and didn't return for five days.[47]

The Doug Williams case was unique not only because the element of racism was clear and overt, but also because it set a precedent for gross managerial neglect and incompetence in failing to enforce rules on acceptable employee conduct. The case is generally misunderstood as a "typical" case of racism in the workplace and how it influenced employee violence. As an illustration of how racism influenced workplace violence, the case is of minimal value because the racism is a bit *too* obvious, almost a caricature of the real thing. Racism in the workplace is rarely that overt; the perpetrators are never that brazen and confrontational in approach, and the restraint is less attributable to the recognition of moral duty or a sense of business ethics, and more attributable to a knowledge that racist behavior would inevitably hurt profits or the bottom line.

In September 1993, Michael E. Rahming, a disgruntled black employee at a facility for the developmentally disabled, was sentenced for the July 30, 1991 murder rampage in which he shot and killed his white supervisor and injured two white coworkers as they ran for cover. Given an opportunity to address the court before the judge imposed sentence, Rahming began his remarks apologetically enough, turning to face the audience of mostly white family members, some of whom were crying. He admitted that "I've ruined your life and my own as well." But then he seemed to lose his train of thought and started to ramble, and his words quickly became accusatory—as if he was also a victim. He claimed that all the victims had constantly taunted and harassed him because he was black. He also took note of the absence of black faces in the courtroom audience, telling them that if they had been "pushed and dumped on and threatened . . . the way I've been threatened," that they would understand why he killed and wounded his three white victims.[48]

He then instructed a few in the audience that if they were so upset over his murder spree, they would be outside the courthouse "rallying with signs" to protest how he had been treated by whites in the system. He concluded his remarks by accusing the judge and the prosecutor—even his own attorney— of "railroading" him and trying to "bury" him alive.[49]

Of the cases in which race was an element, the facts didn't reflect the easy racial Manichaeism of black and white, but a more complex montage of Asians, coloreds, and other nonwhites. On April 26, 2010, Dr. Lishan Wang, 44, stalked and murdered another physician, Dr. Vajinder Pal Toor, 34, a postdoctoral fellow at the Yale School of Medicine, who was studying infectious diseases at the Yale–New Haven Hospital.[50] Wang blamed Toor for getting him fired two years earlier from a position at the Kingsbrook Jewish Medical Center (KJMC) in New York City, where both had worked, and where Wang's motive for the murder took root.[51]

Wang drove to Toor's Connecticut condominium in an old red minivan, and then waited until Toor was leaving for his office at the hospital. Just as Toor was waving goodbye to his wife, Parnetta Sidhu (who was five months pregnant) and their three-year-old son, Wang opened fire with a handgun and then fled in the minivan, leaving Toor to bleed to death on his front lawn as his wife and young son looked on.[52]

Wang had filed a complaint with the EEOC and had sued KJMC in 2009 for wrongful firing. He claimed that hospital administrators had misconstrued his Beijing accent, formal demeanor, hand gestures, and other mannerisms as an "exaggerated excitability" and emotional impairment. He also claimed that "Indian doctors routinely mistreated Chinese residents, humiliating them in meetings and denying them sick leave, while Indian residents were rarely disciplined, even for major infractions like skipping work or errors in patient care."[53]

On April 11, 2012, a Gloucester County, New Jersey, physician, Giocondo Navek, 39, shot and killed another physician, Payman Houshmandpour, 32, as the latter prepared to leave his home in Voorhees, New Jersey, for the Virtua Health System, where he was employed. Navek killed Houshmandpour, a former colleague, because he believed he was behind his dismissal from another South Jersey hospital's residency program a year earlier. Navek evidently parked outside the victim's home, where he ambushed the doctor and then turned the gun on himself to commit suicide.[54]

In the vast majority of these cases, the element of race surfaced more obliquely and more indirectly than was seen in either the Doug Williams or the Lishan Wang case. In these cases, the element of "race" had a significant influence in the formation of the motive, but like other "four-letter" words, the word "race" was never mentioned or discussed out loud. In these cases, the racism had to be identified, analyzed, and assessed only indirectly, by inference and by reading between the proverbial lines. Such was the case of a woman named Arunya Rouch.

On March 30, 2010, Arunya Rouch, 41, a female worker at a Publix food store in Tarpon Springs, Florida, was fired from her job because she had threatened to kill Gregory Janowski, 40, a white male coworker at the store. A few hours after she was fired, she returned to the store's parking lot with a nine-millimeter semiautomatic handgun and shot and killed Janowski as he sat in his car smoking a cigarette and eating lunch.[55] After Rouch shot him, she ran inside the Publix store. Two Tarpon Springs police officers, responding to 911 calls, followed her inside and exchanged gunfire. Rouch was injured during the shoot-out that ensued, was treated at Bayfront Medical Center before being released, and was later charged with first-degree murder.[56]

Rouch, an Asian of Chinese descent, had been hired by Publix three years earlier as a trainer—to visit each new Publix store as it opened to train new personnel on how to manage the seafood department. Married but with no children, Rouch was intensely focused on her job, where she was known as an unrelenting perfectionist.[57] She was so dedicated to her job that she often prepared Asian food and exotic dishes and brought them to work for her coworkers to enjoy during lunch.[58]

But she was also criticized and ridiculed by other coworkers, including Janowski, for her meticulous approach to her job, according to family and friends.[59] She was often dismissed by coworkers as "anal," and advised to "go back and get back into your hole."[60] She was also so dedicated to her job that she occasionally started working before she had officially punched the time clock—which violated Publix policy. On the morning of March 27, 2010, Janowski reported Rouch for violating the Publix policy of not working till officially punched in. Rouch threatened to kill him if she was fired. She was fired three days later,[61] and at noon the next day, she made good on her threat.

Family and friends never alluded to the racial element that could have played a part in how coworkers regarded Ms. Rouch, saying only that she loved her job, and loved making special dishes for her coworkers.[62] Her father-in-law, Kenneth Rouch, said that she "took great pride in her work and . . . family." He also expressed the belief that she just "didn't want to disgrace the family,"[63] a curious aside that invites speculation that the case had actually produced *two* victims, and Arunya Rouch was the first.

The Arunya Rouch case also highlights another aspect of the workplace racial divide, and illustrates how unusual it was that her victim was white. Of the 350-odd cases in this study, just under 7 percent involved Asian Americans—primarily Chinese, Japanese, Korean, and so on. Yet, almost 97 percent of the medical doctors, scientists, and engineers were Asian. And they murdered mostly Asians as well. Dr. Lishan Wang shot and killed Dr. Vajinder Pal Toor. Chicago restaurant owner Keon Suk Oh shot and killed Dong Yu, his female employee, before he committed suicide. Cafeteria worker William Xu shot and killed his supervisor, Jennifer Ying Ying Maik, after she criticized his job performance. When Tuan Nguyen went on a killing spree after losing his job at an electronics company, three of his four victims were Asian. After Soon Byung Park was fired from his job in June 1997, he returned to the company, shot and wounded his boss, Edward Yoon, but then shot and killed his boss's sister, Mee Hua, as she tried to run away. When the South Jersey doctor Giacondo Navek settled a professional grudge against a colleague, the target of his vengeance was another doctor, Dr. Payman Houshmandpour. And when Jiverly Wong went on a killing rampage at an upstate New York civic center in April 2009, ten of his murder victims were Asian.

Of course, Asians occasionally killed members of other racial groups, but these victims numbered fewer than a half dozen, and they were in crowds or passersby. Asian employees rarely killed non-Asians, or members of other racial groups, as a principal or primary target—only other Asians. And although Asian men often killed each other or Asian women, the most surprising discovery in this part of the study was that not a single case was found in which an Asian woman killed, wounded, or even attempted to kill an Asian man. Not a single case.

Still another example of how race influenced workplace murder may be seen in a brief return to the facts of the Amy Bishop case. Her victims, we recall, were the biology department chairman, Gopik Podila, an olive-complexioned Southeast Asian, and professors Maria Davis and Adriel Johnson, both of whom were black. The wounded included a Hispanic professor, Luis Cruz-Vera, who also taught science. In addition to the media's disclosures about Bishop's previous brushes with the law, including the death of her kid brother, the public soon realized that Bishop—the brilliant, Ivy-educated Yankee feminist from Massachusetts—had single-handedly effected a racial "purge" of the UAH's entire science department.

As an often-cited example of workplace murder, the most problematic aspect of the Amy Bishop case is whether her racism (if "racism" it was) was part of her rationale, that is, how she perceived the offending conduct, or whether it was just part of her response. The case of Doug Williams, the white racist from Mississippi, as an example, was unique because the perceived "wrong" that he felt had to be avenged, the cause of his anger and rage, was the mere *presence* of blacks in the workforce. Management hadn't mistreated him, and he hadn't been teased and taunted by hostile coworkers on the assembly line. Indeed, management had tolerated much of his antisocial, racist behavior, to the chagrin of many blacks. He simply got out of bed one morning and, for no other reason than his hatred for blacks, decided to do what he had always wanted to do: kill some black people. In all the other cases of workplace murder, the perpetrator's racism was not the *cause* of the anger and rage (usually some perceived injustice that had little to do with race); the racism was in their *response*.

The same problem surfaced in the much-publicized case of Omar Thornton, 34, a black truck driver for a Manchester, Connecticut, beer distributorship, who was caught stealing beer from a company truck. On August 3, 2010, minutes after a disciplinary hearing, he retrieved two pistols from his locker and then shot and killed eight white coworkers and wounded two others before he turned a gun on himself and committed suicide.[64] All of his victims were white. At the hearing, Thornton had watched a company surveillance videotape of him stealing the beer. He was given the choice of resigning or being fired. During the meeting, he said nothing and didn't argue, but agreed to resign. Although he had never filed complaints or grievances against either the company or any individual employee, it was clear from coworkers, eyewitness accounts, and particularly the transcript of his 911 call[65] that he felt he had been mistreated because of his race.

It's equally clear from the record that his motive for killing his eight coworkers was revenge.[66] Another case in which race played a significant part was that of Anthony Deculit, 37, of Milwaukee, Wisconsin, a black postal worker who on December 18, 1997, shot his supervisor and wounded two coworkers, one of whom died. All of his victims were white, and he (and many of his black coworkers) had complained of racially discriminatory treatment by supervisors and management.[67]

The question for both the Thornton case and a host of others is essentially the same: Was Thornton's murder spree "racist" if he randomly shot every coworker who crossed his path, but because everybody else at the company was white, it only *looked* like a racial murder spree? [68] Could it be said that he was motivated by racism if, during the rampage, he was in cell phone contact with his girlfriend and fiancée, and her mother as well, *both of whom were white*? Was Bishop's murder of three colleagues in fact racially motivated if the same three professors had also voted against her earlier bid for tenure? At what point is a black employee's legitimate interest in raises, promotions, hierarchy, preserving his status in the white pecking order, and so on, trumped by race?

Unlike Thornton and Bishop, some perpetrators left no doubt that they were motivated by race. On September 10, 1994, Oliver French, 47, a black union official at the Ford Motor Company's Rouge plant in Dearborn, Michigan, shot and killed two fellow union officers and wounded another two, all of whom were white. He had worked at the plant for twenty-eight years, and as a skilled electrician was an up-and-coming officer in the local branch of the UAW (United Auto Workers). But he lost a committee election, became disgruntled over the racial and political union infighting, and felt the need to settle old accounts.[69] At his murder trial, his attorney argued (unsuccessfully) that French's "black rage" was a defense. The jury was not persuaded.[70]

Another case in which the racial element shaped the vengeance behind the murder was the Florida case of Clifton McCree, 41, who in February 1996, shot and killed five coworkers and then killed himself after he was fired from his job as a beach maintenance worker for the city of Fort Lauderdale. McCree had held the job for more than eighteen years. After a twenty-day suspension for failing a drug test and behaving rudely to tourists, however, he returned to his job with a .44-caliber Glock pistol and opened fire. He squeezed off ten shots, slapped in another clip, then fired again, "to punish some of the cowardly, racist devils" who were responsible, as he had written in his suicide note.[71]

But far more typical was the case of New York City transit worker Darryl Dinkins, 39, who on February 27, 2004, was arrested for the murder of his two supervisors. Both supervisors had been shot to death. One supervisor, Luigi Sedita, 61, was white, and the other, Clive Patterson, 46, was black. Sedita had been shot twice, in his side and again near his waist. Patterson, the black supervisor, had been shot in the head.

Dinkins had worked for five years as a car cleaner on the midnight shift at the seventy-five-acre rail yard in Brooklyn before he was fired four months earlier for insubordination. He had faced disciplinary charges based on a report by the two supervisors, who stated that they found Dinkins and another cleaner playing dominoes during work hours. Sedita also claimed that Dinkins had once cursed at him and spit in his face, charges that Dinkins denied. Dinkins had had several conflicts with Sedita in the past, and had charged him with racial discrimination. Yet, there was no indication—forensically or otherwise—that he regarded the white supervisor with any more animosity than he did the black.

Most of the cases of workplace murder were influenced by the element of gender, but few were significantly influenced by factors of race. The cases in which the element of race figured prominently were rare, as were those in which the racial issue was subtle and covert. By far the most common, most numerous cases were those in which the racial element was present, but easily (and often) trumped by the traditional issues that govern the workplace for everybody else. These issues included wages, hours, benefits, and the general day-to-day fair treatment that all employees (are entitled to) expect from management, their supervisor or boss.

Chapter Seven

The Problems and Politics of Being the Boss

In this chapter, the classic analytical model of the employee that murders the boss is reversed, to discuss the boss that murders the employee. A surprisingly large number of those who committed workplace murder, it turns out, committed murder after they had worked their way up the organizational ladder to become a supervisor or boss.

This chapter will also assess different types of management and supervision—leadership "personas" and supervisory "styles"—and how different perceptions of these styles influenced the motive to commit workplace murder and shaped the details of the crime. If one boss's management style is subtle and slyly Machiavellian, while another boss's style is more transparently open and frank, is one job site more dangerous, more susceptible or conducive to workplace murder than the other? Does the difference in personal management style make one manager more vulnerable than the other?

BOSSES AND SUPERVISORS—THE VARIOUS MANAGEMENT PERSONAS AND STYLES

The different types of workplace murder, like the circumstances that give rise to the murders, often reflect the personalities of the supervisors and the personas or styles they adopt in the day-to-day management of the company's affairs. Not surprisingly, this broad range of office styles runs the behavioral gamut. They vary from one extreme to the other—from the ultra-feminine, touchy-feely, ladylike approach to the macho violence of threats, guns, and drugs that inform the urban gangsta approach. Appropriately, these two stylistic extremes not only contextualize the discussion of workplace management and murder, but form the structural bookends for this chapter as well.

The broad spectrum of management styles is represented on one end by the distinctly feminine smiley-faced model cheerfully advocated by two former advertising executives, Linda Kaplan Thaler and Robin Koval.[1] At different points in the middle of the spectrum might be the management styles of CEOs like Lee Iacocca, Bill Gates, and Warren Buffet;[2] to the more hands-on, highly detailed micromanagers like Sam Walton and Martha Stewart;[3] to the tougher styles of Carly Fiorina and Donald Trump;[4] to the toughest styles of Don King and Jack Welch;[5] and, finally, to the furthest extreme, probably represented by the gangsta badass CEO style of the notorious Marion "Suge" Knight, the strapping six-foot-four, ex–Oakland Raider football player who founded the Death Row record label.[6]

For Knight, workplace aggression and threats of physical violence were not behaviors to be prevented and avoided at all costs; he fully embraced them as a style and as elements of his own unique persona. He adopted them as an effective management tool, applied them as successful recruitment criteria, and finally used them in a lucrative marketing strategy.[7] This consciously cultivated CEO style reaped tremendous profits for the Death Row record label and its featured rap artists, which once included hip-hop royalty like Tupac Shakur, Biggie Smalls, and Snoop Dogg. The Death Row label was just part of a billion-dollar industry that not only produces rap artists, but also promotes and sells clothes, accessories, alcohol, cars, jewelry, and a dozen other commodities to create and popularize an entire hip-hop lifestyle.[8]

Given this broad stylistic range, the study not surprisingly yielded a large number of bosses, managers, and supervisors who, far from having been victims of workplace homicide, had killed employees themselves. They acted under different names and titles, of course—team leader, section chief, superintendent, deputy chief, head honcho—but their functions were essentially the same. Almost invariably tall, balding white men in their fifties, they usually sat in the biggest corner office, approved the raises, bonuses, and cash awards, and signed off on all requests for everything—from visitors' parking decals, tuition reimbursement, and extra Dixie cups for the annual picnic bash to the authorization of credit cards, travel vouchers, vacation, and maternity leave. And if little has been written on why an employee murders the boss, even less has been written on why a boss murders the employee.

Why, one might ask, would a boss or supervisor murder an employee? Chronic absenteeism? Lack of productivity? Failure to meet a projected deadline? Why resort to murder when the boss or supervisor always has the option of firing the employee under state statutes or the age-old provisions of the common law? As an agent of the owner, the supervisor has more control over the work environment, and is subject to less anxiety and stress. The boss is more attuned to the demands of the employer, certainly more than a low-level employee. And as any Dutch-English dictionary shows, the word "boss" derives from the Dutch word "baas," which literally means "master."[9]

The motives of an employee who snaps and suddenly kills the boss are usually clear, or easily inferred from the circumstances or surrounding facts. The motives are typically "terms or conditions" of employment, like terminations, hours and wages, promotions, benefits, and so on. In fact, news accounts of workplace murders nowadays commonly don't even mention employee motive. This silence is attributable, at least in part, to the knowledge that the underlying conflict isn't wholly personal, but more structural—a Marxist tension so basic to the employer/employee relationship that it need not always be stated; it's correctly assumed.

Not surprisingly, the motive for workplace murder is often more complicated when the killer is the supervisor. The motive is often more nuanced when the killer occupies the large corner office at the end of the hall. And sometimes the motive for murder is just mystifyingly simpler, the *least* complicated, when the evidence is overwhelmingly against the murderer who's also the victim's boss.

BOSSES AND SUPERVISORS WHO MURDERED EMPLOYEES

Perhaps the most straightforward case in this category was that of Atlanta businessman Rolandas Milinavicius, 38, a Lithuanian native who spoke very little English. He owned and operated R. M. Auto International, an auto-supply business on Wilmington Drive near Central Avenue in East Point, just outside Atlanta, Georgia.

The company had only two employees, Inga Contreras, 25, and Martynas Simokaitis, 28, both also from Lithuania. And in the weeks leading up to the murders, they had had several discussions with Milinavicius about a pay raise. On July 27, 2007, the two employees approached Milinavicius again about a pay raise. In addition to the pay raise, Simokaitis also wanted to change the form of his salary from an hourly wage to commission-based payments, and Contreras reportedly asked for a small personal loan.

In response, Milinavicius pulled a nine-millimeter handgun from a file cabinet and shot and killed them on the spot. He shot both in the head, but Simokaitis received eight more bullets to the body as well.[10] Milinavicius's wife discovered the two bodies and called the police, who launched a nationwide manhunt for Milinavicius after he absconded to a nearby mountain resort. He was arrested two days later, after he surrendered to the East Point police.

In custody, Milinavicius promptly confessed to the killings, explaining that the pressures of the business and the mounting debts had finally pushed

him over the edge, and he just snapped after the two employees mentioned
the pay raise still again.[11] He was held without bail, and later tried and
convicted by a Fulton County jury on two charges of murder and several
other criminal counts.[12]

Frank Garcia, 35, was a nursing supervisor at Lakeside Memorial Hospital in Brockport, New York, who was fired after allegations of sexual harassment. Early on February14, 2009, Garcia murdered, execution-style, two
former coworkers, a married couple, in their home. Then he drove to the
hospital, stood in the parking lot, and brandished a .40-caliber Glock handgun before he opened fire. He killed two more former coworkers and
wounded a third as revenge against employees who had made the sexual
harassment charge.[13] He ended the rampage by finally surrendering to the
police.[14]

Ruben Orlando Benitez, 45, was a high-level federal Transportation Security Administration (TSA) official. On or about September 19, 2011, he
stabbed to death a subordinate TSA employee, Stacey Wright, 43, after what
appeared to be a struggle in her ransacked Mississippi apartment, where her
body was found by apartment security personnel. Benitez, who was an assistant federal security director for screening for the TSA in Mississippi, was
arrested on a three-million-dollar bond and charged with the murder.[15]

Stuart Alexander, 39, a mostly self-made man and the Sausage King of
Southern California, had inherited a profitable sausage plant from his father,
who died in 1995. He took over the business, and from the beginning had
problems with the USDA. He claimed that two USDA meat inspectors in
particular were overzealous in their inspection procedures and for more than
a year had harassed him, particularly about the technical processing and the
storage and cooking temperatures of certain meat products for which his
company had become locally famous.[16]

He decided he had had enough. On June 21, 2000, after the two agents
resumed what he regarded as harassment, he locked them out of the plant,
retrieved two handguns from his office, and decided he would finally respond to the harassment. A company video camera captured him chasing the
two USDA agents along with a state inspector, all of whom he shot and
killed. He was later tried and convicted on three counts of homicide, and then
sentenced to death.[17]

Best remembered by the public throughout the 1970s and 1980s for his
"electrified" hairstyle and flamboyant personality, Don King was a celebrity
boxing promoter and the CEO of the extraordinarily successful Don King
Productions. Through his company he brilliantly promoted such memorable
championship bouts as "The Rumble in the Jungle" and the "Thrilla in Mani-
la." He also had long business relationships with former heavyweight boxing
champions and top contenders like Muhammad Ali, George Foreman, Larry

Holmes, Mike Tyson, and Evander Holyfield. But that was a decade later. That Don King wasn't "Don King" yet.

In April 1966, in Cleveland, Ohio, that King was a violent gambler and numbers operator who was owed six hundred dollars by one of his deadbeat employees, named Sam Garrett. The story, recounted in detail in Jack Newfield's biography of King, *Only in America—the Life and Crimes of Don King* (1995), describes how King murdered Garrett, who was

> a sickly man, an abuser, a sufferer from tuberculosis in his left lung, and a man whose kidney had recently been removed in surgery . . . The two men argued at the bar for several minutes, King standing very close to Garrett, using his girth and size and loudness as a form of physical intimidation. Then the dispute spilled out onto the [street where] King began to attack the smaller man. This was not a fight. It was a beating. King outweighed Garrett by a hundred pounds. And King had a gun, while Garrett was unarmed . . . King knocked Garrett down either with a punch or, more likely, with the butt of his gun [and then] King started kicking him in the head, without restraint . . . Blood [soon] smear[ed] Garrett's swelling, mashed face. But King, swept up in the frenzy of the violence, kept on stomping . . . [And after the police arrived, one of the arresting officers] bent over Sam Garrett [whose] eyes were closed and blood was oozing out of his ears. There were bubbles of blood on his lips. 'Don, I'll pay you the money,' Garrett moaned. Then he slipped into unconsciousness . . . After five days in a coma, Garrett died [and] King faced murder charges.[18]

King was tried and convicted of manslaughter in 1966, spent four years in jail before being paroled in 1971, and in 1983 was granted a full pardon by Ohio governor James Rhodes.[19]

BOSSES AND SUPERVISORS WHO COMMITTED SUICIDE

In virtually every instance of boss or supervisor suicide—where the boss/ supervisor visited harm on no one else—the reasons had to do with the workplace. And in the cases like those of Mark Madoff or Clifford Baxter, where the motive for the suicide was depression-related, the depression was centered on the nature of their jobs or the direction their professional goals or careers had taken.

In the case of R. "Bud" Dwyer, there was no question that he wanted to make a point—in addition to preserving his wife's eligibility for $1.28 million in survivor's benefits—when he stuck a .357 Magnum in his mouth before several TV news cameras that were filming the news conference live. Judith Coffin, the only woman supervisor in the study, responded to the workplace harassment and abuse after she was made a supervisor by committing suicide with an insulin overdose. Clifford Baxter's depression stemmed from his role in the Enron scandal, and his scheduled testimony before Congress on the massive criminal fraud perpetrated by Enron against its creditors and the holders of its stock. And Mark Madoff's depression stemmed from the emotional fallout from his father's conviction for running a massive Ponzi scheme that bilked hundreds of investors out of billions in investment funds.

Among the supervisors and bosses who committed suicide, however, must also be included those who committed suicide only after they tried to murder or actually killed an employee. Jack Raglund, 28, was the owner of a small cell-phone company, Classic Communications, Inc., in Coral Springs, Florida. Raglund had just recently fired Victoria Sando, 36, also from Coral Springs, a receptionist at his firm. They had previously been romantically involved, and after he fired her, he agreed to meet at the unemployment office for a hearing on her complaint that the dismissal had been unfair. But before their matter could be heard, the dispute suddenly erupted into a loud argument in which Raglund pulled a gun against his former receptionist/ girlfriend in the agency parking lot.

Ms. Sando had parked her car in the parking lot and then started to walk toward the building when a shot rang out. Then another. And then a few more. It took her a few seconds to realize that bullets had been fired, that bullets were zipping past her, and that she had already been hit—more than once! At least three times. Before she realized what was happening, she was already writhing breathless on the ground, trying to get up, but couldn't. According to eyewitnesses, Raglund had pulled a gun, opened fire on Sando, and then jumped back into his BMW to leave. Sando was lying motionless on the ground, calling out in a whisper, trying to call for help, trying to get up, but couldn't.

But when Raglund saw that she was still moving, obviously still alive, he jumped out of his BMW and ran toward her. He had already shot her at least three times, and she still wasn't dead. He looked down at her and then fired still another shot, point-blank, into her chest. Then he jumped back into his BMW and drove off for good. Sando was later hospitalized and listed in critical condition, but survived the brutal attack.[20] The police found Raglund later that afternoon, in his home alone, where he lay dead of a self-inflicted gunshot wound to the head.[21]

Another case that followed the same scenario of a supervisor's murder/ suicide was that of a Columbus, Ohio, business manager William Evans. On March, 18, 1998, Evans, 51, a manager at the Ohio Bureau of Employment Services, shot and killed Shasta S. Dotson, 40, as she sat in her cubicle casually talking on the telephone. Evans had worked in the building twenty-six years; Dotson was a chief of office services, and she had worked in the building twenty-eight. After Evans shot Dotson three times, he shot himself in the head. Police later found a revolver in his right hand and a semiautomatic in his left.[22]

On October 18, 1993, Arthur Hill, 53, a civilian army-base supply clerk, shot and killed his boss and two coworkers, and wounded two others, after he learned that his temporary promotion to supervisor had recently ended. He had also just learned that he was passed over for a promotion, according to authorities.[23] Hill and all five of his victims were civilian employees at Fort Knox, the home of the nation's gold repository and an army tank training center.

Married with two grown children, Hill had been treated for medical problems at the hospital, but never admitted. Once he arrived at the hospital, he asked for directions to the bathroom, but stopped at an automatic teller machine. A shot was heard about a half hour later. Hill, an army veteran, had worked at the center for eleven years. He had driven forty miles from Fort Knox to the Veteran's Affairs Medical Center in Louisville, walked to the restroom, and then shot himself in the head with the .38-caliber handgun he had used for the earlier slayings. He was later listed in critical condition as a result of self-inflicted gun wounds.[24]

On September 26, 2011, Keon Suk Oh, 46, who owned and operated the Tatami Japanese restaurant in Glenview, a Chicago suburb, shot and killed Dong Yu, 42, who worked as a waitress in the restaurant.[25] Yu, the mother of two, was found shot to death in her Prospect Heights home by the Glenview police, who were responding to several 911 calls which had been made from an apartment at the Lake Run Condominiums, where Yu resided. The 911 calls, later confirmed to be those made by Yu, reported a verbal altercation. Shouting was heard in the background, along with several gunshots, as the caller was being shot as she talked into the telephone. After Suk shot and killed Yu, he turned the gun on himself and committed suicide with a shot to the head. He was found dead in the same fourth-floor corridor as Yu, along with a Ruger .40-caliber semiautomatic handgun also recovered from the scene.[26]

Still another case that followed this scenario was that of John Harrison, 53, a high-level insurance executive at Empire Blue Cross and Blue Shield. His office was on the eleventh floor of a twenty-five-story building at 1440 Broadway near 40th Street in Manhattan. A former FBI agent, he carried more than 250 pounds on his strapping six-foot-two frame. He had left the FBI's Trenton, New Jersey, office twenty years before and worked in the area of insurance fraud investigation and protection.[27]

On the morning of September 16, 2002, at about 8:20 a.m., Harrison summoned two employees to his corner office. Moments later, the two employees, Isabel Munoz, 36, and Vincent LaBianca, 34, took seats in front of his desk. Without saying a word, Harrison pulled a nine-millimeter handgun and a .45-caliber revolver from the desk and began shooting—repeatedly, with both guns, killing both on the spot. Seconds later, he placed the .45 to his head and committed suicide.[28]

Coworkers of the three deceased employees stated that, in the weeks leading up to the tragedy, Harrison was virtually "unhinged," and several other eyewitnesses noted the distinct behavioral changes they saw taking place. During that time, Harrison had restricted himself to a bread-and-water diet in an effort to quickly shed twenty-five pounds. According to friends, he was also likely taking diet pills to boost the effort. A fellow investigator and friend who also claimed to notice the personality change during that period said that Harrison "got real quiet. He stopped saying 'hi' to people." And, according to another friend, his behavior included "brisk walks that took hours." A Harrison colleague, and another vice president in the company, admitted that she too "felt he might have been taking diet pills," adding, "We went to a restaurant and he just sat there and didn't eat a thing . . . and last week, he started acting real moody and strange."[29]

BOSSES AND SUPERVISORS CAUGHT UP IN MURDER, INFIDELITY, AND STAR-CROSSED AFFAIRS

The previous sections of this chapter discussed first those employers who killed subordinate employees, like Rolondas Milinavicius, Stuart Alexander, and Don King. Next were the bosses who committed sole acts of suicide, like Bud Dwyer, Judith Coffin, Clifford Baxter, and Mark Madoff. These bosses were followed by those bosses who committed suicide after they had murdered a subordinate employee, like Jack Raglund, Arthur Hill, and Keon Suk.

The following section, however, will discuss those bosses and supervisors whose acts of murder and suicide took on a more bizarre or personal aspect. Tragic, sadly comic, or heartfelt, the murders and suicides of these bosses and supervisors were motivated not by business concerns, falling profits, economic recessions, or lost market shares. Their troubles stemmed from matters of the heart—love, lust, sex, and forbidden romance.

The workplace has become the place at which millions of people spend most of their awake hours, a development that explains why the rate of on-the-job dating—as well as the rate of adulterous office relationships—has dramatically increased in recent years. According to one study, 15 percent of currently employed executive women admit they had engaged in sexual relations with a higher-ranking colleague, and, moreover, 37 percent said they *still* believed that having sex with the boss paid off professionally.[30]

In a related study, more than 15 percent of female employees had slept with their bosses—adulterously or otherwise—and a third admitted that it paid off professionally.[31] It's hardly surprising that bosses and supervisors, even top CEOs, are especially attractive (and vulnerable) to members of the opposite sex, particularly when they are also subordinate employees.

In this environment, given the rapid growth in office relationships, the growth of murders in the workplace that resulted from failed relationships was inevitable. And for these bosses and supervisors, their crimes were typically desperate attempts to extricate themselves from the clutches of the same private demons of love, romance, and sex. Nor did it matter what *kind* of love was at stake—lost love, star-crossed love, unrequited love, forbidden love, a love that dared not speak its name, or just a torrid but tawdry May-September affair.

In a handful of cases, it was clear from the research that the murderer (always a male) had been motivated by a failed "relationship" with the victim (always a female), especially when the homicide was followed by a suicide. After restaurant owner Keon Suk Oh shot and killed his waitress Dong Yu, and then committed suicide, even after the funerals, the police and other authorities suspected but couldn't confirm a romantic relationship. The authorities were faced with the silence of mourning restaurant coworkers and neighbors who politely refused to talk, and could never confirm the precise relationship between Oh and Yu.[32]

Rubin Orlando Benitez was another boss whose public downfall and disgrace owed to a secret meretricious affair. A high-level Transportation Security Administration official, Benitez had visited his subordinate employee and murder victim Stacey Wright often over a period of several years. He kept this secret rendezvous faithfully, traveling to Mississippi from Chicago, where he still lived with his wife. Wright, who was married but separated, had worked initially as a screener before her last position, and she and Benitez had last worked together at the Jackson-Evers International Airport.[33]

As already noted, on March 18, 1989, William Evans shot and killed his female subordinate at the Ohio Bureau of Employment, Shasta S. Dotson, as she talked casually on the telephone. Evans then turned the gun on himself. The police had reason to believe they had been romantically involved outside the office, and their suspicions were soon borne out. The subsequent probe revealed that Dotson was a 40-year-old mother of two teenage sons, and she was about to marry another man. Indeed, the day before the shooting, she and her fiancé had signed papers to buy a house.[34] In addition, in Evans's apartment the police found his diary and an appointment calendar on which he had noted the date of their breakup. Also discovered was a suicide note, some poetry referring to the suicide, an empty champagne glass, and an opened but nearly full bottle of champagne. The champagne stood next to two martial-arts swords, which had been deliberately crossed—to signal his intention to commit suicide.[35]

The case of John Harrison the insurance executive showed elements of this phenomenon as well—and in much greater relief. In the wake of Harrison's double murder-suicide, investigators soon learned that he was having an adulterous relationship with one of his two murder victims, Isabel Munoz. Indeed, two weeks earlier he had actually left his wife and their marital home in Mount Holly, New Jersey, with the view of solidifying his relationship with Munoz. His sudden, inexplicable preoccupation with weight loss was now revealed for what it was: an attempt to make himself more attractive to Munoz.[36]

The dynamic of the homicidal boss as former lover also played out in the case of Jack Raglund, who, as already noted, was the owner of a small cell-phone company. Raglund had fired his receptionist, Sando, but had also agreed to meet at the unemployment office for a hearing on her claim that her dismissal had been unfair.[37] At the time of the hearing, they were no longer involved, but Raglund apparently snapped and shot Sando four times, saw she wasn't dead, then shot her a fifth time, at point-blank range. In what was apparently a tumultuous relationship, Sando had lived in one of Raglund's houses, but had since moved in with her new boyfriend, Harvey Weisberg, after she broke off the relationship and insisted that it be professional only. She was living with Weisberg at the time Raglund shot her and then later committed suicide.[38]

Hemy Neuman, 49, was a high-level General Electric (GE) executive, an energy manager at the GE unit's quality systems division in Atlanta, Georgia. In November 2010, Neuman put on a fake beard and drove a rented minivan to a suburban Atlanta day-care center. Once he arrived at the day care center, he shot and killed Russell Sneiderman, 36, a former JP Morgan banker who was dropping off his young son.[39] After the shooting, Neuman returned to the minivan and sped from the scene, according to eyewitnesses who made a positive identification of Neuman as the shooter. Neuman, of course, was having an extramarital affair with Sneiderman's wife Andrea, 35, who was also his subordinate at the GE facility.[40]

Russell Sneiderman was dropping his young son off at the Dunwoody Prep preschool when Neuman approached in the rented minivan and opened fire. As an energy manager, Neuman supervised five thousand employees at the GE unit's quality systems division. Andrea Sneiderman, the victim's wife, worked in software systems support. It was speculated, but couldn't be confirmed, that the wife had collaborated with Neuman in planning the crime. But no criminal charges had been filed against her.[41]

Neuman was later prosecuted and stood trial, at which he advanced an insanity defense. He testified that he was only obeying the orders and instructions he heard from an angel and a demon. He had been hearing the voices since he was a young child in an Israeli orphanage, he confessed, but never discussed the voices with anyone else, even though they fairly guided his life. He also testified that the angels had familiar voices: the female angel sounded like Olivia Newton-John, and the male angel had the voice of Barry White.[42]

THE "WHAT-GOES-AROUND-COMES-AROUND" PRINCIPLE

From the management style of Thaler and Koval, who preach a nice and touchy-feely supervisory approach, to the violent neothuggery of a Don King or a Marion "Suge" Knight, there's obviously a lot of behavioral room in which to cultivate a management persona or office style. As the question was put at the opening of this chapter: If a one boss's office style is subtle and shrewdly Machiavellian, while another boss's style is more transparent and open, which office is more susceptible or vulnerable to workplace homicide? Why were some bosses and supervisors viciously stalked, hunted down, and then shot dead on the spot, while others were ignored, overlooked, and even allowed to walk away from the gunfire, to escape and live another day?

The difference may be explained, at least in part, by the vagaries of sheer luck. One Oklahoma postal supervisor never overslept, and had never been late for his shift in more than a decade. Yet, on August 20, 1986, he inexplicably did both, arriving at the post office late only to learn that his inept subordinate Patrick Sherrill had just shot and killed fourteen workers and wounded seven more, and had been *looking for him.*[43] The same eerie scenario took place when the Elgar Corporation's Larry Hansel returned to the plant with his shotgun, looking for the supervisors whose names were on his hit list. Fortunately, most were out of their offices and elsewhere when he showed up on his bicycle with his shotgun and a bandolier of bullets wrapped on his back.[44] But few are that lucky.

A handful of cases, and the Kenneth Tornes case in particular, suggest that it's not always just good luck or serendipity that explains why some bosses survived the bloodiest workplace massacres and continued among the living. Nor was it always just bad luck or tragic misfortune that explained why so many others ended up riddled with bullets and sprawled across their desks, dead.

A number of cases suggest that the best bosses and supervisors, the most talented and highly skilled, were never killed in the workplace. If a supervisor was generally well liked and highly regarded, and everybody sensed that he or she was good at what he or she did, this functioned as a kind of insurance. Even if one malcontent in a factory disliked him enough to kill him, the supervisor's skill and popularity acted as a kind of inhibitor on the potentially violent worker who didn't share the feelings of the group. The worker, as a result, refrained from any violence against the supervisor because the supervisor had accumulated so much interpersonal capital and goodwill with everybody else.

The cases also suggest, not unexpectedly, that the supervisors, managers and bosses who were stalked, hunted down, and shot and killed on the spot also tended to be the least competent, least skilled, and most disliked and mean-spirited toward their subordinates. These supervisors and bosses, moreover, were occasionally hated and disliked even by their peers. In fact, these bosses and supervisors were usually even worse than the facts suggested. Why was this the case? How was this determined?

Much of this argument proceeds on the assumption first articulated in the research of David Grossman, who contended that human beings have an innate aversion to killing another human being. (Grossman's argument and its ramifications are discussed later, in chapter 10.) As a consequence, it takes a lot, psychologically, for a person to overcome this aversion. A person will tolerate a lot of abuse before he or she formulates the desire to kill another human being. In short, people ordinarily don't like killing other people, an aversion rooted in their own sense of self-preservation as a species. And they must be pushed to great lengths before they are provoked to do so.

If a supervisor's mistreatment of an employee was bad enough to provoke that employee to grab a loaded gun and kill, that employee likely had the tacit, unspoken support (if not encouragement) of coworkers and people around him. If a supervisor's treatment of an employee was sufficient to provoke that employee to grab a loaded gun and kill, the desire to kill that supervisor likely existed in the minds of ten other employees as well. Those ten other employees almost certainly had the same homicidal thoughts, but also had the good sense not to translate a criminal thought into a criminal act. They lacked the nerve (or the cojones) to actually commit a horrible homicide.

Scores of cases in the study suggested (or permitted the inference) that a murdered boss was usually disliked by almost everybody. Not a single case, however, suggested that a murdered boss or supervisor was the victim of a lone, deranged malcontent who killed someone who was overwhelmingly adored, respected, and admired by everybody else. Not one case. The murdered boss or supervisor was more typically the least talented, the least competent among his or her peers, the unfortunate victim of a kind of management Darwinism that "thinned the herd" by eliminating the least able, the least adaptive, the least liked, the worst of the worst.

HOW THE BEST BOSSES SURVIVED; WHY THE WORST DIDN'T

Of course, nobody deserves to be murdered, and no supervisor or boss, however incompetent, despised, or vile, should be killed or subject to *any* violence. Even the vaguest suggestion of any kind of violence as a legitimate workplace response is wholly improper and irresponsible in the extreme. Yet the cases suggest a cruelly poetic justice in viewing the violence, resentment, and hatred that resulted in the murder of a supervisor or boss, arguably, as just a reflection of the same violence, resentment, and hatred the supervisor showed in his dealings with subordinates before they responded in kind, and he met his tragic fate.

THE KENNETH TORNES CASE

The case of Kenneth Tornes is significant not only for what the widely reported facts of the case describe, but also for what the facts leave unsaid—which must be inferred. On April 24, 1996, Kenneth Tornes, 32, was an eight-year veteran of the Jackson, Mississippi, fire department. On that fateful morning, Tornes first shot and killed his estranged wife, Glenda, 42, with a .45 semiautomatic handgun. Then he loaded his car with an assault rifle, a TEC-9, and the .45 handgun and drove to the fire station headquarters downtown.

Once inside the fire station, armed with the assault rifle, he made the rounds of several offices, where he also shot and killed four fire chiefs and wounded two more.[45] After the fire station rampage, the police pursued him on a ten-mile chase through downtown Jackson, causing several automobile accidents, before they cornered him in a shoot-out in a suburban shopping mall. During the shoot-out in the shopping mall, Tornes shot and wounded a police officer, and Tornes himself was shot and wounded in the left eye.[46]

Even with five murdered and two wounded, the Tornes case was far from the most violent example of workplace murder. Nor were any of the murders committed in an especially horrific or brutal way. What distinguishes the Tornes case from so many others was the clarity of the surrounding circumstances: the politics of the fire department, the long history of departmental animosity between the supervisors and the rank-and-file. What makes the Tornes case so exceptional is how obviously the firefighters' resentment and hostility were reflected in Tornes's behavior, his motives, his conduct, and his method of carrying out the deaths.

First, Tornes entered the firehouse searching only for those who held the rank of captain or higher, not rank-and-file firefighters like himself. Climbing the stairs, going from office to office with his assault rifle, he brushed past rank-and-file colleagues in blue shirts to hunt down and kill supervisors in white. He consistently avoided harming any firefighter in a blue shirt, looking to kill only the chiefs. When he confronted a female employee in the hallway, he waved her away, saying, "Lady, get back, I'm going to blow this place up." Minutes later, when he bumped into another firefighter with an arson dog, he shouted, "Get out of the way"[47] as he continued up the stairs searching for more chiefs. Before he ran from the fire station, he had shot and killed four supervisors or chiefs and wounded four others, one critically.

Second, Tornes's focus on the chiefs clearly reflected the resentment and dislike that most of his rank-and-file colleagues also felt for the chiefs. Almost to a man, they shared his dislike (if not his murderous hatred) of the chiefs. Surprisingly, they also knew for years that he was planning to avenge what they all regarded as an abusive, petty, and unfair leadership in the department. And Tornes in particular had problems with the chiefs. "He had serious problems with the chiefs," they said.[48]

But Tornes was not alone in this regard. In fact, he likely had the overwhelming (if tacit) support of his rank-and-file colleagues. There was a general tension in the whole fire department between dissatisfied rank-and-file firefighters and the managing chiefs. The chiefs tended to issue reprimands for behavior that the rank-and-file firefighters thought was trivial. And this internal tension had slowly festered into a kind of hate. As a result, most of the firefighters regarded Tornes as a "perfect gentleman except when you got him talking about the chiefs." When it came to the chiefs, he was regarded as a "time bomb waiting to go off." Another rank-and-file firefighter confessed, "I'm surprised it took so long."[49]

Of the reams of facts reported on the Tornes case, in both the local print and televised news media, among the clearest was the fact that the chiefs were almost unanimously hated by their subordinate employees. In all of the news coverage given the tragedy, the flurry of investigations that followed, the funerals and the mournful aftermath, there were few indications by the subordinate, lower-level firefighters that they truly regretted what Tornes had done, and still fewer indications that they truly mourned the murder of the chiefs.

Of the more than three hundred and fifty cases of workplace murder that form the basis of this study, almost all were followed by some degree of shock, surprise, indignation, sympathy, or remorse on the part of coworkers who had survived. These coworkers were grief-stricken, shocked, and often visibly traumatized, and in every case there was condemnation of the act, and expressions of sympathy and pity for the victims, as well as their families and others left behind.

Much like the facts of the Kenneth Tornes case, however, what was stated most eloquently were those thoughts that were barely verbalized at all. In none of these cases did a single coworker lament the murder of a specific supervisor or boss by name! Laments were always expressed on behalf of the group as a whole, and couched in general terms; they were never directed at a particular, personally identifiable supervisor or boss. The shock and indignation were invariably focused on the tragedy of the *event*, or a colleague who would be missed—never over a specific, individual supervisor or boss who was *named*.

The reference here, of course, is exclusively to cases like the Kenneth Tornes case, where supervisors and bosses were specifically sought out and hunted down by armed employees who had murder on their minds. Whatever the news media coverage, coworkers and eyewitnesses always expressed a sadness, pity, and remorse after the incident, often with specific reference to one of the victims, how good and decent he or she was, how easy he or she was to work with, and how much he or she would be missed.

This was rarely (if ever) the case with a murdered supervisor or boss. Have bosses and supervisors in the American workplace treated subordinate employees that badly? Has the history of that relationship been so abusive and unfair that it justifies the conclusion, or even the hushed speculation, that a murdered supervisor—perhaps, just maybe—only got what he deserved?

Perpetrators often responded to their crimes in unexpected ways. In April 2010, Dr. Lishan Wang, 44, ambushed and murdered another physician, Dr. Vajinder Pal Toor, 34, on the doorsteps of his New Haven, Connecticut, home. Wang opened fire, striking Toor with five bullets as his victim's pregnant wife and three-year-old son looked on. It was Wang's revenge for Toor's part in getting him fired from a Manhattan hospital a few years before. Shortly after his capture and arrest, Wang confessed, and then softly apologized to the court, saying that he was "sorry" for what had occurred.[50]

Of course, few perpetrators were that courteous or polite. In September 1993, Michael E. Rahming, a black staff worker with a state agency, we recall, was sentenced after he was convicted of tracking down and murdering his white supervisor as the latter tried to run away. Addressing the court before the judge imposed sentence, Rahming stood up and turned to the all-white courtroom audience, many of whom were family of the victims, and some of whom were crying with grief. Rahming started to apologize for his crimes, but then gradually started to blame his white victims for having provoked him by their racist taunting and discriminatory mistreatment on the job.[51]

Far more typical (and less ambivalent) was the attitude of Larry Hansel, who was convicted and went to jail in 1991 for tracking down two supervisors and murdering them with shotgun blasts from close range. In a 2004 interview, more than a decade after the verdict, Hansel was still angry and filled with hatred and rage. He admitted to the interviewer that he "didn't know the two supervisors that well except that they were upper management," then added: "If I had the chance to do it again I'd respond with *more determination.*"[52]

Nor was Hansel's lack of remorse unusual or unique.[53] Other workplace perpetrators expressed the same sentiment, even years after the crimes. They expressed no regret for having killed a boss or supervisor, or still felt a callous disregard for the lives they took years before. Indeed, like Hansel, many perpetrators—like R. Gene Simmons, Leo Held, Clifton McCree, and

Dan White, et al.—expressed regret that they hadn't killed even *more* people who deserved to die.[54] How do these cases echo the warnings of the Kenneth Tornes case? Though a few perpetrators later showed signs of remorse, the vast majority never showed the slightest contrition, regret, or remorse—even after spending years in jail. Indeed, many were even *more* convinced that they were morally justified and had done the right thing when they murdered their supervisor or boss.

What does this say about management's treatment of the workforce?

Given the Darwinian correlation between a supervisor being well-liked, talented, and skilled and surviving a workplace murder spree, the identification and cultivation of those traits might be a critical priority for management to pursue. A supervisor or boss who's talented, popular, and highly skilled is less likely to be killed in a workplace murder spree; a boss who's incompetent, socially inept, and deeply despised is more likely to be killed in a workplace murder spree—a premise to which Kenneth Tornes and the other subordinate fireman in that Mississippi firehouse would surely subscribe.

In this light, the management philosophy of Linda Kaplan Thaler and Robin Koval—who advocate a business ethos of civility, kindness, and the power of "nice"—deserves a second look. Maybe there's something about this "touchy-feely" "feminine" approach that should be reassessed. At its core, the philosophy is rooted in the notion of reciprocity and the Golden Rule of "Doing unto others as . . . " And what previously sounded like a feminist's touchy-feely, smiley-faced public-relations gimmick, or an impractical Pollyannish marketing ploy, now resonates as a critical behavioral component of any effective business persona or management style.

Of course, the qualities and traits that best serve a manager or boss—like so many other factors that govern the modern, twenty-first-century workplace—vary from profession to profession, factory to factory, even office to office within the same company or firm. One management style might be perfect for one setting or one project, but utterly disastrous for another.

For this reason, a growing consensus is expressed in the belief that each supervisor or boss should be adept at the use of any number of personas or styles—whichever best accomplishes the task at hand. A single persona or style, or the belief that there is a one-style-fits-all model, is not only questionable in a truly diverse workplace, it should probably be discarded as an obsolete half-truth, if not dismissed as a complete workplace myth.

Chapter Eight

Confirming the Facts/Debunking the Myths

Literally hundreds of myths and half-truths about the workplace are accepted as gospel by millions of people who want desperately to enter, survive, and succeed in the workplace environment.

Some workplace myths and half-truths gain such wide currency and deep traction that they earn their own prefixual "ism," spawning theories of productivity and management that shape whole industries, inform public policy, and hold sway for decades.[1] Some foster assumptions about collective employee behavior and purport to fashion new mechanisms for achieving success when they actually just serve vested interests and preserve the status quo.[2] Others describe and diagnose deeply rooted management behaviors that reflect the worst of society and should be adjusted, changed, or even abandoned outright.[3] And still others, containing far more truth than myth, offer the means to a better balance between home and work to create a more balanced and enjoyable life.

A number of these myths and half-truths, far too many, are accepted by the general public as gospel on how to survive and succeed on a job interpersonally. These myths and half-truths typically pertain to behaviors like bullying, "mobbing," and other coercive, inappropriate office conduct. But they are especially numerous, deeply rooted and robust in areas of workplace violence, where, as already noted, so little has been studied, explored, and made available to the public, either to a general readership or to those with a particularized interest in the field or an expertise.

These myths and half-truths are often pondered and whispered about, but are rarely mentioned, and never discussed out loud. The eight myths and half-truths listed below—based as they are on gender, ethnicity, national origin, or race—shouldn't be tolerated as quaint and harmless notions. They should be dispelled, explained, or discarded, whatever the case may be, whatever their pedigree, convenience, popularity, or utility.

WORKPLACE KILLERS ARE MOSTLY SINGLE WHITE MEN IN THEIR EARLY FORTIES WITH SPORADIC EMPLOYMENT HISTORIES WHO WERE TWO OR THREE YEARS ON THE JOB WHEN THEY SNAPPED, WENT BERSERK, AND KILLED THEIR COWORKERS AND BOSS.

That most perpetrators of workplace murder fit a "profile" might be a comforting thought that facilitates classroom discussion and allows many to sleep more soundly at night. Unfortunately, even the most disagreeable, curmudgeonly experts in the field unanimously agree that the modern workplace murderer has no reliable demographic profile, and that the common characteristics that workplace murderers share are still being pondered and sorted out. Of course, many of the early cases of "going postal," particularly from the mid-1980s to the mid-1990s, offered a comfortable stereotype. But even then few elements of the stereotype were challenged as consistently and as persuasively as those of the killer's age and how long the killer had been on the job before he or she exploded in a homicidal rage.

The sporadic employment histories of most of the early perpetrators—like Patrick Sherrill and Jennifer San Marco in the public sector, and Joseph Wesbecker and Mark Barton in the private—only reinforce those elements of the stereotype. Research by criminologist Alan Fox and other experts shows that a "workplace killer is likely to be a 37-year-old single man who has been with the company at least four years."[4] After all, it's not likely that someone would pull a nine-millimeter semiautomatic handgun from their lunch box and open fire, killing a half-dozen people he or she had known for just a few weeks. Joseph Cobb had worked at his company four years before he went berserk; Anthony Deculit had worked for the USPS for about four years before he killed his supervisor and then committed suicide. Yes, it took a relatively long period of time, even two or three years, for the resentment to simmer and boil unnoticed before it spilled over into a homicidal hate.

Yet, even in the late 1980s and 1990s, a closer look at the perpetrators—their ages and how long they had been on the job before they went berserk—reveals workers who bore little resemblance to the relatively youthful, transient slackers the experts had come to expect, and the employers had come to fear.

On August 19, 1983, Perry Smith, who worked at the Johnston, South Carolina, post office, charged into the office with a shotgun and began firing at postal employees, shooting and wounding two and killing the local postmaster. He had resigned only three months earlier, after twenty-five years on the job.[5] On June 9, 1995, Bruce Clark, 57, shot his supervisor in the face, killing him instantly as more than seventy-five coworkers looked on in horror. Clark had been employed by the post office twenty-five years.[6]

On March 6, 1985, Steven Brownlee of the Atlanta, Georgia, post office opened fire on the night shift in the main post office with a .22-caliber pistol and killed a supervisor and a coworker along with wounding a third. He'd been with the post office twelve years.[7] On May 6, 1993, Larry Jasion, 45, a postal mechanic who worked for the USPS in Dearborn, Michigan, went on a deadly rampage in the garage, killing a coworker and another postal mechanic, and wounding a supervisor and an administrative clerk, before he turned the gun on himself and committed suicide, after twenty-four years on the job.[8]

On September 2, 1997, Jesus Antonio Tamayo, 64, of Miami Beach, Florida, shot and wounded his estranged former wife and her roommate as he was leaving his office at the post office and then committed suicide after twenty-one years on the job.[9] On November 28, 2006, Kevin Tartt, 39, employed as a postal worker in San Francisco, went to his supervisor's residence with a revolver and shot her in the back of the head before he killed himself the next day. Tartt had been with the post office facility eighteen years.[10]

On August 10, 1989, John Merlin Taylor, 52, of Escondido, California, arrived at the post office and opened fire on his fellow employees, killing two and wounding another before shooting himself in the head. He had been employed by the post office twenty-seven years.[11] On November 3, 1995, police officer Steven B. Christian drove to a Dallas, Texas, police substation and wounded an officer outside the building in attempting to gain entry and shoot others inside. But he was shot and killed by two fellow Dallas police officers, which ended a bizarre plan hatched by a commended veteran officer who snapped after twenty-five years on the force.[12]

Nor were the post office or public agencies the only work sites for these murders by employees, some of whom were nearing retirement age. Similar murder sprees took place in the private sector as well.

After his supervisors at General Dynamics in San Diego, California, fired him for chronic tardiness and absenteeism, Robert Earl Mack pulled a .38-caliber handgun and shot and killed the company labor negotiator and wounded his former supervisor. Mack had been with the company twenty-five years.[13] Distraught and upset over being fired, Frank Lemos, 56, of Las Vegas went on a rampage, murdering his supervisor by crushing him to death under the bulldozer. Lemos had worked for the Chemical Lime Company's Apex plant for thirty years.[14]

Joseph T. Wesbecker, 47, of Louisville, Kentucky, prowled around the Standard Gravure printing factory in a bloody rampage, killed eight former coworkers and supervisors, and then wounded a dozen others before he placed a gun at his head and committed suicide. He had been with the company eighteen years.[15] In October 1976, Leo Held, 39, of Lock Haven, Pennsylvania, upset with his job and annoyed with the members of his car-pool, drove the family station wagon to the Hammerhill paper plant that morning, where he killed six, including his five supervisors at the plant, where he had worked for more than twenty years.[16]

Lonnie Glasco, on March 24, 2009, gunned down two fellow employees at his bus company before the police fatally shot him in the company parking lot. The police shot and killed him when he refused to drop his gun and leave the building, where he had worked for the company twenty-nine years.[17] And on July 5, 2011, Jeremy "Billy" Davis, 52, of the Louisville Gas and Electric service center, shot and killed his longtime supervisor and then committed suicide. Davis had been employed by the company thirty-one years,[18] and his case wasn't unusual in the number of years of employment that preceded the murder and/or suicide.[19]

Little would be accomplished by an attempt to refute the notion that workplace murderers are young transient drifters with no emotional alle-giance to any given line of employment or to a particular job. Nor would much be achieved by proving that workplace killers were actually a seden-tary corps of geriatric oafs waiting for their retirement benefits and social security checks to arrive in the mail. What the cases in the study show, however, is that the workplace murderer, just like everybody else, has grown older. The average workplace murderer for the twenty-first century is 41.6 years old, has a good attendance record, but has been with the company or office for almost fifteen years.

DISGRUNTLED EMPLOYEES WHO SUDDENLY SNAP AND KILL PEOPLE ON THE JOB HAVE GONE TEMPORARILY INSANE AND AREN'T RESPONSIBLE FOR THEIR CONDUCT, WHICH THEY MAY NOT EVEN REMEMBER THE NEXT DAY.

One of most persistent beliefs in the area of workplace murder is that the disgruntled employee who finally snaps, grabs a Smith and Wesson revolver from his locker, and opens fire on his coworkers has gone temporarily in-sane. Part of this insanity, of course, means that the crazed employee was somehow unaware or even unconscious of what he or she was doing, who he or she was shooting, and what property damage was caused by the homicidal outburst.

This popular notion is reinforced by several real-life workplace massa-cres, like those of Michael McLendon, Mark Barton, Ramon Salcido, Joseph M. Harris, and others. These bloody murder sprees suggested no rhyme or reason, no pattern, and seemed like random mass killings and property destruction. These rampages usually continued until the ammunition ran out, the weapons jammed, somebody in the crowd wrestled them to the ground until the police arrived to place them under arrest, or a SWAT team arrived at the site. These cases spring quickest to mind when we think of workplace murder, perhaps because it's more comfortable to believe that someone who can kill that casually, nonchalantly, and indiscriminately must also be seriously deranged, psychotic, and criminally insane. We also conclude that if people are that crazy, their craziness precludes the rational thinking required for meticulous attention to the minutiae and detail of a bloody attack. This assumption is made even though just the opposite is more likely the case.

This belief persists even in the face of overwhelming factual evidence to the contrary, and scores of eyewitnesses and experts who later testify that the perpetrators didn't just snap and commit "the act of a madman." They were likely "clinically depressed but not deranged. They knew what they were doing,"[20] and the shooting pattern "wasn't random [but] execution-style."[21] The record is filled with examples of men and women who—in the middle of a shoot-out, or while reloading a weapon, or ejecting a clip from an AK-47, or stepping over dead bodies and spent shells—will suddenly, even nonchalantly, do or say something that shows a startling presence of mind, an uncanny focus, or an awareness of what's going on around them, down to the most minute detail.[22]

Examples include the murder spree by John E. List, the Westfield, New Jersey, accountant, we recall, who in November 1971 methodically killed his wife, mother, and three children as each of the three returned home from school. After he shot and killed his wife and mother, he shot and killed his daughter Patricia, 16, with a bullet to the back of her head. Then he shot and killed his younger son Frederick, 13, with a bullet to the back of the head. His older son John Jr., 15, however, had a soccer game that afternoon after school. List casually made himself lunch and then drove to watch John Jr. play in the game. After the soccer game, he drove John Jr. home—where he shot and killed him with several bullets to the back of his head.[23]

Another case in this category was Dan White's November 1978 assassinations of San Francisco mayor George Moscone and city supervisor Harvey Milk. White was angry after his request to be reappointed to his old job was denied. In revenge, he cornered the mayor in his City Hall office, where he fired two bullets into the mayor's chest, placed the gun six inches from the mayor's head, and fired two more bullets into the mayor's earlobes, killing him on the spot. Standing over the mayor's body, White reloaded his revolver with hollow-point bullets, which he had saved especially for Milk. As he burst from Moscone's office, on his way to Milk's office, however, he was spotted by another former colleague, board president Dianne Feinstein, who saw him rushing down the hall and called after him. He gestured for her to wait, and responded briskly but politely, "I have something to do first."

Still other examples of these cases include the massacres by Michael McLendon and E. Gene Simmons, particularly the lurid, ritualistic, and creepy things Simmons did with the corpses around the dinner table over the weekend before he surrendered to the police. These cases often defied explanation, and their perpetrators' heightened sensitivity and awareness during the rampages were arguably better after they went berserk and committed the mass homicides. And just to complicate the analyses, as well as some cases of workplace murder exemplified a random, illogical craziness of events, and other cases exemplified an orderly, systematic efficiency, still other cases fell neatly in neither category, but perfectly exemplified both.

Nor was this enhanced mental state unique to homicidal employees engaged in acts of workplace revenge. This odd mental state is often compared to the concentration achieved by top-level athletes in training for the Olympics or professional sports like the Super Bowl. The same phenomenon has also been recognized by coaches and experts in areas as different as football, gymnastics, even horse-jumping competition. In her insightful work on horse-jumping competition, Elizabeth Letts writes about the mental process of an unlikely jockey whose horse dominated jumping competitions in the late 1950s:

> He visualized the course in his mind's eye, imagining each turn, trajectory, and approach. Show jumping resembles sports like diving and ice-skating: years of training, honing skills and fostering endurance, are sandwiched into a few brief high-risk moments in the spotlight. Every move must be so ingrained, so practiced, so much like breathing that no thought is necessary. Like ice-skaters, who sometimes, upon finishing a flawless round, look momentarily surprised, in high-stakes jumper competitions, after years of training—of sacrifice and striving—moments in the ring pass so quickly that the rider and horse barely register what has happened until they are through.[24]

On October 30, 2007, Natavia Lowery, 25, bludgeoned to death her Manhattan, New York employer, Linda Stein, with a metal gym baton. At her murder trial, as a witness in her own defense, Lowery testified that during the brutal attack her "mind went into shutdown mode."[25] Was this Lowery's attempt to describe the "zoned-out" sensation often described by professional athletes during a perfect game, or in a Super Bowl victory or a championship game? Was this the same sensation described by world-class athletes of being mentally oblivious to the world around them, yet simultaneously more attuned to it? This dynamic of intense, individual pinpoint concentration and focus within a vortex of external confusion and chaos also presents itself—of all places—in the classic discussion of opposing theories of modern acting. In his analysis of the two views, pioneering acting coach Lee Strasberg repeats the age-old doubt (expressed by Diderot and others) that the use of "real" emotion is ever possible on stage. To support their doubts, the nonbelievers "referred to incidents when actors, in the midst of experiencing seemingly real emotions on the stage, had stopped to deal with secondary objects that were not part of the action of the play. How is this possible," they asked, "if the actor is truly involved?"[26]

Lee's explanation, provided by scientists a century later, holds that "these signs of interrupted concentration actually proved the opposite." His explanation also describes the mental state of workplace murderers who are capable of the most startling behaviors as they commit their crimes. "It is usually assumed that when a person's faculties are completely emotionally absorbed, he must be oblivious to everything else. On the contrary," he wrote, "the more intense an experience, the more likely the individual is to attend with mechanical punctiliousness to the minutest trifles of everyday existence." The "intensity of emotional response does not rule out awareness of other things that are going on. In the midst of severe crisis," it was shown, "an individual's attention will often register the smallest details related and unrelated to that crisis."[27]

MEN MAKE BETTER MANAGERS AND SUPERVISORS THAN WOMEN BECAUSE THEY DON'T LET PERSONAL AND DOMESTIC PROBLEMS AFFECT THEIR CONDUCT AND PERFORMANCE ON THE JOB.

A popular website recently posted a list of the nine most common myths of workplace violence, and near the top of the list was the belief that "personal problems of managers and employees don't affect the workplace."[28] But since few can persuasively argue nowadays that personal problems (for either the employee or the boss) don't affect the workplace, the question is dated, and the issue is misconceived. The issue has been resurrected in the age-old argument: "Who makes the better boss, a man or a woman?" Most of those polled believe that men make better bosses. This conclusion is based in part on the popular belief that men are better at not permitting their personal problems to affect their performance on the job. The cases in our study suggest other factors.

First, there are just too many cases of workplace murder—committed *by men*—to argue that they succeed at keeping their private, domestic lives from affecting their conduct and performance on the job. Men commit more than 75 percent of workplace murders, which suggests that they couldn't easily be any *less* skilled in that regard. Second, not only do men commit most of the workplace murders, a closer look at the cases shows that, for many men, the slaughter of former coworkers and supervisors on the job is but a continuation of murders that began even before they left home. In the cases of Charles Whitman, John Merlin Taylor, Dale Burr, Frederick Williams, Mike McLendon, Bruce Alan Miller, R. Gene Simmons, Matthew Beck, and many others, as already noted, the workplace murderer brutally killed his wife, mother, children, grandparents, and everyone in his immediate family before he loaded up the truck with rifles and guns and drove off to kill former coworkers and supervisors at his old job site.

And at this level of human slaughter, the discussion refers only to men. If workplace murder is, by definition, a murder that was motivated by a term or condition of employment, it should be noted that the victims in all of these cases were the financial responsibility of the killer, for whose support the much-hated job was a necessity. Even more noteworthy than the fact that these cases represented 15 percent of all the cases was that (1) they also represented 25 percent of the cases where the male perpetrator was married and (2) not a single case of this type was found—not a *single* case—in which the perpetrator was a female.

Third, given how little inhibition men evidently feel in the expression of their homicidal anger and rage, given how few in the cases were able to modulate their anger, it's unlikely that they would exercise greater restraint in keeping smaller resentments, lesser frustrations, and more trivial annoyances from surfacing in the workplace environment. Even men who have achieved a degree of success in their climb up the organizational ladder, executives and middle management, have often demonstrated an inability to keep their personal problems and private lives from affecting their conduct and performance on the job. Indeed, as we've seen in the previous chapter, this lack of discipline has caused the downfall of many male senior executives, managers, supervisors, and bosses and caused the tragic deaths of many employees as well.

Fourth, studies show that men consistently deny depression and other mental stresses that commonly afflict people in high-pressure, frustrating jobs. The studies also reflect the "fact" that women suffer from depression at a rate four times greater than men. But the actual fact is that men are just far less likely to *admit* their susceptibility to mental stresses. This explains the statistical anomaly of so many women suffering from clinical depression, while men commit 74 percent of the work-related suicides. As already noted in chapter 2, the discrepancy is explained by the fact that women are very good at depression but hopelessly inept at suicide; men are hopelessly inept at depression but great at suicide. As a result, women vent their depression more often, and then choose a method of suicide that allows reflection, second thoughts, intervention, even rescue; men rarely vent their depression, and then choose a method of suicide that's easy, quick, and foolproof—like hanging, leaping from a roof, or a bullet to the head.

The same dynamic supports the notion that men make better supervisors and bosses than women because they're better at keeping their private problems from affecting their conduct and performance on the job. As all the cases of men killing each other suggest, men are no better than women at keeping their private problems from affecting what they do on the job; they're just far less likely *to admit* that the source of their unhappiness, annoyance, and so on, is the home. These men somehow established a deadly link between their home life and family they supposedly loved, and the supervisor and coworkers on the job that they ostensibly hated. And they were adept at hiding it, especially from folks on the job.

That men make better supervisors and bosses than women because they are better able to keep personal problems out of the workplace isn't supported by the cases in the study or any persuasive outside facts. Of course, they could be perceived to be better managers and supervisors for a host of *other* reasons—focus, a dedicated wife at home, good ole gridiron pluck. But their general professional success is definitely not attributable to what the myths hold, or what the public thinks.

GIVEN THEIR MALE-DOMINATED CULTURE, AND THE ANCIENT TRADITIONS OF HARA-KIRI, SEPPUKU, KAMIKAZE, AND OYAKO-SHINJU, ASIAN WORKERS ARE MORE LIKELY TO COMMIT MURDER/SUICIDE ON THE JOB THAN MEMBERS OF OTHER RACIAL GROUPS.

In 2009, 32,845 Japanese people committed suicide, a figure that has remained above the 30,000 mark for the previous twelve years in a row, and the figure shows no indication of changing in the near future. The figure also represents a 35 percent increase in the number of Japanese suicides since 1997.[29] Japan is one of the few countries left in the world where suicide is still considered an act of "honor," a show of sincerity "to expiate . . . shortcomings [during life] and . . . as an act that would restore honor to their name, their family, or organization."[30]

Suicide is such an integral strand in Asian history and the modern sociocultural fabric that a macabre book, *The Perfect Suicide Manual*, has consistently appeared on the regional best seller lists five years after original publication. The author, Wataru Tsurumi, a sociology graduate of Tokyo University, provides clear, easy-to-follow instructions on how to commit suicide—by hanging, self immolation, electrocution, drug overdose, and other means.[31] The author describes and even recommends the perfect location for suicide, which is the Aokigahara Forest, a sprawling, densely wooded area at the foot of Mount Fuji that many have actually chosen as the site for their own suicides. In 1998 alone, the bodies of more than seventy people were found in the infamous wooded area—many were discovered hanging from tree branches, while others had evidently bled to death from slashed wrists, or had succumbed to poisons or an overdose of medications like sleeping pills.[32]

The suicide rates in Asian countries continue to rise, especially in Japan, Korea, and China, and China is the only country in the world in which suicides by women outnumber those by men.[33] Indeed, this trend is likely to continue (and even accelerate in growth and scope), particularly as these countries' economies continue to adjust and respond to the pressures of rapid rural growth and urbanization, a deepening recession, and other global forces beyond their geopolitical control.

Recent economic downturns in Japan, in particular, have been a catalyst in the recent surge in suicides among working men and women. Not coincidentally, suicides by Japanese employees always jump abruptly in March, the end of the fiscal year.[34] Also not coincidentally, popular sites for employee suicides are the cars and stations of the Japanese railway system, when the victims are on their way to or from work.[35]

On April 26, 2000, Dr. Lishan Wang of Atlanta, Georgia, shot and killed Yale physician Dr. Vajinder 44, on the doorstep of his New Haven, Connecticut, home for getting him fired from a Manhattan hospital two years earlier.[36] On June 29, 2000, Dr. Jian Chen, an internist at the University of Washington medical school, shot and killed his mentor and supervisor after learning that his contract for the following year wouldn't be renewed.[37] On November 14, 2008, Zoom Jing Hua Wu, a product engineer with SiPort, Inc., a promising electronics start-up in Santa Clara, California, requested a meeting with the company's top officials, at which he shot and killed three corporate officers, including the CEO Sid Agrawal; Brian Pugh, vice president of operations; and Marlyn Lewis, head of the HR department.[38] Finally, there was the case of William Xu, a cafeteria worker at the University of North Texas whose food preparation was criticized by the food service supervisor, Jennifer Ying Ying Maik. On the morning of August 2, 2009, Xu followed her home, where he held her at gunpoint for three hours before he shot her in the head.[39]

With their highly educated perpetrators, the academic backgrounds, the professional glamour, and striving entrepreneurial ambition, these four cases reflect a critical element of the Asian American's presence in workplace murder. Of all the racial groups, the Asian perpetrators were by far the most highly educated, and included the most scientists, doctors, and engineers. The four doctors alone (each having been fired or dissatisfied with his working conditions) shot and killed seventeen victims. (Since many of the professional Asian male perpetrators tended to kill Asian business partners, medical colleagues, and so on, their *victims* also tended to be the most highly educated and accomplished.)

Those few, however, included two postal workers. Albany, New York, letter carrier Tian Yu Lu; Patterson, New Jersey, postal worker Danny Isku;

Los Angeles bus driver Cathline Repunte; and former Los Angeles sushi delivery man Jiverly Wong of Binghamton, New York. And they also showed men with the lowest regard for female Asian workers.

Asians made up slightly more than 5 percent of the perpetrators (or 18 out of 368). Of the Asian workplace murderers, sixteen were male, two were female. Asian perpetrators killed a total of fifty-six people—fifty-three were killed by males, two by females. Each of the male perpetrators averaged 4.3 deaths per episode, as compared to the national average of about 2.0. There were only two Asian female perpetrators, neither of whom killed another Asian. (Arunya Rouch, who was Chinese, shot and killed a Caucasian male coworker, and Cathline Repunte, a Filipina, shot and killed a Caucasian male coworker.)

Murder/suicides were popular among Asians, but exclusively among males. Only two Asian females qualified for the study, and neither committed suicide. On the other hand, given the cultural prestige and historical importance associated with the act, at least half (or eight out of sixteen) of the male Asian perpetrators ended their episode of workplace violence by committing suicide.

It was no doubt a reflection of the traditional Asian emphasis on striving for excellence and achievement that such a large percentage of Asian perpetrators were also professional men. These included one psychiatrist, three physicians, two electricians, and one engineer. Indeed, of the 350-odd workplace murderers who qualified for this study, virtually *all* of the professionals (or about 95 percent) were Asian (men). It was also a reflection of traditional Asian values that Asians in the workplace tended to kill mostly other Asians. Almost 40 percent of their victims were other Asian men, and almost 25 percent (or twelve out of fifty-five) of Asian males' victims were Asian women.

Chicago restaurant owner Keon Suk Oh shot and killed his waitress (and rumored paramour) Dong Yu, before he took his own life. Electronics technician Tuan Nguyen shot and killed three coworkers, including Thu Theresa Pham, after he was fired from his job. Angry at being fired from an embroidery firm, Soon Byung Park shot and wounded his business partner, Edward Yoon, but also shot and killed Yoon's sister, Mee Hua Hong, as she tried to flee. Cafeteria worker William Xu shot and killed his supervisor, Jennifer Ying Ying Maik, after she criticized his food preparation skills. When Xerox repair technician Byran Koji Uyesugi opened fire on coworkers in a Honolulu Xerox plant, killing seven men, five were Asian. Although Asian men could count at least a dozen Asian women among their murder victims, it's no doubt another sign of the male-centered Asian mentality, and the respect accorded Asian men, that not a single Asian male was ever murdered, wounded, or even shot at by an Asian female.

MEN MAKE BETTER MANAGERS AND SUPERVISORS THAN WOMEN BECAUSE THEY ARE MORE CONSISTENT, CANDID, AND FRANK IN THEIR DEALINGS WITH EMPLOYEES, AND NOT SUBJECT TO DRAMATIC MOOD SWINGS, DON'T GET INVOLVED IN OFFICE POLITICS AND CLIQUES, AND DON'T BRING THEIR PERSONAL LIVES INTO THE WORKPLACE.

According to a 2011 Google-sponsored research project on good management skills, managers have a greater impact on an employee's performance, and how that employee feels about his job generally, than any other single factor. Though much has been written in the last few years on which sex makes the better boss—male or female—few studies have created as much controversy as this research project, conducted by the online recruitment firm www.UKJobs.[40]

What distinguishes this study from the others, however, is the fact that such a substantial number of women were in total agreement with men on a number of critical management issues. For example, almost two-thirds (or 63 percent) of the women polled felt that men made better bosses than women; three-fourths (or 75 percent) of the men felt that other men made better bosses than women.[41] Women generally felt that other women were often a nightmare to work for, which was attributable to the fact that men were far more likely to give the employee straight talk and get directly to the point, which made them easier to deal with.[42]

Other reasons given by women for their preference were that men didn't engage in back-stabbing behavior (like bad-mouthing or gossiping about their staff behind their backs), and men were less likely to play office politics or form cliques. Finally, these women preferred male bosses because men were not subject to dramatic mood swings, and men didn't bring their private lives into the office in a way, or to an extent, that it affected their performance or conduct on the job.[43] Fifteen percent of those polled felt that female bosses tended to be too "sharp-tongued," while 40 percent expressed the view that men were better able to distance themselves and not get involved in office politics and bitching; and 14 percent of the men said they found men to be more reasonable than women.[44]

A review of the cases and the analyses of their facts, however, do not support the results of the Google research project that men made better bosses than women. And at least one critical indication of which gender makes the best boss may be gleaned from a look at the cases to determine who was murdered in the workplace and who did the killing. If we accept the premise that a boss who's murdered by an employee was probably not the best boss, not the most talented and admired boss, we can also accept the premise that a boss who murders an employee is clearly unfit and deserves to go to jail. A determination of which gender makes the better boss— men or women—may be inferred from a look at the cases, as only the cases can tell us which bosses were murdered, or committed murder, more often.

Of the 350-odd workplace murderers included in this study, more than a hundred had murdered their boss or supervisor. These included both men and women employees too numerous to mention. Conversely, at least a dozen bosses and supervisors had "flipped the script" and murdered subordinate employees. These bosses included Rolandas Milinavicius, Don King, Frank Garcia, Jack Raglund, and Arthur Hill, among others. It should also be noted that not a few of these male bosses and supervisors murdered subordinate female employees with whom they had maintained adulterous or otherwise illicit sexual relationships. These included men like John Harrison, Ruben Orlando Benitez, Keon Suk Oh, and Hemy Neuman, among others.

Although there weren't a great many female bosses and supervisors, they too were occasionally murdered by disgruntled employees, a group that included employees like Jacquelyn Ferguson, Yolanda Saldívar, Natavia Lowery, Kim Harris, and a handful more. About a dozen female bosses and supervisors were murdered by subordinate male employees, men like Christopher Shumway, Ronnie Rice, Joseph M. Harris, Henry Earl Duncan, Ryan Jones, Jose Rojas, Joseph Marchetti, William Xu, and Lorenzo Sam. All of these cases shared the single fact that each man had murdered his supervisor or boss, who was a female.

But here the analogy starts to break down. In the cases of employees who murdered their bosses, there was also the flip side of the crime, where the male boss murdered the employee. Yet, even though there were about a dozen bosses who had murdered their employees, and about the same number of employees who had murdered their female bosses, in all the 350-plus cases in this study, there wasn't a single case in which a *female* boss murdered an employee.

Given the number of male bosses who murdered their employees, the fact that not a single female boss murdered an employee clearly reflects positively on women in that role. That male bosses and supervisors were far more violent (and sexually promiscuous) on the job than their female counterparts has already been noted. This discussion suggests that female bosses and supervisors are also generally more balanced emotionally and better able to modulate their anger and rage. And these traits, contrary to the Google research, strongly suggest that women make better bosses than men.

WOMEN MAKE BETTER MANAGERS AND SUPERVISORS THAN MEN BECAUSE THEY ARE BETTER ABLE TO SEE THE WHOLE PICTURE (THE GESTALT), MORE WILLING TO COLLABORATE WITH OTHERS AND MORE WILLING TO INCORPORATE NEW AND INNOVATIVE IDEAS.

Several experts argue that women make better bosses and supervisors than men, including academics like professor Khalid Aziz, a CEO of leadership development consultants the Aziz Corporation, who enumerate ten basic qualities that women have that make them better bosses than men.[45] But few make the case more effectively than Carol Smith, the senior vice president and chief brand officer for the media company the Elle Group, whose interview by Bryant Smith was cited earlier in chapter 4.

In the same interview Smith traces her own obvious success to an experience she had as a little girl in elementary school. She learned the critical "difference between being the boss and being bossy."[46] She states her preference for being straight up and direct in her criticism of an employee's work, which better ensures their future growth and improvement.[47] Significantly, Smith also conceded that men were "definitely better on the 'whatever' side. Things tend to roll off their back. We women take things very personally. We're constantly playing things over in our head—'What did that mean when they said that?'—when they mean nothing . . . So there's a downside to women."[48]

Smith's almost offhanded observation that women tend to take things "very personally," however, becomes the central thrust of other studies, including a study on good management skills conducted by Google's Project Oxygen. As already noted, the study concluded that managers have a greater impact on employees' performance and how they feel about jobs than any other single factor.[49] And a provocative survey by the online recruitment firm www.UKJobs.net revealed that both men and women are in total agreement that men make better bosses—63 percent of the women and 75 percent of the three thousand men interviewed agreed.[50]

Among the reasons for this preference (at least by women) must be included the so-called Queen Bee factor.[51] "A Queen Bee in this context is someone who has worked her way up to the top in a male-dominated organization, and she probably got there by behaving how a man would behave. And this 'male' behavior commonly includes appearing tough and not at all soft and mushy," according to psychologist Cary Cooper of the Lancaster University Management School. "She's unlikely to mentor younger women because she quite likes her unique position, and may feel threatened by younger females rising up the ranks. She had to work hard to get to where she is, so she's not about to give other women a helping hand—they have to work their way up just as she did."[52]

But more critical for our purposes is the explanation offered by feminist blogger Jocelyn Giangrande, who echoes Carol Smith's observation that women tend to take matters too seriously and find themselves unable to move on. With brilliant insight, Giangrande points out that "men can disagree at work, shake hands and go out for beers. [Indeed] some men harbor deeper respect for how well the other man fought the good fight. Women, on the other hand, tend to hold grudges [and] let disagreements sully their relationship, and sometimes that plays out in really unreasonable ways."[53]

In another related study conducted by Jack Zenger and Joseph Folkman in 2011, they polled 7,280 people to assess leadership in a variety of positions—from senior management to "individual contributor." The authors also asked them to rate the leaders in sixteen leadership competencies. Based on their results, the authors discovered that women scored higher than men in all but one of the sixteen competencies, and in twelve of the sixteen, women scored higher by a significant margin. The most surprising finding according to Zenger and Folkman, however, was that the two traits where women outscored men by the widest margin were (1) taking the initiative, and (2) driving for results, both of which have long been regarded as distinctly "male" strengths.

Zenger and Folkman's findings also revealed that on every level women "were rated by their peers, their bosses, their direct reports, and their other associates as better overall leaders than their male counterparts—and the higher the level, the wider that gap grows." The study confirmed that women are seen as better leaders than men by those around them, which was reinforced by other research efforts that show that companies with high female representation in management ranks tend to be more profitable and also have higher employee productivity.[54]

Despite the extraordinarily high ratings of women found by Zenger and Folkman, however, the results of polls and research don't always translate into neatly predictable behavioral patterns. Also, what might be an admirable female trait in the abstract may feel uncomfortable, even threatening, when implemented as expected behavior on a day-to-day basis on the job. Giangrande's observation is thus doubly critical: women too often create grudges over the same matters that men see as professional opportunities and actively cultivate. Whether it takes place on a golf course green, or while discussing the Super Bowl over pizza and beer, there are few substitutes for intraoffice networking and the building of both formal and informal bridges. Women place too much importance on the meritocracy, in the blind faith that simply working hard, even harder than men, and getting great results are what it takes to get promoted. But, in the words of Gershwin's operatic character Sportin' Life, "It ain't necessarily so."[55]

This basic, gender-based difference in perception explains why, despite their high approval ratings, women might not in fact make better bosses than men, which is why women are CEOs of only thirteen of the *Fortune* 500 companies.[56] It explains why Adam Bryant asked Carol Smith, "If women are better managers, how come there aren't more women in the corner offices of corporate America?" And it also explains her blunt answer: "I find it so puzzling. I swear I don't know."[57]

BLACKS RARELY COMMIT SUICIDE ON THE JOB (OR IN GENERAL) BECAUSE OF THEIR DEEPLY ROOTED BELIEF IN THE TRADITIONAL CHRISTIAN FAITH, WHICH TEACHES AN ACCEPTANCE OF THE RIGHTEOUSNESS AT THE CORE OF HUMAN SUFFERING AND A PATIENCE AND FORBEARANCE THAT COME WITH A KNOWLEDGE AND BELIEF IN LIFE EVERLASTING.

One Friday morning in December 2010, the body of Frederick Jermaine Carter, a 26-year-old black man, was discovered hanging from an old oak tree. Suspicions were roused. In the absence of any indication of foul play, the local police ruled the death a suicide. But the local National Association for the Advancement of Colored People was suspicious because that old oak tree was in Greenwood, Mississippi, the state that proudly led the nation in lynching black people for decades after Reconstruction until the end of the modern civil-rights movement.[58]

The suspicion owed not only to a knowledge of Mississippi's deeply entrenched racism, but also to the African American community's stubborn refusal to accept the reality of suicide. If the death retains its official status as a suicide, it will quickly fade as a local statistic, even as suicide currently claims the lives of more black men than ever before. According to Dr. Alvin Poussaint, since "1980, the suicide rate of young black males has doubled, and they are now seven times more likely to commit suicide than black women."[59]

This rise in suicide among blacks is reflected in the workplace, which puts the lie to the widely held belief that African Americans rarely kill themselves and generally reject suicide. As already noted, blacks made up approximately 15 percent of those who qualified for the study. On August 3, 2010, Omar Thornton, 34, a black truck driver, shot and killed eight coworkers and wounded two more, after attending a disciplinary hearing at which he was effectively fired for company theft.[60] All of his victims were white. The Thornton case generated a significant amount of press, principally because of the racial allegations, but the suicide itself was hardly the most controversial element of the incident.

Of the forty-five cases of workplace murder by blacks, twelve out of forty-five (or about 24 percent) ended in suicide—as opposed to eight out of eighteen (or more than 48 percent) for Asians. The average of 3.0 deaths per incident by a black perpetrator was higher than the national average of 2.0 per incident, but still significantly lower than the average of 4.3 deaths per incident by Asian perpetrators.

Some of the smallest statistical groupings in the study included black females who committed suicide: only two, or about 4 percent of the blacks. One was Faedra Rhondelle Satchel, 32, of Miami, Florida, the daughter of a Baptist minister, who on January 3, 2001, shot and killed Carville Eric Walton, 46, a local bail bondsman, following an argument inside Walton's office. She shot him three times in the chest, at close range, then shot herself in the head. The number of black males who committed suicide was much higher, numbering about twelve, or about 24 percent of the blacks included inthe study. And even smaller statistical groupings included the number of Asian women who committed suicide (0.0 percent) and Hispanic women who committed suicide (0.0 percent), even though more than a dozen Asian and Hispanic women were killed by Asian and Hispanic men.[61]

MEN ARE MORE VIOLENT AND AGGRESSIVE IN THE WORKPLACE THAN WOMEN. THEY BRUTALLY MURDER AND WOUND FAR MORE VICTIMS IN THE WORKPLACE MORE OFTEN, AND MORE INDISCRIMINATELY, THAN WOMEN, AND LOVE THEIR GUNS AND OTHER TOYS THAT DESTROY, MAIM, AND KILL.

Without question, men are far more violent than women. They are more aggressive than women, and also have a greater tolerance, even appreciation, for violence, murder, and bloodshed, as ancient artifacts and cave wall drawings depict, and centuries of recorded history have described, documented, and glorified. For these reasons men love their guns, weapons, instruments of torture, and other devices—from firecrackers to intercontinental ballistic missiles—all toys conceived of, designed, built, and perfected to destroy, maim, and kill.

Nor do men become more violent as they grow from boyhood to manhood. They are born that way. It's genetic. Don't agree? Release a group of young children in a large toy store, and boys will always gravitate to the toy gun section (and the girls to the dolls). And even when toy guns are not available, boys will point their little fingers to simulate a gun when playing cops and robbers. (And they learn as early as toddlers to appreciate the ability to aim, hit a target, and direct a line of fire—every time they stand up to pee!)

After losing his job as a technician with a California electronics company, Richard Wade Farley, 40, returned to his old job to talk with a coworker he had been stalking. He wanted her to rescind the restraining order that required him to be in court the next day. If she refused, he decided, he would kill himself. He drove to the building carrying several weapons, including a Benelli semiautomatic shotgun, a .22-250 rifle with a scope, a pump-action shotgun, a Sentinel .22 Winchester Magnum Rimfire revolver, a Smith and Wesson .357 Magnum revolver, a Browning .380 Automatic Colt Pistol, a Smith and Wesson nine-millimeter pistol, a foot-long buck knife, and a smoke bomb. He wore an ammunition vest, inserted a pair of earplugs, and finally put on a leather glove. He had more than one thousand rounds of ammunition.

In a 1991 case, postal worker Joseph Harris went to visit his supervisor to discuss his dismissal, carrying a nine-millimeter handgun, a .22-caliber machine gun with a silencer, several hand grenades, and handmade bombs, along with a samurai sword. And men also like to murder, like Michael McLendon, who murdered ten people, Gene Simmons, who murdered fourteen, Ramon Salcido, eight, Wong Wiverly, fourteen, Edward Burke, thirty-four, etc., etc. No, it cannot be denied, men are definitely far more violent than women.

But women are more lethal.

What's the difference? And why does it matter?

It's a profound difference, and it's rarely recognized or appreciated. And it definitely matters, especially if you're a boss or supervisor or employee who's unlucky enough to find yourself in the middle of a workplace shooting spree. The difference is best illustrated with two different hypothetical fact situations, admittedly exaggerated in some ways, but only slightly, to highlight the behavioral differences. The differences have been distilled from the facts of hundreds of cases, and have never been described before now—the stark differences between men and women, and how differently they murder in the workplace.

THE HYPOTHETICAL MALE MURDERER

In June, Peter Pistoff, 43, a single white man, was fired from his job as an electronics technician at a major aeronautics firm. He had a history of absenteeism, tardiness, and not returning from lunch promptly. Though he received satisfactory performance evaluations over the years, one weekend in May he went on a "weed and wine" binge, smoking a dime bag of Colombian Gold and drinking three bottles of pinot noir. He stumbled into work that Monday morning groggy, annoyed, and hostile. When his supervisor made a comment about his condition, Peter shook his fist at his boss and then screamed an obscenity in his face. He was charged with insubordination, and two days later, on June 19, 2007, he was fired.

In April 2009, two years later, Peter decided to get revenge. He was furious, and had convinced himself that his termination was unfair. He quickly wrote a brief suicide note and left it on his dresser. Then, heavily armed with several weapons hidden under his trench coat, he took a taxicab to his old job to kill his old supervisor. With all of the weight, he stumbled from the taxicab, and he entered the main building through a side door when the elderly security guard went to the men's room.

Under his oversized London Fog raincoat, Peter was carrying two loaded twelve-gauge double-barrel shotguns, a Ruger 210 handgun, two Smith and Wesson revolvers, a Chinese-made AK-47 with three extra banana clips, a Remington single-action M14 carbine rifle, and a chrome-plated .22-caliber Glock semiautomatic pistol. He also wore a heavy-duty Kevlar-lined vest and a shoulder-holstered snub-nosed .38 revolver and carried two homemade ether bombs, and an additional one thousand rounds of long-range rifle ammunition for the Ruger just in case he ran out of bullets. Just to play it safe, he also carried a small twelve-inch machete, two bowie knives, and a pair of brass knuckles—just in case he had to engage somebody in hand-to-hand combat.

Weighted down with all the weapons, Peter lumbered into the company cafeteria just as the workers on that shift were starting to sit down to eat lunch. His old supervisor was luckily out with a cold that day. Since Peter didn't have anybody else in mind that he wanted to shoot, he decided to shoot anybody who crossed his path—including the two gay dudes in shipping and receiving, the three little old ladies in accounting who had always deliberately held up his paycheck, the stuck-up, buxom secretary in HR who dissed him at a Christmas party a few years ago, and the elderly security guard—and then shoot himself in the head.

Peter fired a shot, just to get everybody's attention, then announced to a dozen hungry, confused employees that he was back, that he wanted revenge, and that everybody was going to die in the next thirty seconds. As he spoke, he raised the AK-47 and opened fire, grazing a former coworker as he ducked under a table. Unfortunately, the kick of the AK-47 caused him to lose his balance for an instant, and with the weight of all the weapons under his coat, Peter stumbled and then fell against a table before he fell to the cafeteria floor. As he struggled to get up, all the weight of the weapons held him down, magnet-like, against the floor. And by the time he was on all fours, almost standing again, a little old lady had grabbed his arm, somebody had kicked him in the groin, and a big burly guy in a fez was rushing at him with an upraised metal chair. The last thing Peter remembered was a stinging sensation in his left arm. Three hours later, Peter woke up in the emergency room with a gunshot wound in his arm.

THE HYPOTHETICAL FEMALE MURDERER

Hillary Hadanuff, 37, had worked thirteen years for a small local furniture manufacturer. With only fifteen workers, employee morale was high, and she was liked by everybody—everybody except Rosa, a 20-year-old secretary in the front office who for months had teased Hillary for her size. At five feet one and 160 pounds, Hillary was moderately obese, and she kept careful count of every Rosa put-down, joke, and wisecrack.

It was at the annual office picnic that Hillary finally decided she had had enough. Rosa made another wisecrack, just as Hillary reached for a third slice of almond fudge pound cake. Hillary smiled and said nothing, but returned three minutes later with the tiny .22-caliber pistol she retrieved from her VW Beetle in the parking lot.

Sadly, Rose heard the bang, saw the flash, even caught a whiff of nitrate smoke as the bullet entered her forehead, tore through the upper spinal cords, and then exploded from the back of her neck, killing her instantly. She was dead before she hit the ground.

Of course, neither incident with Peter Pistoff or Hillary Hadanuff actually occurred. They're both fictitious, and the facts are "recounted" here with authorial tongue thrust deep in cheek. But the point *is* a serious one, and it's a critical point that must be made. Men seeking revenge returned to the job on average eight weeks or *two months* after they were fired. (Women returned, on average, after about forty-five minutes or less than an hour.) Even after several months, most men were still angry and resentful (usually even more so), and they almost invariably returned with small arsenals under their coats or on their backs—rifles, shotguns, AK-47s, pistols, revolvers, knives, grenades, and even bombs.

All too typically, the males' intentions were not to wound or kill one or two coworkers they especially despised or hated (as the women did), but to take out the whole accounting department, kill everybody on the board of directors, or destroy a whole wing of a building or plant. They typically wanted to kill not just a particular supervisor or boss, but everybody who crossed their path—coworkers, colleagues, visiting contractors, clients, even strangers they didn't know. But when the dust settled and the body count began, they often hadn't found the person they wanted most to kill, and as often as not, they saved the last bullet for themselves.

Women, on the other hand, always—and without a single exception—returned to their jobs with a single handgun, usually with no extra bullets or thought of the need to reload. *And they killed the person they were looking for.* On this specific, highly particularized goal, they were totally focused, practical, and chilling in their efficiency and resolve; they were never distracted or sidetracked, and sought only to "get the job done."

Fortunately, the cases in the study show that women in the workplace don't kill nearly as often or as indiscriminately as men, and they rarely kill more than one person at a time. However, if you're a widely disliked supervisor or a much-hated boss, or if you're just another employee and the person in the office who hates you most—your archenemy—is the woman running back inside the building from her car in the parking lot with a .357 Magnum in her hand? You may drop to your knees and pray to your god, serenely confident that—as surely as the oceans wave and human life precedes death—within sixty seconds you will be murdered.

Chapter Nine

Deciphering the Language of Workplace Suicide

Homicide and suicide are inextricably linked, wrote American psychiatrist Karl A. Menninger. Not only is suicide actually self-murder, he further observed, but suicides are sometimes committed to forestall the act of murder, and murder is sometimes committed to avert suicide. [1]

Nor is suicide the only kind of murder. As already noted, other types include infanticide (the murder of young children), fratricide (the murder of siblings), matricide (the murder of mothers), patricide (the murder of fathers), regicide (the murder of kings and queens), and genocide (the murder of whole groups of people). And just as homicide has several different expressions, suicide also has a language of its own.

This chapter explores six different ways in which suicide presented itself in the workplace. The psychological and emotional fallout from suicide, of course, can be devastating, and often generates the same losses that flow from workplace murder, including the hidden costs not ordinarily visible to the untrained eye or at first glance. Recent data from the Bureau of Labor Statistics show that workplace suicides in 2008 rose 28 percent over the previous year, [2] and are now the fastest-growing cause of death on the job, growing much faster even than murder. In many ways, in fact, suicide is much worse. It remains perhaps the only conduct nowadays for which everybody may self-righteously blame the victim.

But unlike homicide, suicide has a reversible cultural component that derives its meaning and importance from the context in which it occurs. While in many communities suicide carries a private, unspoken shame, a social opprobrium that never quite recedes into the family past, in other communities it's the very means by which one may absolve and expiate shame, restoring pride and honor to an organization or a family name. [3]

For most of recorded history, moreover, suicide has had a unique application to men as a personal response to utter failure in life. This is especially the case if the man was faced with an inability to earn a livelihood and provide for family, home, and those he protected and loved. A man is thus far, far more likely than a woman to commit suicide after losing his job, as his job is a deeper measure of his worth and dignity as a human being. From antiquity to this day, a man's sense of self-worth is often tied to his employment—having a prestigious, well-paying career, a nice home and car, and maybe even an inground pool in the backyard.

When he loses that employment he essentially loses the basis for his self-esteem, a principal purpose in life, not to mention his sense of himself as a person, and especially as a man. If the man is unmarried or single, the loss also impacts adversely on how attractive he feels in the eyes of others and even how attracted he feels *toward* someone else. To deal with unemployment, in addition to the stresses of money problems and social rejection, may easily be enough to drive a man into a depression that leads to suicide.[4]

A recent study on suicide rates as they relate to male employment shows that for every 10 percent rise in unemployment, there is a 1.47 percent increase in male suicide—with no significant statistical effect on the suicide rate for women.[5] And though women *attempt* suicide more often than men, their suicide rates aren't nearly as high, as they are also more likely to choose methods that (wisely) leave room for second thoughts, intervention, and rescue.[6] In short, and as already noted, women are great at being depressed, but terrible at suicide; men are terrible at being depressed, but great at suicide. As the current recession deepens, and the unemployment rate continues to rise with no sign of hope on the horizon, male suicide is slowly approaching numbers not seen since the Great Depression.

The terms that define behavior and conduct, of course, are highly fluid, always evolving, and always subject to reinterpretation and change. A decade ago, for example, there was no firmly agreed-upon term to describe group behavior we now instantly recognize as "mobbing." Nor was there a vocabulary to describe conduct in which an armed perpetrator forced the police to respond with lethal force, such as "suicide by cop," or "blue suicide." The idea of suicide, its meaning and intent, have also undergone tremendous change in recent years. Which explains not only the rapid rise in workplace suicide in the last decade,[7] but also why suicide has been put to "strategic" use by employees— whether disgruntled, outraged, overmedicated, or chronically depressed.

As we shall see, the facts of some instances of workplace suicide were highly pliable and easily fit into more than one category, serving multiple functions simultaneously. But far more important than categorization was the recognition of how consistently the details of a suicide functioned autobiographically. Suicide, paradoxically, spoke volumes about the deceased's life both as a worker and as a colleague, and their deeper relationship to the workplace.

On June 11, 2005, Bruce A. Miller, 47, was fired by his supervisor after twenty-eight years on the job. That afternoon he returned to his job with a shotgun and shot his way inside the building, looking for his supervisor, who had already left for the day, and then shot his way into her empty office. Once inside her office, he sat down in her swivel chair behind her desk and shot himself in the heart with the shotgun. No one else was injured or harmed.

Given the obvious finality of suicide, one could ask: How did Miller intend to use his suicide as an act of revenge? How could suicide influence a boss or affect a manager if the complainant is dead? The answer lies in that feature of suicide rarely mentioned in scholarly discussions and never cited in the books: the psychological impact of the suicide site itself.

SUICIDE AS PAYBACK OR REVENGE

More than 90 percent of the suicides in this study resulted from a single, self-inflicted gunshot wound to the head—usually to the temple, but sometimes under the chin, or with the barrel lodged straw-like in the roof of the mouth. What made suicide, like in Miller's case, such an effective means of revenge? Why was it guaranteed to make an impression on management or the boss? You need only imagine for a minute that *you* are the supervisor or boss of a disgruntled employee who, like Miller, has just committed suicide—in *your office.*

Even as you assess the need to call 911 to summon the police, you sense the need to remove stacks of blood-soaked documents from your desk, to wipe away the thin red spray that hit your computer screen an instant after the blast, to scrape the mix of blood, brain tissue, and fragments of teeth from your laptop keys. Finding the bullet hole in the wall should be easy enough, but you'll also need to find the spent shell lying in a tiny puddle of blood still dripping on the floor and soaking a section of carpet that now has to be pulled up and replaced. You'll also need to rid your office of the burning scent of nitrate smoke and the fumes from the pieces of burnt flesh and a smoldering clump of hair that plopped like a clump of mud on the floor, and the stench of excrement—the feces from that final bowel movement—now wafting up from the crotch of the corpse, *which still has to be removed from your chair!* As a maintenance crew arrives and your desk is being cleaned, as your eyes fill with tears from the fumes of ammonia and bleach, and as the corpse is finally lifted from your chair, you realize that for weeks and even months to come, you must deal bravely with upset and grieving coworkers, colleagues, and staff. And alongside whatever flicker of sorrow you might feel at this point—and the psychiatric need to erase a horrific image now etched on your psyche—is your reluctance (and inability) to respond to the ten-page suicide note in which the deceased convincingly blames you for everything that went wrong.

Like Bruce Miller, these employees were unabashedly vindictive and open in their quest for payback and revenge. But unlike Miller, who didn't harm anyone else, these suicidal employees typically had no problem killing as many people and causing as much property damage as possible before they committed suicide. And of those employees who committed suicide, almost 75 percent killed at least two other people before they killed themselves.

In early April 1993, Ladislav Antilak was fired from the Sumitomo Electric Light Wave Corporation as a fiber-optic-cable inspector due to frequent problems with coworkers. After a failed attempt to enter the job site, on April 13, 1994, he returned with a firearm and killed two employees and wounded three others before he turned the gun on himself.[8] Nathaniel Brown, 51, an Ohio State University janitor who was about to lose his job for repeated tardiness, absenteeism, and failure to follow instructions, walked into a maintenance building for the early shift and shot two supervisors, killing one, and then opened fire in an office suite with two handguns before he fatally shot himself.[9]

In a handful of cases, the perpetrators succeeded in killing themselves—thinking that their victims were dead—even though their victims miraculously survived the attacks. They typically drove home and, with a self-inflicted bullet to the head, committed suicide, even though they had bungled the earlier homicide. Jack Raglund, 28, the owner of a small cell-phone company, we recall, shot his former receptionist Victoria Sando four times at near-point-blank range before he sped off in his BMW, leaving her for dead. Sando was later hospitalized, listed in critical condition, but survived the attack.[10] The police later found Raglund at his home, however, alone, dead from a self-inflicted gunshot wound.[11]

In other cases, the perpetrators reversed the existential script. They accomplished the homicide, but then bungled the subsequent suicide. For example, in October 1993, Arthur Hill, 53, a civilian army-base clerk, had his temporary promotion to supervisor rescinded, and he had also been passed over for a promotion. In revenge he shot and killed his boss and two coworkers, and severely wounded two others, before he shot himself in the head with a .38-caliber handgun. Miraculously, he survived and was last listed in critical condition according to VA hospital records and available newspaper accounts.[12]

In the vast majority of these cases, however, the suicide wasn't bungled, and the perpetrator bent on suicide succeeded. Another more typical case was that of Howard Trang, 48, who, on April 1, 2008, burst into the office of

Alloy Fabricators of New England and shot a coworker in the left arm and abdomen, and then fled. An hour later Trang was found in his red Toyota RAV4, dead from a single, self-inflicted gunshot wound to the head.[13] On March 6, 1998, Matthew Beck, 35, an accountant who was angry about a salary dispute and his failure to win a promotion after nine years, reported promptly to his office, hung up his coat, and then walked into the executive offices of the Connecticut Lottery. There, he methodically stabbed one top official and shot two others—saying "Bye-bye" to one of them—and then chased the lottery president out of the building and into a parking lot, where he shot and killed him with a semiautomatic handgun, then used the gun to commit suicide.[14]

On December 19, 1997, a Milwaukee postal clerk, Anthony Deculit, 37, killed a coworker he had feuded with and wounded two others, one of whom was a supervisor who had reprimanded him. As coworkers and friends begged and pleaded with him not to pull the trigger, he placed a nine-millimeter handgun in his mouth and did just that.[15] A Santa Fe, California, man, Soon Byung Park, 36, shot and killed a male business partner and the partner's sister before he finally killed himself. He had recently been fired from the embroidery firm, but returned days later with a handgun. He fired at his business partner, who sat behind his desk, then turned and blocked the path of his sister as she tried to flee. "She got down on her hands and knees in front of Park who shot her execution-style,"[16] once in the chest and once in the back of the head.[17] And on Thursday, November 3, 2011, Richard Vance Dixon was fired from his job at an eastern Winston-Salem, North Carolina, gas station by his boss, Alex P. Little. Dixon returned to the station three days later and shot his boss several times, critically wounding him, before he shot and killed himself.[18]

Angry and upset over a series of investment losses, Vincent Dortch, 44, of Newark, Delaware, burst into an executive meeting with two handguns and announced to those sitting at the table, "You have a minute or two to say your prayers" before he opened fire.[19] He had organized the meeting under the pretense that he had two investors, but, minutes after the meeting started, forced the investors to bind the four others with duct tape, saying he had no problem with them. After the two left the room, Dortch opened fire, hitting the four bound men, then said, "I have to finish this job,"[20] before he shot three in the head again, at point-blank range. After the police arrived at the scene, Dortch exchanged gunfire, and then placed a gun at his temple and killed himself.[21]

Still other employees were so consumed and obsessed with hate and rage that any consideration of suicide, or how many other lives would be lost, didn't matter at all. The most dramatic example of this kind of focus was seen in the December 1987, case of David Burke, 35, a former USAir employee who was fired for stealing sixty-nine dollars from his in-flight cocktail receipts. He met briefly with his supervisor and tried to explain the financial hardship that would result from losing his job. But the supervisor flatly refused to reinstate him. The next day, December 7, 1987, Burke bought a ticket on Pacific Southwest Airlines flight 1771, which was a daily flight from Los Angeles to San Francisco. Burke's supervisor was a passenger on the flight, which he took regularly for his commute from San Francisco to Los Angeles. Using his USAir credentials, Burke bypassed the security checkpoint and boarded the same plane with a fully loaded .44 Magnum revolver borrowed from a coworker. Seeing his supervisor on the plane, Burke wrote a note on an air-sickness bag, which read: "Hi, Ray. I think it's sort of ironical [sic] that we ended up like this. I asked for some leniency for my family. Remember? Well, I got none and you'll get none."[22]

As the plane cruised at twenty-two thousand feet above the central California coast, the cockpit voice recorder picked up the sound of two shots fired in the cabin. The cockpit door had been opened and a female flight attendant was heard to tell the crew, "We have a problem." When the captain asked, "What kind of problem?" Burke's voice was heard to announce, "I'm the problem," as he fired three more shots that totally incapacitated the pilots. Seconds later, the cockpit voice recorder picked up increased windscreen noise as the aircraft pitched downward and began to accelerate. A final gunshot was heard, which Federal Aviation Administration experts later speculated was Burke committing suicide. The four-engine British Aerospace 146-200 crashed into the hillside of a cattle ranch in the Santa Lucia Mountains near Paso Robles and Cayucos.

According to eyewitnesses, the plane was "completely intact until impact," crashing into a rocky hillside, nose-first, at seven hundred miles per hour. The only human remains were in small pieces, the largest of which were feet in shoes.[23] The force of impact caused such extensive damage that all the passengers were immediately incinerated, totaling forty-three deaths (thirty-eight passengers and the five-member crew) In fact, twenty-seven passengers couldn't even be identified. Yet, after two days of digging around at the site, a handgun was found that contained six spent bullet casings and Burke's suicide note admitting his responsibility for the crash. Ironically, in a justly incriminating twist of evidence, the FBI was able to lift a single print from a fragment of human finger that was still stuck in the revolver's trigger guard, which positively identified Burke.[24]

SUICIDE AS PROTEST

These employees committed suicide typically to dramatize a wrong or other perceived injustice suffered on the job. The injustice usually resulted from a problem that was structural or systemic, or a change in the status quo. This was often a management policy, or an adverse judicial ruling or agency decision that resulted in a loss of status, benefits, or other entitlement that they felt was unfairly denied or withdrawn.

Judith Coffin, 46, we recall, was a diabetic who had worked for the USPS twelve years when she was promoted in 1993 to project engineer. But the promotion generated so much sexual harassment and verbal abuse by male subordinates and supervisors that she complained to USPS top brass, to no avail. After two years of abuse, she went home one afternoon and wrote a suicide note blaming the USPS for the problem, and died six days later, on August 23, 1995, of an insulin overdose. On March 5, 2007, Jose Mendez, 65, opened fire at the Kenyon Press company in Signal Hill, California, wounding three coworkers and then killing himself after his working hours at the menu-printing plant had been reduced.

On October 18, 1993, Arthur Hill, 53, a civilian army-base supply clerk, went on a killing spree because his temporary promotion to supervisor had been withdrawn. It couldn't be determined what additional benefits or privileges he enjoyed, but the title was sufficiently attractive that its removal was too painful to endure. He shot and killed both his boss and two coworkers, and critically wounded two others before he drove more than forty miles from Fort Knox to the Veterans Affairs Medical Center in Louisville, Kentucky. Once inside the building, he stepped inside a restroom, and then shot himself in the head, in a suicide attempt. Protesting a recent disciplinary action by her superiors, Renita Williams Dozier resigned her position at a Fayetteville, North Carolina, nursing home, but, on October 15, 2005, returned to the home and took two hostages. After a four-hour standoff with the police, she released the hostages unharmed and then killed herself with a gunshot to the chest.

Another protest suicide was that of Patrick Joseph Graves, 51, who had worked for the Goodrich Corporation in Northfield, Minnesota, for three years when he received a poor performance review. He couldn't have been more surprised on Monday, until he was fired the following Thursday afternoon. On September 29, 2011, he matter-of-factly got into his car, locked all the doors, and then fatally shot himself in the head. In another case, Jack Richard Currier was denied a worker's compensation claim through his employer, the Fleetwood Manufacturing Company in San Diego, California, and on July 29, 1991, shot and wounded the company owner and then committed suicide. And on May 18, 2010, Robert Montgomery, 50, an employee at the Boulder Stove and Flooring company, was so infuriated by recent changes in the company's commission and bonus guidelines that he shot and killed the two owners before he shot and killed himself.

As the president of the union local 28, representing employees of the USDA in Los Angeles, David Rothman, 51, had a "stormy" relationship with USDA management, particularly over issues of personal work schedules. He was still attempting to resolve some of those issues when he learned that just two weeks earlier a petition had been circulated among the rank-and-file members of the union to have him removed as president. During an April 22, 1998, meeting, Rothman shot and killed two USDA supervisors before he turned the gun on himself. Found on Rothman's body was a handwritten note in which he apologized to the police, saying, "I am sorry you have to clean up this mess. Don't let it affect your life. The job really sucks." And on the dashboard of his vehicle he wrote: "Reprisal sucks. They never settle EEO complaints. To hell with USDA."[25]

SUICIDE AS THE LAST WORD IN AN ONGOING ACCUSATION, CONTROVERSY, OR DEBATE

The use of suicide as a means of getting the "last word" in an ongoing controversy or debate was chosen by the largest percentage of employees. The need to be heard or listened to easily trumped even the need for payback and revenge. These cases were typically employees who sought a forum, venue, platform, audience, or some other opportunity to address or respond to an accusation, issue, or controversy which they had missed, forfeited, ignored, or been denied. As a result, they typically felt they never had their day in court, or that they were denied the opportunity to present their side of an accusation or controversy. Not surprisingly, they also tended to be marginal employees, the "losers" on the job whose coworkers rarely respected or admired them, or valued or listened to their opinions or what they had to say. Their suicides were therefore much-needed last words at meetings or conferences that were never scheduled, shouted in the ear of despised supervisors or bosses, or the final, eternal "fuck you" screamed in the ear of managements that never wanted to hear their side of the story or listen to what they had to say.

We have already met several employees whose suicides fall within this category. The day before Patrick Sherrill slaughtered his former coworkers at the Edmond, Oklahoma, post office, we recall, he was summoned to a meeting, reprimanded by two superiors, and warned that his termination was imminent. The rampage by Jennifer San Marco was also preceded by several meetings with USPS top brass, which first placed her on "psychological" disability before they fired her outright. And Joseph Wesbecker had long been locked in battle with his company over issues of the workplace before he responded with an AK-47, slaughtering most of his colleagues before he killed himself.

On July 8, 2004, a white bigot, Doug Williams, 48, murdered six people, five of whom were black, after bragging that he could kill African Americans. Considered a racist hothead by coworkers, he was known for his hatred of blacks, and often had run-ins with management and coworkers because of his racial views. Ironically, just minutes before he went on his murder rampage, he had left the company's annual meeting on ethics, at which topics like racial tolerance were likely discussed. It's not known what—if anything—he said at the meeting, or if he got a chance to express his views again. But during the meeting, Williams, dressed in a black T-shirt and camouflage pants, suddenly rose from his chair, went outside to his truck, and returned minutes later carrying a .223-caliber semiautomatic rifle and a twelve-gauge shotgun. He opened fire with the shotgun, leaving four blacks and one white dead, and nine wounded, before he killed himself.

Jacquelyn Ferguson, 51, was hired as a billing clerk in the busy cardiology office of Dr. Jeffrey B. Sack in Sarasota, Florida, and did well for a few months. But the job quickly became a pressure cooker and she started to make costly mistakes. Five months after she was hired, she had a closed-door meeting with Dr. Sack and her immediate supervisor, Denise Keyworth. They drew the line: one more screw-up and she would be fired. What Ferguson said during that critical meeting is not known, but she was deeply depressed and under medication, and the following week she called in sick— three days in a row. When she finally showed up, unannounced, she followed Keyworth into the latter's office, and a moment after she shut the door, gunshots rang out. Ferguson had shot and killed Keyworth, hitting her five times in the upper chest—her lungs, heart, and esophagus. She then drove home, wrote a note which said, "I've never been violent in my life but enough is enough,"[26] and then committed suicide with a bullet to the head.

A quality control manager for a Warwick, New York, factory, Victor M. Piazza, 55, returned to his job nineteen months after being fired for accessing child pornography on his computer. Also facing a parole violation that would surely land him in jail, Piazza's response was to grab a .38-caliber revolver, shooting and wounding three of his bosses before he shot and killed himself. In January 1993, eight months after he was fired from his job at the Fireman's Fund Insurance Company in Tampa, Florida, Paul Calden, 33, returned to his company cafeteria, calmly sat down, and sipped a soft drink— and then shot and killed three of his former supervisors before he shot and killed himself.

On February 8, 2010, Timothy Hendron, 51, shot eight coworkers, killing three, before he also shot and killed himself. An employee of a Saint Louis, Missouri, manufacturer of electric transformers, Hendron believed his supervisors were harassing him, which seems likely since he had joined a pending civil suit against the company and was about to have his day in court. He and his fellow plaintiffs had charged the company with having allowed the workers' pension plan to charge exorbitant fees and expenses without their knowledge and consent, and the trial had just begun that week. On January 2, 1996, Sookhdeo Itwaru, 50, opened fire in a Westchester, New York, auto supply parts store where he used to work, killing his former boss and wounding two others before he shot himself in the stomach. Itwaru had been seething for months, and reportedly haunted the store for months after he quit the job because he had been demoted to driver after serving in a managerial role, and didn't feel his side of the issue had been heard.

In a similarly motivated case, Daniel S. Marsden, 38, of Santa Fe Springs, California, a quality control inspector at a plastics company, on June 5, 1997, shot and killed two men, and injured four others, fatally injuring himself after an argument with a colleague. On January 26, 2005, a Toledo, Ohio, auto-worker, Myles Meyers, 54, after a meeting with his supervisors and union leaders earlier that day, wired a shotgun to his body and burst into a Jeep assembly plant, killing a supervisor and wounding two others before he committed suicide. After suffering years of taunting by coworkers at a news-paper production plant in Providence, Carlos Pacheco, on June 9, 2002, shot and killed two coworkers and injured another before he killed himself. On February 7, 1993, Fernando Ruiz, 30, an employee at a Houston, Texas, produce company, was summoned to his boss's office to be fired for theft and harassing a female employee. Instead of going to the meeting, and faced with a fait accompli, Ruiz retrieved a semiautomatic pistol from his car, and then shot and killed his boss and wounded the female before he shot and killed himself.

On June 1, 2011, Keith Little, 49, killed his supervisor by stabbing him more than seventy times after he was reprimanded and denied a raise in a performance review. Little was no doubt accustomed to having the last word since, according to court records, he had been charged with slaying a co-worker in 2003, but was found not guilty after a jury trial. And it was during a closed meeting at BD Diagnostic Systems in Baltimore, Maryland, on November 17, 2006, that Morris Lyons, 52, shot and killed his supervisor, Harold Creech, 59, and then shot and killed himself.

Wesley N. Higdon, 25, on June 25, 2008, killed his supervisor and four coworkers during a shooting spree at an Atlantis Plastics factory in Hender-son, Kentucky, after an argument about wearing safety goggles and using his cell phone while working at his press machine. Higdon had a reputation for being difficult, and as he was being escorted from the factory by the super-visor, he retrieved a .45-caliber pistol, shot and killed the supervisor, then ran back into the factory, where he shot and killed four other workers before he turned the gun on himself. "He just walked in, looked like he meant business, and started shooting at everybody,"[27] an eyewitness said.

A recently hired employee at the ConAgra meatpacking plant, Elijah Brown, 21, on July 2, 2004, killed six coworkers and wounded two more before he turned the gun on himself. Brown and his victims all worked the second manufacturing shift, which made products like bologna, braunsch-weiger, and processed and sliced meats for deli and sandwich products.

Brown had been teased by several coworkers, and recently had a tiff with another. Just before the shooting, there had been a meeting, but it's not known if Brown said anything at the meeting or remained silent. He clearly disliked some of his coworkers, and the shootings were not random. According to eyewitnesses, he picked exactly who he wanted to shoot, and then shot only those who had confronted or harassed him earlier that week. He even shouted obscenities as he shot them, and at one point walked past coworkers saying, "You haven't done anything to me, so you can go."[28]

On February 2, 2004, a week after being suspended from his job for accessing child pornography on his computer, Darrell L. Kinyon, 49, shot and killed his supervisor. Minutes before the shooting, Kinyon had a meeting with his boss, but flew into a rage, damaged a candy machine, and left the building, returning minutes later, when he shot and killed the supervisor before killing himself.

Omar Thornton, 34, was caught on a company video camera stealing beer from a truck. He worked at a Manchester, Connecticut, warehouse where he was employed as a delivery driver. On August 3, 2010, during a disciplinary meeting, Thornton sat calmly as he watched the surveillance video of him stealing beer from a company truck. He was given the choice of resigning or being fired. According to a company vice president, Thornton "was cool and calm. He didn't yell. He was cold as ice. He didn't protest when we [met] with him to show him the video [and he] didn't contest it. He didn't complain. He didn't argue. He didn't admit or deny anything. He just agreed to resign."[29] (He had complained privately of a coworker who used a racial epithet, and another coworker who drew a racially offensive sketch on the men's room wall, but he never filed a grievance or a complaint against either the company or anyone else.) Then, as he was being escorted from the meeting, he asked to go to the cafeteria, where he retrieved two guns from a lunch box. Although Thornton reportedly had little to say during the disciplinary meeting, he returned from the cafeteria with two pistols, one a Sturm Ruger SR9, and then, "as cold as ice," opened fire, killing eight coworkers and wounding two others before he turned the gun on himself.[30]

As already noted, the facts of some cases were highly pliable, and several of these disgruntled workers had multiple motives, as their conduct fit easily into more than one category and they achieved several ends simultaneously: revenge, protest, and getting in the final word just before they killed themselves. Jeffrey Johnson, 54, had been fired from his job as a Manhattan fashion designer a year earlier. He achieved three ends when, on the morning of August 24, 2012, on a crowded midtown sidewalk, he killed his boss Steven Ercolino, 41, by shooting him repeatedly at point-blank range in front of the Empire State Building[31] and then deliberately raised his gun at heavily armed police officers to achieve the fourth—"blue suicide."[32]

SUICIDE AS CLOSURE ON A LIFE

These employees tended to have the most complicated motives, and their suicides seemed intended not only to end workplace problems with a supervisor or boss, but also as closure on an utterly failed life. Their rampages therefore tended to be among the bloodiest and most violent, with the highest number of victims, and they often started the series of killings with members of their own family, even before they left home for the workplace. These employees also typically had an apocalyptic, end-of-the-world view of what they had to do, and went to great lengths to ensure that nobody, not in-laws or distant neighbors—not even farm animals and pets—survived what they had in mind.

Andrew P. Kehoe, 52, was a Bath Township school board member known about the small Michigan community for his industry and thrift, and his tireless battles against new taxes. He also perpetrated the Bath Massacre on May 18, 1927, in which thirty-eight children (ages 7 through 12) and seven adults were killed, and at least fifty-eight others were injured. He was infuriated by the levy of a property tax to fund construction of a new school building, which led to the foreclosure of his farm. In revenge, he first murdered his wife, and then set his farm buildings on fire—carefully tying up his farm horses and other animals to ensure that they perished in the flames and didn't escape. As firefighters arrived at the site, he detonated a bomb that destroyed the north wing of the school building, killing most of the people inside. (He used a detonator to ignite dynamite and hundreds of pounds of pyrotol, which he had secretly planted inside the school over the course of many months.) As rescuers gathered at the burning school, he casually drove up, stopped, and then detonated a second bomb inside his shrapnel-filled vehicle, committing suicide and killing several others as well, thus ending what remains the deadliest act of school mass murder in American history.

The day before he murdered his coworkers, Mark Barton, 44, murdered his second wife and his two adolescent children by repeated hammer blows to the head as they slept in bed. The next day, July 29, 1999, he drove to the two Atlanta, Georgia, offices at which he was a day trader and had suffered trading losses in excess of 105,000 dollars in the previous two months. At Momentum Securities he shot and killed four coworkers, then walked across the street to the All-Tech Investment Group, where he shot and killed five more. Barton had also been the principal suspect, but never charged, in the 1993 Alabama deaths of his first wife and her mother (also by bludgeoning with a hammer-like object). Hours after the massacres, local police spotted Barton sitting in his vehicle at a gas station, but he shot and killed himself before the police could effect an arrest.

On March 10, 2009, Michael McLendon, 28, went on a shooting spree that spanned three towns in southern Alabama, killing eleven people, including several members of his own family, and wounding six others before he returned to his old job and killed himself after a shoot-out with the local police. McLendon had quit his job at a meat-processing firm, had been fired from a job at a poultry-processing plant, and had also been fired from his job at Reliable Metal Products, a producer of air conditioner parts. He first shot and killed his girlfriend, his mother, and her four dogs in the home he shared with them, and then burned the house down. Extremely well armed with weaponry that included an automatic rifle and a shotgun, McLendon then drove his Mitsubishi Eclipse east to the town of Samson, where he shot and killed his grandmother, his grandfather, and an aunt and uncle. At this point, it seemed he didn't discriminate, and anybody was fair game. Minutes later he shot and killed a tenant on his grandparents' property, then killed a woman, the wife of a deputy sheriff, and her toddler daughter.

After an exchange of gunfire with a pursuing sheriff, he shot and killed two strangers, then sped down Highway 52 toward the town of Geneva and Reliable Metal Products, where he had once worked. Holed up inside the Reliable plant, and surrounded by the police, he fired more than thirty rounds in the shoot-out before he shot and killed himself.

Iowa farmer Dale Burr, 63, whose financial problems had already claimed his farm machinery, his stored grains, and his quarter horses, on December 9, 1985, shot and killed his wife of forty years before he drove to the Hills Bank and Trust Company in Hills, Iowa (population 550). Once at the bank, he shot and killed the bank president, later shot and killed a neighbor, and then shot at the neighbor's fleeing wife and 6-year-old son before he turned the shotgun on himself and committed suicide.

Julian Carlton, 35, was a Caribbean immigrant who worked on the elegant Wisconsin estate of Frank Lloyd Wright. On August 15, 1914, while Wright was out of town, he served Wright's common-law wife and several dinner guests dinner. As they ate, he methodically bolted the windows and doors of the dining room, locked the exits, and then poured buckets of gasoline under the doors before he set the mansion on fire. As the mansion burned, he waited outside with an axe and hacked to death those who jumped from the windows to escape the flames. He was soon captured, narrowly escaping a nearby lynch mob, and two months later had starved himself to death while awaiting trial.

On April 18, 2006, Herbert Chalmers, 55, opened fire at his workplace, Finneger's Catering in Saint Louis, Missouri, killing two coworkers and wounding another, and then turning the gun on himself to commit suicide. His workplace rampage and suicide were launched shortly after he had traveled to two different locations to rape a former girlfriend and murder the mother of his only child. On August 10, 1989, John Merlin Taylor, 52, brought a .22-caliber pistol to his place of employment, the Orange Glen, California, post office, where he shot and killed two coworkers and wounded another before he also killed himself. Earlier that day he had shot and killed his wife at home before he left for work.

On November 27, 1978, former San Francisco supervisor Dan White, 32, shot and killed San Francisco mayor George Moscone, and minutes later shot and killed San Francisco supervisor Harvey Milk. The double assassination made national headlines, as Milk was also one of the nation's first openly gay politicians and an iconoclastic, pioneering leader in the burgeoning gay rights movement of the 1970s. Disappointed with the workings of city politics, and heavily in debt, White resigned from the board but quickly changed his mind when told that his resignation was politically unwise, as it tipped the balance of power on the board to his opponents' constituents. When he asked Milk to reappoint him, Milk refused, a decision that was supported by Mayor Moscone.

In revenge, White met with the mayor in City Hall, and as the mayor mixed two drinks, White pulled his revolver and fired shots at the mayor's shoulder and chest. Moscone fell to the floor as White approached, poised his gun six inches from the mayor's head, and fired two more bullets into his earlobes, killing him instantly. Standing over the slain mayor, White slowly removed the four empty cartridges from his gun and reloaded it with hollow-point bullets that he had saved especially for Milk. When Dianne Feinstein, then president of the Board, saw White quickly exit the mayor's office, she called him, but White sharply responded: "I have something to do first."[33] He quickly intercepted Milk and asked to meet in his office for a moment. Milk agreed, and once the door was closed, White positioned himself between the doorway and Milk, pulled out his revolver, and fired. The first bullet hit Milk's right wrist as he tried to protect himself. White continued to fire, hitting Milk twice more in the chest, firing a fourth bullet in Milk's head, and firing still a fifth bullet at close range, killing him instantly.[34]

White was later tried and convicted by a controversial jury verdict in which the gay community felt he had literally gotten away with murder.[35] After serving five years in jail, White was paroled in 1984, and two years later, in 1986, almost a decade after the double murder, committed suicide.[36]

SUICIDE AS DENIAL, RELIEF, OR EXISTENTIAL ESCAPE

These suicides were probably the easiest to distinguish from the others by their profound sense of embarrassment and humiliation, in their quietly desperate loss of hope, and in the realization of dreams unfulfilled, promise unrealized, and opportunities squandered over the years. These suicides followed lives that were often accomplished, but still somehow misdirected and sometimes even pointless in the end. And they ultimately found life too difficult, too agonizing, to continue the private pain.

On January 25, 2002, Clifford Baxter, 44, while seated in his black Mercedes-Benz in Sugar Land, Texas, shot himself in the head. A former Enron Corporation executive who had sold thirty-five million dollars worth of Enron stock during the company's bankruptcy, Baxter had often clashed with CEO Jeffrey Skilling over questionable business practices, and had agreed to testify before Congress in the Enron case. His suicide note to his wife, hand-printed, but not signed, expressed his despair over the direction his life had taken.

Widely recognized as one of the most skilled appellate lawyers in the country, Mark Levy, 59, was an extremely talented attorney with Ivy League credentials and a dazzling resume, and counted among his close friends a former Yale classmate, Justice Samuel A. Alito, who sat on the US Supreme Court. But when he lost his job at a prominent Washington, D.C., law firm, none of it was enough. On April 30, 2009, before sunrise, Levy left his wife a note in their Bethesda, Maryland, home, parked his Jaguar in the law firm's garage, and then took an elevator to his office on the eleventh floor, where he was discovered an hour later, dead from a self-inflicted gunshot wound to the head.

Another example of this type of suicide was seen in the case of Elizabeth Otto, 31, an employee of the Hewlett-Packard Company who, on December 18, 2000, jumped from the company plane during a flight to San Jose. One of the five other employees on the aircraft attempted to grab her as she was partially outside the rear emergency door. According to reports, Otto was suffering from depression and job-related stress.

In a similar case, Mark Madoff, 46, on December 11, 2010, hanged himself with a dog leash in his Manhattan SoHo apartment as his 2-year-old son slept in a nearby bedroom. Mark Madoff, who was a codirector of trading at the Wall Street firm of Madoff Investment Securities, LLC (founded in 1960 by his father Bernard Madoff), had reportedly grown increasingly distraught and depressed over the enormity of his father's crimes and the effect it was having on his own family. Though no suicide note was found, he had sent several desperate emails to his lawyer and his wife in which he all but said he was going to kill himself. As a *Daily News* source said of a message to his wife, "It basically sounded like he couldn't take the pain anymore."[37]

On May 5, 2005, Houston, Texas, tax attorney Jackie Lee Duke, upset that he was losing his job, wrote a suicide note before he met with his supervising attorney, Paul Hartmann, pulled a .357 Magnum, and shot and killed his supervisor before he raised the weapon and killed himself. On September 29, 1983, James Jenkins, 46, a Minnesota dairy farmer whose farm machinery and livestock had been repossessed a dozen times in the last two decades, shot and killed the local banker and the chief loan officer. The latter was shot in the shoulder, the former shot in the throat, then chased into a ditch, where he was shot three more times by Jenkins and his 18-year-old son. Jenkins said he killed the men after the banker told other bankers in the area that he was a bad credit risk.

SUICIDE AS TORT—THE INTENTIONAL INFLICTION OF EMOTIONAL HARM

These employees committed suicide in ways that seemed deliberately calculated to shock, offend, and antagonize the employer, coworkers, and even the general public. They went to extraordinary lengths to publicize their suicides, to maximize the horror and distress and the chances of their presumed martyrdom. The public became their captive audience as they left long, rambling suicide notes, alerted the news media, and generally did all they could to broadcast their own deaths beforehand. As a result, these suicides typically seemed staged, directed, orchestrated, and "set up," and the circumstances often took on a theatrical aspect as they unfolded in ways guaranteed to achieve the greatest dramatic impact when their bodies were "discovered" by the police.

On July 8, 2005, Bruce Alvin Miller, 46, was fired from his position as an assistant business designer at the Hanover office of the Baltimore Gas and Electric Company in Maryland. Later that day, he returned to the building, pulled a gun and fired shots into his supervisor's office window, and then shot his way inside the building. As coworkers ran and hid for cover, Miller apparently took a seat in his supervisor's empty office, where he was certain she would return, and then fatally shot himself in the chest.

In another case, Patrick Joseph Graves, 51, who had worked for the Goodrich Corporation in Northfield, Minnesota, was disappointed when he received a poor performance review and was fired later in the week. Without saying a word, he matter-of-factly got into his car, locked all the doors, and, while his coworkers stood watching, fatally shot himself in the head. After mailing a long, rambling suicide letter to local newspapers complaining of harassment by his supervisors, Don Mace, 44, on March 25, 1989, got dressed, ritual-like, in his full postal uniform, walked to the main lobby of the Poway, California, post office, took out his .38-caliber revolver, and then killed himself with a bullet to the head. And on June 3, 1992, Roy Barnes, 60, a current postal employee, went to the workroom floor of the Citrus Heights, California, post office armed with a .22-caliber pistol and, almost as if he wanted to outdo Mace's suicide three years before, positioned himself in front of a group of onlookers, and then fatally shot himself in the heart.

In early January 2009, Ervin Lupoe, 35, and his wife were both fired from their positions as technicians at Kaiser Permanente Medical Center in west Los Angeles. Deep in debt, and several months behind in their mortgage payments, they packed the family's sports utility vehicle for a trip to Garden

City, Kansas, to live with his brother-in-law. He even notified school officials that the family was relocating and that three of his five children—Brittany, 8; twin girls Jaszmin and Jassely, 5; and twin boys Benjamin and Christian, 2—would not be returning to attend any more classes that term.

On January 28, he typed a three-page handwritten note in which he described his difficulties on the job and how he and his wife were callously rebuffed by a medical center administrator when they showed up for work. They were told to file a grievance, according to the note, but nothing was done, and two days later they were fired. "They did nothing to the manager who started such and did not attempt to assist us in the matter," the note continued, "knowing we have no job and five children under 8 years old with no place to go." At the bottom of the note he even added, "Oh lord, my God, is there no hope for a widow's son?"[38]

The Lupoe family never made it to Kansas. Indeed, they never left Los Angeles. Ervin Lupoe drove home, where he methodically shot and killed each of his five young children, and then shot and killed his wife. Next, he carefully faxed the three-page typewritten note to local TV news station KABC-TV, and then faxed the same note to the local police. Only minutes later, he sat down near the bleeding bodies, in a haze of nitrate smoke, and finally shot and killed himself, confident that the police were on the way.[39]

Despite the many different ways in which suicides were committed, and the postmortem messages they were meant to convey, several behaviors were similar and widely shared. Of the most noticeable was how reliably the perpetrators gave clear, direct, and unequivocal warnings that they would inflict serious bodily injury or death. They often provided behavioral hints and clues to "telegraph" the deadly act beforehand. This warning conduct was found in almost 90 percent of the cases, and spanned every category and demographic—racial, ethnic, male and female, young and old.

Given the silence on this issue in the literature, one must ask: What caused this behavior? An unconscious desire to be stopped—or get caught—before they actually committed the crime? What were the behavioral warning signs that an employee intended to murder a coworker or kill the boss? The fifty-eight deaths caused by Andrew Kehoe and Nidal Hasan resulted not because the men didn't give behavioral hints and clues, but because the hints and clues were given so subtly, and over such a long period of time, that they were consistently ignored by coworkers and colleagues.

Despite his well-known desire to kill blacks, Doug Williams's coworkers didn't think he would actually commit the act. Although Larry Hansel's activities struck his coworkers as ominous and bizarre, nobody interpreted or read them as a prelude to mass homicide. In both cases, the warning signs were tragically disregarded or ignored.

Chapter Ten

The Warning Signs

The Tick, Tick, Tick of the Human Bomb

"Nobody would've guessed John would do something like that. No way."

"Can you believe that Mortimer could so such a thing?"

"I never knew Fatso was thinking like that. No way, not him. Never!"

Time and again, similar words were mumbled by stunned coworkers and colleagues grieving the sudden loss of another victim of workplace homicide. Most had missed the behavioral hints and clues that a coworker was about to explode in a homicidal rage. Most never suspected that something was amiss, that murder was afoot.

Even when coworkers knew bad blood existed between two workers, or that a coworker had a short fuse, they still expressed shock and dismay after a violent employee was finally pushed to the edge and committed a homicidal act. That this scenario played out so often only highlighted some of the most contentiously debated questions in this area of the law: Do workplace murderers give behavioral hints of what they intend to do? Are these behavioral hints and clues meant—consciously or unconsciously—to "telegraph" the lethal acts beforehand? Do these killers actually want to be stopped?

In his controversial study of killing,[1] Lieutenant Colonel David Grossman argues that the army trains citizens to kill, and that the pervasive violence in the media, and interactive videos, are only civilian replications of this effort. The result is a citizenry that's increasingly desensitized or numbed to violence, especially murder, which explains why the society is so violent and continues to become more violent every day. Drawing heavily from interviews, published accounts, and academic studies on the psychology and economics of killing, the most controversial part of Grossman's research wasn't his central thesis but his underlying assumption: human beings have an innate aversion to killing other human beings. In the formulation of this argument, he relied heavily on the work of US Army general and historian S. L. A. Marshall.[2]

General Marshall claimed, on the basis of extensive surveys, that between 75 and 85 percent of frontline American riflemen had not fired their weapons in combat—even when under attack and at risk of being overrun. He attributed these low firing rates to an instinctive aversion to killing at close range, when the potential victim was clearly identifiable as another human being. After Marshall died in 1977, it was discovered that his research wasn't methodologically sound, and many critics rejected his thesis as fraudulent. But others argued that he had intuitively stumbled on a profound truth. Although his research methods were unsound, evidence of this phenomenon has continued to surface in unexpected places. His basic conclusion that human beings have an aversion to killing other human beings[3] has been amply corroborated by evidence and accounts from other wars as well, including the American Civil War, World War I, and the Falklands War.[4]

Due largely to Grossman's thesis, it's no surprise that the perpetrators' behavioral warning signs arose in several different contexts, and that their warning signs, hints, and clues didn't fall neatly within a single mode of conduct. That they appeared in different contexts and situations not only deflected suspicion and made detection much more difficult, it also required that the behaviors be categorized. The "tick, tick, tick" of the bomb thus varied in "volume" and "decibel" level, and was subject to different contributing factors, some more audible than others.

The first category of warning signs were those given by employees who were in fact quasi trespassers; they still carried keys, access cards, and IDs that permitted access to the job site, even though they were no longer employees. The second category of warning signs came from workers who had been (erroneously) perceived as "model" employees, the ultimate professionals who could do no wrong in the eyes of coworkers and management. The third category came from employees who had never made a clear, direct threat of violence, but whose threat was implied, whose capacity to kill could be inferred from their mercurial temperaments, their volatile personalities, or their dysfunctional domestic circumstances. And the fourth category involved employees who had actually made clear, direct, and unequivocal threats of violence—and soon kept their word

PERENNIAL TRESPASSERS WHO NEVER LEFT THE JOB

Former employees were at the top of the list of most likely workplace murderers not because they made overt threats or committed an affirmative act;

they headed the list because of their status as quasi trespassers whose very presence on the employer's property set the stage for resentment, anger, and violence, which all too often led to murder and death. More than 55 percent of the cases involved former employees who murdered and wounded co-workers on the employer's property—after they had been fired. Soon Byung Park returned to the company and shot his boss, killed the boss's sister, and then killed himself a month after he had been fired. Clifton McCree returned to his job and killed five former colleagues five months after he had been canned. Socorro Hurtado-Garcia of Grand Rapids, Michigan, was allowed back on the job, where he killed his boss, two months after he was fired.

Denis Czajkowski, a psychiatric nurse, returned to the hospital and killed his supervisor a month after he was fired. Andre White returned to his employer's office and killed his supervisor almost two months after he was terminated. Arthur Hasting Wise was permitted back onto company premises, where he shot and killed four former coworkers, two months after he'd been fired. Larry Hansel, we recall, was allowed to return to his old job where he shot and killed his two supervisors more than three months after he was fired.

Dozens of workplace murderers killed coworkers and supervisors (and many also committed suicide) as trespassers, including Perry Smith, Jian Chen, Robert Diamond, Darryl Dinkins, James Simpson, Paul Calden, Ladislav Antilak, Victor Piazza, Gregory Gray, Tom West, Paulino Valenzuela, and Salvatore Tapia. And most of these murders could have been prevented (or at least delayed or thwarted) had the perpetrators not been permitted to return to the job weeks, months, even years after they were fired. We recall that William Baker, who had been scheduled to go to jail for other crimes, returned to his employer General Dynamics on February 5, 2001, carrying a small arsenal, shot and killed four former coworkers and wounded four, almost *six years* after he was fired. [5]

MODEL EMPLOYEES WHO GAVE NO (VISIBLE) WARNING SIGNS

Nobody thought it the least bit odd that John M. Taylor, 51, arrived at the post office that Thursday morning in August 1989 a half hour before his shift was scheduled to begin. He had been with the USPS for twenty-seven years, and had received numerous awards and commendations in recognition of his dedication and work ethic. Just recently, he'd been selected to receive another quarterly performance award, but magnanimously suggested that the award be given to someone else, as he had already won it several times before. According to S. Anthony Baron's account in *Violence in the Workplace*, the gesture was "just like John," whose traits made him one of the most likeable employees in the Orange Glen, California, post office. "He was unfailingly friendly and congenial, always had a smile on his face," one of his supervisors recalled. "If you were to make a composite of a model employee, you'd come up with John Taylor."[6]

On that particular morning, however, Taylor came to work with a handgun. Minutes later, and with no warning, he shot and killed two coworkers and wounded a third before putting the gun to his head and shooting himself. Adding to the tragedy was the discovery that before he left home that morning he had also shot and killed his wife. Given the high praise he received and how much everyone liked him, it's hard to believe that he gave no hints or clues before the shooting that something was amiss. But he did.

Actually, Taylor had a drinking problem, but since it never affected his job, and he was such a "nice" guy, nobody ever gave it a second thought. He had also started to complain about his home life, dissatisfied that his 22-year-old stepson had moved into the house and wasn't looking for a job. (To someone with Taylor's work ethic, this was probably doubly irksome.) And, more revealingly, he had become suspicious about sums of money being placed along his delivery route, and had complained privately that he was being set up by persons unknown to test his professional integrity.[7]

Taylor wasn't the only model employee whose issues remained discreetly behind closed doors and out of sight. Amy Bishop, the Harvard-trained biology professor who shot and killed three colleagues, was privately suspected by colleagues of being bizarre—even "crazy"—before the media publicized her eccentric, violent past and her previous brushes with the law. In fact, few knew that, in the weeks before the shooting, she had even started to take her nine-millimeter handgun to the local firing range.

Behind his respectability as a former policeman and a supervisor, few would have guessed that Dan White would assassinate San Francisco mayor Moscone and minutes later also assassinate supervisor Harvey Milk. Few knew that he was actually dangerously eccentric with a political "dark" side. Sociologist and suicide expert Loren Coleman argues that White's double assassination was inspired in part by the "copycat" effect of the Jonestown mass-murder suicides of almost a thousand followers of Jim Jones in Jonestown, Guyana. Loren reminds us that White had submitted his resignation to the board just two days after the Jonestown massacre.[8] He adds: "White would often go into trances during supervisors' meetings and then impulsively goose-step around the room. His past was filled with mystery, including an enigmatic 'missing year' of 1972. [His] murderous instability appeared to have been set off by the Jonestown murder-suicides and their link to San Francisco."[9]

Among these employees, some behavioral warning signs were given just hours, or even minutes, before the actual attack, by which time, of course, it was too late. On April 17, 1998, Lenda Glass Spencer, 44, a nine-year employee at Preston Engravers, Inc., in East Windsor, Connecticut, finally decided to respond to her boss's persistent racial harassment when she brought a friend's nine-millimeter Smith and Wesson to work. She reportedly drank a half bottle of rum before she arrived at the plant, and then asked her boss if they could speak somewhere in private. They went to a small office, where she stood with her right hand in her right pocket as they spoke. Crying uncontrollably, she asked him to stop harassing her and to stop "looking at her color."[10] When he told her to go to the employee locker room and pull herself together, she refused and then started to pull her right hand out of the pocket. Her boss didn't hang around to see what she was pulling out of her pocket; he ran, and moments later heard shots and knew she was firing at him. She chased him around the plant, firing wildly, and squeezed off seven rounds from a seventeen-round magazine, fortunately missing every shot.[11]

On December 30, 2008, Derik Bonestroo, 24, shot and killed his manager at the Mountain Ski Resort in Boulder, Colorado, where he worked as a ski-lift operator. He reportedly walked into a staff meeting and began a religious rant just moments before he opened fire. During the days leading up to the shooting, his "behavior became increasingly odd, to the point that [his] landlord was very worried. Conversations became bizarre not ordinary talks about Christianity. Boonestroo asked what kind of Bible the landlord owned. Bonestroo said he hoped it wasn't 'Satan's Bible.'"[12]

On July 9, 1995, a City of Industry, California, postal worker, Bruce Clark, 58, exhibited his mental state when, just minutes before he murdered his supervisor, he matter-of-factly punched him in the back of the head, a gesture calculated to provoke the man's anger, which justified Clark pulling his .38-caliber revolver from a paper bag and shooting his supervisor in the face.[13] And in the day or two before San Antonio, Texas, librarian Alan Godin, 64, shot and killed a colleague at Northeast Lakeview College, he quoted lines from movies he had recently seen, particularly those spoken by Hollywood killers, like, "I don't want to get away with it. I just want to do it."[14]

Fortunately, the cases in which the perpetrators gave little or no clear indication that they were contemplating homicide—the John Taylors, the Amy Bishops, and the Dan Whites—were relatively rare. In fact, they represented less than 10 percent of the cases. In the days and weeks leading up to their killings, more than 90 percent of the workplace murderers either gave behavioral warning signs, hints, and clues; openly made deadly threats; or actually "telegraphed" their intention to commit a lethal act.

EMPLOYEES WITH VOLATILE, DYSFUNCTIONAL, VIOLENT BACKGROUNDS

These employees never made clear, direct threats of violence, but it was common knowledge among coworkers that they had volatile tempers, were easily angered, and were capable of violence outside the office and beyond the factory gates. It was commonly known that their private lives were chaotic or dysfunctional, and they were generally perceived to be chronically disgruntled employees who habitually filed grievances without merit or frivolous discrimination lawsuits that were eventually dismissed by the courts.

These employees also often underwent dramatic changes in their private lives or their attitudes, which included any of the following:

1. purchased, borrowed, or bought guns or other firearms and weaponry as their latest interest
2. attended gun shows and exhibits, and collected their own firearms and weaponry at home
3. carried guns in their cars (legal in many states, e.g., Kentucky)
4. started to take target-practice lessons after work
5. joined or participated in activities of extremist political organizations and religious groups
6. shared their secret fantasies of killing/murdering with coworkers, etc.
7. recently lost their homes in foreclosure to the banks; suffered a drop in financial standing, loss of credit, or inability to pay bills; or were awash in debt, etc.
8. suffered the loss of a spouse or long-time partner who abruptly left, took the kids and the cat, and relocated to another state
9. recently received the biopsy test results confirming that they did in fact have an incurable disease
10. became increasingly dependent on alcohol and prescription drugs

We recall the case of Patrick Sherrill, who on August 20, 1986, shot and killed fourteen coworkers and wounded six in an Edmond, Oklahoma, post office before he shot and killed himself. More than any other single individual, Sherrill (and his murder spree) was responsible for the term "going postal." Having lived and worked most of his life in Edmond, he was nicknamed Crazy Pat due to his bizarre behavior, and many suspected he was just a time bomb waiting to explode. According to a newspaper article that appeared after the attack, he "was often seen, sneaking around at night in combat fatigues, tying up dogs with baling wire, peering into neighbors windows, [and] mowing his lawn at midnight. His bizarre behavior was also observed at the many jobs he held throughout his life and by his neighbors."[15] Yet, a careful review of the case shows that he had never formally filed any complaints, and in the days and weeks before the massacre he was never abusive or violent, and never made a single, direct threat to anyone.

Joe Cobb, 54, had worked four years as a truck driver for H&M Wagner and Sons, a food distribution center in Glen Burnie, Maryland. On November 23, 2005, he shot and wounded two former supervisors with a .38-caliber handgun before shot and killed himself. Both supervisors survived the attack, which occurred several weeks after he had been fired. After he wounded the supervisors, he stepped outside and fired a bullet into his head, killing himself on the spot. According to coworkers, Cobb had never made any actual threats of violence, but he was generally known to be hostile with a volatile temper, and people on the job knew he was having family problems at home.

On July 30, 1991, Michael E. Rahming, 40, who worked at a facility for the developmentally disabled in Santa Ana, California, went on a rampage, killing his supervisor and wounding two others. He was known among co-workers as a "troubled, erratic employee who was quick to turn violent and [had] filed frequent discrimination claims that were later deemed unfounded."[16] On August 5, 1997, Robert Shuman, 55, shot and killed two business partners, and later claimed through his attorneys at trial that eight days before the murders he had been prescribed Zoloft, which sent him into a "severe drug-induced agitation" called "akathisia," whose symptoms included explosive violence and a host of suicidal acts. The court rejected the argument. Advancing a similar rationale, army reserve sergeant Rashad Valmont, 29, on August 30, 2010, shot and killed his supervisor while stationed at Fort Henderson, Georgia. He argued, unsuccessfully, that he had been fasting to meet strict military weight guidelines, and that he was dehydrated, exhausted, and delirious as a result of the near-starvation diet which had been ordered by his superior officers if he wanted to advance in the ranks.[17]

On August 1, 2008, a former forklift operator at a Simon and Schuster book distribution warehouse, Robert Diamond, 32, returned to the suburban Philadelphia plant and shot and killed two coworkers before he surrendered to the police. He'd been reprimanded in March for calling a black coworker "boy,"[18] and was fired in April for chronic absenteeism. According to several coworkers, he was a workplace bully who had problems with minorities. One coworker recalled that he "was a nut case, but it was something you kept in the back of your mind that one day he probably would do something like this."[19] Another coworker, responding to the shootings, said, "We [hadn't] seen him in 4 months. We was happy, the warehouse was peaceful cause he picked on everybody in the warehouse. He was just a problem person."[20] According to one report, though Diamond had made it clear to his coworkers that he had a "problem" with blacks and Puerto Ricans, nobody knew that he "was apparently a ticking time bomb."[21]

On April 26, 2010, Dr. Lishan Wang, 44, shot and killed a colleague, Dr. Vajinder Pal Toor, whom he blamed for getting him fired from Kingsbrook

Jewish Medical Center two years earlier. Wang had been fired in 2008 after he went missing for several hours and then lied about his whereabouts. He claimed that Indian doctors routinely mistreated Chinese residents, humiliated them, and denied them benefits while Indian physicians were rarely disciplined even for major infractions like skipping work or committing errors in patient care. Wang had never threatened violence or harm against anyone at the hospital, but at the time of the shootings, senior members of the staff had labeled him as "excitable," "emotional," and unable to "control his anger," and another staff member had even judged him to be "mentally impaired."[22]

EMPLOYEES WHO MADE CLEAR, DIRECT, UNEQUIVOCAL THREATS

The fourth and final category consisted of those employees who actually made clear, direct, and unequivocal threats of violence and death to a co-worker, supervisor, or boss. These employees stood out from all the others not only in their brazen, overtly violent conduct, or the fact that they greatly outnumbered all the others combined, but also because they alone brought out the docility and passivity of both employees and management in responding collectively to the threats. The employee most likely to explode in a violent rage and murder in the workplace:

- shows little humor,
- privately admires or envies infamous workplace killers of the past,
- has difficulty with authority figures and accepting criticism—either from supervisors or peers,
- broods over a recent humiliating life event or a recent sense of being unfairly treated,
- links his self-esteem to the job—even if he is not a particularly good employee,
- definitely needs to "get a life,"
- lacks a social support system, network, or peer group outside work,
- has poor interpersonal skills—particularly poor in conflict-solving,
- has very poor verbal skills (and may often use profanity in everyday chitchat),
- has a history of violence, impulsivity, or making threats,
- currently raises his voice, intimidates, or loses temper with coworkers,
- provides evidence of planning violent activity,
- abuses alcohol or drugs (32 percent or almost a third of all homicides at work have involved alcohol),
- has a history of domestic violence, legal difficulties (bankruptcies, evictions), conflict with coworkers, or making unwelcome sexual advances,

- experienced a recent termination or is expecting termination—this might be in his imagination,
- fits into certain demographics—most violence is perpetrated by poor, young males who live in a violence-prone world; most lethal employees are middle-aged, living alone, and work in blue-collar positions that they have held for a long time, and
- is a relative of an injured or slighted worker "seeking justice" on behalf of his or her family member.

Unlike in so many other cases of workplace murder, nobody was ever the least bit surprised that Thomas McIlvane, 31, would commit an act of violence in the workplace. No protestations were heard that there was a terrible mistake, no heartfelt testimonials from church deacons that McIlvane couldn't have done such a thing, and nobody ever came forward to attest to what a good a father or husband he'd been. In fact, in the days and weeks leading up to his rampage, it seemed he did just about everything—short of running a paid advertisement in the local newspaper—to remind his coworkers that he was a mean SOB capable of violence and bent on revenge. In fact, he repeatedly warned his coworkers that if he wasn't reinstated, he would make Patrick Sherrill's earlier massacre in Edmond, Oklahoma, look like a "tea party" or "Disneyland."[23]

A former marine, Thomas McIlvane was a martial-arts enthusiast who reportedly held a black belt in kickboxing. But whatever his athletic skills, he was an incompetent postal carrier. He had been suspended once for fighting with customers on his delivery route, and was dishonorably discharged from the marines after running over a car with a tank. After several running disputes with postal managers, McIlvane was finally fired in 1990 for insubordination, the culmination of a long list of work-related offenses. He appealed the dismissal through the union grievance procedure, repeatedly warning and threatening coworkers with violence if he wasn't reinstated. "A lot of people thought he had a short fuse," said Edward Fink, 38, a postal clerk,[24] and postal officials acknowledged his threats but shrugged that it was a mail-processing plant, and it was "impossible to keep it locked up at night."[25] There was only so much they could do. Then McIlvane lost the hearing. His dismissal was final. There was no other avenue of appeal.

True to his word, six days later, on November 14, 1991, McIlvane entered the facility with a sawed-off .22-caliber Ruger rifle. He grabbed a woman and placed the rifle at her head but then let her go, saying, "You're not the one I want."[26] He wandered through a maze of offices and cubicles, looking for supervisors in particular. As he fired the weapon, the facility became a scene of utter pandemonium. More than 160 terrified postal workers tried to barricade themselves in offices or escape through windows and doors. In the next ten minutes, McIlvane found a few supervisors, shot and killed three, and injured several former coworkers before he fatally shot himself in the head.[27]

The behavioral warning signs were not always taken seriously, and a few even became the basis for innocent office humor and jokes. On May 4, 1995, James Davis, who worked in a warehouse operated by the Union Butterfield Corporation and Dormer Tools company in Asheville, North Carolina, shot and killed three coworkers and injured another. Few were surprised. In his four years at the warehouse, he had had so many altercations with coworkers that they soon dubbed him Psycho.[28] He drew a knife on one worker, choked and threatened another, and was finally fired after a shoving match. "Among themselves, many [coworkers] had discussed which doors they would use to escape if Davis returned. Some joked: 'If you see James Davis in a Ryder truck, you'd better run.'"[29] Indeed, within hours after Davis was fired, at least two employees advised management that they were afraid he would return and kill people, and a counselor in the company's employee assistance program reportedly warned management that Davis might return and engage in retaliatory physical violence.

On June 29, 2000, Dr. Jian Chen, a pathology resident at the University of Washington, shot and killed his boss and mentor Dr. Roger Haggitt and then shot and killed himself. Although the behavioral warning signs were not as obvious as those in the McIlvane case, they were still noted by coworkers and colleagues. First, it was generally known at the University of Washington's health science complex that Chen's contract wouldn't be renewed for the following year. Second, most also knew that he was having problems with Dr. Haggitt. And third, his behavior had changed, and he was even offered counseling and other help, which he flatly refused. And though he was anything but an avid gun enthusiast or outdoorsman, as early as March, three months before the murder-suicide, several workers and staff heard him talking openly about buying a gun.[30]

On November 2, 1999, Byran Koji Uyesugi, a Xerox service technician working at a Honolulu office, shot and killed his supervisor and six coworkers, and then wounded two others, in the worst mass-murder incident in Hawaii history. A fifteen-year employee, his violent, mercurial temper was well known among colleagues. He had made several threats against coworkers' lives, and was once even ordered to attend anger-management classes after he kicked in and damaged an elevator door.[31] It was also generally known that he owned a large gun collection, with as many as twenty-five handguns registered to his name, dating back to 1982, and possessed an additional eleven handguns, five rifles, and two shotguns that were owned by his father. Realizing that he had "anger" issues which could jeopardize his job, as early as 1985, according to coworkers, he spoke openly of carrying out a mass shooting if he was ever fired.[32]

In the weeks leading up to Larry Hansel's murder of two Elgar supervisors, he immersed himself deeply in right-wing religious and political thinking, and couldn't stop talking about religion and politics to coworkers and anyone else who lent an ear. But it was only in retrospect, according to S. Anthony Baron's account, that management saw what then went unnoticed, was dismissed, or was excused with responses like, "Ah, that's Larry. Sure he's a little strange, but basically he's all right."[33] Baron adds that after "the shootings, others would admit that, yes, Hansel had for months made them feel increasingly uncomfortable with his unsolicited opinions about religion and right-wing politics."[34] He seemed obsessed with both, and often talked interminably on the topics, particularly the Old Testament prophets of doom and gloom. Even away from the office, there were telltale signs. His marital problems had worsened, and he was convinced that UFOs were using his backyard as a landing site, a view he wasn't reluctant to share with people in his neighborhood. According to Baron, a typical reaction from a friend was: "You have to understand Larry. He's just over-intelligent."[35]

On June 4, 1991, three months after he was fired, Hansel returned to the plant—riding a bicycle and carrying a twelve-gauge shotgun. After electronically detonating several homemade bombs, which he had shrewdly set as diversionary distractions, he searched the second-floor hallways for the executives on his hit list. He found at least some of his victims, and shot and killed a vice president and a sales manager. Then, as stunned employees and coworkers looked on, he calmly mounted his bike and pedaled away with the shotgun tucked securely under one arm.[36]

On July 8, 2003, Doug Williams, 48, shot and killed five coworkers and wounded nine others at the Lockheed Martin defense plant in Meridian, Mississippi. Williams, who was white, was known to both coworkers and management for his hatred of blacks, and when he shot and killed six coworkers, few were surprised that five were black. He had a long history of threatening black coworkers, he had attended anger counseling, and only a month before the shootings he had paraded around the plant wearing a head garment that resembled a Ku Klux Klan hood. When told to remove the hood, he chose instead to leave the factory, and didn't return for five days.[37] A white coworker, Hubert Threat, took issue with the claim of racism, arguing that Williams was actually "mad at the world. This man had an issue with everybody. It's not just about race. It was just an excuse he was looking for."[38]

Yet the facts confirm that the killings were indeed racially motivated, and that Lockheed managers should have known beforehand that he was likely to carry out his threats. As revealed in an ABC special news report, Williams had taunted and made death threats to black coworkers as early as a year and a half before he actually carried them out. After he killed his last victim, he shot and killed himself on the factory floor. Many said that his threats against blacks had continued until the day of the killings.[39]

Julian Carlton, the Caribbean butler and handyman who in August 1914 killed seven guests at the Frank Lloyd Wright estate, was known to be "polite and smart," but was also "the most desperate, hot-headed fellow." According to one Wright biographer, Carlton was a good worker but was known to have a violent streak. He reportedly once gave the gardener an "awful calling-down" and said that "if anyone around there ever did him any dirt he would send him to hell in a minute."[40] There was also bad blood between Carlton and one of Wright's draftsmen who worked on the estate. The draftsman reportedly called Carlton a racial epithet after Carlton refused to saddle his horse. And in the days before the murders, according to Carlton's wife, he had been "acting strangely and slept with a hatchet in a bag beside his bed. She said, 'De las' I seen he was runnin' round de house, actin' crazy and talkin' bout killin' folks.'"[41]

Similar behaviors were seen with Kenneth Tornes, the Jackson, Mississippi, fireman who shot and killed two of his supervisors in the firehouse before wounding others. For months he indicated his hatred for supervisors, their arbitrariness, and how they generally treated rank-and-file firemen. And on that fateful day when he arrived at the Jackson firehouse armed with two handguns, he brushed past other rank-and-file firemen in blue shirts on his way to murder the supervisors in white.

RESPONDING TO THE WARNING SIGNS

One of the surprises of this study was the discovery that Marshall's hypothesis that human beings possess an innate aversion to killing fellow human beings might also have a corollary thesis: when coworkers and supervisors see the warning signs that murder may be imminent, they engage in collective denial and do little—or nothing. This typical collective inaction only ensures the bureaucratic inertia that prevents corrective action or any other personnel change that alters or disrupts the status quo.[42]

The McIlvane case illustrates the point. Given McIlvane's direct, clear threats of violence, some coworkers took him seriously enough to draw up escape plans.[43] But there was no formal response from his supervisors or boss, who did nothing to address the likelihood of violence, to ensure that he didn't make good on his threats. Nor was the McIlvane case unique in this respect.

After the December 18, 1997, postal massacre by Anthony Deculit, the president of the local National Association for the Advancement of Colored People in Milwaukee, Wisconsin, reminded postal authorities of his earlier warnings. He had warned postal officials that there was a "a ton of pent-up racial hostility ready to explode." He was referring to more than eighty complaints he had received from black postal workers (including Deculit) in the Milwaukee area over the past few years, especially after many were summarily demoted after complaining about work conditions. But his warnings were ignored. "I told them, 'You're going to have a shooting here,'" he said. "Now, I feel like telling them, 'I told you so.'"[44]

In the months and weeks before Dr. Jian Chen shot and killed his mentor and supervisor at the University of Washington and then shot and killed himself, it was common knowledge around the University's health science center that he was having problems on the job. It was also generally known that his contract as a pathology resident wouldn't be renewed. As a result, his behavior underwent noticeable change. He was offered counseling services and other support, which he flatly refused, and even though he was anything but an outdoorsman or a gun enthusiast who collected guns, as early as March, three months before the tragedy, coworkers and staff had heard him talk openly about buying a gun.[45] What was the response on the part of Dr. Chen's supervisors and colleagues? His supervisor and mentor (and, ironically, his only victim) was the least cautious, as he had decided there was nothing to worry about. But all the others simply avoided Dr. Chen, and discreetly closed their doors whenever he was around.[46]

Management's formal response to workplace murder—and what employees should do if suddenly caught in the middle of a workplace shooting—will be discussed and analyzed in later chapters. For now, the more important need is to identify and isolate those employees most likely to turn into killers. We've already seen that many were in fact trespassers when they murdered their coworkers and colleagues. There are still other situations and circumstances that foster the anger and rage that fuel workplace homicide. Knowledge of these situations and circumstances will not only give focus and clarity to observations of suspicious workplace conduct, but also facilitate detection and prevention long before homicidal thoughts are transformed into homicidal acts.

WHO ARE THE MURDERERS? WHERE DO THEY COME FROM?

A great many murders on the job are committed by strangers with no connection to the deceased employee, and they occur during the commission of a crime. This study, however, focuses on murderers who often worked for (or with) the victims. Indeed, one of the criteria for inclusion in the study was that the perpetrator and the victim be two adults in an employment relationship. As a result, it's perhaps ironic that the next most likely source of workplace killers was not those who were just recently hired, or the rookies on the job, but employees who had already been on the job for a relatively long period of time.

The practical implications of this irony cannot be overemphasized. What it means is that the individual most likely to show up tomorrow morning with a .357 Magnum revolver and kill an employee, or wipe out half the accounting department, is an employee, or, more precisely, a *coworker*. That employee has already been hired. There's no need to beef up the preemployment screening process, or search for the murderer-to-be in the pile of job applications stacked on the supervisor's desk. That employee has already been hired; the potential workplace murderer is already sipping coffee and munching chocolate-glazed donuts in the employee lunchroom. And they didn't just come aboard; they weren't hired just a month ago. With few exceptions, they have been working on the job for quite some time. How long, one might ask, *have* they been on the job?

According to one report, the typical workplace killer "is likely to be a 37-year-old single man who has been with a company at least four years."[47] Other experts agree that it often takes months, even a year or two, to build up enough resentment to murder coworkers and a boss. Our cases, however, suggested a substantially longer period, often as long as five, seven, even ten years. The ticking bomb was not only next door, it was ticking softly for years on end.

How, then, did these employees become workplace murderers? According to the cases, they not only had been on the job for a number of years, but the homicidal urges to which they eventually succumbed obviously took root and grew *after* they were hired. These homicidal urges were not part of their own psychological baggage brought with them when they initially applied for the job. Stated bluntly, the urges typically resulted from years of supervisory abuse and mistreatment on the job.

Research in this area is scant, and not always directly on point, as it tends to focus not specifically on workplace murder but on workplace violence in "general," or the even broader behavioral spectrum of workplace aggression. Still, some of the findings are instructive. In a 2005 study, as an example, Inness, Barling, and Turner tested the traditional assumption that supervisor-targeted aggression was situation-specific. They also investigated the relative impact of situational factors and individual differences in predicting supervisor-directed aggression by employees who held two jobs simultaneously and reported to a different supervisor on each job. What were their findings?

They wrote: "It appears that employee aggressive behavior is contingent on the quality of their experiences in that particular workplace, rather than experiences outside that workplace."[48] They concluded, first, that "employee's aggression toward a supervisor is situation specific," and second, that "both situational factors and individual differences influence the likelihood of workplace aggression, although situational factors have a substantially stronger influence."[49] In other words, whatever personal or psychological "baggage" an employee brought to the job, his or her aggression toward the supervisor was based mostly on how that supervisor treated him or her on the job. The aggression wasn't the result of the employee's poor toilet training as a toddler, nor their juvenile delinquency as a teen, nor the fact that he or she was raised by alcoholic lesbian parents in a cold-water flat with no books on the shelves.

A review of the cases suggests, moreover, that less than 2 percent of the perpetrators had violent tendencies when they first applied for the jobs, and very few would have passed the preemployment screening process if they had had criminal records or histories of mental illness. How, then, did these employees become workplace murderers? The question has been answered by Professor Barling and his colleagues, of course. But it's also been answered before, in a different context, more memorably, and in non-PhD-speak.

In Jonathan Demme's classic movie thriller *The Silence of the Lambs* (1991), FBI agent Clarice Starling (Jodie Foster) meets with Dr. Hannibal Lector (Anthony Hopkins) on several occasions in her attempts to find serial killer Buffalo Bill. During the third meeting, Lector advises her that Buffalo Bill mistakenly thinks he's a transsexual and had probably applied to the three major medical institutions that performed sexual reassignment, but had been rejected by all three. When Starling asks, "On what basis would they reject him?" Lector's answer is responsive to our question as well. He says: "*Our Billy wasn't born a criminal, Clarice. He was made one through years of systematic abuse*" (emphasis added).[50]

Years of systematic abuse. The tick, tick, tick of the bomb, as we've seen, may not be audible to some. And (to continue the time-bomb metaphor), the ticking may reach decibel levels that are beyond everybody's capacity to hear. As we have seen, the warning signs, the hints and clues that a murder is imminent may be unnoticed, disregarded, taken too lightly, even ignored. Yet the cases suggested still another reason so many warning signs went unnoticed or disregarded. The facts clearly revealed why so many behavioral clues went ignored—even by the most perceptive coworkers and supervisors with the most observant eyes.

THE "PUTZ" PARADOX

Time and time again, when faced with a workplace murder, shocked and grieving coworkers mumbled words of surprise and disbelief that a coworker had exploded in a homicidal rage. This was the response, the same tiresome refrain, that was heard even in cases where the shooting was not only foreseeable, but almost predictable. These words were heard even where coworkers knew beforehand that bad blood existed between the perpetrator and the victim, that the perpetrator carried a gun in his briefcase, and that the perpetrator had a bad temper or a "short fuse."

The Yiddish term "putz" does not appear in the *Merriam-Webster's Collegiate Dictionary* (10th Edition, 2001). In its place one is more likely to find another Yiddish term "schmuck." The Yiddish term schmuck is commonly used among American Jews and defined as a "dope," a "jerk," a "boob," or a "clumsy, bumbling fellow." The dictionary omission is due to the fact that "putz" is a far more offensive, pejorative, even obscene term.[51] The word putz literally means penis or the male member. But it's not used as an anatomical reference; the word schmuck serves that purpose. A putz is a man who is pathetically stupid, incompetent, asinine, and dumb. And the word is descriptively analogous to the decidedly non-Yiddish term "dickhead."

The employee most likely to snap and kill coworkers was usually among the most pathetic, most ineffective, socially stunted, teased, and taunted workers in the office or the plant. More than 25 percent of the workplace murderers confess that their killings were a response to having been teased and taunted on the job. In the overwhelming majority of cases, the workplace murderer was also the office loser, the jerk, generally derided as "boob"—a putz.

And therein lies the critical "connection" that's so difficult for the public to process. The connection between the workplace killer and the office putz is so difficult to appreciate and understand largely because it's deeply counterintuitive. That the office putz could—in the sixty seconds it takes to retrieve a pistol from a locker—suddenly become the most powerful individual in the company, the one person in the office whom everybody must now listen to, fear, obey, and respect, is difficult to fathom. And as difficult as it is to fathom, it's even more difficult to accept as a real-life possibility facing virtually every worker every day. This isn't the case of a competent employee slowly rising to his level of incompetence but—in a bizarre, homicidal twist on the Peter Principle—that of an incompetent employee suddenly rising to his level of imagined "competence."[52]

More than any other characteristic or trait, workplace killers like Patrick Sherrill, Jennifer San Marco, Joseph Wesbecker, Mark Barton, and so many others shared a status: they were almost never well liked and respected by the majority of their coworkers and colleagues. Even Amy Bishop, the academically brilliant science professor, was regarded as a nerdy, socially inept outsider who was acutely eccentric, if not crazy.

In almost 20 percent of the cases, the motive for revenge and murder was the constant taunting and teasing by *coworkers*—not a single supervisor or boss. In the cases of Jennifer San Marco and Yvonne Hiller, for example, we recall that both women hunted down and killed women in particular, all of whom were coworkers or colleagues. Not a single supervisor or boss was among the dead. And even in several instances where the perpetrator *did* kill a supervisor or boss, the motive was often to avenge teasing and taunting by coworkers, which the perpetrator felt the supervisor was either responsible for or had tacitly condoned. Why were so few supervisors and bosses murdered for taunting and teasing subordinate employees? For the obvious but often overlooked reason that a supervisor, manager, or boss usually doesn't *need* to tease or taunt.

With few exceptions, workplace murderers were regarded in private as "losers" or the marginal workers on the job. Even in those instances where they *did their jobs well*, they were still regarded patronizingly, with less admiration and respect, if not mild, thinly veiled contempt.[53] They were never the popular, socially skilled, articulate, or more bright and insightful employees in the office, and they obviously were not among those who were adept at modulating their anger and rage. Indeed, had they possessed any of these personality traits, it's unlikely they would have resorted to violence, or felt it appropriate to address a workplace problem by retrieving a .357 Magnum from a truck.

The cases showed dozens of heavily armed perpetrators who, having just murdered the coworkers and supervisors they disliked, casually strolled past fellow employees with whom they had no quarrel. Some even addressed these coworkers cordially, or said "hello" as they continued shooting at someone else or reloaded their guns. They rarely (if ever) shot anyone they liked or those they thought liked them. (Even Sherrill, on the day before he slaughtered his coworkers, warned a single female clerk—the only person in the building who had treated him respectfully—by suggesting obliquely that perhaps she shouldn't come to work the next day.) With very few exceptions, they shot and killed those they disliked, or those they knew disliked them. Part of the reason the really serious mass murderers—like Sherrill, Barton, Farley, and Harris—killed so many was their realization that nobody in the office liked them anyway. If *nobody* in the office likes you, there's no reason to discriminate. As already noted in chapter 7, the cases suggest that the boss or supervisor most likely to be shot and killed was always among the least competent, the least skilled, and the least liked. We now know that the employee most likely to grab a gun and kill that boss or supervisor is often among the least respected and admired, and is often considered the office putz. As the factors that explain why some bosses or supervisors are murdered also explain why some employees are driven to kill, the line of cause and effect is clear, and the dynamic of this deadly connection is complete.

Careful analyses of the cases strongly suggest (or permit the inference) that even though survivors of workplace murders were uniformly shocked and sadly surprised at the death and bloodshed, at the sudden, violent loss of coworkers and friends, they were also equally shocked and surprised at the *identity* of the coworker who wielded the gun.

It was, in a word, the supreme irony that the office jerk, the most pathetically incompetent, the least respected, least admired, who was the butt of the whispered jokes—the office putz!—was also the most likely to arrive at work tomorrow morning with a loaded .357 Magnum revolver and blow your brains out.

Chapter Eleven

Ironies, Trends, and Troublesome Facts

Americans are fascinated with the law, particularly legal entertainment, due largely to television dramas that date from the popular black-and-white TV dramas of a half century ago. The fascination likely started with weekly dramas like *Perry Mason*, which spawned scores of other legal dramas over the next five decades and countless movies on the silver screen. And today even these are supplemented by the broadcast of at least a dozen actual courtroom cases that feature the adjudication of actual cases by actual municipal-court judges, like the ever-popular *Judge Judy*.

AMERICAN WORKERS' FALSE LEGAL KNOWLEDGE AND MISINFORMATION

Americans are thus unique in how long they have been exposed to legal counsel and advice and the hours of legal knowledge absorbed in an adult lifetime. The shows are phenomenally successful, of course, as their plots are driven and ultimately resolved through investigations and points of law—civil or criminal. As a result, virtually every mentally competent adult in the United States has an opinion on many of the most complicated issues in the law, or ever decided by the US Supreme Court, even if they lack an adequate understanding of the underlying legal principles and case law.

As a further result, most adults also think they know their legal rights, especially in an area like employment law, since most people have jobs. And they express their views on matters of hiring, firing, and so on by American companies—from the *Fortune* 500 companies down to the local supermarket staff. The irony, of course, is that much of this knowledge is wrong. Among Western industrialized nations, American workers probably know the least about workers' rights, and studies show a profound lack of knowledge about the exercise of First Amendment freedoms in the workplace. Many have probably lost jobs, or at least earned the ire of a supervisor or two, by insisting on rights they never had, having been terribly misinformed by a close friend or an article they read in the latest issue of *TV Guide*. And the confusion and misinformation are usually greatest in the area of First Amendment rights of free speech and the exercise of religion in the workplace.

First Amendment scholar Bruce Barry writes: "Americans cling to a stubborn, if noble, delusion that a right to speak freely trumps an employer's right to control the expressive activity of its workers. In a national survey on rights in the workplace commissioned in 2001 by the AFL-CIO fully 80 percent of respondents said that it is illegal to fire an employee for expressing political views with which the employer disagrees. Unfortunately, those respondents were wrong—some states have laws protecting employees from being punished for political activity, but most workers enjoy no such protection."[1] Indeed, even if political speech is statutorily protected conduct in the workplace, it's still difficult to prove that the expression of those political views formed the basis for the employer's termination. For this reason, employers enjoy what one labor law expert calls "a nearly untrammeled power to censor and punish their employees."[2]

An example of the employer's power and control over the workplace was recently provided on a matter perhaps even more basic to the workplace than the exercise of free speech. Few workplace features are as basic or taken for granted as the traditional lunch break. This almost universally assumed "right," however, isn't legally required. In fact, the California Supreme Court, traditionally such a progressive, even liberal, appellate court, recently surprised many in the legal community by holding that employers and businesses were not legally required to ensure that workers take a legally mandated lunch break.[3] The unanimous decision, handed down in mid-April 2012, affected many thousands of businesses and millions of workers across the state.

The opinion was issued after workers' attorneys argued that abuses were routine and widespread because many companies were not required to issue direct orders to take lunch. They argued that the employers took advantage of the workers, who were often reluctant to leave their job stations and busy coworkers during a hectic period. The case, originally filed almost a decade ago, was filed by worker organizations, which alleged that many businesses abused the status quo and unfairly denied workers a lunch break. But the court disagreed and sided with the employers, arguing that such a requirement was best formulated, ratified, and ultimately administered by the workers themselves.[4]

This general lack of knowledge, or misinformation, on the part of most American workers leads all too often to the Hansel Syndrome, named after a workplace murderer, Larry Hansel who, like many employees, had no idea how few legal rights employees typically have against their employers, especially in right-to-work states. Some of the gripes often heard from disgruntled workers include "I was wrongfully fired," "I have a right to see my file," "I demand my coffee break now," "I'm working in a hostile environment," "I exercised my First Amendment rights," "My boss invaded by privacy," "I was retaliated against after I complained," and "I was discriminated against because my boss doesn't like me." In fact, however, unless a worker resides in Montana—the only state in the nation with a law that specifically states that an employee can be fired only "for cause"—none of these rights are enjoyed by American workers in the private sector, and not all apply even in the public sector. [5]

Larry Hansel was an electronics technician for the Elgar Corporation who, in early June 1991, shot and killed the two Elgar executives responsible for his termination. He had been fired two months earlier for grossly inappropriate office behavior, which included the open espousal of extremist views in politics and religion (he often quoted at length from the Old Testament prophets of doom) and his political involvement with right-wing activist groups. [6] The first tragedy of the Hansel case, of course, was the death of the two executives. But the second tragedy was Hansel's mistaken belief that the executives had fired him illegally. They hadn't fired him illegally—for the simple reason that Hansel never had those rights in the first place. Is it possible that Hansel murdered two corporate executives, and will spend the rest of his life in jail, solely because he misunderstood something he read in *TV Guide*?

The practical effect of the Hansel Syndrome is that employees are falsely emboldened or empowered in their day-to-day dealings with management. And when they meet with failure or fall short of stated goals, the sense of frustration and loss is only deepened or enhanced. The realization that they started out with a lot less than they thought only doubles the sense of collective disenfranchisement and loss. It also inhibits future collective efforts to preserve those few rights that do exist—both for individual workers and for workers collectively as part of a bargaining unit.

LET 'EM EAT CAKE: TOUGHER BOSSES AND TOUGHER MARKETS

This general lack of knowledge extends as well to other areas of the employment relationship, including the day-to-day mundane affairs of the office and the workings of the assembly line. Many workers don't realize, for example, that the law protects such antisocial conduct as a boss or supervisor yelling, screaming, bullying, tearing doors from the hinges, and berating employees in front of coworkers and the whole office. Nor is the scope of permissible supervisor/boss office behavior tolerated as a mere function of socioeconomics, education, culture, and class—the last resort of drunken sailors, longshoremen, truck drivers, teamsters, and grooms at the track.

On July 30, 2010, Kevin Morrissey, 52, committed suicide after several weeks of what was reportedly relentless office bullying by his boss. Morrissey, the managing editor of the award-winning literary magazine *Virginia Quarterly Review*, was so distressed that he made more than eighteen telephone calls during the two weeks before he finally committed suicide. He sought help from the department of human services, the university ombudsman, and even the faculty/employee assistance center, but none came. Though Morrissey had suffered from depression for years, both his sister and his coworkers insisted that the suicidal element arose only after the bullying by his boss, Ted Genaways, BA, MA, MFA, PhD, a brilliant translator of Spanish poetry, an expert on Walt Whitman, a Guggenheim fellow, and the editor of seven volumes of poetry.[7] Though Genaways was later cleared by the university of any wrongdoing, he left the position in late May 2012.[8]

The law, unfortunately, does not protect an employee from a bad, ill-tempered supervisor or boss. With all the laws and regulations that govern and restrict so many other areas of modern life—from rent-controlled apartments, drugs, cars, medicine, advertising, tobacco, and medicine to the manufacture and shipment of foods in interstate commerce—the American workplace remains, ironically, a behavioral Wild West. In the absence of a contract for a term of employment, the "employment at will" doctrine rules. This means that an employer may terminate or fire an employee at any time and for any reason (so long as it isn't an illegal reason), just as the employee can (at least in theory) quit or leave the job for any reason. But because the employer can terminate the worker at will, it can do anything short of termination as well—such as making the job an unpleasant place to work, even a living hell.[9]

The broad behavioral latitude afforded the boss in the American workplace, however, assumes a different guise, and serves different purposes, in an increasingly competitive and globalized economy in which the marketplace requires increased productivity with fewer personnel hours. As a result, more businesses and employers, as an example, now advocate a harder, tougher stance in what everyone concedes is a tougher, much more competitive market.

This new mood is perhaps best personified by business leaders like George Cloutier, the 63-year-old founder and CEO of American Management Services and an author whose hard-nosed advice is directed to small and medium-sized businesses.[10] Cloutier's tough-as-nails, take-no-prisoners approach isn't likely to be accepted by everybody, and his philosophy is bound to alienate others. His essential rules of thumb and business advice include always pay yourself first; never hire relatives, because they have a sense of entitlement; never hesitate to fire a poor performer; the recession is just an excuse for poor performance; fear is the best motivator, the idea of loving your employees couldn't be more crazy or insane; teamwork is grossly overrated; and so on. [11]

Cloutier's business philosophy might be difficult to accept, and definitely wouldn't be taught at the Wharton School. But his message, according to some, is a "gift to the millions of business owners who face financial mediocrity or failure, and need some serious tough love to pull themselves back into solvency." [12]

Whatever the long-term effects of Cloutier's philosophy, the clear impact is to increase the anxiety and tension that now pervade the American workplace, which only enhances the resentment and rage that fuel workplace homicide. An employee who's ignorant of his or her workplace rights; who labors under an abusive, bullying supervisor who's itching to fire the employee; is in a situation that only nudges the employee closer and closer to anger, to aggression, and finally to violence.

As the legal system generally tolerates management behavioral excesses and abuse in the workplace, Congress and the various state legislatures are understandably reluctant to fashion a general tort law for the workplace. The rationale is that, however necessary such a statute might be to prohibit and curb growing problems like office "mobbing," bullying, and so on, such a statute would also constitute a questionable intrusion into the marketplace and an interference with market forces.

A general tort law for the workplace, the argument continues, would also deny employers and businesses an effective management tool and an incentive to prod or nudge an unproductive or complacent workforce to become more competitive in a global market. Congress and the various legislatures share the belief that these decisions should remain within the exclusive business judgment and expertise of the boss, and any interference with the underlying dynamic would be inadvisable as against both common sense and long-standing public policy.

THE RISING STAKES OF UNEMPLOYMENT/THE PERILS OF LOSING A JOB

In the absence of a general tort law for the workplace, the wide behavioral latitude afforded management also influences the methods and procedures used to recruit and hire new employees. In recent years, a number of employers have quietly adopted the policy of hiring only those applicants that are *already employed*. In other words, if the job applicant is unemployed, he or she won't even be considered for employment, and only those applicants who already have a job will be considered for the position.

Though this callous hiring criterion appears at first glance to affect only those outside the workforce or without jobs, the practical effect is significantly broader. Much like the Cloutier philosophy, this practice, despite its appearance, actually impacts almost as negatively on employees who are already on the job. By requiring that job applicants be currently employed, the employer also raises the stakes of being fired in the minds of those already on the job—who now have an even greater fear of being replaced. This dynamic of fear and dread of losing one's job serves only to feed the insecurity, anger, frustration, and rage that fuel workplace violence and ultimately homicide.

Again, the point that must be emphasized is that these management behaviors, though functionally discrete and divorced from the crisis of workplace murder, nevertheless enhance the anger, frustration, and insecurity of those already on the job, which fuels the violence that leads almost inexorably to bloodshed and workplace homicide. If securing gainful employment is only made more difficult if the applicant doesn't already have a job, the stakes of losing one's job are raised that much higher in the minds of those already employed. And it gets worse.

If people are understandably upset when they're fired from their jobs, they will likely react even more angrily, even violently, if they're fired in states and cities where debtors' prisons are slowly, gradually, but inexorably making a comeback. In a growing number of states, losing one's job or getting fired may ultimately be a matter not of life and death, of course, but of physical liberty and going to jail—which often amounts to *civil* death. Losing one's job can now be a matter of freedom or imprisonment, because people who fall behind in their debts and can't pay their bills—even relatively small amounts—can now be arrested, handcuffed, and hauled off to jail.

Though the United States abolished debtors' prisons in the 1930s,[13] more than a third of the states now authorize state and local police to arrest people and haul them off to jail if they haven't paid overdue bills. These outstanding bills range from bills for health care services and auto loans to maxed out credit cards. In parts of Illinois, in fact, "debt collectors commonly use publicly funded courts, sheriff's deputies, and county jails to pressure people who owe even small amounts to pay up."[14]

Under some of these statutes—enacted in seventeen states, including Georgia, Louisiana, Michigan, Ohio, and Washington—the American Civil Liberties Union found that growing numbers of people were being incarcerated. These debtors turned inmates included a woman who was arrested on four different occasions for failure to pay $251 in fines and court costs related to a minor misdemeanor or conviction, and a mentally challenged juvenile who had been imprisoned by a local judge over a prior conviction of theft of school supplies.[15] In Herrin, Illinois, for example, a breast-cancer survivor, Lisa Lindsay, ended up in jail because she owed a 280-dollar medical bill, which she had erroneously been advised she didn't have to pay. [16]

Of course, a number of debt collectors, as well as local governments, take advantage of several statutory loopholes and argue, creatively, that the debtors aren't being arrested and imprisoned for nonpayment of bills, but *technically* for failing to pay various legal fines or failure to appear in court. These are often couched in terms like "contempt of court" fees. These courts are flourishing across the country, and lawmakers in the Illinois House of Representatives, for example, have recently enacted measures that prohibit the imprisonment of state residents if they cannot pay their bills. [17]

Still other states require "poverty penalties," including late fees, payment plan fees, and exorbitant interest rates when people cannot pay all of their debts at once, according to a report by New York University's Brennan Center for Justice. Alabama, as an example, charges a hefty 30 percent collection fee, while Florida, not to be outdone, allows private debt collectors to add a 40 percent surcharge on the principal or original debt. And several Florida counties use these "collection courts," where debtors are legally subject to imprisonment but have no constitutional right to counsel or a public defender. [18]

In an era of shrinking municipal budgets and state fiscal shortfalls, double-digit unemployment and the pervasive effects of a recession, local governments are desperately seeking new sources of revenues to subsidize the funds raised by an already overburdened property-tax base. In response, many states now impose new and frequently onerous "user fees" on individuals with criminal convictions, according to the authors of the New York University Brennan Center report. The authors warn that "far from being easy money, these fees impose severe—and often hidden—costs on communities, taxpayers, and indigent people convicted of crimes. They create new paths to prison for those unable to pay their debts, make it harder to find employment and housing, as well as to meet child-support obligations." [19] As these practices proliferate and gain a foothold in state and local governments across the country, they slowly raise the stakes of getting fired, and they intensify tenfold the dire consequences of losing a job. Even more critically, however, they also gradually, almost imperceptibly, start to *criminalize poverty*.

How do these practices raise the stakes of getting fired? And how do the raised stakes of getting fired increase the violence in the workplace? They raise the stakes in two ways. First, where John Doe, an angry employee, once contemplated a nonviolent response to a workplace indignity or slight, since he now faces almost-certain termination anyway, there's less incentive *not* to be aggressive on the job. Second, even though he's safely employed, the thought of losing his job, the consequences of facing life without food, money, and so on, is so frightening and scary that he now both values the job as the source of his safety and security, but also hates it, too, as a deepening imprisonment and enslavement—from which, in either case, he will never escape.

RISING LEVELS OF CLINICAL DEPRESSION

As millions of Americans, both employed and unemployed, continue to suffer the worst unemployment in a generation, as the economy continues to stall and job creation and growth peter out, workplace anxiety and insecurity feed workplace anger and frustration, and people also become depressed. Jeffrey Pfeiffer, noting the nexus between workplace anger and workplace violence, writes: "When people lose their jobs, they get angry and depressed . . . Angry and depressed people who believe they have been treated unfairly can lose psychological control and exact vengeance on those they deem responsible."[20]

That millions of American workers suffer from depression is a deeply troubling fact, yet it's not surprising, especially given the growing use of prescription drugs, particularly antidepressants. What *is* surprising about these findings, however, is how the demographics for both the diagnosis and treatment for depression have changed in recent years. Given the high percentage of workplace murderers who were clinically depressed, or at least under the influence of antidepressant medications at the time they committed their crimes, the changing demographics do not bode well for a decrease in workplace murder in the foreseeable future.

The rapidly increasing number of people who suffer from depression, according to Daniel Goleman, author of the best-selling *Emotional Intelligence*,[21] is virtually overshadowed by the fact that those who suffer from the disease are getting younger and younger. Goleman argues that the demographics for the onset of clinical depression are getting younger and younger every year. And, as already noted, this is critical in light of the number of workplace murderers who were on prescribed antidepressant medication at the time they snapped in a homicidal rage and killed in the workplace.

Goleman writes:

> Although the likelihood of becoming depressed rises with age, the greatest increases are among young people. For those born after 1955, the likelihood they will suffer a major depression at some point in life is, in many countries, three times or more greater than for their grandparents. Among Americans born before 1905, the rate of those having a major depression over a lifetime was just 1 percent; for those born between 1945 and 1954, the chances of having had a major depression before age thirty-four are ten times greater than for those born between 1905 and 1914. And for each generation the onset of a person's first episode of depression has tended to occur at an ever-earlier age.[22]

Each of these five factors—employees' ignorance of how few rights they actually enjoy in the workplace, a falsely emboldened workforce in which many are addicted to antidepressant drugs, the absence of a general workplace tort law, the criminalization of poverty, and the revival of debtors' prisons—may seem as separate and discrete as the five fingers and seem to bear little if any relationship to violence on the job. But all five factors actually function together, like fingers on a hand, to cause, encourage, and perpetuate the crime of workplace homicide.

MORE GUNS IN THE WORKPLACE—FOR EVERYBODY, EVERYWHERE

Although some of the major battles between gun-control advocates and members of the National Rifle Association (NRA) and others have been waged on the national stage, current battles are now being waged over access to firearms by employees in the workplace. Several states—like Georgia, Mississippi, Maine, Florida, Kentucky, Utah, and Arizona—have enacted so-called workplace protection laws. These laws permit gun owners with licenses to carry concealed weapons, to keep handguns and other firearms in their personal vehicles while parked on their employer's parking lot or in a parking garage.

The rationale for these legislative initiatives is that private citizens feel the need to assume some responsibility for their own protection and safety, especially during difficult economic times when a recession tightens local budgets and reduces local municipal services like fire and police protection. They argue that employees "should be permitted to keep guns in their vehicles at work in order to protect themselves while traveling to and from work and during their personal breaks away from work, such as lunch."[23]

And, of course, there's merit to both sides of the issue, as opponents of these laws argue that "allowing employees to keep guns in their cars will increase both the instances of workplace violence and the associated costs."[24] The opposition points out that in cases in which an employee loses his or her temper, even level-headed, mature employees may have rash thoughts, and with a loaded firearm so easily available, there's no cooling off period during which they can change their minds or reconsider their plans. As one business owner put it: "I don't want to be staring at the gun of someone who comes back into the building after being terminated. Even law-abiding individuals do crazy things in a highly charged moment. Getting into their car and seeing that gun . . . who knows what could happen."[25] Businesses and other employers also oppose the laws as a governmental intrusion on their property rights, since they can no longer control what can or cannot be brought onto their property. In short, the "rights of the gun owner trump the right of the property owner and that is bad for business."[26]

Some of the states have gone further, not only permitting the employee to keep a firearm in the vehicle while on the employer's property, but also providing a cause of action to the employee, who can sue the employer who doesn't permit him or her to keep the firearm in the vehicle while on the employer's property. Some states also award damages and attorney's fees to those employees who prevail in court against an employer.[27]

Of course, during the two years' research in this study, not a single newspaper account was ever found of a licensed gun owner, either in Kentucky or elsewhere, who was armed with a firearm in his or her car and foiled or prevented a robbery or other crime during his or her lunch break. On the other hand, dozens of cases were found in which a just-fired employee merely stepped to his or her vehicle in an adjacent parking lot, retrieved a firearm, returned to the work site, and then shot and killed coworkers and/or bosses just minutes after a disciplinary hearing, a reprimand, or some other perceived insult.

On June 25, 2008, Wesley N. Higdon, 25, a press operator in Henderson, Kentucky, shot and killed five coworkers at a plastics plant in the rural western Kentucky town and then committed suicide. Angry and upset, he retrieved a handgun from his car just two hours after an argument with his supervisor about wearing his safety goggles and talking on his cell phone while on the assembly line. Higdon kept a .45-caliber pistol in his car, which was/is legal under Kentucky's workplace protection law.[28]

The language in workplace protection statutes varies widely from state to state, and not every state has enacted these measures, but the company will generally be in full compliance by observing approximately seven different steps.[29]

The NRA and other pro-gun lobbyists and groups, however, did not stop at the interiors of cars and trucks that sit in the employer's parking lot. They have aggressively pushed and prodded various state legislatures to enact measures that are even more far-reaching. And the trend is growing. In Ohio, for example, an individual with the appropriate license can walk into a bar and order a drink with a fully loaded .357 Magnum tucked inside his windbreaker. And the groups didn't stop at Ohio. In just the last three or four years, more than twenty-two "states have weakened or eliminated laws restricting the possession of concealed weapons [and also eased the] eligibility and testing requirements for obtaining a permit, opening up public places to concealed weapons, and expanding legal protections for those who put their guns to use."[30]

As Luis Tallek has stated, "In a society where 45% of households have at least one gun," increasing numbers of people will act out their anger by using a gun. Since a third of those guns are also loaded and unlocked at all times, "guns immediately up the ante" in any confrontation. What could have been a loud shouting match or even a fistfight is now life threatening.[31]

As this trend permits more guns into more places—restaurants, classrooms, bars—more states allow more freedoms in this area than they did just a decade ago. Indeed, federal legislation reportedly currently awaits the president's signature before it becomes law to allow each and every state to recognize every other state's permit to carry weapons, much as they recognize each other's drivers' licenses. The greater availability of guns, in a greater number of places, will definitely contribute to the rise of workplace violence. And that "violence" with guns on the job almost always assumes the form of workplace homicide.

WORKPLACE MURDER AS A PRIVATE FAMILY AFFAIR, OR *OYAKO-SHINJU*

Among the 350-odd cases that make up the basis for this study, some occasionally revealed fact patterns that were ultimately so gender-slanted or male- or female-exclusive that one gender or the other was statistically invisible. Such was the case with the following line of workplace homicides, in which the total absence of women is a statistical exclusion that justifies the exclusive use of the male pronoun.

The fact pattern of most of these cases consisted of a man who, after being laid off or fired, returned to his job and killed the manager or boss he felt was responsible for his misfortune. The fact pattern that distinguished the following cases from all the others was what the man did just before he packed his shotguns and rifles in the car and drove to the workplace: he went back into the bedroom and brutally murdered his wife or girlfriend, or his mother, along with the children and other members of the family, sometimes even Fido the dog. Only then did he drive to the workplace, where he proceeded to kill his supervisor and coworkers who got him fired from the job. In these cases, the private, family murders were a kind of deadly prologue to the workplace murders. And they may represent a troublesome trend.

As already noted, a man is far more likely than a woman to commit suicide after losing his job—usually the sole means by which he provides for his family, his home, and those he cares for and loves. In this situation, the man murders his family, then commits suicide. This behavior is akin to a ritual in the Japanese tradition where despondent parents not only take their lives, but take those of their children as well. Known as oyako-shinju, the parent-child suicide is considered an act of mercy and the last demonstration of the parents' wish that their children not become financial burdens to society or charges of the state. Men in the US typically are not burdened with a cultural legacy of ritualistic suicide, but the effect is the same.

These men are angry, desperately unemployed, and burdened with mortgage payments, medical bills, and other debts typically incurred to maintain a wife and family, including a modest home, insurance, and a car. They are also heavily armed. And all too often, the dynamic becomes one in which a man with a .357 Magnum—unable to exact revenge against the evil boss who eliminated his job—turns the gun *away* from the boss, toward the burden itself, to eliminate what made the job so painfully indispensable in the first place: the wife and kids.

In early January 2009, Ervin Lupoe, 35, and his wife were both fired from their positions as technicians at Kaiser Permanente Medical Center in West Los Angeles. Deciding that he had no options, and faced with a wife and five young children, Ervin Lupoe shot and killed his wife and each of his five young children (all between ages 2 and 8), and then committed suicide.[32]

The perpetrator of the infamous Bath Massacre in May 1927, Andrew P. Kehoe, as already noted, was angry about a property tax that was levied for construction of a new school building. Before he exacted revenge by blowing up the school, killing thirty-eight children (ages 7 through 12) and injuring fifty-eight others and then committing suicide, even before he left his kitchen with the bomb materials waiting in his car, he first went back into his bedroom and bludgeoned his wife to death.[33]

On August 1, 1966, Charles Whitman, 25, a student at the University of Texas at Austin and an ex-marine, shot and killed fourteen people and wounded thirty others during a shooting rampage on and around the Austin campus. He killed three people inside the university tower before he took an elevator up the tower and killed ten more victims from the twenty-ninth floor of the observation deck. Just hours before his rampage atop the tower, however, he had murdered first his mother and then his wife at their respective homes just a few blocks away.[34] In early August 1989, John Merlin Taylor brought a .22-caliber pistol to work at the Orange Glen, California, post office, shot and killed two coworkers, and then wounded a third before he committed suicide—having shot and killed his wife at home an hour before he left for work.[35]

We recall the bankrupt Iowa farmer, Dale Burr, 63, whose financial problems had claimed his farm machinery, his stored grains, and his beloved quarter horses. On December 9, 1985, Burr drove to the Hills Bank and Trust Company of Hills, Iowa (population 550), raised his twelve-gauge shotgun and killed bank president John Hughes, then shot and killed a neighbor before he shot and killed himself. Earlier that morning, however, he had shot and killed his wife of forty years.[36] There's also the case of Frederick Williams, 41, a Memphis, Tennessee, fireman who in July 2000 summoned the local fire department and police after he set his house on fire. When the firemen (his colleagues) arrived, he opened fire, killing three firemen and a police officer before they found the body of his new wife, whom he had killed just before he set the fire.[37] John E. List, 44, a devout Lutheran accountant who had just lost his job, explained why he methodically shot and killed his wife, mother, and each of his three adolescent and teenage children. That was his only option—otherwise they would end up on public assistance or welfare and receiving food stamps, which would subject them to community derision and ridicule.[38]

The victims of these cases were almost always female—wives, girlfriends, mothers, children, and other members of the family—and the cases often ended with the man's suicide. These cases of workplace murder were, of course, among the bloodiest, and included the cases of Michael McLendon, Kenneth Tornes, Bruce Alvin Miller, Gene R. Simmons, Mark Barton, Ramon Salcido, Tracey Moss, Juan Rolon, Steven Harold Smith, and John Merlin Taylor, among others.[39]

In one sense these preworkplace murders signaled a no-turning-back decision by the perpetrator. The murder of a wife and family members even before the murderer left for the workplace means that he had not only crossed the Rubicon psychologically, but the future murders he had planned were now all but inevitable. For reasons not readily apparent, these men had created a deadly nexus between their home lives and the family members they supposedly loved, and the workplace, whose supervisors and other employees were the objects of their hate.

By far the most troublesome aspect of this trend was not that it represented a large percentage of the cases in the study. Clearly, it did not. Though numerically significant enough—representing about 5 percent of the cases—the most distressing points to note here are that (1) these perpetrators represent almost 30 percent of the workplace killers who were married, and (2) not a single case in this especially violent, bloodthirsty group—not a single case—involved a perpetrator who was female.

OCCUPYING WALL STREET AND THE VULNERABILITY OF THE CEO

On September 22, 2008, Lalit Kishore Chaudhary, the CEO of Graziano Transmission of India, agreed to meet with more than a hundred former employees to discuss and negotiate the status of fifteen workers who had been fired a few months before. During the negotiations, however, a brawl erupted, more than thirty people were injured (including two company managers who received serious head injuries), and Chaudhary was killed from a blow to the head.[40]

Of the ten CEOs that were murdered in the last decade, only three were targets of disgruntled employees. Those were Indian CEO Sid Agrawal, who was murdered by a laid-off engineer (one of the perpetrators in this study);

another Indian CEO, Lalit Kishore Chaudhary, who was brutally beaten to death by a crowd of disgruntled factory workers; and Maurice J. Spagnoletti, a Puerto Rican banking CEO who was shot down, likely because he had ordered the auditing of a particular Puerto Rican bank in which there had likely been some fiscal chicanery. And of the three CEOs who were killed by former employees over "terms and conditions" of employment, only Sid Agrawal was murdered in the United States.

Workplace violence is on the rise in countries like India,[41] and violent clashes between workers and management have started to erupt even in the remote regions of China. This violence not only reflects the growing economic and industrial power of the two countries, it also reflects a corresponding rise in expectations that the newly developed power fosters in members of the workforce, both as individuals and as workers in a collective group. Each sector—capital, labor, government—consciously flexes its muscles in the global marketplace. And, as the clashes show, not even the highest levels of management can always escape the violence that ensues. Except in the United States.

Rarely is grassroots worker violence inflicted on those at the highest levels of American corporate management, the senior managers—or the CEO. And this type of murder—or boardroom "assassination"—to which Sid Agrawal fell victim is still a very rare occurrence in the United States.[42] The face of billionaire CEOs in America is misleading. That face is now a friendly composite of men like Warren Buffet, the avuncular, plainspoken midwesterner who gives millions every year to philanthropic causes and dispenses homespun wisdom and investment homilies from the porch of the house in which he's lived for thirty years. The image is completed by men that include media mogul Ted Turner, or the still boyish Mark Zuckerberg, the "boy-next-door" titan behind the phenomenon known as Facebook. All are highly likeable, photogenic men who consistently draw the biggest applause at commencement exercises, come across as decent human beings, and annually donate billions of philanthropic dollars to causes all over the world.

What goes virtually unnoticed is that none of the highly visible, familiar billionaire CEOs in America come from the financial/banking sectors. Where are *those* CEO billionaires? Who's the CEO of BankAmerica? CitiBank? Capital One? Or American Express? Most Americans don't even know their names, let alone what they look like or where they live. That they're generally unknown and anonymous to the American public of course is no accident. They know (if the public doesn't) that they have made their billions in ways that create unemployment, home foreclosures, bankruptcies, and unpaid bills and that drain and cheat the middle class. They also know that their best protection—from both public scorn and even criminal prosecution—is to remain faceless, anonymous, and unknown.

But this may change. Ever since the Occupy Wall Street (OWS) movement sprang into existence in the spring of 2011, it has remained more or less in the headlines for its protests and calls to the citizenry to "confront the ruling class" and to focus attention on the unprecedented economic inequities that exist and continue to grow across the country. Along with the media publicity, however, it has also been justly criticized for several sound reasons.

First, the OWS movement lacks both a coherent ideology and an identifiable formal leadership that can impose an orthodoxy. Second, its membership is a loose hodgepodge of those too easily inclined toward the "fun" aspects of political movements rather than the drudgeries required to effectuate socioeconomic change. Third, there is only passion and excitement, and no indication of a serious attempt to organize a formal movement bent on true socioeconomic change. "Given a choice between, say, drafting a legislative proposal to help the poor versus walking down the middle of the Brooklyn Bridge to instigate a media-circus police confrontation, the latter wins every time."[43] Finally, the OWS movement lacks a concrete agenda and an established set of attainable goals, and without this incentive, there can be no payoff. Besides, "who can get excited over researching the impact of the minimum wage on poverty? But five minutes on the local 6:00PM news and screaming 'police brutality' is such great fun—enough fun to keep doing it, at least for a day or two more."[44]

Many of the perpetrators included in the study who were fired, or suffered some other economic catastrophe—like Andrew Kehoe, Charles Whitman, Merlin Taylor, John E. List, R. Gene Simmons, Mark Barton, Ervin Lupoe, and others—could rarely name a specific individual or person who was directly responsible for their loss. The loss resulted instead from a series of coldly detached business decisions and market "forces" that dictated the layoffs, shutdowns, plant closings, and other cutbacks that caused the losses of so many others as well. For others, however, the nature of the business—or the structure of the corporate leadership—is such that a specific individual *can* be named and identified.

If, despite all odds, OWS gains momentum, increasing numbers of citizens will make the critical connection between their worsening economic plight and the economic upheaval of the last decade, on the one hand, and the decisions that reflect the policies of Wall Street and the *Fortune* 500 CEOs, on the other. As more citizens recognize the relationship between their worsening plight (unemployment; the bankruptcies, evictions, repossessed cars, and unpaid medical bills); and the deepening inequities brought by the titans of Wall Street and the CEOs, they may conveniently—eventually—focus their anger, rage, and energies on the real battlefield: Wall Street, and the real enemies of the shrinking middle class. Including the CEO.

THE CHANGING BASIS FOR WORKPLACE VIOLENCE

When Amy Bishop was denied tenure by the UAH faculty, she filed a sex discrimination suit with the EEOC in 2006. The EEOC is the federal agency charged with hearing and adjudicating employment issues, and in fiscal 2011 the agency received nearly 100,000 complaints of employment bias, the most in its forty-six-year history. But the nature of the agency's most recent complaints is revealing. They reflect a changing dynamic in the American workplace, and in the direction of workplace violence as well.

Amy Bishop's case notwithstanding, the number of cases filed with the EEOC in 2011 that alleged racial discrimination fell by 1 percent, those based on sex discrimination dropped by 2 percent, and sexual harassment cases dropped by 3 percent.[45] The notable difference, however, was that charges of bias based on ancestry or country of origin didn't drop at all—they rose by a whopping 9.5 percent, by far the largest increase in any category.[46] Experts explain the rise in these specific areas as due to the growing diversity of the nation's workforce. Former general counsel for the EEOC Ron Cooper explains, "We're seeing more workers from India, Pakistan and other countries that bring additional religious complexity to the workforce."[47]

These demographic changes have already started to play themselves out in the workplace. That these shifting demographic and religious behaviors have already generated acts of physical aggression in the workplace should not be a surprise. Nor should it be a surprise that the aggression will escalate to physical violence and the physical violence will fuel homicides. Many cases of what the EEOC euphemistically refers to as "harassment" are in fact barely disguised cases of assault. The EEOC itself concedes "that the increase in religious harassment charges since 2001 can be attributed to retaliation from the attacks of September 11, 2011"[48] and the victims of these acts of "harassment" were "perceived [by their coworkers and supervisors] to be Muslim, Arab, South Asian or Sikh."[49]

The case of Susan Bashir illustrates the point. Susan Bashir, a 41-year-old married mother of a teenage daughter, sued the telecommunications giant AT&T for what she claimed was a pattern of offensive and discriminatory conduct. She claimed that the discriminatory conduct by her supervisors began when she converted to Islam in 2005, six years after she had been hired by the prestigious *Fortune* 500 company as a network technician.[50] After Bashir started to wear a religious head scarf known as a *hijab*, and also started to attend Friday mosque services, her managers and coworkers at the Kansas City office called her names, including "terrorist," and told her she was going to hell. One of Bashir's managers at AT&T repeatedly told her to remove her *hijab*, insulted her for wearing it, and once even physically grabbed her and tried to rip the *hijab* off her head, according to documents filed in the suit.[51]

Bashir complained to AT&T's office of human resources, and then filed a formal complaint with the EEOC in which she charged the company with discrimination based on her religion. She was later fired, in 2010. After several days of hearing testimony and deliberation, a jury in Kansas City, Missouri, ordered AT&T to pay Bashir $5 million in punitive damages, in addition to 120,000 dollars in actual damages.[52]

Bashir said that in March 2005, before she filed her charges with the EEOC, she had called AT&T's employee help line, and also asked the company to provide sensitivity training for her coworkers. "It was a worthless call," she said. "Nothing ever changed." The harassment by her managers and coworkers only continued, and after she filed the complaint, some of her coworkers got angry with her, which led to a final encounter with her boss. Bashir said she became so stressed out that she couldn't return to work, and had even requested a transfer within the company, which didn't happen.[53] Of course, the inherent irony of the case was the intolerance shown Bashir by her Kansas City coworkers, many of whom were Christians. But the irony also obscures the true danger of the AT&T manager who, in attempting physically to remove her religious headwear, actually committed a physical *assault.*

As already noted, the number of discrimination complaints filed with the EEOC that were based on race and sex has dropped in recent years. But the number of complaints based on ancestry and country of origin (which includes religious practices) has dramatically and substantially increased. In this light, the hostile, aggressive conduct by Bashir's manager at AT&T may well represent the start of a still another troublesome trend, one that changes the bases for future acts of violence on the job, which only heightens the anger and rage that fuel workplace murder and willful homicide.

Chapter Twelve

Employer Response, Responsibility, and Resolve

No two companies are the same, even those that make identical widgets for the same market, compete for the same market shares, and vie for the same consumer dollars. Nor do companies respond to workplace murder in the same way. Companies and businesses have very different approaches to workplace violence, and the differences shape and reflect their priorities and goals. The differences also shape their response and responsibility to those employees victimized by workplace homicide.

For this reason, a comparison of how two very different companies responded to similar workplace murders will be instructive. It should illustrate, first and foremost, that since companies do their best to respond to the crisis, the difference between success and failure is often found not in kind—but degree. The difference between success and failure wasn't found in *what* a company did, but rather in how it was done, how quickly, and how long that effort was sustained.

TWO CASE STUDIES

The McDonald's Restaurant

On the morning of July 18, 1984, James Oliver Huberty, 44, left his apartment in the San Ysidro section of San Diego, California, and headed for a neighborhood McDonald's restaurant to grab a bite to eat. Two weeks earlier, he had been fired from his job as a security guard, and he was feeling depressed. Earlier that day, he had commented to his wife that "society had its chance,"[1] and as he left for the McDonald's she asked him where he was going, and he said, "Hunting humans."[2]

She thought nothing of these comments, even though she knew from her own domestic problems that he was violent, and had once shot their dog in the head after a neighbor complained of the barking. Nor could she later explain why she didn't think his behavior that morning was bizarre, especially since he was a hardcore "survivalist," and left for the McDonald's carrying a nine-millimeter Uzi semiautomatic, a Winchester pump-action twelve-gauge shotgun, and a nine-millimeter Browning handgun.

As a self-proclaimed survivalist, James Huberty saw signs of trouble in America, which was on the brink of ruin, in his view, because of government meddling and overregulation that ruined businesses, including his own. He also believed that the country was headed for disaster because a cabal of international bankers purposefully manipulated the Federal Reserve System, which bankrupted the nation. To prepare for the inevitable apocalyptic collapse, he also collected a half-dozen guns, including those he brought with him to the McDonald's restaurant that afternoon.[3]

Looking for a good target, Huberty had reportedly first visited a Big Bear supermarket, and later checked out the local post office, but decided the McDonald's was the best target. It was located in a neighborhood densely populated with Mexicans and Mexican Americans, and was crowded that Wednesday afternoon with local residents, including families with babies, toddlers, pregnant women, teenagers, and even a few elderly senior citizens. At approximately 3:40 p.m., Huberty stepped inside the crowded McDonald's, raised the nine-millimeter Uzi, and opened fire.

At that very moment—2,100 miles away—Dick Starmann was driving his wife to an elegant restaurant, the International Club, in Chicago's Drake Hotel. Starmann and his wife were making plans to celebrate her upcoming birthday. After they were seated, shown menus, and ordered dinner, a waiter brought a telephone to their table. Starmann was the vice president of the McDonald's food corporation, and the caller was their 13-year-old son. The kid had just seen a TV news bulletin about a shooting at a McDonald's restaurant somewhere in California.[4]

Starmann's first thought was that it was a local story, not a crisis that demanded his direct attention, at least not immediately. A few minutes later, his son called again, this time to report that four people had been confirmed dead, shot and killed by a gunman at that McDonald's store. Another call reported six confirmed dead, and still another call brought the number of deaths to eight. And local authorities were still counting. Starmann realized this wasn't a "local" story. Before their food was served, they rushed from the hotel and drove to the McDonald's home office in Oak Brook, Illinois.

During the thirty-minute drive, they heard the final details on the car radio. James Oliver Huberty had shot and killed twenty-two men, women, and children, and wounded another nineteen, at a San Diego McDonald's restaurant. He had spent 257 rounds of ammunition before he was fatally shot by a SWAT team sniper. The massacre had lasted for seventy-seven minutes, and the dead included babies, pregnant women, several teenagers, and elderly men. Also killed were four McDonald's employees: Elsa Herlinade Borboa-Firro, 19, Paulina Aquino Lopez, 21, Margarita Padilla, 18, and a store manager, Neva Denise Caine, age 22. It was the bloodiest massacre in the history of an American corporation.

None of the company's top officers had any experience handling a mass murder, and none knew how exactly to deal directly with the poor Mexican American community of San Ysidro, San Diego. Still, as soon as Starmann reached his office, he was on the telephone with the McDonald's marketing chief and another vice president, who decided, first, to suspend all advertising for several days. In the next twenty-four hours, Starmann gave more than sixty interviews to the press, and he appeared on every network TV news that night—for fifteen hours straight.[5] The next day several top executives met and quickly approved a one-million-dollar contribution to the survivors' fund, which had been organized by the widow of the company founder, who also donated the first one hundred thousand dollars.

The decision was also made that the company's senior executives fly to San Ysidro to attend a funeral held the next day for eight of the victims, even though it had to be done outside the eye of the media in order to avoid the charge of grandstanding. There was much debate on whether the restaurant should remain open, which might appear callous or disrespectful of the dead, or if it should be closed, which would send a message of "defeatism."[6] But the store was permanently closed after they learned that many of the survivors had returned to the site with flowers, statues, and votive lights and candles and the store had quickly become a local shrine.

With virtually every decision, on every issue, on every controversial fact, meetings and conferences were held by McDonald's top brass to ensure that every move they made was the best, strategically and otherwise, and served the best interest of the company.

More than a month later, McDonald's executives met with community leaders to donate the property to the people of San Ysidro and the city fathers, and to assure the community that its only motive was to do what was right. Donald P. Horwitz, an executive vice president, later explained that, "We decided to do what we thought was morally right, not what was necessarily legally correct nor financially sound nor even proper from a communications standpoint. We had a moral obligation to do the right thing, no matter what the right thing was."[7]

The company's handling of the crisis received much praise, many compliments, and hundreds of positive letters, and also prompted scores of favorable newspaper editorials both locally and beyond.[8] The stellar McDonald's image was successfully separated in the public's mind from the murders at the store. The public's confidence and trust in the McDonald's brand was not only restored, but *raised* from where it had been before.

Despite all the press releases and the carefully worded statements for the evening news, one still could not help but wonder if the company's *actual* priorities and goals were otherwise. In a telling corporate postscript, McDonald's senior management was quick to reassure the San Ysidro community (and, presumably, its stockholders) that today McDonald's "operates a new store just three blocks from the old one, and its sales are running one-third higher than those of the outlet it replaced."[9]

Amidst the compliments and praise, it was crystal clear throughout that the top priority of the McDonald's company was the protection of its own interests, which left a number of questions unanswered. One can only guess how the McDonald's food company responded to the claims of the many survivors, particularly the parents and families of the three teenage employees and the 22-year-old manager of the store. [10]

But if the McDonald's company was far more concerned with public relations, and the employees were probably given short shrift, the following case shows just how differently companies respond to workplace murder. The case also admirably demonstrates that there's always more than one way to "do the right thing."

The Law Firm of Pettit and Martin

On Thursday, July 1, 1993, just before 3:00 p.m., a well-dressed businessman, Gian Luigi Ferri, 55, carrying two large briefcases, entered the elevators of the office building at 101 California Street in San Francisco. He was headed for the law firm of Pettit and Martin on the thirty-fourth floor. Once the elevator reached the thirty-fourth floor, Ferri took off his suit jacket and then placed a set of ear protectors over his head. [11]

Pettit and Martin had represented him in several business matters, and he was now furious with the attorney who had handled the matter. He also held a grudge against the firm. With his jacket removed, he revealed two nine-millimeter Intratec DC9 semiautomatic machine pistols, carried in shoulder straps, and each loaded with fifty-round magazines. He also carried a smaller .45-caliber semiautomatic handgun and hundreds of rounds of ammunition loaded into dozens of magazines carried in his innocent-looking lawyer cases. [12]

Ear protectors in place, and without saying a word, Ferri opened fire on a glass-enclosed conference room where a deposition was underway, killing one lawyer and the lawyer's client. He killed another person on the thirty-fourth floor, and then went down a flight of stairs, where he resumed gunfire. By the time he stopped shooting, he had killed eight and wounded six. As the

San Francisco police closed in, he turned the gun on himself and committed suicide. Among the dead were three attorneys, a law student, two legal secretaries, and a young mother. [13]

On Ferri's body was found a rambling semiliterate four-page typed letter in which he had listed the names of his "enemies," including those labeled "criminals," "rapists," "racketeers," and lobbyists. He had also compiled a long list of complaints about different aspects of his life, ranging from the medieval motivations behind why lawyers practice law the way they do [14] to the conspiracy behind increased public consumption of the popular flavor enhancer monosodium glutamate, or MSG. [15]

A spokesman for the law firm, however, explained that lawyers in the firm had advised Ferri on several real-estate deals in the Midwest years earlier, in the late 1970s and early 1980s, but hadn't represented or had any contact with him since then. [16] And, in the tragic irony of the massacre, none of the murdered and wounded victims had any connection with Ferri, and none of their names was among the thirty-odd names that made up his "enemies" list of those targeted for his personal wrath. [17]

What distinguished Pettit and Martin's response to workplace murder from those of so many other companies wasn't what it did, but how it was done, how quickly, and how long that effort was sustained. And the response was remarkable. Broken down into four general steps, the partners and management of Pettit and Martin did the following.

First, Pettit and Martin's personnel manager, Karen Wilson (as soon as she learned there was a heavily armed madman firing guns in the building), organized several other employees to barricade the doors of their office suite with file cabinets. Since there was no other way of learning what was happening, she turned on the radio to hear the preliminary reports of the siege as it unfolded. Then, realizing that the firm would need immediate help in dealing with the disaster, Wilson called workshop psychologist Bobbi Lambert. The critical point to emphasize here is that Wilson was thinking about counseling sessions for grief-stricken, mourning employees while bullets were still echoing in the corridors. She was already laying the groundwork for everything that followed—*while Ferri was still on the loose*!

Second, the next day, Friday, July 2, an office-wide, preliminary mourning-and-grief session was held at a nearby hotel for grief counselors to talk with survivors, many of whom were still in a state of shock. As the grief counselors conducted their first counseling sessions, cleanup crews had already started to arrive at the offices of Pettit and Martin a few blocks away. They would labor around the clock that weekend to remove all evidence of the massacre—repairing broken windows, cleaning up debris and shards of glass, pulling up and replacing bloodstained carpets, and repairing bullet-punctured walls. During that weekend, as people attended funerals and visited hospital wards and emergency rooms, the staff of five grief counselors had already been assembled, formally retained, organized, and prepped, and was ready to meet the survivors Monday morning.

Third, Monday morning the staff of five grief counselors was waiting in the lobby of Pettit and Martin, ready to offer consolation to the employees, many of whom, returning to work for the first time, were having flashbacks of the incident, were convulsed with tears, were visibly upset, or couldn't stop crying. As part of the grief-counseling process, Pettit and Martin permitted employees to place flowers at every spot where someone had been killed, and also encouraged the maintenance of journals in which people were free to write their memories of the victims. (Lambert had wisely advised Pettit and Martin to avoid the temptation to pretend nothing had happened.)

Fourth, Pettit and Martin kept the staff of five grief counselors on the payroll—and at the office—picking up the tab for unlimited counseling services, available to any employee who felt the need. Now that the initial shock had subsided, almost everybody experienced some kind of posttraumatic stress syndrome, which is expressed in many different, often conflicting ways. As part of Pettit and Martin's long-term responsibility for its employees' recovery, it kept the staff of five grief counselors on the site (and the payroll) for two weeks, and granted time off to every employee who asked.

Despite Pettit and Martin's remarkable response, it never recovered. The firm continued to lose attorneys and decline financially. Less than two years later, in 1995, and in the middle of a sluggish California economy, the law firm disbanded. Former partner Sheldon M. Siegel was philosophical: "After that . . . I don't think it would've been possible to keep the firm going on much longer." And he was also the practical realist, adding: "There was just sort of this sadness, this pall in the air." [18]

THE EMPLOYER'S RESPONSIBILITY TO THE EMPLOYEE BEFORE THE SHOOTING

Adopt a Zero-Tolerance Violence Plan

Under current Occupational Safety and Health Administration (OSHA) guidelines, employers are required to provide a safe work environment for the employee who works on the property, whether it's a factory, warehouse, office, or business complex. And even before the shooting occurs, the best preventive approach is to *already have* a "zero-tolerance" policy in place. This policy should make clear that any form of violence or physical aggression is strictly forbidden and unacceptable, and that violations carry disciplinary consequences, from reprimands and suspensions to termination. Every new and current employee should also be instructed on the procedure for how to report such conduct, and management should take steps to ensure that employees feel comfortable filing such reports.

Since the cases show that the employee most likely to kill has already been hired, is already on the job, it's absolutely critical that this information be made available to the older, veteran employees as well. After all, these veteran employees, whose orientations took place years ago, are likely far less knowledgeable and thus in greater need of notice than the new rookie employees just coming aboard.

Create and Enforce a Gun-Free Environment

The creation of a gun-free work environment that prohibits employees from carrying firearms on the employer's property provides the greatest protection to employees and others who visit the employer's property. A comprehensive policy that strictly prohibits firearms on the property offers the most consistent protection and also reduces the risk of legal liability should a shooting incident actually occur. The potential legal liability of a shooting that does occur without this prohibition is simply too great to ignore. Another benefit of a gun-free policy is that it projects a public image of safety and security for the workplace, which can boost worker morale, and so on. And the establishment of the policy is both easy and inexpensive.

Firearms and other weapons can be excluded from the workplace or other property by posting a simple notice at each public entrance. The technical requirements for what constitutes official notice (like phrasing and definitions) vary from state to state, so it is advisable to check the law of the particular state in which the workplace is situated. And though the enforcement of the gun-free policy raises questions about employer liability, the questions are easily resolved in the employer's favor.

Employer enforcement doesn't require the employer to search clients, contractors, or other visitors to the workplace, nor does it *require* weapons detection technology. A simple notice that all visitors to the workplace carrying concealed weapons must leave the weapons outside is legally sufficient to deter law-abiding citizens, and employees will already know that any violation of the policy will result in serious discipline or even termination.

Nor should the employer worry that adoption of a gun-free policy will invite lawsuits if a workplace shooting occurred and somebody was murdered. Since such attacks are generally regarded as unforeseeable, the employer isn't likely to be held liable for not preventing them, and even with the gun-free policy in place, the appropriate response to a threatening situation is to summon security or to call the police.

Implement a Detailed Termination Procedure

The employer's second responsibility is to formulate a procedure for the firing or termination of an employee—with compassion and dignity. Firing an employee (for whatever reason) can be a routine procedure, or it can be a volatile event. It's therefore critical that the employee being fired is allowed to maintain his or her dignity while minimizing the possibility that he or she will retaliate and become violent.

It's not difficult to imagine the number of murders and injuries that could have been prevented had the perpetrator been terminated with a little more dignity and compassion and not treated like a leper—or like the criminal they ultimately became. In fact, a number of cases in the study strongly suggest that the spark that ignited the murderous rage wasn't so much the basis or the reason for the firing, but the embarrassment and humiliation of *how* the perpetrator was fired.[19]

In almost 80 percent of the cases, the principal motive to kill stemmed from the anger and rage that resulted from having been fired or laid off. The rage often lasted weeks, months, and in a few instances even a year or longer. As economic news worsens and unemployment climbs, the fear, pressure, and anxiety facing newly terminated workers could turn a routine firing into a homicidal tragedy.

What follows is an easy, ten-step guide for employers to ensure the safe but effective termination of an employee from the job. And it's important to note here that, even though care must be taken to ensure a dignified termination, the focus is not on the feelings of the employee being fired—but on the safety of everybody else.

> If you are in doubt about the risk, an experienced consultant should be hired. Choose a neutral environment for the termination, such as a conference room. The room should have a lot of windows, be closest to the entrance, and have a minimum amount of furniture.
>
> Create a safe environment. Clear the table or desks of any objects that can be used as weapons (pens and pencils are atop the list of objects that can be used as weapons).
>
> Have a male and a female in the room to handle the termination. Only one person actively communicates the termination. The second person does not participate but is present only as a witness and to provide assistance if needed.
>
> Depersonalize the situation. When/if possible, emphasize that the termination is about the position, not the person.
>
> Control your emotions. Remain as neutral as possible and focus on the situation, not the person.
>
> Ensure that all company property has been retrieved and that the employee's property is being packed and inventoried. The employee should sign for his or her property and be given his or her personal belongings at the completion of the termination. Employees should not be allowed to return to their offices or workstations after termination.

Separate completely. Any termination process with a high-risk individual should strive for a complete separation in which there is no opportunity to reestablish a relationship with the company.
At all costs, avoid the walk of shame! Respect the person's dignity.
Adopt a "Goodbye-but-don't-come-back" rule.

An effective termination should also include notice to the employee that the termination or firing is absolute and complete. It must be made clear that the employee—once fired—may not return to the job. This may not initially rate high as a factor in preventing workplace violence, particularly murder—not until we recall that *almost half the workplace killers were former employees who returned to the job site after they had been fired.* Businessman Soon Byung Park returned to his job and wounded his boss, shot and killed his boss's sister, then killed himself, a month after he was fired. And Clifton McCree returned to his job and killed five coworkers five months after he was fired.

Men like Socorro Hurtado-Garcia, Denis Czajkowski, Andre White, and Larry Hansel had little in common in terms of childhood, family background, choice of weapons, motives, or modus operandi. Yet the single fact they all shared was their status as former employees who were permitted to return to the workplace. Others include Perry Smith, Jian Chen, Robert Diamond, Darryl Dinkins, James Simpson, Paul Calden, Ladislav Antilak, Victor Piazza, Gregory Gray, Tom West, Paulino Valenzuela, and Salvatore Tapia, who killed scores of coworkers (and often also committed suicide) after they returned to the site of jobs from which they had been fired.

Although female murderers were typically more impatient than men when it came to exacting revenge (and didn't murder as often or as indiscriminately), they too often killed former coworkers by forcing their way back onto employer property after they had been fired or laid off. We recall that Jennifer San Marco returned to the mail-processing center months after she had been fired and she killed several former coworkers, Yvonne Hiller returned to the Kraft baking plant and killed two coworkers only minutes after she had been suspended, and Jacquelyn Ferguson also returned to her job at the cardiologist's office and killed her supervisor after she had been fired. Still other females included Arunya Rouch, who returned to the Publix food store parking lot to kill a coworker just hours after she was fired, and the list goes on and on, to include the murders and/or suicides of other females like Mozella Dansby, Kim Harris, and Renita Dozier.[20]

WHAT THE EMPLOYEE MUST DO DURING THE SHOOTING

Of course, the employer isn't required to bear the whole burden of ensuring the safety of an employee suddenly caught in the middle of a workplace shooting. Listed below are six commonsense points to consider in such an event. Some are "common sense" but also counterintuitive, and must therefore be performed consciously or deliberately, especially when acting instinctively or "doing what comes naturally" may result in injury, even death. The six points are as follows:

Respond to the sound of gunfire according to your situation. If you can see the shooter, run in the opposite direction or evacuate the building, leave your belongings behind, visualize your entire escape route before you start, and avoid elevators and escalators. But running away should be your first plan. At twenty feet from the assailant, you're still within lethal range, but at about fifty feet you'll be a more difficult target, even for an assailant who's experienced with a gun.

If the assailant shoots at you as you run, don't run in a straight line. Run in a zigzag pattern and wave your arms or bend down every few strides, anything to make yourself a more difficult target. To reduce your chances of being hit with a bullet, look for a door or window, or hide in a room, preferably with windows, which will allow escape if necessary.

If you're trapped and can't evacuate the building, hide in a secure area (preferably a designated shelter location), lock the door, blockade the door with heavy furniture, cover all windows, turn off all lights, turn on all the alarms, silence all electronic devices, lie down on the floor, remain silent, and lie flat, which will protect your vital organs, since horizontally you're a more difficult target, and if you lie flat on the ground, the shooter might think you're already dead.

If the assailant is about to shoot you, do anything you can to stop them. You may try talking to the shooter if you know him or her, unless, of course, you know the shooter hates you because you have teased and taunted the shooter since he or she was first hired nine years ago. Remember, attacking an armed shooter is *never* a smart thing to do. If the shooter has a gun, he or she likely has already decided to kill people, and anything you do might just cause more bloodshed.

As a distraction, you might throw something at the assailant—anything that can be lifted, like chairs, laptops, or fire extinguishers—or set off the sprinkler system or fire alarm. You'll risk getting injured or even killed, but the more people rush the assailant at once, the greater the chances are that someone will take the shooter down. Unarmed individuals who band together have a greater chance of surviving the attack.

If you're barricaded in a room with others, have them spread out as widely as possible—get down on the floor behind the furniture or any other cover. People have a natural tendency to huddle together in a crisis, but in a shooting situation, this only makes everybody one big, stationary target. Spreading out and getting down low makes everyone a more difficult target. [21]

THE EMPLOYER'S RESPONSIBILITY TO THE EMPLOYEE AFTER THE SHOOTING

After a workplace shooting, many employees never return. For those who stay, recovery can be excruciatingly painful and slow, and, for the employer, very expensive. The overwhelming majority of employees take from a week to a few years to return to previous levels of productivity. And this is expensive for the employer because, in the interim, mistakes multiply, recruiting new employees suddenly becomes difficult, and the same clients who had been understanding and sympathetic during the first days after the tragedy quickly grow impatient and curt. [22]

As Mike France writes:

> As soon as the shock wears off, almost everybody experiences some form of post-traumatic stress syndrome. But it manifests itself in a wide variety of ways. After the shooting at Navistar in Melrose Park, Illinois, on Feb. 5, about 20 percent of the plant's workforce of 850 took the next day off. Among the people who went to counseling sessions the next day, "some were just still stunned," says William B. Bunn, Navistar's vice-president for health, safety, and productivity. "Some were outright grieving for their friends. Some were feeling guilty; they were saying, 'I know that when he stopped to reload, I could have grabbed him.'" [23]
>
> In this [mental] state, employees are almost incapable of returning to their normal routines. After a gunman killed five people at the Atlanta office of day-trading firm All-Tech Investment Group on Thursday, July 29, 1999, the office reopened on the next Monday. "The [employees] came. But they weren't doing anything. They were just milling around," recalls Bruce T. Blythe, CEO of Atlanta's Crisis Management International, which counseled All-Tech. "The [firm] called us and said, 'Something needs to happen . . . Nobody is working.'" [24]

Faced with this situation, All-Tech responded much like the other professionally counseled corporations : they gathered everybody together and painstakingly reviewed the details of the event. This provokes discussion of the incident and the recognition that others had the same reaction—the first step toward moving beyond the tragedy.

These sessions are typically followed up with private counseling, where employees plagued by recollections often go through a specialized therapy known as eye movement desensitization and reprocessing or EMDR. This is a form of psychotherapy that helps people heal from the symptoms of emotional distress that result from traumatic or very disturbing life experiences, like witnessing a bloody shooting massacre in which friends and colleagues were murdered just a few feet away. Studies show that the use of EMDR can afford a psychological relief that once took years. The therapy works on the principle that the mind can actually heal from psychological trauma just as effectively or even as quickly as the body recovers from physical trauma. And there are typically eight phases of treatment.

For example, when you cut your finger, your body and its blood work to close the wound. And if a foreign object or repeated injury irritates the original wound, it festers and causes pain. However, once the block is removed, the healing process resumes. EMDR therapy posits that a similar process occurs with mental injury. "The brain's information processing system naturally moves toward mental health [and] if the system is blocked or imbalanced by the impact of a disturbing event, the emotional wound festers and can cause intense suffering. [But once] the block is removed, healing resumes. Using the detailed protocols and procedures learned in EMDR training sessions, clinicians help clients activate their natural healing processes."[25]

Such steps help most employees get up and running, however shakily, within about two weeks. But not everybody heals so fast. Lambert recalls walking the halls of Pettit three weeks after the shooting to check up on people. "They would seem normal, but then you'd look inside somebody's office and see tears going down their cheeks," she says.

Alongside the difficulty of counseling grief-stricken, mourning employees who have just suffered a traumatic event, however, is the problem of how senior managers and supervisors handle the problem. Since, as a practical matter, much of what the employer should provide is done through senior management, the aftermath of a workplace murder always presents a serious management challenge.

As personnel grieve and staff members mourn and undergo grief counseling, the day-to-day work of the office inevitably suffers. Mistakes increase and orders are confused, and as news of the tragedy spreads in the business community, recruiting becomes more difficult. Clients are also lost. In the beginning, they're always gracious and understanding, waiving deadlines, sending elaborate floral arrangements to the funeral homes. But as the days turn into weeks, the same clients understandably grow impatient and irritable, and want to move on, return to business as usual.

A sense of camaraderie and team spirit often pervades the office, and members of the work team often grow closer. With the office having shared a powerful emotional experience, the rigidity of the traditional organizational hierarchy dissolves. CEOs and top-echelon managers hug and embrace secretaries and receptionists, talk is more informal, relations among the employees more collegial, the usual petty workplace rivalries are abandoned, and age-old jealousies are forgotten. But these feelings of goodwill soon wear off. And when the bosses and supervisors gradually return to their focus on productivity and the bottom line, subordinate employees may regard them as hypocrites, or feel betrayed.

Customers, clients, and suppliers, who were always so sympathetic, understanding, and even gracious in the days after the shooting—sending elaborate floral arrangements to the funerals, waiving deadlines, and so on— soon grow impatient and curt since, no matter how tragic the shooting might have been, they still have businesses to run, which means they must now return to business as usual. According to Bobbi Lambert, the grief specialist who was contacted minutes after the Ferri massacre erupted, "Clients usually can't do enough for you during the first week or two." Lambert, who runs the Kentfield, California, consultancy Confidante, Inc., and who has advised a number of businesses that have suffered acts of workplace violence, adds: "Then it's like 'We need to get back to work, and we don't really want to hear anything more about it.'"[26]

In the midst of these changes, managers and supervisors in particular are called upon in ways that are more challenging and very new. As few managers and supervisors have experience handling mass murders, in the area of grief counseling, most don't have a clue. "Within minutes of one of the most harrowing experiences of their lives," Mike France astutely observes, "they're suddenly confronted with a series of conflicting demands that they had never imagined, much less prepared for."[27]

And these demands are typically so riddled with contradiction, complexity, and internal tensions that many often resist any kind of resolution at all. As employees undergo long-term grief counseling, and others gradually return to their old levels of productivity, other problems loom.

THE EMPLOYER'S CONTINUING RESPONSIBILITY— LITIGATION AND BEYOND

The problems are only multiplied and exacerbated once civil suits are filed by the victims' families, especially if the perpetrator was an employee of the company (as is often the case), or the company could have done more to ensure the security of the premises (which is virtually always the case). As a gesture of heartfelt sympathy, the employer may want to pay funeral expenses or establish a small college scholarship fund, especially if the estate includes young children. But corporate counsel may advise against the gesture, as it may be misconstrued as a tacit admission of liability or, worse, an attempt to induce the employee/plaintiff not to pursue a claim in court. And their attorneys will proceed under any of a number of legal theories of liability.

The OSHA Standards—and the General Duty Clause

Under the Occupational Safety and Health Act of 1970 (OSHA), every employer is required to provide employees with both work and a work environment that's free from recognized hazards that cause or are likely to cause death or serious physical injury. This general, prophylactic provision serves in the absence of specific OSHA criteria for the prevention of workplace violence. Under this general "duty" provision an employer may be found liable if it knew (or should have known) violence would occur. Violation of this general duty clause may also subject an employer to penalties, especially if it can be proved that the employer or the industry knew of the hazard and knew its inherent danger, and a feasible abatement method existed.

The Doctrine of *Respondeat Superior* ("Let the Master Answer")

A Latin term which means "let the master answer," the *respondeat superior* doctrine carves an exception out of the general rule that people aren't responsible for the acts of others. Originally construed to permit recovery from the employer for injuries caused by an employee, the rationale was that the former ordered or approved the employee's acts. The modern view modifies the requirement that the employer specifically authorize or approve the act. In most states, the employer is liable for any employee act. Once the relationship and scope of employment are established, the employer becomes "strictly liable"—which eliminates the requirement of negligence by the employer.

The Doctrine of Negligent Hiring ("He Shoulda Never Been Hired")

Under this theory of liability, the plaintiff contends that the employer failed to conduct proper investigation into personal and job references, criminal histories, and other background information that would have revealed the employee's misconduct. The employer was therefore negligent for putting a person with a criminal or otherwise dangerous tendencies in a position where they could pose a threat to others. Thirty-six of the fifty states allow people to bring cases against employers for negligent hiring, and the standards for establishing a claim vary from state to state.

The Doctrine of Negligent Retention ("He Shoulda Been Fired")

Closely related, conceptually, to the doctrine of negligent hiring, this theory of liability is based on negligent retention—that is, the negligence occurred *after the employee was hired* and for the period he or she remained employed. The tort of negligent retention requires that the employer became aware or should have been aware of problems with the employee that indicated his or her unfitness for the job but failed to take any action, like a background check, investigation, discharge, or reassignment. (It's under this theory of liability, of course, that the survivors of Amy Bishop's murders stand a better chance of successfully suing the University of Alabama.)

Whatever theory of liability the plaintiff's attorney elects, management will encounter problems with its employees. The employees' allegiance will be split or seriously compromised as they sue their own bosses and testify against them in court. And as these cases proceed to jury trial, Michael France aptly observes, "employee witnesses are often forced to choose between their company and their colleagues, and the finger-pointing can get ugly."[28]

As the number of doctrinal choices increase for a plaintiff's attorneys seeking a day in court, the employer's responsibility (and liability) for employee conduct expands and grows as well. This is particularly evident in cases of workplace murder that involve stranger-on-stranger crime, and in which the employer—like all big employers—is a substantial property owner as well.[29] Much of the wealth of companies like McDonald's and Burger King, for example, isn't found in the millions of cheeseburgers they sell every day, but in their vast real-estate holdings, represented by the many thousands of properties across the country that they own and lease to their many thousands of entrepreneurial lessees.

What steps does the employer take to prevent a shooting in the workplace itself? How can the workplace site—whether a plant, factory, office building, classroom, or even a vacant lot—be protected against workplace homicide? And what steps does the employer take to ensure that a potential workplace murderer, however provoked, motivated, or well armed, is prevented from translating homicidal thought into a homicidal act?

Chapter Thirteen

Guidelines for Workplace Safety, Security, and Control

The last chapter focused on the employer's first duty and responsibility to ensure the safety and well-being of the employee—not only before and during a workplace shooting, but after a workplace murder as well. The employer's response ranged from the timely detection of behavioral signals that a violent act was imminent to recognition of the need for grief counseling and other means of achieving closure.

That discussion also recommended several approaches by management to ensure that the employee's work environment didn't lend itself to violence, particularly with firearms and other weapons, which invariably resulted in injuries and often death. These recommendations were (1) the institution of a "zero tolerance" for all workplace violence, (2) the creation of a gun-free work environment, (3) the implementation of an effective termination procedure, and, finally, (4) the adoption of a "don't come back" rule to address the problem of former employees returning to the job to exact revenge, often months after they were fired.

But these four measures, by themselves, perform only part of the effort required to detect and thwart workplace shootings and prevent workplace homicide. They address certain elements of the problem, and reflect certain imperatives that cannot be ignored. Yet they work far more effectively only in conjunction with another, fifth element that completes the whole preventive approach.

THE POLICIES AND PRACTICE OF PREVENTION

The employer's duty to ensure employee safety is only the first of two obligations imposed by the rules and regulations in this area of the law. This chapter will focus on the employer's need to maintain the safety and security of the employee while the employee is inside or on the employer's property. This includes the safety and security of the physical plant, office, and every job site—from the plush penthouse executive suite on the top floor of corporate headquarters downtown to the rural warehouse and storage facility behind the garage and above the leaky men's room with the wobbly toilet seat.

Each of the four management initiatives listed above addresses a critical imperative in the workplace, and all four reflect vital policies that change the day-to-day behaviors of everybody on the workforce. When the young UAH nursing student (back in chapter 4) asked, in effect, if Amy Bishop's act of triple murder was preventable, and also wondered by inference if such tragedies could be prevented in the future, the authorial answer was an unqualified, enthusiastic yes. After all, a workplace that (1) is violence-free, (2) strictly prohibits firearms, (3) terminates employees in a way that's compassionate and dignified, and (4) makes the fired employee understand that he or she must never return, is a workplace that statistically will never experience the tragedy of a workplace homicide.

Still, as effectively as the implementation of these four initiatives alone will prevent workplace murder, the task is made even easier—and the possibility of workplace homicide is virtually eliminated—when implementation of the four policies is simultaneously reinforced and buttressed by the appropriate technology.

Workplace murder, of course, is a serious crime, and weapons detection technology is extensive. This technology includes an array of measures that reflect different views and strategies on how best to achieve optimum results. These include closed-circuit TV, electrified fencing, security guards, the deployment of stationary or mobile canine units, building access-control devices, vehicle identification decals, and so on. Yet there exists an incredible irony, a grand paradox. On the broad spectrum of workplace violence, though murder is the most extreme form of workplace violence, the prevention of workplace murder is also the least labor-intensive and the easiest to achieve. With reference to the prohibition of firearms, and nine-millimeter handguns in particular, the effort to prevent workplace murder carries still another unexpected dividend: it's also the least expensive.

Almost 85 percent of the workplace killers in the study used firearms, and the vast majority of those chose the nine-millimeter semiautomatic handgun. (As already noted, among women who used firearms, the nine-millimeter handgun was virtually the *only* weapon used.) Inasmuch as this study focuses exclusively on workplace murder, there's no need to discuss the prevention of other, less extreme forms of workplace violence, whether "mobbing," bullying, or exchanging surly glances at the watercooler.

The exact location of Amy Bishop's triple-murder on the University of Alabama's Huntsville campus—the scene of the crime—was 369R, a smallish conference room on the third floor of the Shelby Center for Science and Technology. The Shelby Center is a sixty-million-dollar state-of-the-art structure, which was formally dedicated on Sunday, October 14, 2007, and hailed by many in the crowd as only the first step in a process that would make the Shelby Center the "MIT of the South." [1]

Housing both the mathematics and biology departments, the four-story, 200,000-square-foot building boasts eighteen teaching laboratories, fifteen research laboratories, two auditoriums, thirteen classrooms, and additional space for offices and comfortable student and faculty lounge areas. The Shelby Center is also outfitted with the most sophisticated research and teaching tools, safety features, and wireless computer technology—complete with open fume hoods, an often overlooked but critical feature for scientists who conduct in-classroom experiments that involve fire, ignitable chemicals, or flames. [2]

On the day of the murders, February 11, 2010, the Shelby Center had been in use for more than two years, and there's no indication that the building or any of the surrounding acreage had been secured with any device or technology capable of firearm detection. Bishop's approach and entry into the building, including her movement once inside the building, with a concealed nine-millimeter semiautomatic handgun had not been recorded or filmed by any camera system. Nor was her movement inside the building restricted or hampered in any way, either electronically or by security personnel. And there's no indication that that lack of restriction didn't exist at other building properties on the Huntsville campus as well.

Different high-tech devices and equipment are widely available, of course, and existing technologies are being developed, improved, refined, and simplified almost daily. As already noted, many are practical, non-labor-intensive, environmentally responsible, visually unobtrusive, and also surprisingly inexpensive. Many more are highly technical, complicated, and sophisticated systems whose manuals probably require an advanced degree in engineering or physics to understand. Still, among the least expensive, user-friendly means by which the university could have prevented Amy Bishop from entering the sixty-million-dollar Shelby Center with her nine-millimeter handgun and murdering three professors was one that would have cost the university about seventy dollars plus tax. [3]

WORKPLACE TECHNOLOGIES AND PROTOCOLS

Illegally concealed guns and other weapons are a major threat to both the business community and law enforcement. Existing firearms detection systems, especially metal detectors, however, have a limited special range and a relatively high false-alarm rate.[4] The protection of academic or commercial office buildings, including building environments, and equipping them with the best, most effective, cost-efficient technologies in weapons detection, is a daunting task. Even after the selection is made, the installation, operation, and plans for future maintenance are all functions that will challenge even the best technical staff.

Property or building environments, of course, vary widely, and even if two buildings were architecturally and structurally identical, the underlying real estate could significantly alter the security problems and the technological options. That only one of two otherwise identical buildings was built on a slightly sloping hillside, or bordered a lake, or was subject to easements, and so on, is a factor that can (and often does) change the required technology and how and when it's installed, operated, and even maintained in the years to come.

A modern science building, like the Shelby Center, for example, raises security questions that are very different from those raised by other buildings with different purposes and different physical layouts. And those buildings would, in turn, vary significantly from those presented by still other buildings like nuclear facilities, power plants, hotel or apartment complexes, bridges, tunnels, government agencies, financial institutions, and so on.

Of course, none are impervious to security breaches or beyond physical vulnerability. History teaches that gunmen bent on murder are an especially creative, inventive bunch. They may strike from anywhere—from behind the curtain of a balconied theater box during the performance of a play to the sixth-floor window of a book depository overlooking a grassy knoll or a public square.

Fortunately, the problems are not insuperable. Although the identification and assessment of a property will always be unique to that location, some physical security actions are applicable to many property types. Some of the most generally applicable security actions, of course, include the installation of alarms, closed-circuit TV systems, electrified fencing, security guards, and even the deployment of canine units.

Still other means exist, of course, but they focus, for example, on factors like access-control systems; electronic manipulation of elevators; heating, ventilation, and air conditioning systems; water sprinkler devices; and motion-sensitive optics. These technologies are beyond the scope of this discussion because they focus mostly on the capture, apprehension, neutralization, or deactivation of a threat after the threat has been realized. The focus of this discussion is essentially one of prevention, making consideration of these means unnecessary, and obviating the need to discuss technologies designed to address threats that have already been realized.

And the appropriate technologies are widely available, being improved upon every day.

The New York City police, with assistance from the Pentagon, for example, recently tested a scanning device that has the remote capacity to detect concealed firearms. "The device measures the natural radiation that's emitted by people, and can detect when this flow of energy is impeded by an alien object, such as a gun."[5]

This technology has shown considerable promise in the detection of weapons and obviates the need for an actual physical or hands-on body search. Commonly known as terahertz imaging detection, the technology functions much like night-vision goggles, which simply detect infrared radiation. However, unlike infrared radiation, the terahertz wavelength is not blocked by layers of clothing or other coverings. With terahertz, you will be able to identify a gun as a gun," according to John Federici, a physics professor at the New Jersey Institute of Technology.[6]

This technology is being developed in conjunction with a US Department of Defense counterterrorism unit, which has expressed an interest in the technology's capacity or potential to thwart suicide bombers and similar threats for which a concealed weapon is required. A prototype device was recently tested at a Bronx, New York, shooting range, where it was proved effective at distances of up to sixteen feet, and developments are ongoing to extend that capacity to more than eighty feet.[7]

The companies that specialize in the design, manufacture, and sale of these technologies are usually listed for public reference. Sago Systems, Inc., as an example, develops, manufactures, and sells state-of-the-art passive millimeter-wave imaging systems for security operations. Their proprietary cameras detect and image contraband that goes undetected by conventional metal detectors. With patented cameras, Sago joins a number of other companies whose products have successfully imaged such contraband as suicide vests, plastic explosives, knives, and ceramic guns. And their products are affordable, noninvasive (absolutely no radiation), and compatible (or interoperable) with existing security systems and infrastructures.

Among the available technologies is Sago's ST-150, a standoff detector that can be deployed at mobile checkpoints, at building entrances, as a perimeter security device, or as a covert contraband system. The "standoff" option is appropriate for preventing shootings like that committed by Amy Bishop, who likely would have shot and killed any security guard manning the portal system as she headed for the third floor of UAH's Shelby Center.[8] Several units have been purchased by agencies of the US government to determine optimal use. The ST-150 in particular is designed for mobility. On Monday morning, it's deployed at the Shelby Center, for example, but during the following weekend (when human traffic is minimal) the system is deployed at the main entrance to the campus athletic center for a basketball game. The ST-150 is lightweight and quickly sends data to a remote command center, or the operator can be within a few feet of the people being imaged. The ST-150 is user-friendly and ready to be installed in a commercial or academic setting.[9]

As with most new technologies, however, the laws that accommodate the new development lag behind, and the ST-150, as well as other technologies, may not be invasive physically, but they are very invasive legally. And given the technology's legal invasiveness, it's not surprising that it has also provoked controversy. However appropriate and innocuous the ST-150 may appear in its deployment as a portal in the lobby of the Shelby Center, for example, it's not difficult to imagine situations in which the technology might lend itself to potential abuse. Civil liberties experts, for example, have assumed a cautious stance on these developments, which they find "intriguing and worrisome," says Donna Lieberman, executive director of the New York Civil Liberties Union.[10]

This is hardly surprising. The potential for abuse is clear, as the technology can, on the one hand, easily make the job of law enforcement much easier by conducting a "virtual" "stop and frisk" without first restricting the movement of a suspect. But, on the other, it may also abridge an individual's ability and right to walk down the street free from an arbitrary pat down. According to Lieberman, it clearly intrudes upon that individual's expectation of privacy.[11] In addition to the legal ramifications, there are more medical concerns about this new technology and the danger it poses in the emission of radiation, which physicists like Federici argue wouldn't be at a high enough level to cause concern. "This is a lot different than nuclear radiation or X-rays," he said. "It doesn't really cause any damage."[12]

The appropriate technology, of course, will vary from case to case, situation to situation, reflecting the different needs of the occupant. One relatively small nineteenth-century wooden, two-story museum with a single primary entrance for the general public may require a single electronically equipped portal with one part-time attendant, while another building, twelve stories of steel-girded tinted glass with nine entrances strung along an underground parking facility, will raise different security issues, require different problem solving, and necessitate more sophisticated technologies with different contingency planning, diagrams, and personnel.

The number and types of building environments, and the best weapons detection system for each environment, are far too numerous to mention (let alone discuss) here. The most prudent course is to pursue all available options with a local expert whose access to the building's construction history, floor plans, and so on will inform their best judgment, and who will then advise the client accordingly.

Other than the most general descriptions of buildings and offices, little was available in the research of the cases to permit an assessment of the security precautions that were taken (or not taken) by the employer or the owner of the workplace property on which the murder occurred. A rare exception was the case of William Evans.

Evans, 51, was the director of business management at the state employment agency in Columbus, Ohio. On March 18, 1998, while wielding a gun in each hand, Evans shot and killed coworker Shasta S. Dotson, 40, as she sat in her cubicle casually talking on the telephone. After he killed Dotson, he then shot and killed himself, the police arriving minutes later to find a revolver in his right hand and a semiautomatic in his left. [13]

The bizarre murder/suicide occurred on the second floor of a six-story office building that housed more than five hundred accounting, auditing, and other employees, and though the building owner had apparently posted a security guard in the lobby, no metal detectors or weapons detection system were in operation at the time.

The reportorial detail of the Evans murder/suicide was relatively rare, but not as rare as the facts themselves. Evans was the only case in the study in which a white-collar supervisor in the public sector was engaged in a secret relationship outside the office with a subordinate female employee whom he later killed before committing suicide in a large public building. (The research yielded at least a half-dozen such relationships that ended in suicide. Although this factual scenario was found a few times in the public sector, most of these perpetrators were in the private sector.) [14] The building had no weapons detection system whatsoever, despite its urban location and the substantial volume of daily human traffic. Since Evans had access to (and throughout) the large office building (with two handguns on his person), and had likely entered the building at least once every (business) day for the previous twelve years (he started working in the building in 1984), it's easy to see how even the cheapest, simplest weapons detection device would have had a valuable deterrent effect.

Of course, it can't be determined how often Evans brought the weapons to work, or if he stored the guns at the office, and so on. But from what we know about the building, its size, its occupants, and its location, it seems unlikely that Evans was the only man who carried deadly weapons on his person when he went to work and walked throughout the building during the course of an average day. And the likely flow of firearms throughout the building might have been higher had it been a factory or warehouse, which were the more common work sites for the murders that occurred in the cases included in the study.

More than 56 percent of the perpetrators in the study (about 180 out of 350) were blue-collar workers, and more than 56 percent of their murders were committed in either a factory or a warehouse (more than three times more often than in any other location); 17 percent occurred in office buildings; 10 percent in open commercial spaces, like malls and parking lots; 8 percent in universities, colleges, or schools; 4 percent in vehicles or cars; and 5 percent in "other." Still, it's difficult to generalize, and there were always glaring factual exceptions that occasionally threatened to invalidate the rule.

One truly exceptional case was that of Jiverly Antares Wong, 41, a naturalized ethnic Chinese immigrant from Vietnam who lived in Johnson City, New York. Unlike most of the Asian perpetrators in the study, Wong was not a professional; he wasn't a physician, an engineer, or the president of a promising electronics startup seeking investors for the firm, and he didn't have an impressive résumé listing an Ivy League MBA. In fact, Wong likely never even finished high school, and he had a minor criminal record, having been convicted in 1992 on a misdemeanor charge of fraud.

Wong had worked for almost seven years delivering sushi for a local catering company, and had also worked at a local Shop-Vac vacuum cleaner plant before it closed its doors in November 2008. Wong also dispelled a popular Asian stereotype, because the record suggests he wasn't good at math, and, unlike most of the Asian men in the study, who spoke slightly accented but grammatically sound English, Wong's English skills were terrible in every respect.[15]

On April 3, 2009, Jiverly Wong shot and killed thirteen people and wounded four others in the American Civic Association immigration center in Binghamton, New York, before he turned a gun on himself and committed suicide.[16] At 10:30 a.m. that Friday morning, he drove his father's car and barricaded the rear door of the building, which had neither a metal-detection device or even a security guard. After he barricaded the back door of the building, he armed himself with two guns, a nine-millimeter Beretta pistol and a .45-caliber Beretta. Wearing a bulletproof vest, a bright green nylon jacket, and dark-rimmed sunglasses, he burst through the *front door* of the building and opened fire.[17]

That there was no weapons detection system or device, or even a security guard in the lobby, is suggested by the fact that within a minute or two after Wong opened fire, at least a half-dozen 911 calls were made. All were made by three civic center receptionists, one of whom died minutes after she made a 911 call and was shot in the head. Another, Shirley DeLucia, a 61-year-old, remained on the line for almost forty minutes despite her gunshot wound, courageously relaying information to the police until she was finally rescued.[18] And there's not a single word in the record that refers even obliquely to the presence of a security guard, or to any personnel who returned fire or otherwise responded when Wong burst into the building lobby and opened fire.

The police arrived exactly three minutes after the first 911 call, and when the dust settled, they determined that Wong had shot and killed thirteen people, including several fellow Asian immigrants, and had seriously wounded four more as many sat in their classrooms studying English as a second language from their books. Wong's motive for the rampage included feelings of having been "degraded and disrespected" by people in general, his poor English language skills, and frustration at having recently lost his job.[19]

The Wong case was not only among the most violent cases of workplace murder found in the study, it was also one of the cases in which the perpetrator had shown much premeditation and planning beforehand. Before he killed his thirteen victims and then turned a gun on himself, the record reveals that he barricaded the rear door of the center with his father's car. The record also suggests that he was familiar with the physical layout of the American Civic Association center building, knew the main entrances and exits for ingress and egress, knew there was no emergency evacuation plan in effect, knew there were no security measures in force, no security guards to confront, and no metal-detection device at the main entrance.

The record also reveals that he had even envisioned his physical movements inside the building—where he would go, which classrooms he would visit—before he actually arrived at the center and burst through the front door with both guns ablaze.[20]

Yet it's the extent to which Wong had planned his workplace murders that also makes the case a factually receptive context in which to illustrate the value of just a few simple administrative steps. These preventative steps show how effectively just one system or protocol, had it been in place on April 2, 2009—the day *before*—would have definitely prevented one of the worst cases of workplace murder ever to occur in the United States.

What practical, easy steps could have been taken, what simple administrative measures could have been adopted, to prevent the facts of the Wong case from happening in the first place? And how could the facts of such a tragedy be recognized—before they actually take place?

Those steps are listed very simply below. The following steps work most effectively, however, only when launched in a workplace environment that has already instituted (1) zero tolerance for all violence, (2) a detailed termination procedure, and (3) a "goodbye but don't come back" rule. With those three initiatives already an established fact, the employer is advised to:

1. Conduct a security assessment to determine the building's vulnerability to a workplace shooter.

2. Identify different escape routes (and post or publicize these routes in accessible places or conspicuous areas of the building), being sure to take into account those employees with special physical needs or disabilities.
3. Designate shelter locations with especially thick (bulletproof) walls, solid doors with locks, minimal interior windows, first-aid emergency kits, communication devices, and duress alarms.
4. Designate a point of contact who has a good knowledge of the building and its security procedure and the building's floor plan, and who will be in contact with the police or other law enforcement in the event of a shooting incident.
5. Incorporate this procedure into any already established fire or emergency preparedness program. (The considerations for an effective response to a workplace shooting are strikingly similar to those for a fire and even some natural disasters.)
6. Vary the security guards' patrols and reconnaissance patterns in and around the building and its facilities.
7. Limit access to blueprints, floor plans, and other documents that contain sensitive security information (like access codes, combinations, etc), but make sure these documents are available to law enforcement personnel who will be responding to the incident.
8. Establish a central command station for building security.
9. Put in place (a) an elevator system that may controlled or shut down from a central command station and (b) a communications system that allows for building-wide, real-time messaging.[21]

A good faith implementation of the foregoing nine recommendations—along with a commitment to zero tolerance for workplace violence and the institution of a detailed termination procedure, along with a "no return" rule—will forever eliminate the possibility of workplace murder, both as a tragedy for the employee and as a serious management concern.

SURVIVAL—CONTROLLING THE AFTERMATH

There remains, however, one final element of the preventive process that should be addressed. As critical as it is for management to ensure workplace safety and security, in this area, however, is management's effort to ensure workplace control. What is this final element of control, and how is it important to the overall process of preventing workplace murder?

A brief return to the facts of the Jiverly Wong case will be instructive. And more important than a mere repetition of the violent facts is a closer look at the timeline of events—by the perpetrator, Wong, after he entered the building and started to shoot people as he went from classroom to classroom; by the three receptionists who made the first 911 calls that were directed to the police; by law enforcement, including a SWAT effort; and by the hostages and occupants of the center as a heavily armed Wong holed himself up in the building and held the SWAT force and the police at bay.

Wong first entered the lobby of the civic center, both guns blazing, at 10:30 a.m.; the first 911 calls were received within sixty seconds, and the local police started to arrive at the scene within three minutes, at 10:33 a.m. Forty minutes later, at 11:13 a.m., members of a SWAT team had arrived and started to evacuate the building. Some of the occupants had escaped to a basement, while more than a dozen others remained hidden in the building, huddled in a first-floor closet. Local police remained at the perimeter of the property, having locked down the nearby (Binghamton) high school and several streets in the area as extra precautions.

It should be noted that, at this point, Wong had already shot and killed several people and had fired ninety-nine rounds—eighty-eight from his nine-millimeter Berretta and eleven from his .45-caliber pistol—but nobody outside the building knew his whereabouts, or where in the building he was hiding. Approximately ninety minutes later, at 12:00 noon, ten people had evacuated the building, and at 12:40 another ten followed them safely from the building into the hands of medics, EMT personnel, and the police. (Wong's body was later found in a first-floor office, where he had committed suicide, and on his body the police found a bag of ammunition, unspent magazines, an empty magazine with a thirty-round capacity, and a firearm laser light.)

It was not until 2:33 p.m., or two hours after Wong opened fire, that the SWAT team had completely evacuated the civic center and all involved were safely in the hands of law enforcement and the police.

It was during this period that the various witnesses, former hostages, and occupants were provided first aid, were transported to local hospitals for treatment, or to the morgue, and were individually processed and debriefed by law enforcement, including SWAT and the local police. It was also during this period, in the *aftermath* of the murders, ironically, that the employees and occupants faced the very real danger of being seriously wounded or even killed—this time by law enforcement and the police.

This irony owes to the fact that the occupants don't have time to think and consider the mindset of the police and other law enforcement during this tense period, and as a result are often shocked and offended by their treatment by the police after they have escaped from the building, away from the shooter, and find themselves safely outside again, in the hands of the police. How will they be treated by the police? And why?

After the police arrive, don't expect to be treated civilly or even with respect. Until the police actually confirm the identity of the shooter, or place the shooter in custody, they will treat *everybody* like the shooter, and will probably handcuff you and everybody else who comes running from the building. The reason is that they don't know who the shooter is, and it could easily be the shooter who shrewdly runs from the building, pretending to be an innocent hostage running from the building toward the police.

For this reason, once the employee has escaped from the building and is detained by the police, the employee should refrain from any sudden, alarming movements and quickly lie facedown on the ground, with arms spread away from his or her body, palms open and upward, facing the police, and with fingers spread apart so that the police can see even from a distance that his or her hands are empty. The employee should be fully cooperative; should not argue, protest, or object; and should tell the police everything he or she knows.

The employee need only consider that, whatever the police instruct him or her to do, and however much they shout and scream, even if they handcuff the employee, it's being done only as a way of securing the workplace environment and to get the situation under control. The police aren't being mean or racist or insensitive. The employees need only remind themselves that the police and other emergency personnel, in a highly tense situation, have been highly trained to handle virtually every contingency, but they will be on edge, on high alert, and tense. Realize that they might have to shoot and kill in a split-second moment of life and death in order to protect you and the others, and to neutralize the danger.

Nor should the employee be disappointed if the police and the members of the SWAT effort don't immediately charge like the cavalry into the building and rescue everybody, the way it's often done on TV and the Hollywood movie screen. Remember again that they have been trained to first survey and assess the situation before they make a move. And they realize that they won't be able to help or rescue anyone if they do their jobs incorrectly and get themselves injured or killed.

Whatever else may be said about the prevention of workplace violence, it provides a safe, secure, and stress-free environment in which the vast majority of workers spend most of their days. But the implementation of the suggested recommendations will not only eliminate workplace murder as a management/employee concern. There are other benefits as well. Indeed, the benefits abound.

A gun-free workplace, along with zero tolerance for violence, insulates an employer from possible legal liability if a workplace shooting *does* occur. A workplace based on this policy also projects a public image of safety and security, both of which inure to the benefit of employees as the security allays employee fears and boosts worker morale. As already noted, a third of American workers go to work every day "afraid,"[22] and many are as fearful *for* their jobs as they are *on* the job. At the end of the day, however, the most important benefit derived from this policy is the positive effect it has on workplace industry, efficiency, productivity, creativity, and—ultimately— profits and the bottom line.

Although the recommendations made here require the complete prohibition of firearms in the workplace, they don't endorse the argument that private gun ownership should be banned or even restricted among the citizenry. Arguments for the abolition of private gun ownership, the curtailment of the right to bear arms, or a more restrictive reading of the Second Amendment by the Supreme Court are not only foolhardy but also impractical, even shortsighted. Guns are a vitally important, even profound symbol of our birth as a sovereign nation, our national politics, culture, and our foreign policy— from the eighteenth-century Minutemen at Concord to the deployment of "drones" as a viable military strategy in twenty-first-century Afghanistan and Iraq.

CHICKS AND GUNS—A NEW CONSUMER MARKET, OR ARTISTIC FREEDOM AT WORK

So intertwined are the issues of private gun ownership and American culture, for example, that the two cannot always be separately analyzed and discussed. This feature complicates virtually every discussion and debate, including the simplest judgments about politics, economics, even art. For example, the single most surprising discovery in this study was that women in the workplace who used a firearm always—without exception—used only a single handgun. In almost three years' research, in which thousands of cases, newspaper articles, clippings, and blurbs were reviewed, not one instance of workplace murder was found in which a woman used a rifle, carbine, or shotgun. Indeed, not a single case was found in which an ambidextrous woman used two handguns. Every woman used only a single handgun. Never anything more.

Then something bizarre happened. In an incredible coincidence, in late 2011 an unusual book appeared on the local library shelves. The book was titled simply *Chicks with Guns*, by photographer Lindsey McCrum.[23] A giant, lavishly produced coffee-table affair, the book features about eighty stunningly beautiful glossy plates of women—young and old, of every race, in every setting, some with young children, toddlers, even one in a wheelchair, and all female. Of these eighty-odd plates, about twenty depict women holding various types and models of handguns, but more than sixty (or about 75 percent) of the photographs depict women holding every conceivable gauge and caliber of, you guessed it, carbine, rifle, and shotgun. And in many of the photographs of women holding handguns, standing in the background is a cabinet, shelf, or rack that's filled with rifles, carbines, and shotguns.

Is it the height of cynicism to suspect a secret marketing strategy, or an elaborate but clandestine corporate effort to expand an already saturated consumer market, secretly bankrolled by the National Rifle Association? Or is the book exactly what it purports to be: an unusually stunning photographic achievement and a profoundly compelling visual essay?[24] *Chicks with Guns* will likely popularize rifles, carbines, shotguns, and assault weaponry among women, both in the workplace and beyond. A clearer, more effective advertising campaign to induce women to buy more rifles and shotguns is hard to imagine. Yet the book is actually the result of a legitimate, indeed commendable, artistic vision and achievement, which only seeks a readily receptive audience for guns that seems to grow every day.

As already noted in chapter 11, in the last few years a number of legislative initiatives succeeded nationwide that were designed to increase the public's access to firearms. The rationale for enactment of these laws was that private citizens increasingly feel the need to assume some responsibility for their own safety and protection. This is especially the case, the argument goes, during difficult economic times, when recessions tighten local budgets and reduce local municipal services like fire and police protection. In addition, the argument continues, employees should be permitted to "keep guns in their vehicles at work in order to protect themselves while traveling to and from work and during their personal breaks away from work, such as lunch."[25]

Of all the arguments advanced to support increased access to guns, however, this argument is probably the least persuasive, indeed, even specious. In the three years of research that preceded this study—the thousands of cases reviewed and the many hundreds of newspaper articles, clippings, and blurbs that were meticulously clipped and catalogued—only two cases were found in which an employee foiled a bank robbery or thwarted a serious crime during his lunch break because he was carrying a concealed weapon or had fortuitously stashed a loaded firearm in the glove compartment of his car. This is hardly a sufficient statistical basis to justify the expansion of concealed weapons legislation.

Perhaps the second-least persuasive argument advanced by so-called gun advocates is that shooting incidents like that that occurred in Arizona would have been foiled or even prevented had people in the audience also been armed. Even assuming for the sake of argument that this premise is valid,[26] an exception should be made for the workplace. The workplace is the only locale (even excepting a church, synagogue, temple, mosque, or other place of worship) in which the ban on firearms should be across the board, total, and complete. Why should the workplace be regarded so differently? Why should a work environment be the sole exception to the rule?

GUN CULTURE AND THE QUEST FOR PERSONAL CONFIDENCE, "TALENT," AND SELF-ESTEEM

Almost as devastating as the effects of an individual murder in a specific workplace are the far-reaching effects of a gun mindset, a gun "culture," or the socioeconomic context in which the murders occur. The gun culture, after all, is infinitely more than target practice in the backyard, or shooting tin cans off a rack to win a giant teddy bear at the county fair. The gun culture has a tremendous effect not only on the community, but also on the individual members of that community, their politics, their economics, and the way in which they conduct their daily lives and view the world. This includes how a community and its members regard the workplace—whether it's a factory, warehouse, assembly plant, or an office building, storefront, or high-rise executive suite. It also includes how efficiently, productively, and creatively an individual member of that community performs on the job. And it should be noted here at the outset that this is not an argument for stricter gun control, but a call to recognize how critical it is that the mindset that invariably *accompanies* gun ownership not be allowed to affect the workplace.

In one of his best-selling crime novels, author Laurence Shames describes the personality and outlook of one of his low-rent mobsters when he writes that "whenever he carried his gun, he always felt like he had talent." This is a deeply profound insight, shrewdly observed, and applies as well to Graham Greene's film noir characters as it does to fictional characters in darkly humorous novels about the Mob. Such is the power of the gun.

In the book *Chicks with Guns*, we recall, eighty women were beautifully photographed holding different types of guns. Of the women who describe how owning and holding a gun made them feel, virtually all describe the feeling as one of "talent," "power," and "satisfaction," and the word used most often is "confident." Could those same feelings be derived, perhaps more genuinely and durably, from completing a course at the local community college, starting a hobby, serving breakfast at a homeless shelter, painting the kitchen, or finally cleaning out the garage? Would the social costs be significantly less if these feelings were achieved in a way that didn't involve the purchase, use, and maintenance of a deadly rifle, assault weapon, or other firearm?

That gun ownership and possession makes a person feel talented, empowered, satisfied, and confident is fine; the problem, however, is that gun ownership and particularly gun possession also poses dangerous threats to individuals and to the community at large, killing thousands of people every year, and certainly causes more deaths than enrollment in a community college, taking up a hobby, or finally cleaning out a cluttered garage. For better or worse, the fact is that gun ownership, and particularly gun *possession*, changes you. The average person from Anywhere, USA, will almost invariably walk, talk, and interact differently with people, both in private and in public, if he or she is carrying a concealed gun. It's only human nature.

In a recent study conducted by professors at Notre Dame University, it was found that whatever the effects of gun ownership, the ramifications of gun *possession* were very different, with wider, greater potential for conflict, injury, and death. [27] The study showed that a person who carried a gun was far more likely to think that other people were also carrying guns. [28] Moreover, the study showed that possessing a gun made a person far more likely to use a gun against a perceived threat or danger than if the gun were easily accessible or merely laying nearby. [29]

These findings explain what occurred in the Amadou Diallo case of New York City a few years ago and, in short, support the view that gun possession affects how the gun possessor perceives the world, responds to other people and situations, and resolves issues that may arise. [30] And if gun ownership is not problematic, gun possession is a much more delicate issue, and gun possession in or near the workplace presents the dangers at their very worst.

Chapter Fourteen

Conclusion

Gun Culture, Productivity, and Profits

GUN CULTURE, THE MYTH AND THE REALITY

In 2000, Michael A. Bellesiles wrote a book entitled *Arming America—The Origins of a National Gun Culture* (Knopf). In the book he argued that contrary to popular belief, guns and firearms didn't figure as prominently in the nation's culture and history as almost everybody believed.

Bellesiles contended that most Americans didn't even own a gun until after the Civil War, and that the roots of the American gun culture were not nearly as deep, pervasive, or immutable as everyone had assumed or been taught. An Emory University history professor, he spent a decade searching and reviewing probate and other legal records, court documents, military and business records, travel accounts, personal letters, hunting magazines, and even fiction, looking for references to guns.

His research led him to conclude that "almost no guns were made in America prior to the 1820s,"[1] and prior to the 1860s, "guns were not . . . a significant component of America's national identity, essential to its survival."[2] America's "core values" at the time, he argued, were "either religious or liberal sensibilities" and the "prosperity and survival of the United States depended on the grace of God, or civil virtue, or the individual's pursuit of self interest."[3] Bellisiles concluded, in short, that "America's gun culture is an *invented tradition*."[4]

As this view was radically different from the accepted history of gun ownership, not surprisingly the response ignited still another bitter and raucous debate over the nature and scope of Second Amendment rights. The nasty political debate soon became a scholarly investigation, however, when the book's critics discovered dozens of factual errors, questionable sources, and instances in which Bellesiles had deliberately misconstrued primary sources to support his own academic agenda and advance his own political views.[5]

The uproar led to an independent panel of three prominent historians who concluded in 2002 that Bellesiles was "guilty of unprofessional and misleading work" and also raised questions about falsified data.[6] Columbia University promptly took back the Bancroft history prize it had awarded the book, and Bellesiles resigned from the Emory University faculty. He and his supporters, however, still maintain that the uproar was "politically motivated" because his errors were minor, and that he became the target of a "swiftboating" campaign that was financed by the National Rifle Association.[7]

There is no question that an astronomically high level of gun deaths separates the United States from every other industrial nation on the face of the earth, and that 2 million violent crimes and 24,000 murders occur every year in the United States. Indeed, as Bellesiles notes, more Americans are killed by guns in a typical week than in all of Western Europe in a year. Given this level of human slaughter, and the level of public indifference, the role played by the "gun culture" in American history, and how far back it extends in the national past, pose the wrong questions. And as they pose the wrong questions, the answers might be correct but inevitably still miss the point.

Bellesiles's book and the controversy it provoked accomplished little except to energize and further polarize an already polarized public debate. The question isn't how deeply the gun culture is a part of the national past or how widely it's been embraced; the more critical inquiry is how the gun culture will figure in America's *future*—specifically America's economic role in the twenty-first-century global workplace.

The shelves are filled with studies and polls that assess and measure the cause-and-effect relationship of gun ownership and crime, gun ownership and gun injuries, gun ownership and accidental death, and so on. But few studies focus on the relationship between gun ownership and other behaviors, other qualities and traits that are indispensable to the workings of a viable twenty-first-century workplace. Whatever behaviors were attributed to or caused by gun ownership in the frontier past, however deep its roots or pervasively embraced, it's clear what the gun culture does *not* do, and what it does *not* achieve.

The gun culture does not unleash the human drive toward productivity and efficiency, nor does it release the spark of ingenuity and creativity that are now indispensable elements in the twenty-first-century workplace; all of which translate into greater human capital, and ultimately generate higher profits and a healthier bottom line. How and why—anthropologically—is the gun culture antithetical to human industry and the work ethic? Why is the gun culture inimical to the principles that serve a productive, viable twenty-first-century workplace?

GUN CULTURE AND THE AMERICAN CHARACTER—ACROSS THE FIFTY STATES

The concept of culture, of course, is difficult to define. Yet the distinctive features and significant characteristics of the American gun culture consistently negate or nullify every trait that's indispensable to a profitable twenty-first-century workplace. The two are in opposition, behaviorally, and rarely meet. This tension is best illustrated by contextualizing the two different sets of behaviors, and then comparing them as they exist (or don't exist) in America, among the populations of the various fifty states.

The extent to which the inhabitants of different states have embraced the gun culture may be reflected in the official state records of gun ownership and gun registration. Studies show, for example, that states like Alaska, Wyoming, Montana, North Dakota, South Dakota, West Virginia, Arkansas, Alabama, and Kentucky lead the nation in firearm registration and ownership.[8] Not surprisingly, these same states, where the gun culture is most pervasive and the most deeply rooted, also lead the nation in gun deaths.[9]

What remains surprising, however, is how routinely and frequently scholars and pollsters establish the relatively easy, commonsense connection between gun ownership and gun deaths, but consistently ignore the relationship between gun ownership and other behaviors, outcomes, and circumstances—other pursuits and values that have become critically important in modern American life.

What, for example, is the relationship between the states with very high rates of gun registration and ownership and, say, the states that rank highest on the lists of the best places for retirement,[10] job creation, starting a business,[11] technology,[12] job opportunities,[13] physical/environmental health,[14] raising a family,[15] educating children,[16] and quality restaurants,[17] or whose residents are the most literate,[18] or the healthiest and most physically fit.[19] How do the "gun" states stack up against the other states—in other areas? It's surprising how often the states that lead the nation in gun ownership and gun deaths also tend to be at the bottom of the lists of quality-of-life criteria. Conversely, the states that consistently rank highest on the lists of quality-of-life areas tend to rank lowest on those lists that rank gun registration, ownership, and death.[20]

Of course, recognition of these connections and relationships isn't a "science," and no claim to either scientific accuracy or even objectivity will be made here. In addition, there are stark, glaring examples—exceptions—that fly in the face of anyone with a hardened statistical agenda. A number of states that rank high on the lists of gun registration and ownership, like Alaska and Idaho, for example,[21] also rank fairly high on the lists of the best states in which to start a small business.[22] Montana, for example, is near the top of the lists for states with high gun ownership,[23] yet stands justifiably proud (if virtually alone) as a proworker state in which an employer must have a darn good "reason" for terminating an employee.[24]

But these statistical dead ends are too few and far between to invalidate or even obscure an unmistakable, clearly discernible pattern. This pattern shows a strong connection — or nexus—between states in which the gun culture is pervasive and deeply rooted and the behaviors that are inimical to, even destructive of, a workplace environment that's also profitable in an increasingly globalized twenty-first-century economy. For better or worse, the states that lead the nation in gun ownership and gun-inflicted injuries and death also tend to be the states that are the drunkest,[25] the fattest,[26] the laziest,[27] the dumbest,[28] and the most nicotine-addicted,[29] with the worst drivers[30] and the worst schools.[31]

And how significant is it, statistically, that West Virginia, Arkansas, Mississippi, and Kentucky, for example, lead the nation in gun ownership and the adoption of the gun culture, but are also the four "dumbest" states in America?[32] These less fortunate states consistently rank at or near the bottom of the lists that rate the best places to raise a family, educate children, start a business, and other pursuits that bear on the quality of modern American life. And, even more unfortunately, when these states do not occupy the very bottom of the quality-of-life lists, they seldom occupy the middle, and never rank near the top.

Whatever impact the gun culture has on workplace safety and security, these comparisons show unmistakably that it's also antiwork ethic and not conducive to a profitable workplace. The comparisons show that the gun culture does little to spur productivity, efficiency, creativity, and drive, which ultimately affect profits and the bottom line. Bellesiles's answers and conclusions were not only biased and falsified, he had asked the wrong questions. Whatever role the gun culture played in the history of American economic might, it wasn't always an indispensable element in American economic development, or a necessary feature of economic creativity, productivity, and growth.

GUN CULTURE AND THE ECONOMICS OF NINETEENTH-CENTURY WHALING

For almost two centuries, American whale oil lit up the world—financing the start of the Industrial Revolution and laying the groundwork for American domination of an enterprise that founded the global economy. From its humble beginnings as a local economic enterprise in the late seventeenth century until its decline in the decades following the Civil War, the American whaling industry mapped millions of miles of uncharted ocean and opened new seaways and markets around the world. In this respect, the men in the whaling industry were much like twentieth-century astronauts in space travel and interplanetary exploration. In addition, the whaling industry employed the world's most multicultural workforce and shrunk the globe by bringing once remote reaches of the earth into contact with each other as never before.[33]

The breadth and scope of the American whaling industry even captured the popular imagination. As space-age travel by astronauts inspired Stanley Kubrick's pioneering film opus *2001: A Space Odyssey*, so whaling inspired Herman Melville's literary masterpiece *Moby Dick*, whose first two hundred–odd pages are dedicated largely to detailed descriptions of the most arcane and technical aspects of whaling.

At about the time Melville was completing the final pages of *Moby Dick*, the whaling industry was a booming worldwide enterprise, and the United States was the global behemoth— dominating the industry in what was the first truly global market. In the 1850s, New Bedford, Massachusetts, was more than the harbor for Melville's fictional character, Ishmael; it was in fact the center of the whaling business. According to one newspaper, New Bedford was the richest, most affluent city per capita in the United States, possibly the world.[34] In 1846, the titans of the whaling industry owned more than 640 whaling ships, which was more than *triple* the number of whaling ships owned by all the other countries in the world.[35]

In an age before electricity, whale oil was the primary illuminant for lamps, and the primary lubricant for machinery. (Thomas Jefferson preferred to read with lamps filled with spermaceti, a highly refined whale oil, because it produced far less soot when it burned.) Whale oil lit the streets of London and Paris and produced ambergris (actually, whale vomit) for ladies' perfumes, and whales also yielded baleen, a bone-like substance that was highly moldable and widely used for umbrellas and corsets, much the way plastic is used today. The whaling industry grew by a factor of fourteen between 1826 and 1850.[36]

But in the decades following the Civil War, as the costs of whaling (and worldwide competition) grew, wealthy capitalists funneled their investment dollars into other domestic industries, like railroads, steel, and oil. In 1859, for example, the United States produced less than two thousand barrels of oil a year; by 1900, the US produced that amount of oil every seventeen minutes.[37] At its height, the whaling industry contributed more than ten million dollars to the gross domestic product (in 1880 dollars!), which made it the fifth-largest sector in the economy.[38]

Barely fifty years later, the whaling industry was all but dead.[39] Historians still disagree over what caused the relatively rapid demise—rising costs, declining demand, overhunting, an 1846 conflagration that razed much of Nantucket, the California Gold Rush, and so on. But there's little disagreement that the whaling industry was started, organized, financed, managed, owned, controlled, and dominated by New England Quakers—plainspoken, pious, religious pacifists who opposed all violence and all wars and eschewed the ownership and use of guns.

The whaling industry of the eighteenth and nineteenth centuries was not the only American business enterprise that took root and then flourished outside the prevailing gun culture. Nor were the Quakers alone in their rejection of guns and violence which released a creative energy and entrepreneurial drive that laid the foundation for global markets, tremendous profits, and wealth. Another example of this phenomenon arose in the late twentieth century, in the poorest neighborhoods of New York City's infamous South Bronx, in the unlikely origins and growth of rap music and hip-hop.

GUN CULTURE AND THE ECONOMICS OF RAP MUSIC AND HIP-HOP

Since its humble beginnings in the mid-1970s in the poorest sections of the South Bronx, New York, rap music has grown exponentially, creating a hip-hop culture and lifestyle that spawned a multibillion-dollar industry whose influence is worldwide.[40] While much has been written about that success, little has been written about the poor, jobless teenagers and the environment that gave rise to the music—the abject poverty, the unemployment, street crime, gang violence and armed warfare, guns and lack of opportunity. These were gifted teenagers with "plenty of imagination but little cash [who] began to forge a new style from spare parts."[41] Theirs was a music of "pure street-wise ingenuity,"[42] part of a "generation that refused to be silenced by urban poverty."[43] "They didn't have money to pay for admission to the expensive midtown and downtown clubs, so they had their own parties. Along the way, clubs, house parties, and block parties sprang up all over New York ghettos, giving birth to the neighborhood DJ and MC."[44]

These teenagers "came from poverty and desolation,"[45] "the poorest of the poor inner city areas,"[46] and rap music was a politicized music that evolved with the "downfall of the Black Power movement of the 1960s and 1970s, [and] organically fill[ed] a void for young people, allowing them to create a cultural expression and meaningful existence of their own."[47] The music allowed them a "creative outlet . . . to escape from the financial crisis that had over taken their neighborhoods and eliminated . . . many of the social programs upon which they had come to depend."[48] Poor, unemployed high school dropouts who were often literally penniless with no economic opportunities, many of the first rappers threw street parties that were wholly spontaneous affairs hosted by DJs with makeshift turntables and oversized speaker systems, and as often as not, "the power source for these sound systems was the nearest street light."[49]

From 1968 to 1972, gangs and street violence in the South Bronx spread like wildfire, and peaked in 1973.[50] When Malcolm X famously offered the choice of "the ballot or the bullet,"[51] these teenagers accepted the "ballot" option, but on their own terms—by politicizing their words and music to address the issues and problems of their day. But they also flatly rejected the option of the "bullet," and abandoned the gun culture that figured so prominently in their lives. The godfather of rap music, Afrika Bambaataa, himself once a gang member like so many of his peers,[52] rejected the gun culture in favor of creating a new music, and they "used hip-hop as a way to speak out against the negative gang culture that had developed among many poor inner-city black groups."[53] They rejected the gun culture, and then compensated for their lack of money with creativity, industry, and a work ethic that was second to none.[54]

Even the "gangsta" rappers, like Ice-T, who often wrote the most incendiary lyrics like "kill the cops," were just "talkin' the talk" but not "walkin' the walk." In lyrics like those in Ice-T's "Mic Contract," even the microphone is seen as a symbol of power, a phallic extension or "gun" which enabled rappers to fight it out. But it's a "*sublimated* warfare,"[55] fought in lieu of the real thing. To this day, decades later, detractors still argue that the lyrics of rap music, especially "gangsta" rap, only incite teenagers to commit more crime.[56] But the detractors miss the point. While Ice-T and other gangsta rappers were exhorting listeners to "kill the cops," something extraordinary was happening (or *not* happening) in the real world, on the nation's streets.

If we consider the thirty-year period from 1975 to 2005 as the time it took rap music to evolve into a mature, popular art form, we can better assess what influence it was having on the street. A look at the national murder rate from 1975 to 2005 shows little variation, averaging just under twenty thousand per year,[57] but with dramatic increases in almost every other serious crime.[58] Yet the murder rate in New York City (including the South Bronx) during that same period not only dropped, but dropped *dramatically!*[59] And not just the rate for homicide dropped, but the rates for every other category of serious crime: forcible rape,[60] aggravated assault,[61] burglary,[62] larceny-theft,[63] vehicular theft,[64] and robbery.[65] A similar drop in homicides over the same period was seen in Los Angeles, the other birthplace of rap music, whose youth had immersed themselves in this new art form![66] In short, while the national crime rates in the seven most serious crimes had generally climbed, those same crimes in New York (including the South Bronx) and LA had consistently dropped, even *plummeted!*

This "coincidence" in timing, of course, suggests that it was exceedingly difficult for a typical Bronx teenager of that period to rhyme rap lyrics, compose music, practice a new art form, mix and scratch for gigs at block parties, compete with other kids in other neighborhoods, prepare for local auditions, and work toward signing a record deal, all during the day—and then commit felonies at night. There simply weren't enough hours in the day. Something had to give.

Little has been written on this neglected aspect of the origins of rap music, how brilliantly and creatively the first rap artists "made something out of nothing."[67] They embraced a strong DIY (do-it-yourself), entrepreneurial work ethic that has since produced scores of young black millionaires and created jobs in the industry—on both the creative and technical sides—that lifted thousands of young blacks into the middle class.

In Ben Stiller's film *Tropic Thunder* (2008), Tom Cruise not only revived his dormant movie career but also stole the movie with his portrayal of Les Grossman, a pudgy, balding white media mogul with a filthy mouth—and a firm belief in a business philosophy he lifted from the lyrics of rap music. Nor was the Les Grossman character just the far-fetched creation of an inspired scriptwriter. The same rap lyrics have inspired at least one real-life millionaire CEO/investment analyst to take similar note. A prominent, highly successful venture capital investor in Silicon Valley, Ben Horowitz believes that rap lyrics hold a trove of lessons for would-be tech entrepreneurs. Throw the business seminars and textbooks out the window, Horowitz says, and listen carefully to rap lyrics instead.[68]

In the mid-1970s, a handful of black teenagers in the South Bronx with no money but a lot of talent, imagination, creativity, and drive rejected the gun culture and the violence it bred in their neighborhoods. They fought the system by creating words and music instead, to address the politics and issues of their times. And what was the result? In a single generation they unleashed a creative energy and force that spawned a cultural revolution, politicized popular music, and touched the souls of disenchanted youth all over the world, generating a multibillion-dollar industry that sells music, clothes, and accessories, and markets a "lifestyle" that spread around the globe.

GUN CULTURE, ECONOMIC GROWTH, AND THE "PEOPLE" FACTOR

As already noted, gun ownership/possession often changes how the owner regards other people, how he or she responds to situations and perceives danger, how he or she interacts with others and the outside world. And these changes are not always for the good. Rooted in fear, suspicion, and insecurity, the ownership and possession of a gun may provide a faux sense of "talent," "power," and "confidence," as it did with many of the women featured in Lindsay McCrum's brilliant photographic essay *Chicks with Guns*. But it also fosters suspicion and a very real need to protect, defend, even kill. The gun culture does little to foster those traits essential to a collaborative effort, to a common work ethic, to connecting and engaging with someone else. In virtually every recent case of mass murder (even the unemployed killers who didn't qualify for this study) the killer was heavily armed, *never* gainfully employed, and *always* later described by neighbors as a "loner" with *few friends*.

The Google-sponsored study—Project Oxygen—only confirmed that technical skills alone were not nearly as important in the twenty-first-century workplace as the ability to make a "connection with other people," to collaborate, to be accessible face-to-face.[69] Carol Smith, we recall, espouses a hiring philosophy that requires meeting a job applicant three times, "and one of them better be over a meal. You learn so much in a meal."[70] And what do employees value most? "Even-keeled bosses who made time for one-on-one meetings, who helped people puzzle through problems by asking questions, not dictating answers, and who took an interest in employees' lives and careers."[71]

Economics development expert Richard Florida writes that 30 percent of the American workforce now consists of a demographic that will determine how companies are organized, what companies will prosper and thrive, and which will wither, go bankrupt, and fail. He calls this growing demographic the "creative" class, and he argues that it's not about technology, government, management, or even power anymore, it's all about *people* and their dynamic and emergent patterns of relationships.[72]

Relatively recent advances, particularly in information technology, of course, have reduced the need to deal personally or face-to face with potential customers, buyers, and clients. How people in business interact with each other has dramatically changed as a result of e-mail, cell telephones, and text messages. Although these changes no longer *require* close proximity to people you want to do business with, Florida and others argue that the economics of "agglomeration" explain why creative, productive, and successful firms continue to choose locations where *other* creative, productive, and successful companies do business, and that this only underscores the importance of *people* dealing face-to-face in dynamic *relationships*.[73]

Investment dollars and capital, along with economic growth and prosperity, it seems, follow these people wherever they cluster to live, work, play, raise families, and settle down. And where do they typically choose to do all these things? With few exceptions, they settle in states that rank highest on the lists of quality-of-life issues—cities and states whose inhabitants place the highest value on environmental health, neighborhood schools, and top-quality restaurants, cities whose citizens are the most literate, most educated, most racially and gender tolerant, and physically fit. In other words, members of the "creative" class avoid those states with a deeply rooted gun culture and rank highest on the lists of gun possession and ownership. [74]

Scores of traditionally-managed companies whose business ethos was based on the gun culture, whose modus operandi reflected the frontier mindset, are no longer around. One-third of the firms in the *Fortune* 500 in 1970, for example, no longer existed just a dozen years later in 1983—killed off by merger, acquisition, breakup, or bankruptcy. [75] This is because the gun culture consistently inhibits and even prevents the human drive toward hard work, industry, productivity. The gun culture rarely inspires or encourages industry, efficiency, and creativity—all of which are essential elements of a human capital that's so vital in the twenty-first-century workplace. These elements of human capital have already shown their value, and will continue to shape how the modern workplace is conceived, staffed, organized, and managed. More and more, they will also affect, even determine, which companies take root, grow, prosper, and flourish, and which will go bankrupt and fail.

GUN CULTURE AND ECONOMIC GROWTH IN THE GLOBAL MARKETPLACE

The gun culture's adverse effects on economic growth and prosperity are not limited to the American experience and its fifty states. The phenomenon also has global implications, as the rejection of the gun culture and its accompanying mindset of violence may be seen in examples worldwide. Ghandi's rejection of violence, of course, released a creative energy and political drive that led to India's independence from a heavily armed British imperialist presence in 1947. And many argue that Mahatma Ghandi's philosophy of passive resistance spawned the modern civil rights movement in the United States starting in the mid-1950s and inspired the leadership of Dr. Martin Luther King Jr.

Indeed, a study of most modern empires—for example, the Dutch in the seventeenth century, Spain and Portugal in the eighteenth, Britain in the nineteenth, and the United States in the twentieth—suggests that their true power rested not so much on military strength but *economic* primacy. [76] Many argue that US world dominance didn't end in the rice paddies of an ignominiously abandoned South Vietnam. That was a "military" defeat, of course, but America still remained a formidable if not the supreme power on the world stage. America's fall from a world power actually came later, in the mid-1980s—on September 16, 1985, to be exact—"when the [US] Commerce Department announced that the United States had become [for the first time in its history] a *debtor* nation." [77]

As the global economy grows smaller, and markets become more competitive, the effects of the gun culture on economic growth will only be seen in greater relief. The gun culture's negative effect on individual and collective industry, productivity, and creativity can also be seen internationally, when the comparisons are made not between the fifty US states but between the world's 178 sovereign nation-states.

In this regard, it's not surprising that the only nation in the world whose economic power now equals (if not surpasses) that of the United States—China—is also the country with the strictest gun laws in the world. "Possession of a single gun in China can yield a three-year prison sentence, while perpetrators of gun crimes are often executed."[78] Nor is it surprising that, generally, the countries that have either recently achieved economic superpower status or now approach that status—Japan, India, Brazil, Indonesia, Singapore, Korea, and so on—are all societies in which guns and firearms are strictly regulated, restricted, or nearly banned.

The true force of this argument, however, is found in the specifics, which are even more illuminating. In a Wikipedia list of 178 countries and their respective rates of gun ownership,[79] the United States tops the list at number one, with 88.8 guns per one hundred residents. At the very bottom of the list is Tunisia at 178th, with 0.10 guns (or one-tenth of a gun) per one hundred residents. When this list is placed alongside other lists, like those that rank national economic growth and potential, the comparisons say much about the incompatibility of the gun culture with economic growth and potential. The ten "economic" powerhouses—Japan, Malaysia, Vietnam, China, the Philippines, Singapore, Indonesia, South Korea, Cambodia, and Laos—for example, average 126th or near the bottom of the Wikipedia gun ownership list,[80] with only 1.9 guns per one hundred residents.[81]

On a list of the twenty "hottest growing" economies in the world,"[82] eighteen of the twenty countries average 1.6 guns per one hundred residents, and average about 129th on the Wikipedia gun list.[83] On the World Bank's list of the twenty-nine "hottest economies in the world for the next two years,"[84] twenty-five of the twenty-nine countries average about 139th on the Wikipedia gun list, with an average of less than 1.3 guns per one hundred residents.[85] And on the list of the ten "fastest-growing economies in the world for the next forty years,"[86] nine of the ten countries average 132nd on the Wikipedia gun list, with an average of only 2.2 guns per one hundred residents.[87] In other words, with one or two exceptions, the twenty hottest growing economies in the world, and the fastest-growing economies in the world for both the next two years and the next four decades, are all societies that are virtually *without guns*!

Those who disagree with these statistical conclusions might point to the example of Switzerland, which generally has the second-highest rate of gun ownership in the world (after the United States) but, incredibly, also has virtually *no crime*. But the reference to Switzerland here is misplaced for two reasons. First, as one of the few countries in the world that doesn't maintain a standing army, the Swiss government requires every able-bodied male to own and maintain an assault weapon, this as part of an effective national militia.[88] Second, the relationship under discussion here isn't between gun ownership and crime, but gun ownership and *economic growth and productivity*. And even with its low crime rate, the Swiss's possession of so many guns comes with a heavy price. Switzerland, after all, is hardly a world economic power, and what, the cynic might ask, have the Swiss contributed to the modern world except the chocolate bar and the cuckoo clock?[89]

Of course, these statistical comparisons are not drawn to insult or to disparage any nationality or group of people, whether residents of the state of Mississippi, the province of Alberta, or the canton of Ticino. Yet it seems a fair generalization, if not an incontrovertible fact, that the gun culture and the work ethic are the behavioral equivalents of oil and water: they don't mix. It seems that the realization of financial prosperity and economic growth rarely occurs where a gun culture has taken hold. When you tap the countries anywhere on the globe with the smallest number of guns per capita, and then tap the places whose economies are the most vibrant and productive with the most consistent growth, you've tapped the same places twice.

The effects of the gun culture on workplace safety and security, of course, are a legitimate basis for management concern. Yet what may be as important to the twenty-first- century workplace is how adversely the gun culture affects productivity, industry, and efficiency, how it inhibits creativity, thwarts personal industry, and discourages a striving for individual excellence—all of which reduce profits and ultimately impact on the bottom line.

In each of the three cases already discussed—the Quakers, the rap musicians, and the different societies across the globe—a particular, discrete group of people affirmatively rejected or consciously abandoned the gun culture before the economic energy was unleashed or took root. But the gun culture may be so inimical or so poisonous to workplace success, so destructive of economic growth and prosperity, that there's no need for it to be consciously rejected or formally abandoned. Other value systems may serve in its stead, and other behavioral norms may have already taken root. Indeed, in some instances it seems that the absence of the gun culture alone may virtually *ensure* economic success.

One example of this phenomenon abounds in almost every large American city, and thrives in our society, today, at this very moment. This example is as close as the nearest inner city, on every other corner it often seems, in virtually every neighborhood, especially in those neighborhoods that are densely populated by Hispanics, blacks, and other minority groups.

GUN CULTURE AND THE ECONOMICS OF EGG ROLLS, CHICKEN WINGS, AND SHRIMP FRIED RICE

More than just a place to buy quick, inexpensive takeout, the small Chinese restaurant is now a neighborhood institution. The local Chinese restaurant has thrived for decades in the so-called inner-city ghetto—much like the Pentecostal storefront church, the bodega, the beauty parlor, the liquor store, and the barbershop. One blogger has even posed the question of whether "The Chinese Restaurant [is a] Ghetto Indicator." "If your block has a Chinese restaurant where you order from a tiny slit in a wall of bulletproof glass," he observes, "that's a good sign that you are in the ghetto. If the most popular item is chicken wings and fried rice, you are most definitely in the 'hood." However, if "the restaurant specializes in a particular kind of Chinese cuisine—Szechuan, dim sum, Taiwanese—you have left the ghetto."[90]

No formal research has been done on the economics of the small Chinese restaurant in urban inner cities nationwide. In the absence of this research, however, it shouldn't be assumed that McDonald's is the most ubiquitous restaurant experience in America. In fact, there are more Chinese restaurants in the United States than McDonald's, Burger King, and Wendy's *combined*.[91] Although this informal network has monopolistic features in its supply and distribution methods, it still shares much with the "mom-and-pop" business model which has all but disappeared from the retail scene. But that's where the similarities end, as each of these thousands of small businesses, located primarily in impoverished inner-city ghettos, often generate as much as a quarter million dollars in income every year.[92] Why was this multibillion-dollar network, this lucrative inner-city institution not started by the enterprising white male titans of the *Fortune* 500? Why have these restaurants not since been gobbled up—like the "mom-and-pop" businesses— by multinational conglomerates hell-bent on a national franchise or a world-wide retail chain? Among other factors,[93] the principal reason was twofold: the American gun culture and its history, and how that history was reflected in a white male-oriented business ethos and its predictably skewed investment sense.

First, the Chinese Exclusion Act of 1882 not only restricted immigration and prevented Chinese men from becoming citizens, it also effectively barred them from jobs in agriculture, mining, and manufacturing. The result was that Chinese men opened laundries and restaurants. Cleaning and cooking, after all, were considered a "woman's" work, and these jobs did not threaten white men. This occupational demasculation of the Asian man was also achieved culturally, and gained wide acceptance and popularity in the fictional (and later TV) character of Charlie Chan. The character, Mr. Chan, was a submissive Chinese-Hawaiian detective "who was the type of Asian that whites did not fear. He spoke English with a heavy accent and walked like a woman. He was not assertive and [he] was docile and obedient, and perpetuated the stereotype of the Asian man as feminine and asexual."[94]

Second, given the long history of blatant racism against blacks and other minority groups that now live in the inner city, few (if any) whites would ever see the potential investment opportunity in such a locale. Nor would white entrepreneurs choose to start a small business whose customer base consisted almost exclusively of blacks, Hispanics, and other nonwhite minority groups. Whites were understandably fearful and suspicious, and their fear and suspicion were more than justified. Burdened with the guilt of slavery and its legacy of racism, and the plausibility of black revenge, whites dared not venture, entrepreneurially, where hordes of poor but guilt-free Chinese settled in, worked hard, and soon flourished economically.

The Chinese effectively embraced another mindset, another nonconfrontational culture. Where other racial and ethnic groups—the Irish, African Americans, Hispanics—often resorted to violence, civil disobedience, or public protest, the Asians were the "model minority." The Asians were supposed beneficiaries of a cultural exceptionalism[95] who seemed never to raise their collective voice, never engaged in public protest, and never took to the streets. Excluded from a society which embraced the gun culture—and its attendant paranoia, suspicion, and fear—Chinese workers started thousands of these small businesses across the country, thousands of tiny restaurants that specialized in quick take-out, whose egg rolls, chicken wings, and white Fold-Pak cartons of shrimp fried rice now generate billions of dollars in cash annually.

GUNS, PRODUCTIVITY, AND PROFITS IN THE MODERN WORKPLACE

The stakes, then, are much higher than just workplace murder and homicide. In the final analysis, at the end of the day, what hangs precariously in the balance is also the success or failure of a business or company which must compete in a highly competitive twenty-first-century global marketplace.

As the cases show, the least competent, least people-skilled, and least liked boss or supervisor is statistically more likely to be murdered by a disgruntled employee. In this light, it might also follow that a workplace whose employees are suspicious, insecure, paranoid loners who can't "connect" with coworkers and colleagues will soon, almost inevitably become less efficient and productive, and fail. It will fail even sooner in a highly competitive global marketplace. And it will fail even if nobody is ever shot and killed on the job, even if nobody ever "snaps" in a homicidal rage and murders a hated coworker or an abusive boss.

With the waning influence of churches, voluntary clubs like the Rotary, the Kiwanis Club, the Elks, and the local PTA, fraternal and professional organizations and unions, fewer and fewer venues are left in which adults of different backgrounds can mingle and socialize together. Barbershops, local taverns, and beauty salons are typically segregated, and even religious congregations are typically very homogeneous, with the vast majority of worshippers reporting that all or nearly all of their fellow worshippers are of their own race.

Virtually alone among these once-popular venues of democracy and social capital, however, is the modern workplace—what Cynthia Estlund aptly describes as "a veritable hotbed of sociability and cooperation, of constructive and mostly friendly interactions among co-workers day after day, and often year after year . . . where adults interact with each other [in places that are] likely the most demographically diverse."[96] In what American institution today are so many different ethnicities, races, ages, cultures, sexual orientations, creeds, and colors thrown together and expected not only to treat each other civilly, even courteously, but also to work together, toward a common goal? Only one place. Our jobs. Where we work.

Why, it's often asked—given the possibility, even the likelihood, that an act of workplace murder will not occur—should all the extra effort, energy, funding, and allocation of other resources be focused on something that occurs only in the worst-case scenario? Why should virtually everybody on the workforce—from the CEOs and upper management to the wage-grade "temps" on the factory floor—be informed about workplace violence, particularly workplace homicide?

There are many answers to this question, and some hopefully were provided on the preceding pages. But for those questions that were raised and not answered, for those that have yet to be raised, and for those that resist the quick, rote reply, the shortest answer is also the most accurate and the most readily understood.

Because the workplace—like murder—is different.

Appendix of the Perpetrators in the Study

A
Adams, Keith
Alcantara, John Jesus
Alexander, Stuart
Allaway, Edward Charles
Allman, Shareef
Anderson, Shane
Antilak, Ladislav
Arechavalet, Taureax
Arias, Juan Lopez
Arrington, Natasha
Asgharalam, Najma
Ashley, John
Austin, Mary Barbara
Avalos, Ernesto Hernandez
B
Badasci, Jim
Baker, Debra
Baker, William
Barber, Dupree
Barnes, Roy
Barnett, David
Barton, Mark
Baxter, Clifford J.Beck, Brian Carl
Beck, Matthew
Beckwith, Holmes

Benitez, Ruben Orlando
Bernard, Thomas
Betancourt, Mario
Bishop, Amy
Bonestroo, Derik
Boyd, John Jr.
Bradford, Thomas Eugene
Brattin, Michael
Bright, Richard Dean "Rusty"
Brittain, Nathaniel
Bromwich, John Jay
Brooks, James
Brooks, Joseph
Brown, Benny Ray
Brown, Elijah
Brown, Kerri Fae
Brown, Nathaniel
Brown, Ritchie Arthur
Brownlee, Samantha Estelle
Brownlee, Steven
Burke, David
Burnam, Jason
Burr, Dale
C
Calden, Paul
Callaway, Auburn
Campbell, Randy Lee
Carciero, Jay
Carlton, Julian
Carter, Russell
Case, William
Cayce, Wilma Ward
Chalmers, Herbert, Jr.
Charland, Arthur
Chen, Jian
Chiu, Tommy
Christian, Gregory
Christian, Rocky
Christian, Steven
Clark, Bruce
Clark, Raymond
Clegon, Christopher
Clemons, Gerald

Clifton, Karan Vanae
Cobb, Joe
Coffin, Judith
Coleman, Carl "Rick"Cowan, Frederick William
Cox, Owen
Cox, Stephen
Cruz, Cornelius
Cruz, Kevin
Culbertson, Linda
Cunningham, David
Currier, Jack Richard
Czajkowski, Dennis
D
Dansby, Mozella
D'Arcy, Jonathan Daniel
Davis, Alex
Davis, James
Davis, Jeremy "Billy"
Davis, Ronald Dean
Dayton, Jessica
Deculit, Anthony
Diamond, Robert
Dinkins, Darryl
Dixon, Richard Vance
Dortch, Vincent
Dozier, Renita Williams
Duke, Jackie Lee
Dunan, Marlene
Duncan, Henry Earl
Dutra, Sara
Dwyer, R. "Bud"
E
Edeen, Karl
Edwards, Reggie
English, Julian
Errasti, Pelayo
Espinal, Eddy
Evans, William
F
Fajardo, Darlin
Farley, Richard Wade
Ferguson, Jacquelyn
Ferguson, Joseph

Ferri, Gian Luigi
Fiedler, Paulette
Findlay, Calvin
Firvida, Francisco
Flenaugh, Sebron, Jr.
Flores, Emilio (& Filberto)
Flores, Victor Rodriguez
Ford, Michael Julius
Foster, Femesha
Foster, Mark Stephen
French, Oliver
Friedlander, Robert Nathan
G
Gallaher, Grant
Garcia, Ezekial
Garcia, Frank
Gardner, John
Geisenheyner, Mark
Gilbert, John
Gillane, John
Givens, Donald
Glasco, Lonnie
Godin, Alan
Godineaux, Craig
Gomez, Martin
Gonzalez, Fidel
Gonzalez, Marco
Graves, Patrick Joseph
Gray, Gregory
Green, Christopher
Gunter, Elisabeth
H
Hallamore, Eileen
Hammett, Mansel (Sonny)
Hansel, Larry
Harmon, Herman
Harris, Joseph M.
Harris, Kareem
Harris, Kim
Harris, Robert Wayne
Harrison, Cadian Jerome
Harrison, John
Hartmann, Michael Paul

Hasan, Nidal Malik
Hastings, Arthur
Hawkins, Robert
Held, Leo
Helfer, Robert "Scott"
Helsley, Christopher
Hendron, Timothy
Hernandez, Ernesto
Hessler, Jerry
Hester, Darrell E.
Hickman, Shontay Joyner
Higdon, Wesley Neal
Hilbun, Mark R.
Hill, Arthur
Hiller, Yvonne
Hill, Stephen
Hoover, Brewer, Jr.
Horowitz, Wayne L.
Hua, Tung Ngoc
Huh, Howard
Hunter, Alfred J, III
Hurtado-Garcia, Soccoro
I
Iglanov, Ilya
Isku, Danny
Itwaru, Sookhdeo
Izquierdo-Leyva, Silvi
J
Jack, John
Jackson, Joe
Jasion, Larry
Jenkins, James (& Stephen)
Jennings, Charles
Jerolaman, Kenneth
Johnson, Angela
Johnson, Jr., James
Johnson, Jeffrey
Johnson, Patrick L.
Johnson, Terrell
Jones, Ryan
Jordan, Emanuel
K
Kashoual, Akouch

Kehoe, Andrew
Kellerman, David
King, Don
Kinyon, Louis Derrell
Kirkpatrick, Eric Allan
Knight, Marion "Suge"
Kropf, Steven
L
LaCalamita, Anthony
Landin, Randy
Laurel, Imelda Molina
Leary, Edward
Leeds, Lee Isaac Bedwell
Lee, Jerold
Lee, Robert Yachen
Lemos, Frank
Lett, Alexander L.
Levy, Mark I.
Lewicki, Jonathan
List, John E.
Little, Keith D.
Logsdon, David W.
Lowery, Natavia S.
Ludlam, Joseph H.
LuPoe, Ervin
LuPoli, Dominic
Lu, Tian Yu
Lyons, Morris
M
Mace, Don
Mack, Robert Earl
Madoff, Mark
Maldonado, Jose Luis
Maines, William D.
Mapp, Claudius
Marchetti, Joseph
Marsden, Daniel S.
Matthews, Richard
McCall, W.A.
McCree, Clifton
McDermott, Michael
McIlvane, Thomas
McLendon, Michael

Mei, Xiubin
Mendez, Jose
Meyers, Myles
Milinavicius, Rolandas
Miller, Bruce Alvin
Miller, Alan Eugene
Mitchell, Colleen P.
Mitchell, Eddie
Mitchell, Jolly
Moncke, Rodney James
Monroe, Thomas Eugene
Montgomery, Robert
Moore, George Edward
Morena, Saul Gastelum
Morrissey, Kevin
Moss, Tracy
Munoz, Lydia
Murphy, Warren
Murray, Matthew
Myers, Myles
N
Navek, Giocondo "Joe"
Neale, Joseph
Neuman, Hemy
Nguyen, Tuan
Norwood, Brittany
O
Oh, Keon Suk
Otto, Elisabeth M.
P
Pacheco, Carlos
Palmer, Donnell
Parades, Jaime
Parera, Leonardo
Parish, John Felton
Park, Soon Byung
Pearson, Michael
Perez, David
Phillips, William Arthur
Piazza, Vincent M.
Powell, Jerry
Price, Tyrone
Prince, Arlene

Provance, Gary
Q
Quintanilla, Jesse A.
R
Raglund, Jack
Rahming, Michael
Ramirez, Mario
Ray, Erika
Repunte, Cathline
Rice, Ronnie
Riley, Willie
Rincker, James
Rivera, Marco Gonzalez
Roberts, Donnell
Roberts, Earl
Robinson, Benjamiin
Robinson, Christopher J.
Rodriguez, Jason
Rojas, Jose R.
Rolon, Juan
Rothman, David
Rouch, Arunya
Ruiz, Fernando
Russell, Jonathan
S
Salcido, Ramon
Saldivar, Yolanda
Sam, Lorenzo
Sangco, Edilberto "Eddie"
Sangthavong, Chanthin "Bobby"
San Marco, Jennifer
Satchel, Faedra Rhondelle
Savage, Lonnie
Scherkenback, Corey P.
Schill, Julius F.
Schumerth, Shane
Shadle, Ricky
Shell, Walter V.
Sherrill, Patrick Henry
Shuman, Robert
Shumway, Christopher
Silva, Simon
Simmons, R. Gene

Simpson, James
Smith, Perry
Smith, Steven Harold
Solanas, Valerie
Spencer, Lenda Glass
Steadman, James
Stiger, Anthony
Stiles, Joseph Gerard
T
Tamayo, Jesse Antonio
Tapia, Salvador
Tartt, Kevin
Taylor, John "Benji"
Taylor, John Merlin
Taylor, Melvin D., Jr.
Teague, Elizabeth
Thomas, Ronald
Thornton, Omar S.
Tillery, Edgar
Tracy, Betty Lou
Trang, Howard
Tran, Phong Thuc
Tornes, Kenneth
Torres, Arturo Reyes
Tripp, Kenneth
Tuduj, Tom
Turner, Andre
U
Ullery, Roxanna
Uyesugi, Byran
V
Valcarel, Victor
Valenzuela, Paulino
Vallejos, Dominic
Valmont, Rashad
Vanegas, Gustabo DeJesus
W
Waddy, Walter
Wang, Lishan
Warren, Jesse James
Webb, James A.
Wesbecker, Joseph T.
West, Tom

White, Dan
White, Jeffrey
White, Levi Andre
Whitman, Charles Joseph
Whitt, John
Wilhelm, David
Williams, Doug
Williams, Frederick
Winterbourne, Alan
Wise, Arthur H.
Wissman, Robert
Wong, Jiverly
Woods, Clarence
Woods, Willie
Wu, Jing Hua
X
Xu, William
Y
Yarborough, Maceo

_____

Total: 368

Notes

INTRODUCTION

1. Frank E. Kuzmits, "Workplace Homicide: Prediction or Prevention," *SAM Advanced Management Journal*, Sunday, March 22, 1992, p. 1.

2. "Is Workplace Violence on the Rise?" *HR Hero Line*, November 13, 2009, http://hrhero.com/hl/articles/2009/11/13/is-workplace-violence-on-the-rise/.

3. Michael G. Harvey and Richard A. Cosier, "Homicides in the Workplace: Crisis or False Alarm?" *Business Horizons*, March–April 1995, p. 2, http://findarticles.com/p/articles/mi_M1038/is_n2_v38/ai_16793706/. "Today workplace homicide is the second leading cause of work-related deaths [and it] is the leading cause of death for women on the job."

4. Charles Montaldo, "It's Official: 'Going Postal' Is Epidemic." Montaldo writes that "workplace violence has reached epidemic proportions, according to the U.S. Department of Justice, with an average of three or four supervisors killed each month in the United States." *About.com guide,* undated, http://crime.about.com/od/issues/a/aa040717.htm. "Violence in the Workplace Has Become an Epidemic," according to an official American Federation of State, County and Municipal Employees (AFSCME) announcement. Also see http://www.afscme.org/news/publications/workplace-health-and-safety/fact-sheets/pdf/workplace-Violence-AFSCME-fact-sheet.pdf. The Centers for Disease Control (CDC) also regards workplace violence as an "epidemic." See http://www.cdc.gov/niosh/docs/2002-101/.

5. See Marleah Blades, "The Workplace Violence Epidemic," *Workplace Violence* (undated). Also see http://workplaceviolencenews.com/2012/03/20/the-workplace-violence-epidemic/ and Bill Lewinsky, executive director of the Force Institute, an organization that specializes in the study and analysis of police strategy, who writes: "The disturbing fact is that we now know that workplace violence is epidemic." Also see "The Lethal Employee," April 20, 2007, reprinted from *The Park Marksman* .

6. See Marx Howell, "The Postalization of Corporate America," Marx Howell and Associates, 2011, http://www.marxhowell.com/The-Postalization-of-Corporate-America-Workplace-Violence-howell-&-Mount.lhtml.

7. Nick Turse, "Economic Fallout Has Spurred an Epidemic of Murder and Suicide That Has Gone Largely Unnoticed," *AlterNet*, August 31, 2010, http://www.alternet.org/module/printversion/140455.

8. David Lohr, "Florida Woman Gunned Down by Stalker, Police Say," *AOL News*, February 12, 2010, http://www.aolnews.com/2010/02/12/florida-woman-gunned-down-by-stalker-police-say/.

9. Edecio Martinez, "Emcore Shooter Robert Reza Kills Two, Self, Say Police," *CBS News*, July 12, 2010, http://www.cbsnews.com/8301-504083_162-20010291-504083.html, and Trip Jennings, "Two Women Killed by Shooter Monday Were Victims of Chance, APD Chief Says," *New Mexico Independent*, July 13, 2010, http://newmexicoindependent.com/59273/two-women-killed-by-shooter-monday-were-victims-of-chance-apd-chief-says.

10. Patricia King and Julie Solomon, "Waging War in the Workplace," *Newsweek*, July 19, 1993, http://www.newsweek.com/1993/07/18/waging-war-in-the-workplace.print.html.

11. Ibid.

12. Harvey and Cosier, note 3 *supra*, p. 2.

13. Most of these authors focus exclusively on killers whose crimes have received the most publicity and news coverage. See, e.g., *The Will to Kill: Making Sense of Senseless Murder*, James Alan Fox et al., Prentice Hall, 2011, in which the authors' analyses focus on the likes of Susan Smith, Theodore Kaczynski, Erik and Lyle Menendez, Andrew Cunanan, Eric Harris, and Dylan Klebold, etc.—all of whom are "celebrity" killers—without regard to vast differences in case histories, forensics, motives, provocation, etc.

14. Mike France, and Michael Arndt, "Office Violence: After the Shooting Stops," *Businessweek*, March 12, 2001, http://www.businessweek.com/print/magazine/content/01_11/b3723113.htm?chan=mz.

15. Isaac Arnsdorf et al., "Clark Charged in Le GRD '13 Murder," *Yale Daily News*, September 17, 2009, http://www.yaledailynews.com/news/2009/sep/17/clark-charged-in-le-grd-13-murder/.

16. *Wikipedia*, s.v. "Pacific Southwest Airlines Flight 1771," http://en.wikipedia.org/wiki/Pacific_Southwest_Airlines_Flight__1771.

17. During the mid- and late 1970s, Wayne Williams and John Wayne Gacy were responsible for dozens of homicides apiece; both were ultimately convicted of multiple charges. Williams was sentenced to spend the rest of his life in jail, and is still serving his jail term. Gacy, who had raped and killed more than thirty-three teenage boys, was convicted for the murder of twelve, was sentenced to death in an Illinois court, and in May 1994 was executed by lethal injection. See *Murderpedia*, s.v. "John Wayne Gacy," http://www.murderpedia.org/male.G/g1/gacy-john-wayne.htm.

18. *Wikipedia*, s.v. "Valerie Solanas," http://en.wikipedia.org/wiki/Valerie_Solanas.

19. Larry Smith et al., "Woman Shot at Boss, Police Say," *Hartford Courant*, April 17, 1998. Also see http://articles.courant.com/1998-04-17/news/9804170262_1_worker-police-racial.

1. MURDER IN THE WORKPLACE

1. Romauld A. Stone, "Workplace Homicide: A Time for Action," *Business Horizons*, March–April 1995.

2. Susan M. Heathfield, "Workplace Violence: Violence Can Happen Here," About.com, undated, http://humanresources.about.com/od/healthsafetyandwellness/a/workviolence_3.htm.

3. Michael G. Harvey and Richard A. Cosier, "Homicides in the Workplace: Crisis or False Alarm?" *Business Horizons*, March–April 1995.

4. Michael Harvey, "Tech Engineer Kills Three Bosses at Silicon Valley Start-Up after Being Sacked," *Times Online*, November 16, 2009, http://www.timesonline.co.uk/tol/news/world/us_and_americas/article5167198.ece.

5. See *Wikipedia*, s.v. "Charles Whitman," http://en.wikipedia.org/wiki/Charles_Whitman.

6. See *Wikipedia*, s.v. "Columbine High School massacre," http://en.wikipedia.org/wiki/Columbine_High_School_massacre.

7. See generally, *Wikipedia*, s.v. "Virginia Tech massacre," http://en.wikipedia.org/wiki/Virginia_Tech_massacre.

8. Kathryn Marie Dudley, *Debt and Dispossession: Farm Loss in America's Heartland* (University of Chicago Press, 2000).

9. Osha Davidson, *Broken Heartland: The Rise of America's Rural Ghetto* (University of Iowa Press, 1996).

10. Joseph Amato, *When Father and Son Conspire: A Minnesota Farm Murder* (Iowa University Press, 1988); also see Jeff Baenen (Associated Press), "Minnesota Bank Officers Killed: Book Examines 'Farm Crisis' Murders," *Los Angeles Times*, May 22, 1988.

11. Bruce Brown, *The Lone Tree Tragedy: A True Story of Murder in America's Heartland* (Crown Publishers, 1989).

12. Ibid.

13. See generally *Wikipedia*, s.v. "Colin Ferguson (convict)," http://en.wikipedia.org/wiki/Colin_Ferguson_(convict).

14. Ibid.

15. See generally, *Wikipedia*, s.v. "Ted Kaczynski," http://en.wikipedia.org/wiki/Ted_Kaczynski.

16. Ibid.

17. William Styron, *The Confessions of Nat Turner* (Random House, 1967).

18. Ibid., at 429.

19. Beckwith's murder victim, was Dean J. Herman Wharton, after whom the University of Pennsylvania graduate school of business and finance is named.

20. The Postal Reorganization Act of 1970, Pub. Law 91-375, was signed into law by President Richard M. Nixon on August 12, 1970, abolishing the US Post Office Department, which had been part of the cabinet. Under the Act, the US Postal Service (USPS) became a corporate-like independent agency which was granted an official monopoly on the delivery of the mail in the United States.

21. See Thomas Evans, *The Education of Ronald Reagan: The General Electric Years and the Untold Story of His Conversion to Conservatism* (Columbia University Press, 2008).

22. Ibid.

23. Christopher R. Martin, *Framed—Labor and the Corporate Media* (ILR Press, 2004), p. 21.

24. "Since the Reagan Revolution, life has become quantifiably worse for most Americans—more work, less pay, far less leisure time, less security, exponentially greater stress, a massive shift of wealth from the middle-class to the very top layer of the plutocracy, all whitewashed by a culture that celebrates these violent appropriations as if it's all just swell, and only losers complain. Just to give one telling statistic: in 1978, CEOs of large US corporations made on average 30 times their workers' salaries; by 2001, CEOs made 571 times their average workers' salaries. American workers work 184 hours more per year than 30 years ago, but they earn almost the exact same in real terms, with far fewer benefits." See "Mark Ames—Going Postal," AbeBooks.com, undated, http://www.abebooks.com/docs/authors-corner/mark-ames.shtml.

25. Ibid.

26. Felicity Barringer, "Postal Officials Examine System after Two Killings," *New York Times*, May 8, 1993; also see Mark Ames, "Excerpt: Breaking Down at the Post Office," *AlterNet*, October 3, 2005.

27. Loren Coleman, *The Copycat Effect: How the Media and Popular Culture Trigger the Mayhem in Tomorrow's Headlines* (Simon and Schuster, 2004), p. 151. Also see Associated Press, "Postal Worker Held in Death of Postmaster," *Ocala Star-Banner*, December 3, 1983.

28. Coleman, ibid., at 152–53.

29. Ibid., at 153–54.

30. Ibid., at 154.

31. See Rachael Bell, "Workplace Homicide." TruTV.com (undated), http://www.trutv.com/library/crime/notorious_murders/mass/work_homicide/4.html; also see Coleman, note 27 *supra* at 148–52; *Wikipedia*, s.v. "Patrick Sherrill," http://en.wikipedia.org/wiki/Patrick_Sherrill. And also see *Murderpedia*, s.v. "Patrick Henry Sherrill," http://murderpedia.org/male.S/s/sherrill-patrick-henry.htm.

32. "California: Another Fatal Attraction," *Time*, February 29, 1988, http://www.time.com/time/magazine/article/0,9171,966785,00.html?ppromoid=googlep; "An Obsession with Lau-

ra," National Institute for the Prevention of Workplace Violence, http://www.workplaceviolence911.com/docs/20010406-19.htm.

33. See Coleman, note 27 *supra*, at 152–53.

34. Associated Press, "Mail Handler Shoots Three at Post Office," *Los Angeles Times*, December 15, 1988, http://articles.latimes.com/1988-12-15/news/mn-524_1_post-office. Also see "3 Shot in New Orleans as Suspect Holes Up," *Washington Post*, December 15, 1988, http://www.highbeam.com/coc/1P2--1295435.html. Also see Coleman, note 27 *supra*, at 153.

35. See Coleman, note 27 *supra*, at 153–54.

36. Tom Gorman and Richard Serrano, "Postal Employee Kills Wife, Two Co-Workers," *Los Angeles Times*, August 11, 1989, http://articles.latimes.com/1989-08-11/news/mn-207_1_postal-employee . Also see Coleman, note 27 *supra*, at 154.

37. Associated Press, "Worker on Disability Leave Kills Seven, Then Himself, in Printing Plant," *New York Times*, September 15, 1989, http://www.nytimes.com/1989/09/15/us/worker-on-disability-leave-kills-7-then-himself-in-printing-plant.html?scp=1&sq=September%2015,%201989%20Kentucky%20shooting&st=cse. Also see Associated Press, "Records Show Killer Having Mental Illness," *Victoria Advocate*, September 24, 1989, http://news.google.com/newspapers?=wb8LAAAAIBAJ&sjid=cVYDAAAAIBAJ&pg=3936, 4855278&dq=joseph+wesbecker. Also see Mark Ames, *Going Postal—Rage, Murder, and Rebellion: From Reagan's Workplaces to Clinton's Columbine and Beyond* (Soft Skull Press, 2005), pp. 7–27.

2. WHY SO LITTLE IS KNOWN ABOUT THE PROBLEM

1. Jill Andresky Fraser, *White-Collar Sweatshop—The Deterioration of Work and Its Rewards in Corporate America* (W. W. Norton and Co., 2002), p. 28.

2. Ibid.

3. Arlie Russell Hochschild, *The Time Bind—When Work Becomes Home and Home Becomes Work* (Henry Holt and Co., 1997), pp. 24–34.

4. Ibid.

5. Cynthia Estlund, *Working Together: How Workplace Bonds Strengthen a Diverse Democracy* (Oxford Press, 2005).

6. Charles C. Heckscher, *The White Collar Blues: Management Loyalties in an Age of Corporate Restructuring* (Basic Books, 1996).

7. See generally Robert D. Putnam, *Bowling Alone: The Collapse and Revival of American Community* (Simon and Schuster, 2001), and an earlier work that addresses similar themes of urban alienation and postmodern angst, David Riesman, *The Lonely Crowd* (Yale University Press, 1953).

8. "The lines between entertainment and not-entertainment are disappearing. Entertainment pervades the economic landscape and, in so doing, is reshaping every business that it touches . . . In the end, few businesses will be able to escape the impact of entertainment." Michael J. Wolf, *The Entertainment Economy* (Times Books, 1999), p. 51.

9. The film's only false note is a mercifully brief, feel-good moment when another fired employee (played by J. K. Simmons) is so inspired by his pink slip that he momentarily ponders a return to cooking school, ostensibly to realize a dream abandoned thirty years ago.

10. Not only does Reitman pull a few cinematic punches, it's noteworthy that he starts out on the side of the recently unemployed, but because his true allegiance is to corporate management, he ultimately sides with the Clooney character and the others who are gainfully employed. Of course, it's virtually impossible to assess or even quantify the influence exerted over American movie studios and the Hollywood establishment by the office of Joseph Breen (1890–1965) under Will Hays (1879–1954). For decades the office, which now survives organizationally as the Motion Picture Association of America (MPAA), served as the censor or "morals watchdog" over the movie industry. Although the position of the office was clear on topics like Communism, racial bigotry, anti-Semitism, extramarital sex, masturbation, adultery, homosexuality, and drug addiction, less clear was its view on depictions of worker dissatisfac-

tion and expressions of violence against management. The situation was only exacerbated after the postwar decade of the 1950s, and the breakup of the studio system in the early 1960s, which paved the way for the wave of independent filmmakers of the late 1960s and early 1970s and the highly decentralized industry model that prevails today.

11. Bruce Shipkowski, Associated Press, "Black People Must Leave, NJ Walmart Announcer Says," *Yahoo!Finance*, March 18, 2010. http://finance.yahoo.com/news/Black-people-must-leave-NJ-apf-1749619349.html?x=0. A manager of the store, located in Washington Township in southern New Jersey, quickly got on the microphone and apologized for the remark, though it wasn't clear whether an employee or a rogue patron was responsible for the comment.

12. See, e.g., S. Anthony Baron, *Violence in the Workplace—A Prevention and Management Guide for Businesses* (Pathfinder Publications, 2000); Gerald W. Lewis, *Workplace Hostility* (Taylor and Francis, Inc., 1999); Kim Kerr, *Workplace Violence: Planning for Prevention and Response* (Elsevier Science, 2010), Kristine Empie, *Workplace Violence and Mental Illness* (LFB Scholarly Publishing, LLC, 2003); Carol Wilkinson, *Violence in the Workplace* (Government Institutes, 1998); Gerald Lewis and Nancy Zare, *Violence in the Workplace—Myth and Reality* (John Doe Pubs, 1998); Daniel Farb and Bruce Gordon, *Workplace Violence Guidebook* (University of Health Care, 2005); David Adriansen, *Workplace Violence Prevention Training* (VDM Verlag, etc., 2008); Marc McElhaney, *Aggression in the Work-place* (AuthorHouse, 2004); P. A. J. Waddington, *The Violent Workplace* (Willan, 2006); and Nicole Spracale, "Violence in the Workplace: Preparation, Prevention and Response," dissertation, 2002, Dissertation.comUSA.

13. See Bernadette H. Schell and Nellie M. Lanteigne, *Stalking, Harassment, and Murder in the Workplace* (Greenwood Press, 2000).

14. See, e.g., Michele A Paludi, Rudy V. Nydegger, and Carmen A. Paludi, *Understanding Workplace Violence—A Guide for Managers and Employees* (Praeger, 2006).

15. See, e.g., S. Anthony Baron, *Violence in the Workplace—A Prevention and Management Guide for Businesses* (Pathfinder Publishers, 1993). Closer to the mark, and the only book out of hundreds that attempts to focus exclusively on workplace homicide, however, is Michael E. Kelleher, *New Arenas for Violence—Homicide in the American Workplace* (Praeger, 1996). Unfortunately, the book devotes only a single chapter (pp. 49–99) to a discussion of more than twenty-odd cases of workplace homicide, which, of course, precludes an in-depth analysis of the issue.

16. These books are either autobiographical works whose authors were courageous survivors of a bloody massacre, or the product of investigative reports that recount the murder years after the fact with a new narrative angle or forensic twist. The best of these autobiographical works includes Brent C. Doonan, *Murder at the Office—A Survivor's True Story* (New Horizon, 2006). Doonan was shot five times but still survived the infamous July 1999 Atlanta, Georgia, murder rampage by Mark Barton, which left twelve dead and thirteen wounded. This format also includes Carmina Salcido, *Not Lost Forever—My Story of Survival* (HarperCollins, 2009). Carmina Salcido was the sole survivor of the April 1989 Sonoma, CA, massacre by her father Ramon B. Salcido, who killed seven people, including his boss, his wife, and two of his three daughters.

17. J. Anthony Lukas, *Big Trouble: A Murder in a Small Western Town Sets Off a Struggle for the Soul of America* (Simon and Schuster, 1998).

18. See *Wikipedia*, s.v. "J. Anthony Lukas," http://en.wikipedia.org/wiki/J._Anthony _Lukas.

19. Iris Chang, *The Rape of Nanking—The Forgotten Holocaust of World War II* (Penguin Group, 1998).

20. See *Wikipedia*, s.v. "The Rape of Nanking (book)," http://en.wikipedia.org/wiki/ The_Rape_of_Nanking_(book)

21. Karen Silkwood (February 19, 1946–November 13, 1974) was an American labor union activist and chemical analyst whose controversial evidence against her former employer, the nuclear-fuel conglomerate Kerr-McGee, accused it of numerous violations of health regulations, including the exposure of its employees to dangerous levels of plutonium. After protracted, high-publicity litigation, the case was headed for retrial when Kerr-McGee decided to

settle with the Silkwood estate by agreeing to pay $1.38 million in damages, after Silkwood was killed in an automobile accident that many still claim was suspiciously suggestive of murder. Kerr-McGee shut down its nuclear-fuel plants in 1975. See generally *Wikipedia*, s.v. "Karen Silkwood," http://en.wikipedia.org/wiki/Karen_Silkwood.

22. Erin Brockovich (born June 22, 1960) is an American legal assistant and environmentalist who, without a formal law school education, or any other legal education, was instrumental in building a case against the corporate giant Pacific Gas and Electric Company (PSE&G) of California in 1993. She currently is the president of Brockovich Research and Consulting, a consulting firm focusing on personal-injury claims for asbestos exposure, and Shine Lawyers in Australia. See generally *Wikipedia*, s.v. "Erin Brockovich," http://en.wikipedia.org/wiki/Erin_Brockovich.

23. See Arthur F. Licata, esq., "Confidentiality Agreements—Listen . . . Do You Want to Know a Secret," http://www.alicata.com/CM/Press/Backup_oF_CONFIDENTIALITY_AGREEMENTS.pdf.

24. Ibid.

25. Ibid.

26. Licata correctly observes that "confidentiality agreements are against public policy and should be treated as such by the courts. The settlement terms of a court proceeding should be available to the public and to the press. What happens in the courts is the public's business. Confidentiality agreements should be prohibited absent a showing of specific harm after an evidentiary hearing. The court should require that personal injury cases settled prior to trial, at trial, and/or after trial should not be the subject of secrecy agreements." Ibid. Licata is not alone in his criticism. Courts have long acknowledged the problem of confidentiality agreements and their disservice to the public interest. The Third Circuit Court of Appeals, for example, has observed that "courts routinely sign orders which contain confidentiality clauses without considering the propriety of such orders or the countervailing public interests which are being sacrificed by the orders." *Pansy v. Borough of Stroudsburg*, 23 F.3d 772,785 (3d. Cir. 1994).

27. Elizabeth Wurtzel, *Bitch—In Praise of Difficult Women* (Doubleday, 1998), p. 259.

28. See, e.g., Studs Terkel, *Working: People Talk about What They Do All Day and How They Feel about What They Do* (New Press, 1997).

29. See *Wikipedia*, s.v. "Valerie Solanas," http://en.wikipedia.org/wiki/Valerie_Solanas.

30. Ibid.

31. See Randy Shilts, *The Mayor of Castro Street—The Life and Times of Harvey Milk* (Saint Martin's Griffin, 1988).

32. See Stephanie Madoff Mack (Mark Madoff's widow), *The End of Normal* (Blue Rider Press, 2011).

33. Emphasis added. See James Alan Fox, "Workplace Homicide: What is the Risk?" *Crime and Punishment*, August 5, 2010, www.jamesalanfox.com.

34. Ibid.

35. See generally Franklin E. Zimring, *The Great American Crime Decline* (Oxford University Press, 2008).

36. See Eric F. Signbatur and Guy A. Toscano, "Work-Related Homicides: The Facts," *Compensation and Working Conditions*, Spring 2000, p. 3.

37. See Jared Wade, "Workplace Murder on the Decline," *The National Law Review*, April 13, 2012, http://wwwnatlawreview.com/article/work;lace-homicides-decline, citing Tanya Restrepo and Harry Shuford, "Violence in the Workplace," NCCI research brief, January 2012, http://www.caepv.org/membercenter/files/ncci_violence_in_the_workplace_report_%28jan_2012%29.pdf.

38. Ibid.

39. "Man Convicted of Killing 7 Co-Workers," *New York Times*, April 25, 2002, http://www.nytimes.com/2002/04/25/us/man-convicted-of-killing-7-coworkers.html. Carey Goldberg, " A Deadly Turn to a Normal Work Day," *New York Times*, December 28, 2000, http://www.nytimes.com/2000/12/28/us/a-deadly-turn-to-a-normal-work-day.html, and Michael Ellison, "Gunman Kills Seven at Net Firm," *Guardian*, December 27, 2000, http://www.guardian.co.uk/world/2000/dec/27/usgunviolence.usa.

40. Ibid.

3. DEFINITELY NOT YOUR AVERAGE GIRL NEXT DOOR

1. See Gary Davis, "Biology Professor Amy Bishop Kills Three, Wounds Three in Shooting Rampage in Alabama," *Yahoo!Voices* , February 13, 2010, http://voices.yahoo.com/biology-professor-amy-bishop-kills-three-wounds-three-5468309.html?cat=8. Also see *Wikipedia* , s.v. "2010 University of Alabama in Huntsville shooting," http://en.wikipedia.org/wiki/2010_University_of_Alabama_in_Huntsville_shooting.

2. Ibid.

3. Ibid. Of the 350-plus perpetrators included in the study, only one other case involved a teacher whose motive was an obsession with tenure. On May 22, 1990, Donald Givens, 50, a science teacher at Centerville High School in Centerville, TN, shot and killed the school principal, Ron Wallace, 41. The principal was shot and killed minutes after he surprised Givens, who was secretly preparing to blow up the school. Several of the school's 850 students had complained about Givens and his inability to "get along with the kids," and he was afraid he would lose his job—even though he had tenure. See "Teacher Charged in Slaying," *New York Times*, May 22, 1990, http://www.nytimes.com/1990/05/22/us/teacher-charged-in-slaying.html.

4. Ibid.

5. Ibid.

6. Ibid.

7. Ibid.

8. At the time Bishop was charged with the triple murder, only four women sat on Alabama's death row, three for having killed their minor children, and another for having killed her husband, according to the Alabama Department of Corrections. See Verna Gates, Colleen Jenkins and Peter Bohan, "Accused of Murder, Alabama Professor Faces Death Penalty," *Yahoo News* (Reuters), May 26, 2011, http://news.yahoo.com/s/nm/20110526/us_nm/us_crime_alabama.

9. See John Holusha and Randal C. Archibold, "Ex-Employee Kills 6 Others and Herself at California Postal Plant," *New York Times*, February 1, 2006, http://www.nytimes.com/2006/02/01/national/01postal.html.

10. A deputy clerk for the city of Milan, New Mexico, where San Marco moved in 2004, said that she had "applied for a business license in 2004 for a publication called *The Racist Press* that she said she planned to launch." See "Postal Shooter's Bizarre Behavior," *CBSNEWS,* http://www.cbsnews.com/2100-201-_162-1272077.html.

11. "Those who knew her recalled her hostility toward minorities, particularly Asians." See Katherine Ramsland, "Female Mass Murderers: Major Cases and Motives," *CrimeLibrary*, undated, http://www.trutv.com/library/crime/notorious_murders/mass/female_mass_murderer/1.html. All but one of her victims were nonwhite, and one former "plant worker . . . recalled that San Marco, who was white, seemed particularly hostile to Asians while working for the postal service." Tim Molloy, "Racism in Postal Rampage," *Chicago Sun-Times*, http://www.suntimes.com/output/news/cst-nws-post02html .

12. See Halusha and Archibald, note 9 *supra*.

13. See Ramsland, note 11 *supra*.

14. Ibid.

15. Martin Kasindorf, quoting Professor Alan Fox, in "Woman Kills 5, Self at Postal Plant," *USA Today*, February 1, 2006, http://www.usatoday.com/news/nation/2006-01-31-postal-shooting_x.htm.

16. See note 10 *supra*.

17. See note 9 *supra*. In the relatively rare instances where women committed suicide after a workplace rampage, the number of murder victims never exceeded two, and the rampage thus didn't qualify as a "massacre."

18. The only case that comes close, factually, is that of Nathaniel Friedlander, a white accountant with the University of Miami's admissions office. In revenge for a written reprimand by his black supervisor for swearing in public, Friedlander dripped liquid mercury at different points in the supervisor's cubicle. The chemical caused a serious skin rash over much

of the supervisor's body which required several days' hospitalization. However, as the chemical was not ingested orally, it will not here be considered a poisoning, but rather a kind of physical "assault and battery"; that is, an offensive "touching." See Associated Press, "Miami Employee Charged with Trying to Poison Boss with Mercury," *7News.wsvn.com*, September 30, 2006, http://www.wsvn.com/news/articles/local/M130134.

19. Trish Mehaffey, "Jessica Dayton Found Guilty of First Degree Murder," *Eastern Iowa News*, April 21, 2010, http://www.easterniowanewsnow.com/2010/04/21/jessica-dayton-murder-trial-first-day/.

20. Matthew Walberg, "Waitress Sentenced in Murder of Leona's Manager," *Chicago Tribune*, April 1, 2010, http://articles.chicagotribune.com/2010-04-01/news/ct-met-leonas-restaurant-murder-20100.

21. Robin Benedick, "Jury Clears Ullery of Murdering Boss," *Orlando Sentinel*, March 31, 1988, http://articles.orlandosentinel.com/1988-03-31/news/0030080146_1_ullery-bobryk-murder-charge.

22. See Lena Sullivan, "Florida Woman Samantha Brown Charged with Killing Boss in Pinellas Park," Associated Press, January 27, 2012.

23. See Jennifer Bonnett, "Convicted Murderer Sarah Dutra Released from Prison," *Lodi News-Sentinel*, August 26, 2011, http://www.lodinews.com/news/article_b4e2bd6a-d038-11e0-8450-001cc4c03286.html.

24. Two books were written about the case: Brian J. Karem, *Marked for Death—the Cold-Blooded Seduction and Murder of Larry McNabney* (HarperCollins Publishers, 2005), and Carlton Smith, *Cold-Blooded—A True Story of Love, Lies, Greed, and Murder* (Saint Martin's Press, 2007).

25. Ibid.

26. Ibid.

27. Greg Argos, "School Cafeteria Workers Accused of Trying to Poison Boss," *WCNC.com*, March 2, 2011, http://www.wnc.com/news/local/Police-say-school-employees-tried-to-poison-coworker--117197733.htm.

28. The only case that fell into this category was a Wendy's multiple murder and robbery case and its two perpetrators, John B. Taylor, 38, and his friend and partner Craig Godineaux, 30. See Eun Lee Koh, "2 Indicted on Charges of Murder at Wendy's," *New York Times*, June 30, 2000, http://nytimes.com/2000/06/30/nyregion/2-indicted-on-charges-of-murder-at-wendys.html. Also see Sarah Kershaw, "A Verdict of Guilty Is Uttered 20 Times In Wendy's Killings," *New York Times*, November 20, 2002, http://www.nytimes.com/2002/11/20/nyregion/a-verdict-of-guilty-is-uttered-20-times-in-wendy-s-killings.html. Two other cases also come close, factually, but were strictly family affairs. The first was the father-son case of Filiberto Flores, a factory worker at the O&G Spring and Wire Form Specialty Company in Chicago who, after a quarrel with a coworker on April 30, 2008, returned a few minutes later with his two sons, one of whom, Emilio, shot and killed the coworker. "Man, 49, Charged in Co-worker's Death," *Chicago Tribune*, May 4, 2008, http://articles.chicagotribune.com/2008-05-04/news0805030052_1_co-worker-police-custody. The second case was that of James Jenkins, 46, a Minnesota farmer, and his teenage son who, on September 29, 1983, shot and killed two bankers who had foreclosed on the family's farm. See Dan Cryer, "Futility And Murder On Fertile Rural Ground," *Orlando Sentinel*, May 7, 1986, http://articles.orlandosentinel.com/1986-05-07/lifestyle/0220140028_1-jim-jenkins-blythe-ruthon.

29. See generally, Terrence Real, *"I Don't Want to Talk About It": Overcoming the Secret Legacy of Male Depression* (Better World Books, 2006).

30. Kim Wessel, "Doctor Testifies Harris Was Insane—Defense Finishes Case in Slayings at Nursing Home," *Courier-Journal*, February 2, 2001, www.raven1.net/mcf/news/harris-insane.hrm.

31. Ibid.

32. Ibid.

33. Melissa Buscher, "Hostage-Taker At Fayetteville Nursing Home Commits Suicide," *WRAL.com*, October 15, 2002, www.wral.com/news/local/story/1030961.

34. Allison Pearson, "Gary Speed: The Last Taboo Is the Agony of Distress," *Telegraph*, November 30, 2011, http://www.telegraph.co.uk/health/men_shealth/892586Gary-Speed-the-last-taboo-is-the-agony-of-distress.html.

35. Ibid.

36. *Wikipedia*, s.v. "Bath School disaster," http://en.wikipedia.org/wiki/Bath _school _disaster.

37. See "Prelude to the Tower Shootings," *Wikipedia*, s.v. "Charles Whitman," http://en.wikipedia.org/wiki/Charles_Whitman.

38. See Tom Gorman and Richard Serrano, "Postal Employee Kills Wife, 2 Co-Workers," *Los Angeles Times*, August 11, 1989, http://articles.latimes.com/189-08-11/news/mn-207 _1_postal-employee.

39. Emily Yellin, "Officer and 2 Firefighters Die in Ambush at Memphis House," *New York Times*, March 9, 2000, http://www.nytimes.com/2000/03/09/us/officer-and-2-firefighters-die-in-ambush-at-memphis-house.html.

40. See Kevin Sack, "Shootings in Atlanta: The Overview," *New York Times*, July 30, 1999, http://www.nytimes.com/1999/07/30/us/shootings-in-atlanta-the-overview-gunman-in-atlanta-slays-9-then-himself.html?scp=2&sq=Barton Shooting Atlanta 1999&st=cse.

41. See Associated Press, "Firefighter Kills Wife and 4 Officials," *New York Times*, April 25, 1996, http://www.nytimes.com/1996/04/25/us/firefighter-kills-wife-and-4-officials .html?partner=rssnyt&emc=rss.

42. See Mark Ames, "Workplace Massacre in Alabama: Did Endless Downsizing and Slashed Benefits Cause the Rampage?" *AlterNet,* March 13, 2009, http://www.alternet.org/story/131201/workplace_massacre_in_alabama%3A_did_endless_downsizing_and_slashed_benefits_cause_the_rampage . Also see Larry Copeland, Donna Leinwand, and Andrea Stone, "Alabama Gunman Kept a List of Those Who Had 'Done Him Wrong,'" *USA Today*, March 12, 2009, http://usatoday.com/news/nation/2009-03-10-alabama-shooting_N.htm. Also see *Wikipedia*, s.v. "Geneva County massacre," http://en.wikipedia.org/wiki/Geneva_County_massacre.

43. See Angela Swanlund, *The Encyclopedia of Arkansas History and Culture*, undated, http://www.encyclopediaofarkansas.net/encycolopedia/entry-detail.aspx?entryID=3731, also see *Wikipedia*, s.v. "Ronald Gene Simmons," http://en.wikipedia.org/wiki/Ronald _Gene_Simmons.

44. Nursing student Caitlin Phillips's questions at Jay Reeves and Greg Bluestein, "Amy Bishop's Alleged Attack: Angry Professor Shot Colleagues Methodically, Says Survivor," *Huffington Post*, February 16, 2010, http://www.huffingtonpost.com/2010/02/16/amy-bishops-alleged-attac_n_464686.html.

4. THE LIMITS OF THE HUMAN RESOURCES FUNCTION

1. See Alan Downs, *Corporate Executions—The Ugly Truth About Layoffs, etc.* (Amacon Press, 1995).

2. Ibid.

3. Ibid.

4. Ibid.

5. Ibid.

6. Ibid.

7. Tamar Lewin, "Dean at MIT Resigns, Ending a 28-Year Lie," *New York Times*, April, 27, 2007, http://www.nytimes.com/2007/04/27/us/27.mit.html, and Associated Press, "MIT Admissions Dean Resigns after Claims About Resume Surface," *Fox News.com*, April 27, 2007.

8. Ibid.

9. Ibid

10. See Floyd Norris, "Radio Shack Chief Resigns after Lying," *Nytimes.com*, February 21, 2006, and Chris Noon, "Radio Shack's Edmondson Apologizes for Resume Flubs," *Forbes.com*, February 16, 2006.

11. See Margaret Heffernan, "Does Your Resume Tell the Truth?" *CBS MoneyWatch*, CBS *News*, May 8, 2012.

12. See Tom Coyne, "Scandal Stuns Irish—O'Leary Admits Falsifying Resume, Resigns as Coach," Associated Press, *LJWorld.com*, December 15, 2001.

13. See Margaret Kane, "Veritas CFO Leaves on MBA Lie," *CNET*, October 3, 2002.

14. See Mike Ricciuti, "Lotus CEO Papows Resigns," *CNET*, January 2000.

15. Rachel Zupek, "Infamous Resume Lies," Career Builder.com. The top nine ways job applicants fib on their resumes, according to Forbes.com, are (1) lying about getting a degree, (2) exaggerating numbers, (3) increasing previous salary, (4) playing with dates, (5) inflating titles, (6) lying about technical abilities, (7) claiming language facility, (8) providing a fake address, and (9) padding grade point averages. Nowhere in the top reasons was the concealment of a criminal record, and the obvious reason is that that information is automatically retrieved by computer from a database and typically does not rely, for verification, on human agency.

16. See Lisa Takeuchi Cullen, "Getting Wise to Lies," *Time*, April 24, 2006, http://www.time.com/time/magazine/article/0,9171,1186550.html.

17. Ibid.

18. Ibid.

19. See Frank James, "Amy Bishop Allegedly Hit Woman at IHOP over Booster Seat," *NPR*, July 27, 2012, http://npr.org/blogs/thetwo-way/2010/02/amy_bishop_unprovoked _allegedl.html. Also see Jay Reeves and Greg Bluestein, "Amy Bishop's Alleged Attack: Angry Professor Shot Colleagues Methodically, Says Survivor," *Huffington Post*, February 16, 2010, http://www.huffingtonpost.com/2010/02/16/amy-bishops-alleged-attac_n_464686.htm.

20. See Donovan Slack and Shelly Murphy, "Bishop Indicted in Brother's Death," *boston.com*, June 17, 2010, http://www.boston.com/news/local/massachsetts/articles/2010/06/17/bishop_indicted_in_brothers_death/.

21. Conflicting newspaper accounts of her husband's knowledge in this regard may suggest that he didn't know she owned or had access to a gun.

22. See Jay Reeves and Greg Bluesein, "Ala. Prof's Story Begins with Brother's 1986 Death," *boston.com*, February 16, 2010, http://www.boston.com/news/nation/articles/2010/02/16/survivor_ala-prof_in_slayings_shot_methodically/.

23. It could not ordinarily be determined from the cases in this study, collected and compiled as they were largely from newspaper and magazine accounts, if the perpetrators had prior criminal records of violence or histories of assaultive conduct before they committed the murders that qualified them for the study. Mark Barton was one of only five or six biographical exceptions, due largely to the fact that his massacres generated so much publicity, including at least two biographical books. See *Murder in the Office—A Survivor's Story* by Brent C. Doonan (New Horizon Press, 2006) and *Guns and Day Trading*, by Sondra London (Emporium, 1999).

24. Former boxing promoter Don King was another of the exceptions in this respect, about whom much has been written. Biographies, both authorized and unauthorized, have been written about his flamboyant, often controversial life and lifestyle. For an unauthorized biography of Don King that couldn't be less flattering, see *Only in America—the Life and Crimes of Don King* by Jack Newfield (William Morrow & Co., 1995).

25. See the Immigration Reform and Control Act, 8 USC section 1324.

26. See James M. Shaker, "Preemployment Screening Methods: How Much Do You Really Want to Know?" Ryan Swanson, www.ryanswansonlaw.com.

27. Anthony Bourdain, *Kitchen Confidential—Adventures in the Culinary Underbelly* (HarperCollins Publishers, 2000), p. 96.

28. The Google engineers were surprised to learn that, according to the study, factors like commitment, honesty, and enthusiasm were far more important in workplace success than skills alone—even in work sites where a highly technical expertise was typically a minimum requirement. "We'd always believed that to be a manager, particularly on the engineering side, you need[ed] to be as deep or deeper a technical expert than the people who work[ed] for you."

But it "turns out that that's absolutely the least important thing. It's important, but [it] pales in comparison [to] making a connection and being accessible." Sunny Bindra, "What Google Can Teach Us about Leadership Skills," *Sunwords.com*, May 30, 2011, citing Adam Bryant of the *New York Times*, March 12, 2011, http://www.sunwords.com/2011/05/30/what-google-can-teach-us-about-leadership-skills/.

29. See, e.g., the survey conducted jointly by Mitch Ditkoff and Tim Moore of Idea Champions, Carolyn Allen of Motivation Solution Center, and Dave Pollard of Meeting of Minds, which reveals that "most people would rather have inexperienced people with a positive attitude than highly experienced people who lack enthusiasm, candor, or commitment on a collaborative work team." Carolyn Allen, editor, *California Green Solutions*, at http:// www.californiagreensolutions.com/cgi-bin/gt/tpl.h,content=1075. "Survey Suggests Attitude Is More Important than Experience," http://www.ideachampions.com/downloads/collaborationresults.pdf.

30. See Adam Bryant's interview of Carol Smith, etc., "No Doubts; Women Are Better Managers," *New York Times*, July 25, 2009, http://www.nytimes.com/2009/07/26/business/26corner.html?pagewanted=all.

31. Also see "Before Ala., Prof Marred by Violent Past," *CBSNews*, February 14, 2010, http://www.cbsnews.com/2100-201_162_62045588.htm, and "Police: Ala. Professor Killed Brother in 1986," *NBCNEWS*, February 14, 2010, http://www.msnbc.msn.com/id/35372168/ns/us_news-crime_and_the_courts/t/police-ala-professor-killed-brother/.

32. The official review of Bishop's tenure file included the faculty's conclusions that her scholarly publishing had been insufficient, that she hadn't secured enough research grants, and "there were also concerns about her personality." See Paul Basken and David Glenn, "Accused Alabama Shooter Was a Bright Scientist With Career Ups and Downs," *The Chronicle*, February 15, 2010, http://chronicle.com/article/Accused-Alabama-Shooter-Was/64202/.

33. Ibid. Also see *Wikipedia*, s.v. "2010 University of Alabama in Huntsville Shooting," http://en.wikipedia.org/wiki/2010_University_of_Alabama_in_Huntsville_shooting. One experienced observer noted that whatever the faculty's "formal" reasons for its decision, "the real reason she was turned down for tenure was that people thought she was nuts." Roger Schank, "How the U of Alabama at Huntsville Murder Story Highlights the Disaster that Is Our University System," *Education Outrage*, February 15, 2010, http://education.blogspot.com/2010/02/how-u-of-alabama-at-huntsville-murder.html.

34. Ibid.

35. See *Wikipedia*, s.v. "2010 University of Alabama in Huntsville Shooting," http:// en.wikipedia.org/wolo/2010_University_of_Alabama-in_Huntsville_shooting, note 33 *supra*.

36. Ibid.

37. See Desiree Hunter and Jay Lindsay, "Alabama Suspect Fatally Shot Her Brother in 1986," *AolNews*, February 13, 2010, http://www.aolnews.com/2010/02/13/3-dead-in-shooting-at-university-of-huntsville/.

38. See Jay Reeves and Greg Bluestein, "Ala. Prof's Story Begins with Brother's 1986 Death," *boston.com*, February 16, 2010, http://www.boston.com/news/nation/articles/2010/02/16/survivor_ala-prof_in_slayings_shot_methodically/.

39. See "Accused Alabama Prof Shot, Killed Brother in 1986," *Newsmax*, February 13 2010, http://www.newsmax.com/us/alabama-professor-AmyBishop-shooting/2010/02/13/id/349836.

40. See Laurence M. Cruz, "Murder-Suicide at Wash. Hospital," *HighBeam*, June 29, 2000. "Colleagues of [the] medical resident who killed himself after fatally shooting his supervisor locked their doors when the man was around, a faculty member said . . . But his supervisor, Dr. Rodger Haggit, apparently did not share their fears. His door was unlocked . . . when Dr. Jian Chen walked in for a meeting and shot Haggit, 57, four times in the torso before shooting himself in the head." See http://www.highbeam.com/doc/1P1-29698472.html.

41. For the general facts of Dr. Jian Chen's murder/suicide, see Charles E. Brown, Eli Sanders, and Christine Clarridge, "Two UW Doctors Killed in Shooting," *Seattle Times*, June 29, 2000, http://community.seattletimes.nwsource.com/archive/?date=20000629&slug=4029355 and "Resident Kills a Medical Chief, Himself in Seattle," *Los Angeles Times*, June 29, 2000, http://articles.latimes.com/2000/jun/29/news/mn-46184.

42. See Julian Barling, "Understanding Supervisor-Targeted Aggression," *Journal of Applied Psychology* 90, no. 4, pp. 73–139.

43. For one of the best articles written on why and how workers are driven to murder unscrupulous bosses and supervisors, see Mark Ames's "This Is Why Workers Shoot Their Employers," *The Exiled*, September 1, 2009, http://exiledonline.com/this-is-why-workers-shoot-their-employers/.

5. SOME WERE CRAZY, SOME NOT SO CRAZY

1. Justice Potter Stewart's famous take on "obscenity," stated in his concurring opinion in *Jacobellis v. Ohio*, 378 US. 184 (1964), in which the US Supreme Court struck down an Ohio statute that prohibited the exhibition of the French movie *The Lovers*. The Ohio court held the movie obscene, and the Court reversed the decision, ruling that the movie fell within the protective scope of the First Amendment and therefore was not obscene.

2. Associated Press, "Police Look for Motive in Deadly Postal Shooting," *MSNBC*, January 31, 2006, http://www.msnbc.msn.com/id/11107022/, and Randall C. Archibold et al., "Death Toll Climbs to 8 in California Postal Plant Rampage," *New York Times*, February 2, 2006, http://query.nytimes.com/gst/fullpage.html?res=9F04E7D91F3FF931A35751C0A9609C8B63.

3. See John Holusha and Randal C. Archibold, "Ex-Employee Kills 6 Others and Herself at California Postal Plant," *New York Times*, February 1, 2006, http://www.nytimes.com/20006/02/01/national/01postal.html?_r=2&oref=slogin&pagewanted.

4. Rachael Bell, "Workplace Homicide," *TruTv*, no date indicated, http://www.trutv.com/library/crime/noorious_murders/mass/work_homicide/4.html.

5. See *Wikipedia*, s.v. "Patrick Sherrill," http://en.wikipedia.org/wiki/Patrick_Sherrill, p. 1.

6. See S. Anthony Baron's *Violence in the Workplace*, p. 58.

7. Ibid.

8. See Kevin Sack, "Shootings in Atlanta: The Overview," *New York Times*, July 30, 1999, http://www.nytimes.com/1999/07/30/us/shootings-in-atlanta-the-overview-gunman-in-atlanta-slays-9-then-himself.html?scp=Barton. Also see *Wikipedia*, s.v. "Mark O. Barton," http://en.wikipedia.org/wiki/Mark_O._Barton.

9. Several biographical works on Frank Lloyd Wright cover the Carlton massacre. For the most comprehensive analysis of the murder and its motives, see William R. Drennan's *Death in a Prairie House: Frank Lloyd Wright and the Taliesin Murders* (University of Wisconsin Press, 2007). Also see Meryle Secrest, *Frank Lloyd Wright—A Biography* (Knopf, 1992); also see Nancy Horan, *Loving Frank* (Ballantine Books, 2007), which focuses more on the controversial romance between Wright and Mamah Borthwick Cheney, one of Carlton's victims, for whom Wright had left his wife and children, and with whom he lived at the well-known Wisconsin estate.

10. See "California: Another Fatal Attraction," *Time*, February 29, 1988, http://wwwtime.com/time/magazine/article/0,9171,966785,00.html?promoid=googlep. Also see National Institute for the Prevention of Workplace Violence, "An Obsession with Laura," http://www.workplaceviolence911.com/docs/w0010406-19.htm. Also see *Wikipedia*, s.v. "Richard Farley," http://en.wikipedia.org/wiki/Richard_Farley.

11. See "Woman Convicted in Death of Sacramento Lawyer Released from Prison," *CBS Sacramento*, April, 26, 2011, http://sacramentocbslocal.com/2011/08/26/woman-convicted-in-death-of-sacramento-lawyer-released-from-prison/.

12. See *Wikipedia*, s.v. "Murder of Larry McNabney," http://en.wikpedia.org/wiki/Murder_of_Larry_McNabney

13. Ibid.

14. Ibid.

15. Ibid.

16. On Warhol's mistaken suspicion that Solanas's work was actually a police trap, see "How Did Andy Warhol Die?" *CarlyGoogles*, June 9, 2011, http://carlygoogles.blogspot.com/2011/06/how-did-andy-warhol-die.html; also see "Hang Him on My Wall," *ARTCITY21*, undated, http://www.artcity21.com/com/magazine/andy_warhol/andy_warhol.htm.

17. Valerie Solanas was later charged with and convicted of attempted murder and other crimes. At her trial, Warhol refused to testify against her, and after serving a brief period of incarceration, she was released from prison in 1971. Briefly lionized as an iconic feminist leader by some, but derided as a "crazed lesbian" by others, she soon drifted back into obscurity, in and out of mental hospitals, and on April 25, 1988, at the age of 53, died of emphysema in a San Francisco, CA, hotel. Also see *Wikipedia*, s.v. "Valerie Solanas," http://en.wikipedia.org/wiki/Valerie_Solanas.

18. See Robert Reinhold, "Seeking Motive in the Killing of 8: Insane Ramblings Are Little Help," *New York Times*, July 4, 1993, http://www.nytimes.com/1993/07/04/us/seeking-motive-in-the-killing-of-8-ubsabe-ramblings-are-little-help.html; also *Wikipedia*, s.v. "101 California Street shootings," http://en.wikipedia.org/wiki/101_California_Street_shootings. Also see Mike France and Michael Arndt, "Office Violence: After the Shooting Stops," *Businessweek*, March 12, 2001, http://www.businessweek.com/print/magazine/content/01_11/b3723113.htm?chan=mz.

19. See "Services Conducted for New Jersey for Slain Postal Service Workers," *New York Times*, October 15, 1991, http://www.nytimes.com/1991/10/15/nyregion/services-conducted-in-new-jersey-for-slain-postal-service-workers.html.

20. Ibid.

21. See http://www.fdungan.com/usps5.htm. Sometime earlier, Harris, who had been born in prison and had a lifetime of psychiatric problems, had also avenged his loss of as much as ten thousand dollars by a broker, Roy Edwards. Dressed in a black ninja costume, he entered Edwards's Montville, NJ, home and handcuffed the family. After sexually assaulting Edwards's wife and two daughters, he shot and killed Edwards. As hundreds of investors had lost money in their dealings with Edwards, the police never had reason to connect Harris as a suspect in Edwards's death as well, not until after he had killed the postal workers and his supervisor in 1991. Harris, who had been born in prison, had a lifetime of psychiatric problems. For more biographical information and a detailed account of his mass murder rampages, see *Murderpedia*, s.v. "Joseph M. Harris," http://murderpedia.org/male.H/h/harris-joseph-m.htm.

22. See generally *Wikipedia*, s.v. "Stuart Alexander (businessman and mass murderer)," http://en.wikipedia.org/wiki/Stuart_Alexander_(businessman_and-mass-murderer). See Office of Inspector General, "California Man Arraigned for Murder of USDA Employees," news release, October 27, 2000, http://www.usda.gov/iog/webdocs/oig56.html.

23. Ibid.

24. Ibid.

25. Henry K. Lee, "Sausage King Dies in his Cell on Death Row/Cause of Death Not Known for Man Who Murdered 3," *SFGate.com*, December 28, 2005.

26. See *Wikipedia*, s.v. "Ramon Salcido," http://en.wikipedia.org/wiki/Ramon_Salcido. Also see *Murderpedia*, s.v. "Ramon Salcido," http://murderpedia.org/male.S/s/salcido-ramon.htm. Also see the autobiography of Ramon's daughter who survived the massacre, and whose childhood memory of the murders is included in the book: Carmina Salcido, *Not Lost Forever: My Story of Survival* (HarperCollins, 2009).

27. See *Wikipedia*, s.v. "Ronald Gene Simmons," http://en.wikipedia.org/wiki/Ronald_Gene_Simmons; also see Angela Swanlund, *The Encyclopedia of Arkansas History and Culture*, http://www.encyclopediaofarkanss.net/encyclopedia/entry-detail.aspx?entryID=3731.

28. Ibid.

29. Simmons was later tried and convicted of fourteen counts of capital murder and then sentenced to death. After receiving a brief stay of execution on appeal, Arkansas governor (later president) Bill Clinton signed Simmons's second execution warrant, shortly after which he died by execution on death row. See *Wikipedia*, s.v. "Ronald Gene Simmons," http://en.wikipedia.org/wiki/Ronald_Gene_Simmons; also see Angela Swanlund, *The Encyclopedia of Arkansas History and Culture*, http://www.encyclopediaofarkanss.net/encyclopedia/entry-detail.aspx?entryID=3731.

30. See *Murderpedia*, s.v. "Leo Held," http://murderpedia.org/male.H/h/held-leo.htm.

31. Ibid.

32. Ibid.

33. Ibid.

34. Ibid. Held died hours later in the hospital, but not before explaining why he did what he did. All the victims had irked or annoyed him in some way or another, and there was only one person he regretted not having killed, a 70-year-old neighbor, a fact he regretted even on his deathbed. Also see *Murderpedia*, s.v. "Leo Held," www.Murderpedia.com.

35. See S. Anthony Baron, *Violence in the Workplace—A Prevention and Management Guide for Businesses* (Pathfinder, 1993), p. 8. Also see Stephanie Armour, and Tom Ankner, "Inside the Minds of Workplace Killers," *USA Today*, July 14, 2004, http://www.usatoday.com/money/workplace/2004-07-14-workplace-killings_x.htm.

36. Ibid.

37. See Carey Goldberg, "A Deadly Turn to a Normal Work Day," *New York Times*, December 28, 2000, http://www.nytimes.com/2000/12/28/usa/a-deadly-turn-to-a-normal-work-day.html. On McDermott's subsequent trial and conviction, see "Man Convicted of Killing 7 Co-Workers," *New York Times*, April 25, 2002, p. A18, http://www.nytimes.com/2002/04/25/us/man-convicted-of-killing-7-coworkers.html.

38. The jury deliberated for nearly sixteen hours over a period of three days. As Massachusetts does not have a death penalty statute, McDermott is currently serving several life sentences with no possibility of parole.

39. See *Wikipedia*, s.v. "John List," http://en.wikipedia.org/wiki/John_List, p. 2. John List was not eligible for inclusion in the study because he didn't meet the criterion that the perpetrator be employed at the time of the crime, nor was his murder spree motivated by "revenge." His case is noted despite its exclusion only because no case better illustrates how detailed and meticulous a killer can be in covering up his incriminating, telltale tracks.

40. Ibid.

41. Ibid.

42. Ibid.

43. Ibid.

44. Jarrett Murphy, "Six Dead in Mississippi Massacre," *CBSNews*, July 9, 2003, http://www.cbsnews.com/stories/2003/07/national/main562301.shtml; also see Matt Volz, "Gunman Opens Fire at Lockheed Martin Plant in Mississippi; Six Dead including Shooter," Associated Press, July 8, 2003, http://www.boston.com/news/daily/08/plant_shooting.htm; and Brian Ross and David Scott, Lockheed Workplace Murders Targeted Blacks," *ABCNews*, May 12, 2005, http://abcnews.go.com/CleanPrint/cleanprintproxy.aspx?1288639049703.

45. See Mark Ames, *Going Postal—Rage, Murder, and Rebellion* (Soft Skull Press, 2005), pp. 7–27.

46. Ibid.

47. Ibid.

48. Ibid.

49. Ibid.

50. See S. Anthony Baron, *Violence in the Workplace—A Prevention and Management Guide for Businesses* (Pathfinder Publishers, 1993), p. 47–48.

51. Ibid.

52. For Willie Brown's account of the assassinations of Mayor Moscone and Supervisor Milk, see James Richardson's biography of the legendary California politician (who himself was on White's hit list, and was leaving Moscone's office as White burst in), *Willie Brown—A Biography* (University of California Press, 1996), pp. 253–54.

53. For a more detailed, forensically more graphic account of the assassinations of Mayor Moscone and Supervisor Milk, see Randy Shilts, *The Mayor of Castro Street—The Life and Times of Harvey Milk* (Saint Martin's Press, 1982), pp. 267–72.

54. Ibid., at 268.

55. Ibid., at 324–25.

56. At the trial, the jury returned a highly controversial verdict of guilty, but on a lesser included offense of involuntary manslaughter. Most in the gay San Francisco community felt

that White had quite literally gotten away with murder. After serving five years in jail, he was paroled in 1984, and two years later, in 1986, was found dead, having committed suicide by toxic inhalation while seated in his car, which was parked in his ex-wife's garage. See *Wikipedia*, s.v. "Harvey Milk," http://en.wikipedia.org/wiki/Harvey_Milk.

57. James C. McKinley Jr. and James Dao, "Fort Hood Gunman Gave Signals Before Rampage," *New York Times*, November 8, 2009, http://www.nytimes.com/2009/11/09/;us/09reconstruct.html?_r=2&hp; also see "Investigators look for Missed Signals in Fort Hood Probe," *CNN*, November 10, 2009, http://www.cnn.com/2009/CRIME/11/09/fort.hood .shootings/. Also see *Wikipedia*, s.v. "Fort Hood shooting," http://en.wikipedia.org/wiki/Fort_Hood_shooting.

58. Ibid.

59. Ibid.

60. Ibid.

61. See *Wikipedia*, s.v. "Bath School disaster," http://en.wikipedia.org/wiki/Bath_School_disaster.

62. Ibid.

63. See William K. Stevens, "Official Calls in Press and Kills Himself," *New York Times*, January 23, 1987, http://query.nytimes.com/gst/fullpage.html?. Also see *Wikipedia*, s.v. "R. Budd Dwyer," http://en.wikipedia.org/wiki/R._Budd_Dwyer.

64. Ibid.

65. Ibid.

6. THE INFLUENCE OF GENDER AND RACE

1. Sigmund Freud espoused a model of human nature in which certain immutable features—like gender, race, and age—are believed to determine our course in life, and in which different groups of people were fundamentally different because of the accident of their birth into a certain category (or ascribed status, versus those features over which a person has control—achieved status).

2. This oddity will inevitably change, given the greater exposure of increasing numbers of women to the use and maintenance of heavy, high-caliber weaponry like rifles and AK-47s as required for their on-the-ground military roles in the recent US conflicts around the world, including Iraq and Afghanistan.

3. See Troy Graham, Mike Newall and Michael Brocker, "Before Kraft Shooting Rampage Growing Alarm over Suspect's Behavior," *Philadelphia Inquirer*, September 11, 2010, http://www.philly.com/inquirer/front_oage/201009911_BeforeKraft_shooting_rampage_growing_alarm_over_suspect_s_behavior.html. Also see Sean Alfano, "Suspended Female Employee Guns Down Two Shooting Spree at Kraft Factory in Philadelphia," *NY Daily News*, September 10, 2010, http://www.nydailynews.com/news/national/2010/09/10_suspended _female_employee_opens_fire_at_kraft_foods_facility_in_philly_killing_t.html.

4. Ibid.

5. Ibid.

6. Jon Cassidy, "Death Sentence Upheld in Fatal Burning," *Orange County Register*, March 12, 2010, http://www.ocregister.com/common/printer/view.php?db=ocregister&id=238948. Also see S. Anthony Baron, *Violence in the Workplace—A Prevention and Management Guide for Businesses* (Pathfinder, 1993), p. 18.

7. Jon Cassidy, "Death Sentence Upheld in Fatal Burning," *Orange County Register*, March 12, 2010, http://www.ocregister.com/common/printer/view.php?db=ocregister&id=238948.

8. Ibid.

9. See Jon Cassidy, note 6 *supra*. D'Arcy was convicted of first-degree murder by an Orange County jury and sentenced to death. On appeal, his lawyers argued the inadmissibility of certain photographic evidence, and also pointed out that D'Arcy had had a deeply troubled

childhood, including a mother who once forced him to eat his own feces as punishment for soiling his pants. The court rejected the appeal. See Jon Cassidy, note 7 *supra*.

10.   The only other case found in which fire was used as a weapon occurred in Britain (U.K.), in October 2008. The perpetrator was Russell Carter, 53, a disgruntled truck driver who believed his boss, Kingsley Monk, 45, owed him three thousand pounds in back wages. After four hours of arguing, he murdered his boss by beating him with a metal pipe and strangling him with his own necktie, and then attempted to murder three employees (who had witnessed the murder) by dousing them with gasoline and setting the building on fire. The three survived the attack, and Carter was later convicted and sentenced to thirty years' imprisonment. See Luke Salkeld, "Vietnam Veteran Killed Boss in Reservoir Dogs–style Attack after Slipping into UK Despite String of Convictions," *MailOnline*, October 23, 2009, http://www .daily-mail.co.uk/news/article-1222501/Disgruntled-lorry-driver-killed-boss-Reservoir-Dogs-style-attack-jailed-life.html.

11.   .See Isaac Arnsdorf et al., "Clark Charged in Le GRD '13 Murder," *Yale Daily News*, September 17, 2009, http://www.yaledailynews.com/news/2009/sep/17/clark-charged-in-le-grd-13-murder/.

12.   See Christina Ng, "California Yogurt Store Owner Allegedly Locks Diaper-Clad Employee in Box," *ABCNews*, August 29, 2011, http://abcnews.go.com/US/california-yogurt-store-owner-allegedly-locks-diaper-clad/story?id=14404292.

13.   See Carol Costello, "When Co-workers Kill: Workplace Violence on the Rise," *CNN*, October 7, 2009, http://amfix.blogs.cnn.com/2009/10/07/preventing-workplace-violence/. Also see Associated Press, "Maine Man Convicted in Brutal Coffee Shop Killing," August 31, 2006, http://www.foxnews.com/printer_friendly_story/0,3566,211518,00.html.

14.   See "Ex-KFC Worker Admits Killing Boss," *Journal Gazette*, January 18, 2011, http:// www.journalgazette.net/apps/pbcs.dll/article?AID=/20110118/NEWS07/110119492/-1/ NEWS09.

15.   In this regard, it should be noted that literally minutes after Joseph Harris killed his supervisor with the sword, he crept downstairs to the basement, where he killed her live-in boyfriend by shooting him in the back of the head—*with a gun*.

16.   Tim Minton and Jonathan Dienst, "Going Postal: Mail Sorter Charged With Stabbing Boss at JFK," *NBCNewYork.com*, June 19, 2010, http://www.printthis.clickability.com/pt/ cpt?action=cpt&title=Going=Postal%3AMail, and Will Cruz, "Postal Service Worker Stabs Boss with Scissors at Kennedy Airport: Sources," *NYDailyNews.com*, http://www .nydaily-news.com/fdcp?1294161681390.

17.   Arrested three months later, Duncan was tried and convicted of murder, and then sentenced to death, which was later reduced on appeal to life imprisonment without parole. In this regard, it should be noted that of all the cases included in the study, Matthew Beck, 35, was the only perpetrator (male or female) who killed one of his supervisors with both a gun *and* a knife. An accountant, Beck was outraged over his job, salary, and inability to get a raise in the several years he had worked for the Connecticut Lottery. On March 6, 1999, he shot and killed three lottery officials and shot and stabbed a fourth. Though one of the officials was a female, it doesn't appear from the record that she was Beck's immediate supervisors, but rather a political appointee with general managerial functions and oversight responsibilities for the office as a whole. See Jonathan Rabinovitz, "Rampage in Connecticut: The Overview; Connecticut Lottery Worker Kills 4 Bosses, Then Himself," *New York Times*, March 7, 1998. http:// www.nytimes.com/1998/03/07/nyregion/rampage-connecticut-overview-connecticut. Also see Richard Weizel, "Town of the Lottery Killings," *New York Times*, March 15, 1998, http:// www.nytimes.com/1998/03/15/nyregion/town-of-the-lottery-fillings-html?ref=matthewbeck.

18.   Janet Shan, "Top Mississippi TSA Official Rube Orlando Benitez Arrested for Stabbing Death of Stacey Wright, Being Held on $3 Million Bond," *Hinterland Gazette*, September 21, 2011. http://hinterlandgazette.com/2011/09/top-mississippi-tsa-official-ruben.html.

19.   Of course, men killed or wounded male supervisors by stabbing. On May 16, 2006, Tom Tuduj of Chicago stabbed and killed his company's CEO after a poor job review. On July 26, 2010, Claudius Mapp stabbed and wounded his supervisor at an Atlanta, GA, postal facility. Two months later, Willie Riley stabbed and wounded his boss at a New Orleans paper company in order to avoid drug testing. On June 1, 2011, Keith D. Little stabbed his supervisor

at a Bethesda, MD, hospital seventy times, killing him, after receiving a poor performance review. And in May 2007, Martin Gomez murdered his boss on a suburban Chicago horse farm, stabbing him more than 111 times. A few men even killed (or attempted to kill) their female supervisors with guns. Joseph Marchetti shot and wounded a female supervisor, while William Xu, Lorenzo Sam, and Melvin D. Taylor Jr. all shot and killed their female supervisors. But these scenarios were relatively rare, and not nearly as common as those in which men used guns or other firearms to kill other men. The only other possible explanation is that men felt more confident that they could overpower a woman without a weapon or gun. Women typically were not as strong as men, for whom a deadly weapon that could be used from a safe distance just made more sense.

20. Frank Lemos, 56, had worked at the Chemical Lime Company in Las Vegas, NV, for thirty-six years without any problems. But on November 10, 1998, upset over being fired, he went on a rampage, chasing his supervisor in a company bulldozer, crushing him repeatedly with a 196,000-pound front loader, and destroying company buildings and smashing vehicles before the police arrived at the plant and shot and killed him. See Glenn Puit and Joe Schoenmann, "Worker Goes Berserk, Kills Using Bulldozer," *Las Vegas Review Journal*, November 11, 1998, http://www.reviewjournal.com/lvrj_home/1998/Nov-11-Wed-1998/news/1021668.html.

21. Of the relatively rare cases in which a disgruntled male employee killed his female supervisor or superior, only about a half dozen involved the use of a gun or other firearm. These included the cases of Joseph Marchetti, William Xu, David Barnett, and Lorenzo Sam.

22. On November 28, 2010, Thomas Bernard of Saint Lucie County, FL, choked his boss, tax attorney Ashley Pollow, 58, and then doused the body with drain-cleaning chemicals to hasten decomposition before locking the body in his storm cellar. The body was found on December 7, 2010. Bernard's girlfriend, Michelle Lockridge, 58, has been charged as an accomplice. See Will Greenlee, "Ex-employee Arrested in St. Lucie County Attorney's Killing," *TCPalm*, January 28, 2011, http://www.tcpalm.com/news/2011/jan/28/ex-employee_arrested-in-st-lucie-county-killing/. Another possible example of a male murdering another male with his bare hands, though it's not altogether clear if the case qualifies, is boxing promoter Don King's 1966 murder of his employee by stomping him to death. The record suggests that King actually beat the man with a handgun as well. See Jack Newfield, *Only in America—The Life and Crimes of Don King* (William Morrow and Co., 1995), pp. 4–8.

23. See *Wikipedia*, s.v. "Ramon Salcido," http://en.wikipedia.org/wiki/Ramon_Salcido. Also see "Daddy Dearest," undated, http://www.mayhem.net/Crime/salcido.html. The surviving daughter, Carmina, later authored her autobiography (with Steve Jackson), Carmina Salcido, *Not Lost Forever—The Story of a Survivor* (HarperCollins Publishers, 2009).

24. Ibid.

25. See *Wikipedia*, s.v. "Ronald Gene Simmons," http://en.wikipedia.org/wiki/Ronald_Gene_Simmons; also see Angela Swanlund, *The Encyclopedia of Arkansas History and Culture*, http://www.encyclopediaofarkanss.net/encyclopedia/entry-detail.aspx?entryID=3731.

26. Ibid. Simmons later laid the bodies in neat rows around a table in the lounge, in what was possibly a drunken attempt to duplicate the scene of the Last Supper. He then spent the weekend watching TV and guzzling beer, surrounded by the corpses, waiting for Monday morning, when he would leave the house and resume the violence at his former place of employment.

27. See Kevin Sack, "Shootings in Atlanta: The Overview," *New York Times*, July 30, 1999, http://www.nytimes.com/1999/07/30/us/shootings-in-atlanta-the-overview-gunman-in-atlanta-slays-9-then-himself.html.?scp=2&sq=Barton. Barton had also been the principal suspect, but was never formally charged, in the deaths of his first wife and her mother six years earlier in 1993 (also by bludgeoning with a blunt, hammer-like object) in Alabama. Hours after the 1999 massacre, Barton was spotted by the local police, but turned a gun on himself and committed suicide before they could make an arrest. And if his life ended at that moment, the discovery of evidence that implicated him in other murders didn't. Hours after his suicide, the police found the remains of his family in his girlfriend's apartment in the Atlanta suburb of Stockbridge. Also see Brent C. Doonan, *Murder at the Office—A Survivor's True Story* (New Horizon, 2006).

28. Ibid.
29. See note 25 *supra.*
30. See Rachael Bell, "Workplace Homicide," *TruTV.com*, http://www.trutv.com/library/ crime/notorious_murders/mass/work_homicide/4.html. Also see http://murderpedia.org/ male.S/s/sherrill-patrick-henry.htm. Also see J. Anthony Baron, *Violence in the Workplace*, note 6 *supra* at p. 58.
31. The view that women can be more "lethal" in the workplace, of course, only lends credence to author Richard Condon's literary creation of Irene Walker, a talented female "hit man," in his darkly comic Mafia romance, *Prizzi's Honor*, which spawned a movie of the same name. The story involves the Prizzi family's hit man, Charley Partanna (played by Jack Nicholson), who falls in love with a beautiful blonde "tax consultant" he meets at a wedding, Irene Walker. He doesn't know that she's also a mob assassin who was hired by the Prizzi family to rub out a family enemy. But when he learns that his beloved is not only a talented hit man, but that she has also swindled seven hundred thousand dollars from the Prizzi family, he's confronted with a tragic choice: either marry the woman with whom he's so quickly fallen in love, or fulfill his professional duty to his employer, the Prizzi family, and whack her. Of course, he reluctantly decides to do his job. What does he choose as his murder weapon? A knife, of course.
32. See Azadeh Moaveni, "Man Fatally Shoots Worker, Then Himself," *Los Angeles Times*, December 10, 2003, http://articles.latimes.com/2003/dec/10/local/me-workshoot10.
33. See Amy Wallace and H.G. Reza, "2 Executives of Firm Slain in Office: Violence: Laid-off Worker Stalked Victims at San Diego Electronics Company, Witnesses Say," *Los Angeles Times*, June 5, 1991, http://articles.latimes.com/1991/06-05/news/mn-217_1_san-diego-electronics. Also see Stephanie Armour, "Inside the Minds of Workplace Killers," *USAToday*, July 14, 2004, http://www.usatoday.com/money/workplace/2004-07-14-workplace-killings_x.htm.
34. See Jeffrey Collins, "Hastings Wise a 'Volunteer' for Execution; His Is Scheduled for This Evening," *Times and Democrat*, http://thetandd.com/news/article_931d7ad1-28eb-53a8-aa06-cd5bf8d05595.html, also see Joshua Quinn, "Arthur Hastings Wise Put to Death for Aiken Murders," *NBC Augusta*, August 16, 2007, http://www.nbcaugusta.com/news/ocal/ 1835431.html.
35. See Charles Hill, "Trucker Kills 6, Hurts 5 in Texas Rampage," *Saint Petersburg Times*, August 10, 1982, also see Associated Press, "Texas Killing Spree Ends in 5 Deaths at Hand of Angry Man," *Miami News*, August 10, 1982, p. 6.
36. For the underlying facts of the Ladislav Antilak case, see *AmicusAttorney*, March 7, 2000, *Robblee III v. Budd Services, Inc.*, 136 N.C. App. 793 (2000), No COA99-348, http:// caselaw.findlaw.com/nc-court-of-appeals/1069826.html.
37. See Associated Press, "Five Workers Die in Shooting Rampage at Chicago Navistar Plant," *Lubbock Avalanche-Journal*, February 6, 2001, http://www.lubbockonline.com/stories/ 020601/nat_020601041.shtml.
38. Ibid.
39. See Shelly Barclay, "Murder at Frank Lloyd Wright's Home in Wisconsin," *Bukisa*, July 16, 2009, http://www.bukisa.com/articles/123301_murder-at-frank-lloyd-wrights-home-in-wisconsin. Also see Meryle Secrest, *Frank Lloyd Wright—A Biography* (Knopf, 1992), pp. 216–20.
40. See Doonan, *Murder at the Office*, at note 27 *supra*, p. 79.
41. See "3 Slain by Gunman at Café in Tampa," *New York Times*, January 28, 1993, http:// www.nytimes.com/1993/01/28/us/3-slain-by-gunman-at-cafe-in-tampa.htm. Also see "Lethal Grievance," *SunSentinel.com*, February 27, 1994.
42. See Saint Louis County Police, "Press Release: Warrants Issued on 48 Year Old Man Suspected of Office Shooting in Earth City," October 22, 2004, http://www.co.st-louis.mo.us/ scripts/P/d/press/view.cfm?ViewMe=5255. Also see Associated Press, "Nation in Brief," *Washington Post*, October 24, 2004, http://pqasb.pqarchiver.com/washingtonpost/access/ 721913001.html?FMT=ABS&FMTS=ABS:FT&date=Oct+24%2C+2004&author=&desc =NATION+IN+BRIEF.

43. See "Suspect, Victims in Safeway Shooting Rampage Identified," *DenverChannel.com*, June 26, 2006, http://www.thedenverchannel.com/news/9424239/detail.html.

44. See Jace Radke, "Rampage Brings Death to Industrial Plant," *Las Vegas Sun*, November 11, 1998, http://www.lasvegassun.com/news/1998/nov/11/rampage-brings-death-to-industrial-plant/.

45. Jarrett Murphy, "Six Dead in Mississippi Massacre," *CBS News*, July 9, 2003, http://www.cbsnews.com/stories/2003/07/09/national/main562301.shtml; also see Brian Ross and David Scott, "Lockheed Workplace Murders Targeted Blacks," *ABCNews*, May 12, 2005, http://abcnews.go.com/CleanPrint/cleanprintproxy.aspx?1288639049703; also see Matt Volz, Associated Press, "Gunman Opens Fire at Lockheed Martin Plant in Mississippi; Six Dead including Shooter," *Boston.com*, July 8, 2003, http://www.boston.com/news/daily/08/plant_shooting.htm.

46. Ibid.

47. Ibid.

48. See Rene Lynch, "Man Gets 60 Years for Deadly Shooting Spree," *Los Angeles Times*, September 4, 1993, http://articles.latimes.com/1993-09-04/local/me-31559_1_fairview-center.

49. Ibid. Whether the judge acted out of restraint, or whether he allowed himself to be annoyed by Rahming's accusatory, self-serving ramblings, is not known, but he imposed a sentence of sixty years to life imprisonment.

50. See Patrick G. Lee, Kerry Burke, and Helen Kennedy, "Madman Stalks & Murders Yale Doc," *NY Daily News*, April 27, 2010, p. 7. Also see Barry Leibowitz, "Confession in Yale Doctor Vajinder Toor's Murder? Lishan Wang Says He Was There and He's Sorry, Claim Cops," *CBSNews*, April 30, 2010. Also see http://www.cbsnews.com/8301-504083_162-20003891-504083.html.

51. Ibid.

52. Ibid. Thanks to quick-thinking neighbors who called 911, Wang was arrested only minutes later in the minivan, in which the police found printouts on two other people who were involved with Wang's dismissal, along with a wig, a hammer, a knife, one thousand rounds of ammunition, and two handguns. Wang was formally booked, was held on a two-million-dollar bond, and after confessing to the shooting, according to the arresting officers, softly said, "I'm sorry." See Leibowitz, note 50 *supra*.

53. See Patrick G. Lee et al., note 50 *supra*.

54. See Jason Nark, "Authorities: South Jersey Doc Kills Ex-colleague, Self," *Inquirer/Daily News*, April 12, 2012, http://articles.philly.com20212-04-12/news/31331529_1_voorhees-girlfriend-neighbors.

55. See Demorris A. Lee, Rita Farlow, and Jamal Thalji, "Before Publix Worker Was Shot and Killed, He'd Been Threatened at the Store," *Tampa Bay Times*, March 31, 2010. http://www.tampabay.com/news/publicsafety/crime/shooting-incident-reported-at-tarpon-springs-publix/1083848. Also see Demorris A. Lee and Rita Farlow, "Woman Accused of Killing Publix Coworker in Rare Company," *Tampa Bay Times*, April 12, 2010, http://www.tampabay.com/news/publicsafety/crime/woman-accused-of-killing-publix-coworker-in-rare-company/1086728.

56. Ibid.

57. Ibid.

58. Ibid.

59. Ibid.

60. Ibid.

61. Ibid.

62. Ibid.

63. Ibid.

64. See Ray Rivera and Christine Haughney, "Amid Mourning, Eerie Details Emerge about Connecticut Shootings," *New York Times*, August 4, 2010, http://www.nytimes.com/2010/08/05/nyregion/05shooting.html?pagewanted=1&_r=1. Associated Press, "Police: Conn. Warehouse Gunman Targeted Managers," *Fox News*, August 4, 2010, http://foxnews.com/us/2010/08/03/dead-wounded-conn-workplace-shooting/. Also see Associated Press, "9 Dead in Shooting at Connecticut Beer Distributor," *MSNBC*, August 4, 2010, http://www.msnbc.msn.com/id/

38535909/ns/us_news-crime_and_courts. Also see Emily Friedman, "911 Tapes from Connecticut Shooting Describe Gunman's Deadly Rampage," *ABC News*, August 4, 2010, http://abcnews.go.com/US/connecticut-shooter-omar-thornton-chased-victims-beer-distributor/story?id=11322281&page=1. Also see Stephen Singer, "9 Killed in Shooting at Conn. Beer Distributorship," *Yahoo!News*, August 3, 2010, http://news.yahoo.com/s/ap/20100803/ap_on_re_us/us_beer_distributor_shootings. Also see Stephen Singer, "9 Killed in Shooting at Conn. Beer Distributorship—Gunman Claimed Racial Harassment, but Never Filed a Claim with His Union," Associated Press, August 4, 2010, http://www.chieftain.com/article_110a4e1c-9f86-11df-b6d6-001cc4c03286.html?mode=story. Also see www.murderpedia.com, including the transcript of Omar Thornton's 911 call to the police (released on August 5, 2010, two days after the shooting) at http://murderpedia.org/male.T/t/thornton-omar.htm.

65. Ibid.

66. Ibid

67. See "Postal Worker in Milwaukee Shoots 3 and Kills Himself," *New York Times*, December 20, 1997, http://www.nytimes.com/1997/12/20/us/postal-worker-in-milwaukee-shoots-3-kills-himself.html.

68. Many were convinced that Thornton was motivated solely by factors of race, which was downplayed by the press. Christopher Donovan, "Hate-Fueled Black Mass Murderer in Connecticut Spun as 'Disgruntled Man' by Media," *Occidental Observer Blog*, http://theoccidentalobserver.net/tooblog/?p=3073&cpage=2.

69. See "Auto Worker Kills 2, Wounds 2 in Shooting; Victims Were on a UAW Committee," *Chron/Houston Chronicle Archives*, September 11, 1994, http://www.chron.com/CDA/archives.mpl/1994_1225305/auto-worker-kills-2-wounds-2-in-shooting-victims-w.html.

70. See "Ford Union Official's Murder Trial Opens, Race Will Play a Major Role," *Luddington Daily News*, March 27, 1995, p. 2, http://news.google.com/newspapers ?nid=19950327&id=dRQAAAAIBAJ&sjid=UFUDAAAAIBAJ&pg=4899,7435854.

71. Mike Clary, "Fired Employee Guns Down Co-Workers, Kills Himself," *Los Angeles Times*, February 10, 1996, http://articles.latimes.com/1996-02-10/news/mn-34334_1_fired-kills-workers.

7. THE PROBLEMS AND POLITICS OF BEING THE BOSS

1. See Linda Kaplan Thaler and Robin Koval, *The Power of Nice: How to Conquer the Business World With Kindness* (Crown Publishing Group, 2006). Also see Ronald M. Shapiro and Mark Jankowski, with James Dale, *The Power of Nice* (John Wiley and Sons, Inc, 2001).

2. See, for instance, Lee Iacocca, *Where Have All the Leaders Gone* (Scribner, 2008) and Lee Iacocca, *Iacocca—An Autobiography* (Bantam, 2007), Jonathan Gatlin, *Bill Gates—The Path to the Future* (HarperCollins Publishers, 2009), Marc Aronson, *Up Close: Bill Gates* (Penguin Group, 2008), Ken Torrin, ed., *An Unauthorized Biography of Warren Buffet* (Webster's Digital Services, 2011), respectively.

3. For some insight into the more hands-on management styles of Sam Walton and Martha Stewart, see, for instance, Karen Blumenthal, *Mr. Sam: How Sam Walton Built WalMart and became America's Richest Man* (Penguin Group, 2011), and Christopher Byron, *Martha, Inc.* (Wiley, John & Sons, 2002), respectively.

4. To glean some indication of the management styles of Hewlett-Packard's CEO Carly Fiorina, see, for instance, Peter Burrows, *Backfire: Carly Fiorina's High-Stakes Battle for the Soul of Hewlett-Packard* (Wiley, John & Sons, Inc., 2003), and for that of Donald Trump, see Donald J. Trump with Tony Schwartz, *Trump—The Art of the Deal* (Random House, 2004).

5. The hardest, take-no-prisoners management style of Don King may be seen in Jack Newfield's unflattering portrait of the former boxing promoter. See note 18 infra., and accompanying text. For the equally hard (but button-down collar) management style of Jack Welch, see, for instance, Thomas F. O'Boyle, *At Any Cost: Jack Welch, General Electric, and the Pursuit of Profit* (Knopf, 1998).

6. Jake Brown, *Suge Knight: The Rise, Fall, and Rise of Death Row Records: The Story of Marion "Suge" Knight, A Hard Hitting Study of One Man, One Company that Changed the Course of American Music Forever* (Amber Communications Group, Inc., 2001).

7. See Ronald D. Brown, "The Politics of Mo' Money, Mo' Money, and the Strange Dialectic of Hip Hop," review/ essay/comment on *The Hip Hop Generation—Young Blacks and the Crisis in African American Culture* by Bakari Kitwana, *Vanderbilt Journal of Entertainment Law and Practice* 5 (2003), 59, 60.

8. Ibid.

9. The word "boss" derives from the Dutch word "baas," which literally means "master."

10. Associated Press, "Car Dealer Accused of Killing 2 Workers," *USA Today*, July 31, 2007, http://www.usatoday.com/news/nation/2007-07-31-car_dealer-killings_N.htm. Milinavicius was sentenced to two consecutive life terms plus ten years, and both the sentence and the earlier pretrial proceedings were later upheld by the Georgia Supreme Court.

11. Ibid.

12. Ibid.

13. See Ben Dobbin, "Frank Garcia Guilty of Murder Rampage," *Huffington Post*, December 16, 2009, http://www.huffingtonpost.com/2009/12/16/frank-garcia-guilty-of-mu_n_394172.html. Also see Ben Dobbin, "Frank Garcia Guilty: Valentine's Day Killer Convicted," *Huffington Post*, November 30, 2009, http://www.huffingtonpost.com/2009/12/01/frank-garcia-guilty-valen_n_375066.html.

14. Ibid.

15. See Cynthia Hodges, "Chicago Native, Top TSA Official Charged with Murder,"*examiner.com*, September 22, 2011, http://www.examiner.com/article/chicago-native-top-tsa-official-charged-with-murder . Also see Jerry Mitchell, "Former TSA Manager at O'Hare Charged with Murder in Mississippi," *Chicago Sun-Times*, September 22, 2011, http://www.suntimes.com/news/metro/7811334-418/former-tsa-manager-at-ohare-charged-with-murder-in-mississippi.htm.

16. See Jim Herron Zamora, "'Sausage King' Goes on Trial for Murder," *San Francisco Chronicle*, April 27, 2004, http://www.sfgate.com/chi-bin/article.cgi?f=/c/a/2004/04/27/BA-GIL6/bDQM1.DTL. Also see *Wikipedia* , s.v. "Stuart Alexander (businessman and mass murderer)," http://en.wikipedia.org/wiki/Stuart_Alexander_(businessman_and_mass_murderer).

17. Stuart Alexander was never executed after he received the death penalty. He died, instead, of natural causes in December 2005, found dead in his San Quentin jail cell as he awaited execution on death row.

18. See Jack Newfield, *Only in America—The Life and Crimes of Don King* (William Morrow and Co., 1995), pp. 4–8.

19. Ibid.

20. See Lisa Locker, "Ex-boss Shoots Woman 4 Times, Kills Himself Dispute Over Dismissal Ends In Gunfire," *SunSentinel.com*, May 20, 1988, http://articles.sun-sentinel.com/1988-05-20/news/8801300976_1_parking-lot-unemployment-office-wound. Miraculously, Sando was soon taken off the "critical" list and survived her bullet wounds. See "Shooting Victim Better," *SunSentinel.com*, May 25, 1988, http://articles.sun-sentinel.com/1988-05-24/news/8801310820_1_parking-lot-boss-intensive-care-unit.

21. Ibid.

22. For the facts surrounding the Williams Evans murder/suicide, see "Job Agency Murder-Suicide Tied to Failed Relationship, Police Say," *Toledo Blade*, March 26, 1998, http://news.google.com/newspapers?nid=1350&dat=19980326&id=90BPAAAAIBAJ&sjid=IgMEAAAAIBAJ&pg=4200,3501733; also see "@marilloGlove-News: 2 Killed in Shooting at State Employment Headquarters," *@marillo.com*, March 19, 1998, http://amarillo.com/stories/031998/LA0675.001.shtml.

23. See "Civilian Kills 3, Hurts 2 and then Shoots Himself," *Star-News*, October 19, 1993; also see "Worker at Fort Knox Kills 3, then Shoots Himself," *New York Times*, October 19, 1993, http://www.nytimes.com/1993/10/19/us/worker-at-fort-knox-kills-3-then-shoots-himself.html.

24. Ibid.

25. Todd Shield, "Restaurant Owner Kills Self, Employee in Prospect Heights," *Chicago Sun-Times*, November 11, 2011, http://glenview.suntimes.com/news/7944646-418/glenview-restaurant-owner-kills-employee-self-in-prospect-heights.html.

26. Ibid.

27. See Heidi Evans and Tracy Connor, with Richard Weir and Michele McPhee, "Killer's Tortured Last Days Ex-FBI Man in Times Sq. Bloodbath Left Wife, Didn't Eat," *Daily News*, September 18, 2002, http://www.nydailynews.com/2002-09-18/news/18202089_1_john-harrison-isabel-munoz-diet. Also see Associated Press, "N.Y. Executive Kills 2 Co-Workers, Himself," *Los Angeles Times*, September 17, 2002, http://articles.latimes.com/2002/sep/17/nation/na-nyshooot17. Also see "Shooting Leaves 3 Dead at Empire Blue Cross and Blue Shield," *Insurance Journal*, September 18, 2002, http://www.insurancejournal.com/news/east/2002/09/18/23184.htm.

28. Ibid.

29. Ibid.

30. See Jason Buckland, "Women Still View Sex with the Boss as a Way to Get Ahead," *EverydayMoney*, August 30, 2010, http://www.everydaymoney.ca/2010/08/not-unlike-malt-shops-bellbottoms-and-the-integrity-of-the-emmy-awards-the-notion-that-a-woman-needs-to-sleep-with-her-boss.htm. Also see Sylvia Ann Hewlett, "How Sex Hurts the Workplace, Especially Women," August 24, 2010, http://blogs.hbr.org/hbr/hewlett/2010/08/how-sex_hurts_the_workplace_es.html.

31. See Alyson Shontell, "15% of Women Have Slept with Their Bosses—And 37% of Them Got Promoted for It," *Business Insider*, August 25, 2010, http://articles.businessinsider.com/2010/08-25/strategy/30337940_1_female-executives-affair-work-life-policy.

32. See notes 28 and 29 *supra*.

33. See note 18 *supra*.

34. See note 25 *supra*. "Job Agency Murder-Suicide Tied to Failed Relationship, Police Say," *Toledo Blade*, March 26, 1998, http://news.google.com/newspapers?nid=1350&dat=19980326&id=90BPAAAAIBAJ&sjid=IgMEAAAAIBAJ&pg=4200,3501733; see note 25 *supra*.

35. Ibid.

36. See note 30 *supra*. The problem, of course, was that Munoz clearly did not feel as strongly for Harrison as he evidently felt for her. And his "dreams" were dashed when she sent him a "Dear John" e-mail, indicating that she had not "signed on for anything serious" and that she didn't think it wise that he split from his wife.

37. See notes 23 and 24 *supra*.

38. Ibid.

39. Laurence Veile Davidson, "Ex-GE Manager Claims Insanity in Atlanta Killing of Former JP Morgan Banker," *Bloomberg*, March 9, 2012. http://www.bloomberg.com/news/print/2012-03-09/ex-ge-manager-claims-insanity-in-atlanta-killing-of-former-jpmorgan-banker.html.

40. Ibid.

41. Ibid.

42. Ibid.

43. Marc Bovsun, "Mailman Massacre: 14 Die after Patrick Sherrill 'Goes Postal' in 1986 Shootings," *Daily News*, August 15, 2010, http://articles.nydailynews.com/2010-08-15/news/27072662_1_part-time-letter-carrier-howard-unruh-spree-killings, also see William Robbins, "The Loner: From Shy Football Player to 'Crazy Pat,'" *New York Times*, August 22, 1986, http://www.nytimes.com/1986/08/22/us/the-loner-from-shy-football-player-to-crazy-pat.html.

44. Hansel had been looking for "three supervisors in particular." And during his search of the building he approached a male employee, poked his gun into the man's chest, and asked where the supervisors were. When the man proved unhelpful, Hansel let him run away, unharmed. See Amy Wallace, H. G. Reza, and Nora Zamichow, "Gunman Kills 2 SD Executives: Terror: Laid-off Worker, Armed with Shotgun Explodes Bombs and Then Stalks Executives while Terrified Employees Flee Electronics Firm, Officials Say," *Los Angeles Times*, June 5, 1991, http://articles.latimes.com/1991-06-05/news/mn-164_1_top-executives.

45. See Associated Press, "Firefighter Kills Wife and 4 Officials," *New York Times*, April 25, 1996, http://www.nytimes.com/1996/04/25/us/firefighter-kills-wife-and-4-officials.html? partner=rssnyt&emc=rss. Also see www.murderpedia.com, http://murderpedia.org/male.T/t/ tornes-kenneth.htm.

46. Ibid.

47. Ibid.

48. Ibid.

49. Ibid.

50. See Barry Leibowitz, "Confession in Yale Doctor Vajinder Toor's Murder? Lishan Wang Says He Was There and He's Sorry, Claim Cops," *CBSNEWS*, April 30, 2010, http://www.cbsnews.com/8301-504083_162-20003891-504083.html.

51. See Rene Lynch, "Man Gets 60 Years for Deadly Shooting Spree," *Los Angeles Times*, September 4, 1993, http://articles.latimes.com/1993-09-04/local/me-31559_1_fairview-center.

52. See Stephanie Armour, "Inside the Minds of Workplace Killers," *USA Today*, July 14, 2007, http://www.usatoday.com/money/workplace/2004-07-14-workplace-killings_x.htm (emphasis added).

53. In January 1992, General Dynamics employee Robert Earl Mack shot and killed a labor representative and his supervisor during a disciplinary hearing. In February 2012, years after his conviction and imprisonment, and decades after the crimes, he was interviewed by Dr. Steve Albrecht, who found that he was still incapable of admitting his responsibility for the deaths, still unable to show remorse for his crimes, and still angry and resentful at what he still believed was his mistreatment by management. See Steve Albrecht, "My Interview with a Double Workplace Murderer," *Psychology Today*, February 21, 2012, http://www.psychologytoday.com/blog/the-act-violence/201202/my-interview-double-workplace-murderer.

54. Hansel was not alone in his belief that his victims only got what they deserved. The mass murderer R. Gene Simmons not only never apologized for his murders, but expressed his disdain for the entire criminal justice system by knowingly waiving all rights to appeal and resisting all assistance of counsel, and even wrote letters to the court refusing any and all aid that would delay his execution. Leo Held is another example. After Held killed his five supervisors, he was later fatally shot by the police in a shoot-out. Not only did he never show the slightest remorse, on his deathbed he explained his motives and also expressed regret that he still had another person he wanted to kill but couldn't find that person during his rampage. More than one perpetrator expressed his or her lack of remorse posthumously, like Clifton McCree, who killed all five of his white coworkers after he was fired, and then killed himself, but expressed his disdain and hatred for his victims in a nasty suicide note. And there was also Dan White, who in November 1978 assassinated San Francisco mayor George Moscone and supervisor Harvey Milk. Years after the double assassination, after he was released from prison, he reportedly not only confessed, but also expressed regret that he hadn't also killed two other politicians, and that he should have killed all four. See *Wikipedia*, s.v. "Dan White," http://en.wikipedia.org/wiki/Dan_White. It should be noted here that the number of incarcerated perpetrators who were still resentful and lacking in remorse was actually much higher than indicated. In more than a dozen interviews, the perpetrators (as inmates) typically had little incentive to be candid and totally truthful to the reporter, and they always spoke in ways that were guarded and self-serving in the extreme—in ways that wouldn't jeopardize pending criminal appeals, or put them in a "bad" light the next time they appeared before a parole board.

8. CONFIRMING THE FACTS/DEBUNKING THE MYTHS

1. Taylorism was a theory of management that analyzed and synthesized work flows. The principal objective was to improve economic efficiency, especially labor productivity; it was one of the first attempts to apply science to the engineering of processes and to management. Named after Frederick Winslow Taylor (1856–1915) and at its peak of popularity between 1910 and 1915, it's now mostly discredited, as it fails to recognize that individuals learn

differently and are motivated differently, and that the divergent interests of management and workers frequently result in resentment, if not sabotage.

2. Boulwarism is a negotiation strategy named after General Electric's former vice president Lemuel Boulware (1895–1990), whose negotiations with labor unions provided an offer or counteroffer that wasn't meant to be negotiated. A basically "take it or leave it" tactic, when faced with a strike Boulware is famous for having informed the union leaders at the outset that the company had already evaluated the workers' needs and was putting forth its "first, last, and best offer" on the table. A GE tactic between 1949 and 1960, this philosophy of negotiating has been largely rejected. The National Labor Relations Board, as an example, rejects the tactic because it doesn't encourage negotiation between management and labor, but inhibits it.

3. The "organization" man is from a 1956 best-selling book, William H. Whyte, *The Organization Man*, considered by many to be one of the most influential books on management ever written. White basically conducted extensive interviews with many CEOs of the major American companies, like GE and Ford, and a central tenet of the book is that average modern Americans subscribe to a collectivist ethic, not to the prevailing notion of rugged frontier individualism. White observed that this system led to risk-averse executives who faced no consequences and could expect jobs for life as long as they made no egregious missteps. The book led to deeper examination of the concepts of "commitment" and "loyalty" within corporations and matched its fictional equivalent, Sloan Wilson, *The Man in The Gray Flannel Suit*, in inspiring criticism that those Americans who were inspired enough to win World War II returned to an empty conformity and the pursuit of the dollar.

4. See Stephanie Armour, quoting Alan Fox in "Inside the Minds of Workplace Killers," *USA Today*, July 14, 2004, http://www.usatoday.com/money/workplace/2004-07-14-workplace-killings_x.htm.

5. See Felicity Barringer, "Postal Officials Examine System after 2 Killings," *New York Times*, May 8, 1993, http://www.nytimes.com/1993/05/08/us/postal-officials-examine-system-after-2-killings.html?pagewanted=all. Also see Mark Ames, "Excerpt: Breaking Down at the Post Office," AlterNet, October 3, 2005, http://www.alternet.org/media/24798/excerpt:_breaking_down_at_the_post_office/.

6. Ted Johnson and John M. Glionna, "Postal Supervisor's Shooting Death Baffles Employees," *Los Angeles Times*, July 11, 1995, http://articles.latimes.com/1995-07-11/local/me-22544_1_postal-workers.

7. See Felicity Barringer, "Postal Officials Examine System After 2 Killings," *New York Times*, May 8, 1993, http://www.nytimes.com/1993/05/08/us/postal-officials-examine-system-after-2-killings.html?pagewanted=all. Also see Associated Press, "Clerk Kills Fellow Worker, Wounds Two in Shooting Spree at Atlanta Post Office," *Los Angeles Times*, March 7, 1985, http://articles.latimes.com/1985-03-07/news/mn-34494_1.

8. "Post Office Murders," *Time*, May 17, 1993, http://www.time.com/time/magazine/article/0,9171,978524,00.html.

9. "Postal Worker Shoots 2 and Then Kills Himself," *New York Times*, September 3, 1997, http://www.nytimes.com/1997/09/03/us/postal-worker-shoots-2-and-then-kills-himself.html?scp=1&sq=September%203rd,%201997%20Jesus%20Antonio%20Tamayo&st=cse.

10. Jaxon Van Derbeken, "Postal Workers Remember Slain Supervisor and Dead Carrier," *San Francisco Chronicle*, December 14, 2006, http://www.sfgate.com/cgh-bin/article.cgi?f=/c/a/2006/12/14/BAGHCMVH381.DTL.

11. See Tom Gorman and Richard Serrano, "Postal Employee Kills Wife, 2 Co-Workers," *Los Angeles Times*, August 11, 1989, http://articles.latimes.com/1989-08-11/news/mn-207_1_postal-employee.

12. See "Psychiatry Causes Senseless Violence," *Scientology against Drugs*, November 8, 2007, http://scientologyagainstdrugs.wordpress.com/category/psychiatry-causes-senseless-violence/.

13. See Alan Abrahamson, "Accused Killer Haunted by Disturbing Visions: Crime: Robert Earl Mack, Charged in Convair Shootings, Says He Had Intended to Shoot Himself," *Los Angeles Times*, June 21, 1992, http://articles.latimes.com/1992-06-21/local/me-1321_1_robert-earl-mack.

14. See Jace Radke, "Rampage Brings Death to Industrial Plant," *Las Vegas Sun*, November 11, 1998, http://www.lasvegassun.com/news/1998/nov/11/rampage-brings-death-to-industrial-plant/.

15. For the factual particulars of Westbecker's murder rampage, see http://murderpedia.org/male.W/w/westbecker-joseph.htm; also see *Wikipedia*, s.v. "Standard Gravure Shooting," http://en.wikipedia.org/wiki/standard_Gravure_shooting.

16. See "Pennsylvania: The Revolt of Leo Held," *Time*, November 3, 1967, http://www.time.com/time/magazine/article/0,9171,837437-1,000-html; also see www.murder pedia.com, http://murderpedia.org/male.H/h/held-leo.htm, and the book that was written about Held's murder rampage, Don Sarvey, *Day of Rage: Model Citizen turns Cold-Blooded Killer in a Small Pennsylvania Town* (Stackpole Books, 2011).

17. See Tony Perry, "Man Shoots 2 Co-workers; 1 Dies," *Los Angeles Times*, March 25, 2009, http://articles.latimes.com/2009/mar/25/local/me-briefs25.S2; also see John Wilkens, Angelica Martrinez, and Greg Gross, "3 Dead in MTS Shootings—Police Gun Down Man Who Shot Co-workers," *Sign on San Diego*, March 25, 2009, http://www.utsandiego.com/news/2009/mar/25/1n25mts1011213-3-dead-mts-shootings/.

18. See Matt Thacker, "Murdered Clarksville Man Remembered by Co-workers," *nt*, http://newsandtribune.com/local/x971903788/Murdered-Clarksville-man-remembered-by-co-workers.

19. Also noteworthy in this respect was Bruce Alvin Miller who, recently fired from his job, shot and killed himself in his boss's office after he had been with the company 28 years. See "Worker Kills Self in Boss's Office," *HR.BLR.com*, July 11, 2005, http://hr.blr.com/HR-news/Health-Safety/Violence-in-Workplace/Worker-Kills-Self-in-Bosss-Office/. And still another case was that of Oliver French, a black senior union official in the UAW at the Ford Motor Company's Rouge plant in Dearborn, Michigan. After French lost a local election, and then lost favor with the local union leadership, he shot and killed two coworkers and fellow union officers, and then shot and wounded two others. He had been on the job twenty-eight years. See "Auto Worker Kills 2, Wounds 2 in Shooting/Victims Were on a UAW Committee," *Houston Chronicle* (archives), September 11, 1994, http://www.chron.com/CDA/archives.mpl/1994_1225305/auto-worker-kills-2-wounds-2-in-shooting-victims-w.html. Also see "Ford Union Official's Murder Trial Opens, Race Will Play a Major Role," *Luddington Daily News*, March 27, 1995, p. 2, http://news.google.com/newspapers?nid=19950327&id=dRQ AAAAI-BAJ&sjid=UFUAAAAIBAJ&pg=4899,7435854.

20. See "Lethal Grievance," *SunSentinel.com*, February 27, 1994, which discusses the case of Paul Calden, a recently fired employee of the Fireman's Fund Insurance Company. On January 27, 1993, Calden methodically shot five of his former supervisors, three of whom died, and then committed suicide (http://articles.sun-sentinel.com/1994-02-27/features/9402090322_1_workplace-violence-paul-calden-tampa-bay).

21. Gary Davis, "Biology Professor Amy Bishop Kills Three, Wounds Three in Shooting Rampage in Alabama," *Yahoo!Voices*, February 13, 2010, http://voices.yahoo.com/biology-professor-amy-bishop-kills-three-wounds-three-5468309.html?cat=8. Also see *Wikipedia*, s.v. "2010 University of Alabama in Huntsville shooting," http://en.wikipedia.org/wiki/2010_University_of_Alabama_in_Huntsville_shooting.

22. This was especially true in what was likely the perpetrators' first decision: who they wanted to kill. Only about 15 to 20 percent of the cases in the study present facts that suggest the shootings were random; the vast majority present facts that strongly suggest conscious decision making in this regard. Indeed, some perpetrators—like Larry Hansel, Kenneth Tornes, Paul Calden, and Leo Held—literally brushed past or walked by fellow employees in order to search the building to kill a supervisor or boss. Other perpetrators—like Jennifer San Marco—shot and killed *only* fellow employees and didn't shoot a single supervisor or boss. A few—like Bryan Uyesugi—killed only men. And still other perpetrators—like Doug Williams, Oliver French, and Omar Thornton—shot and killed only those of a certain race.

23. See *Wikipedia*, s.v. "John List," http://en.wikipedia.org/wiki/John_List, p. 2.

24. Elizabeth Letts, *The Eighty-Dollar Champion: Snowman, the Horse that Inspired a Nation* (Random House, 2011), p. 222.

25. Patrice O'Shaughnessy, "How Personal Assistant Natavia Lowery Killed Celebrity Realtor Linda Stein, Who Wouldn't Back Down," *NY Daily News*, February 28, 2010, http://www.nydailynews.com/fdcp?1293144210750.

26. See Lee Strasberg, *A Dream of Passion—The Development of the Method* (Little/Brown, 1987).

27. Ibid., at p. 35.

28. See "Violence and Harassment in the Workplace: The 9 Most Common Myths of Workplace Violence," McClure Associates, undated, http://www.mcclureassociates.com/info/myths.html.

29. Edwin Karmoil, "Japan—Suicide Rate Takes a Worrisome Jump," *L atimes.com*, August 4, 1999.

30. Ibid.

31. Ibid.

32. Ibid. Also see Alex Wong, "The Asian Suicide Phenomenon," *Hardboiled*, April 30, 2012, http://hardboiled.berkeley.edu/archived-issues/issue-12-6/the-asian-suicide-phenomenon/.

33. Ibid.

34. Ibid.

35. Ibid.

36. See Barry Leibowitz, "Confession in Yale Doctor Vajinder Toor's Murder? Lishan Wang Says He Was There and He's Sorry, Claim Cops," *CBSNEWS*, April 30, 2010, http://www.cbsnews.com/8301-504083_162-20003891-504083.html.

37. See Charles E. Brown, Eli Sanders, and Christine Clarridge, "Two UW Doctors Killed in Shooting," *Seattle Times*, June 29, 2000, http://community.seattletimes.nwsource.com/archive/?date=20000629&slug=402935.

38. See Michael Harvey, "Tech Engineer Kills Three Bosses at Silicon Valley Start-Up After Being Sacked," *Times Online*, November 16, 2009, http://www.timesonline.co.uk/tol/news/world/us_and_americas/article5167198,ece.

39. See "Man Changes Plea to Guilty in Murder of Boss at UNT," *Dallas Morning News*, September 27, 2010, http://www.dallasnews.com/news/community-news/denton/headlines/20100927-man-changes-plea-to-guilty-7462.ece.

40. By Liz Hull, "Men Are the Best Bosses: Women at the Top Are Just Too Moody (And It's Women Themselves Who Say So)," *MailOnline*, August 12, 2010, http://www .dailymail.co.uk/femail/article-1302096/Men-best-bosses-Women-just-moody .html#ixzz1vMZBKacf.

41. Ibid.

42. Ibid.

43. Ibid.

44. Ibid.

45. See, e.g., Professor Kahlid Aziz, "Why Women Make Better Bosses," *Management Issues*, August 24, 2010, http://www.management-issues.com/2010/8/24/blog/why-women-make-better-bosses-asp.

46. See Adam Bryant's interview of Carol Smith, etc., "No Doubts; Women Are Better Managers," *New York Times*, July 25, 2009, http://www.nytimes.com/2009/07/26/business/26corner.html?pagewanted=all.

47. Ibid.

48. Ibid.

49. Debra Cassens Weiss, "Google Statisticians Study Performance Reviews for Good Manager Skills; Expertise is Low on the List," *ABAJournal*, March 15, 2011, http://www.com/mews/article/google_statisticians_study_performance_reviews_for_good_manager _skills_expe.

50. See "Most Women Prefer Working for Men," *Telegraph*, June 10, 2012, http://www.telegraph.co.uk/news/uknews/6020123/Most-women-prefer-working-for-men.html.

51. By Jill Foster, "Why a Female Boss Can Be a Woman's Worst Nightmare," *MailOnline*, July 26, 2011, http://www.dailymail.co.uk/femail/article-2018776/Why-female-boss-womans-worst-nightmare.html#ixzz1rwcPkw9T.

52. Ibid.

53. See Jocelyn Giangrande, "Are Women Harder to Work for? The Truth Revealed," *The Confident Woman*, January 15, 2011, http://jocelyngiangrande.com/2011/01/15/are-women-harder-to-work-for-the-truth-revealed.

54. Jack Zenger and Joseph Folkman, "Are Women Better Leaders than Men," *Harvard Business Review*, March 15, 2012, http://blogs.hbr.org/cs/2012/03/a-study_in_ leadership _women_do.html.

55. The character Sportin' Life sings "It Ain't Necessarily So" in George Gershwin's opera *Porgy and Bess* (1935), expressing his doubts about and disbelief of several statements in the text of the Bible.

56. Del Jones, "Women CEOs Slowly Gain in Corporate America," *USAToday*, January 2, 2009, http://www.usatoday.com/money/companies/management/2009-01-01-women-ceos-increase_N.htm.

57. See note 47 *supra*. "No Doubts; Women Are Better Managers," *New York Times*, July 25, 2009, http://www.nytimes.com/2009/07/26/business/26corner.html?pagewanted=all.

58. Jerry Mitchell, "Black Suicide Remains Unspoken Crisis," *Journey to Justice*, December 8, 2010, http://blogs.clarionledger.com/mitchell/2010/12/08/black-suicide-remains-unspoken-crisis/.

59. See generally Alvin F. Poussaint and Amy Alexander, *Lay My Burden Down—Suicide and the Mental Health Crisis among African Americans* (Beacon Press, 2001).

60. See Ray Rivera and Christine Haughney, "Amid Mourning, Eerie Details Emerge About Connecticut Shootings," *New York Times*, August 4, 2010, http://www.nytimes.com/2010/08/05/nyregion/05shooting.html?pagewanted=1&_r=1. Also see Associated Press, "Police: Conn. Warehouse Gunman Targeted Managers," *Fox News*, August 4, 2010, http://www.foxnews.com/us/2010/08/03/dead-wounded-conn-workplace-shooting/; Associated Press, "9 Dead in Shooting at Connecticut Beer Distributor," *MSNBC*, August 4, 2010, http://www.msnbc.msn.com/id/38535909/ns/us_news-crime_and_courts; and Emily Friedman, "911 Tapes from Connecticut Shooting Describe Gunman's Deadly Rampage," *ABC News*, August 4, 2010, http://abcnews.go.com/US/connecticut-shooter-omar-thornton-chased-victims-beer-distributor/story?id=11322281&page=1.

61. In fact, in the entire study, only one Hispanic woman was found who had even *attempted* to kill a boss. On August 18, 2008, a Houston, TX, woman named Lydia Munoz, 30, broke into the home of her former employer, Ronald Williamson, 42, as he and his wife lay sleeping in bed. At about 3:00 a.m., Munoz broke into the house and started to stab him repeatedly, and continued the attack until his wife grabbed a baseball bat and knocked Munoz to the floor and kept her there until the police arrived. Munoz was later arrested and charged with aggravated assault and burglary of the Williamson's Sugar Land home. See Eric Hanson, "Sugar Land PD: Houston Woman Stabbed Ex-boss," *Chron.com*, August 18, 2008, http://www.chron.com/neighborhood/fortbendnews/article/Sugar-Land-PD-Houston-woman-stabbed-ex-boss-1600902.php.

9. DECIPHERING THE LANGUAGE OF WORKPLACE SUICIDE

1. See Karl A. Menninger, *Man Against Himself* (New York: Harcourt, Brace & World, Inc., 1938). "But suicide is also a murder *by* the self. It is a death in which are combined in one person the murderer and the murdered" at p. 23. "Suicide must be regarded as a peculiar kind of death which entails three internal elements: the element of dying, the element of killing, and the element of being killed" at 24. "And so it is that one who nourishes murderous wishes also feels, at least unconsciously, a need for punishment of a corresponding sort. We see the truth of a statement made by [Sigmund] Freud many years ago that *many suicides are disguised murders* . . . for the reason that murder alone justifies in the unconscious the death penalty, even when both are acted out upon the self" at 50 (emphasis in original).

2. See "Bureau of Labor Statistics—Consensus of Fatal Occupational Injuries," August 2009, http://www.bls.gov/iif/oshwc/cfoi/osar0010.pdf, which states in pertinent part: "Prelimi-

nary data from the 2008 Census of Fatal Occupational Injuries (CFOI) program reported 251 workplace suicides, their highest level since the inception of the CFOI program in 1992. The 2008 count is 28 percent higher than the 196 suicides recorded in 2007."

3. Among the several types of ritualistic suicide in Japan is the practice of "oyako-shinju," which requires that the life of one or both parents as well as the child or children also be taken. In her criticism of the practice, Caroline Ouyang writes: "Bearing in mind that the Japanese tend to lack social values such as welfare, the thought of a parentless child left to fend for [itself] typically le[ads] the parents to take their children with them in death rather than have the offspring live as abandoned outcasts. Many cases of oyako shinju occurred with Japan's defeat after World War II. In 1954, four hundred cases of this type of suicide were reported, averaging out to more than one instance per day." Caroline Ouyang, "Kamikaze without a Cause— Suicide in Japan," *The Worldly*, 2004, http://www.theworldly.org/ArticlesPages/Articles2004/April04Articles/Kamikaze.html .

4. Mark Howarth, "Shock 15% Rise in Suicides since the Recession as Unemployment and Bankruptcy Take Their Toll," *MailOnline*, May 24, 2012, http://www.dailymail.co.uk/news/article-2149663/Shock-15-rise-suicides-recession-unemployment-bankruptcy-toll.html.

5. Dean Baker and Kevin Hassett (from the *New York Times*), "Opinion: The Human Disaster of Unemployment," *Unemployed Nation Hearings*, May 14, 2012, http://depts.washington.edu/unemploy/node/46.

6. Menninger also writes: "So far as they go, statistics . . . indicate that among civilized people suicide is much more common among males, although women try to commit suicide more frequently than men do." See *Man against Himself* by Karl Menninger (Harcourt, Brace & World, Inc., New York, 1938), p. 15. Also see Allison Pearson, "Gary Speed: The Last Taboo Is the Agony of Distress," *Telegraph*, November 30, 2011, http://www.telegraph.co.uk/health/men_shealth/892586Gary-Speed-the-last-taboo-is-the-agony-of-distress.html.

7. See Bureau of Labor statistics at note 2 *supra*.

8. For the facts of the Ladislav Antilak case, see *Robblee III v. Budd Services, Inc.*, 136 N.C. App. 793 (2000), at http://caselaw.findlaw.com/nc-court-of-appeals/1069826.html and http://www.aoc.state.nc/www/public/coa/opinions/2000/990348-1.htm.

9. See Associated Press, "Ohio State Janitor's Gunfire Kills Co-Worker, then Self," *Newsmax*, March 9, 2010, http://www.newsmax.com/PrintTemplate?nodeid=352147.

10. "Shooting Victim Better," *SunSentinel.com*, May 24, 1988. http://articles.sun-sentinel.com/1988-05-24/news/8801310820_1_parking-lot-boss-intensive-care-unit. Another case in which the perpetrator committed suicide under the mistaken assumption that they had murdered someone—someone who had miraculously survived—was that of Richard Vance Dixon. See note 18 *infra* and accompanying text.

11. Lisa Ocker and Jim McNair, "Finances, Romance Blamed In Attack," *SunSentinel.com*, May 21, 1988, http://articles.sun-sentinel.com/1988-05-21/news/8801310059_1_raglund-critical-condition-unemployment-office.

12. See "Civilian Kills 3, Hurts 2 and then Shoots Himself," *Star-News*, October 19, 1993; also see "Worker at Fort Knox Kills 3, then Shoots Himself," *New York Times*, October 19, 1993, http://www.nytimes.com/1993/10/19/us/worker-at-fort-knox-kills-3-then-shoots-himself.html. Also see "Civilian Kills 3, Hurts 2 and then Shoots Himself," *Wilmington Morning Star*, October 19, 1993, p. 2A, http://news.google.com/newspapers?nid=1454&dat=19931019&id=ia0sAAAAIBAJ&sjid=5RQEAAAAIBAJ&pg=6501,1211925.

13. See 1 Dead, 1 Wounded in Workplace Shooting," *Boston Channel.com*, April 1, 2008, http://www.thebostonchannel.com/news/15760103/detail.html. Also see, "Family of Randolph Shooting Victim Gropes for Answers," *EnterpriseNews.com*, April 1, 2008, http://www.enterprisenews.com/homepage/x325171363; also see John R. Ellement and Andrew Ryan, "Man Kills Self after Shooting Co-worker in Randolph, Prosecutor Says," *Boston.com*, April 1, 2008, http://www.boston.com/news/local/breaking_news/2008/04/man_shot_by_cow.html.

14. Matthew Beck is the only perpetrator included in the study (male or female) who used both a gun *and* a knife in the same instance of workplace murder—and on the *same victim*). See Jonathan Rabinovitz, "Connecticut Lottery Worker Kills 4 Bosses, Then Himself," *New York Times*, March 7, 1998, http:www.nytimes.com/1998/03/07/nyregion/rampage-connecticut-

overview-connecticut-lottery-worker-kills-4-bosses-then.html. Also see www.Murderpedia .com, http://murderpedia.org/male.B/b/beck-matthew.htm.

15. Associated Press, "Postal Worker Kills Self After Fatal Rampage," *Los Angeles Times*, December 20, 1997, http://articles.latimes.com/1997/dec/20/news/mn-521. Also see "Milwaukee Postal Worker Kills 1 and Self," *New York Times*, December 19, 1997, http:// www.nytimes.com/1997/12/20/us/postal-worker-in-milwaukee-shoots-3-kills-himself.html.

16. Nicholas Riccardi and Douglas Shuit, "2 Dead, Firm's Owner Hurt in Fired Worker's Rampage," *Los Angeles Times*, June 14, 1997, http://latimes.com/1997-06-14/news/mn-3158_1_santa-fe-springs.

17. Ibid.

18. See "Police: Fired Worker Shoots Boss, Kills Himself at Gas Station," *News Record*, November 7, 2011, http://www.news-record.com/content/2011/11/06/article/police_fired _worker_shoots_employee_kills_himself_at_gas_station.

19. See Richard G. Jones, "Gunman Kills 3 Members of Investment Firm and Himself," *New York Times*, February 14, 2007, http://www.nytimes.com/2007/02/14/us/14board.html. Also see Adam Taylor, Terri Sanginiti and Andrew Tangel, "Bear Man Kills 3, Himself Over Deal Gone Bad," *Delaware Online*, February 14, 2007, http://www.delawareonline.com/article/20070214/NEWS/70214061/Bear-man-kills-3-himself-over-deal-gone-bad.

20. Ibid.

21. Ibid.

22. See "David Burke–Pacific Southwest Airline Flight 1771," *Storm2k.org*, June 10, 2012, http://www.storm2k.org/phpbb2/viewtopic.php?f=6&t=94200. Also see *Wikipedia*, s.v. "Pacific Southwest Airlines Flight 1771," http://en.wikipedia.org/wiki/Pacific_Southwest_Air lines_Flight_1771.

23. Ibid.

24. Ibid.

25. Jean Merl and Tracy Johnson, "Routine Turns to Tragedy," *Los Angeles Times*, April 24, 1998, http://articles.latimes.com/1998/apr/24/local/me-42505.

26. Latisha R. Gray, "Report Describes What Led to Killing," *Herald-Tribune*, December 14, 2007, http://www.heraldtribune.com/article/20071214/NEWS/712140500.

27. Beth Smith, "Rampage at Atlantis Plastics Ends with Six Dead," *Gleaner.com*, June 26, 2008, http://www.courierpress.com/news/2008/jun/26/rampage-atlanits-plastics-ends-six-dead/

28. Sandy Smith, "Six Killed in Kansas City Workplace Shooting," *EHSToday*, July 6, 2004, http://ehstoday.com/news/ehs_imp_37089/.

29. Associated Press, "Gunman, 8 Others Fatally Shot in Conn. Warehouse," *Azcentral.com*, August 3, 2010, http://www.azcentral.com/news/articles/2010/08/03/20100803con-necticut-workplace-shooting-html.

30. Ibid.

31. See Jamie Schram, Larry Celona, and Dan Mangan, "11 Shot—Mayhem at the Empire State Building," *New York Post*, August 25, 2012, pp. 1–2.

32. "He knew what he was doing," according to an eyewitness who worked in the Empire State Building who noted Johnson's calm, serene facial expression, and who suspected Johnson was planning a suicide by cop. "He knew he was going to die. He didn't want to live." See Aaron Feis, Bill Sanderson, and Todd Venezia, ibid., p. 5.

33. For a summary of White's double assassination of San Francisco mayor Moscone and Supervisor Milk, see notes 52–56 of chapter 5 *supra* and accompanying text; for a forensically detailed account of the double assassination see Randy Shilts, *The Mayor of Castro Street—The Life and Times of Harvey Milk* (Saint Martin's Press, 1982), pp. 267–72.

34. Ibid.

35. Ibid.

36. Ibid.

37. See Stephanie Madoff Mack, *The End of Normal* (Blue Rider Press, 2011), pp. 303–36.

38. See Bonnie Buck, Jonathan Lloyd, Olsen Ebright, and Thomas Watkins "SoCal Murder-Suicide Father Awash in Debt," *NBC Southern California*, January 28, 2009, http:// www.nbclosangeles.com/news/local/BREAKING-NEWS-Bodies-Found-in-Wilmington-

Home.html. Also see Jennifer Lawinski, "California Dad in Family Killings Left Suicide Note Citing Loss of His, Wife's Jobs," *Fox News*, January 28, 2009, http://www.foxnews.com/printer_friendly_story/0,3566,483645,00.html.

39. Ibid.

10. THE WARNING SIGNS

1. Dave Grossman, *On Killing: The Psychological Cost of Learning to Kill in War and Society* (Little, Brown and Co., 1995).

2. S. L. A. Marshall, *Men Against Fire: The Problem of Battle Command* (University of Oklahoma Press, 2000).

3. Though Marshall's methodology was criticized as bogus, others have been more forgiving and point out that, however intuitively, Marshall stumbled across a profound truth. "Numerous independent studies have since found similarly low firing rates among Japanese and German riflemen, as well as among the frontline soldiers of World War I, the American Civil War, and several other conflicts. For whatever reason, the Pentagon took Marshall on faith and initiated a decades-long human-improvement campaign. By the Korean war, in the 1950s, surveys showed that fully half of the frontline riflemen who saw the enemy fired their weapons in response. In Vietnam, the number rose to 90 percent despite the unpopularity of the war and the low morale among troops. Of course, to fire at someone is by no means to hit him. The 90 percent figure was undermined by a significant number of intentional misses (a common phenomenon that is difficult to assess and quantify), and it was inflated by a battle doctrine called 'Quick Kill,' which taught American soldiers to spray masses of automatic fire rather than take careful aim. As a result of that doctrine, in Vietnam US infantrymen fired 50,000 rounds of ammunition for each kill they made—a ratio that would have encouraged even conscientious objectors to go ahead and shoot. The firing rates for Vietnam are therefore somewhat skewed. But compared with Marshall's claimed rates for World War II they do seem to show that the US military had made strides in conditioning the infantry to kill." William Langewiesche, "The Distant Executioner," *Vanity Fair*, February 2010, p. 6, http://www.vanityfair.com/politics/features/2010/02/sniper-201002.

4. Ibid.

5. See Alex Rodriguez, Jon Yates, and Gary Marx, "Convicted Ex-worker Kills 5 in Melrose Park," *Chicago Tribune*, February 6, 2001, http://articles.chicagotribune.com/2001-02-06/news/0102060231_1_wound-engines-gunshot; See also Associated Press, "Five Workers Die in Shooting Rampage at Chicago Navistar Plant," *Lubbock Avalanche-Journal*, February 6, 2001, http://www.lubbockonline.com/stories/020601/nat_020601041.shtml. See also "Former Chicago-area Factory Worker Kills 4, Self, Police Say," *CNN.com*, February 5, 2001, http://edition.cnn.com/2001/US/02/05/plant.shooting.04/, and Kate Randall, "Another Workplace Shooting in the US: Five Dead at Chicago Navistar Plant," World Socialist Web Site, February 10, 2001.

6. See Robert Welkos and Tom Gorman, "Disgruntled Postman Goes on Shooting Spree: 2 Slain, Escondido Gunman Is Brain Dead," *Los Angeles Times*, August 10, 1989, http://articles.latimes.com/1989-08-10/news/mn-497_1_brain-dead and Tom Gorman and Richard Serrrano, "Postal Employee Kills Wife, 2 Co-Workers," *Los Angeles Times*, August 11, 1989, http://articles.latimes.com/1989-08-11/news/mn-207_1_postal-employee. Also see, S. Anthony Baron, *Violence in the Workplace—A Prevention and Management Guide for Businesses* (Pathfinder, 1993), p. 33.

7. Ibid., Baron, at 39.

8. Loren Coleman, *The Copycat Effect—How the Media and Popular Culture Trigger the Mayhem in Tomorrow's Headlines* (Paraview–Pocket Books, 2004), p. 69.

9. Ibid., at 69–70.

10. Larry Smith, Bill Leukhardt, Paul Marks, and Eric Ferreri, "Woman Shot at Boss, Police Say," *Courant*, April 17, 1998, http://articles.courant.com/1998-04-17/news/9804170262_1_worker-police-racial.

11. Ibid.

12. Associated Press, "Officials: Ski Resort Shooter Killed Cat, Committed Suicide," *Fox-News.com*, January 1, 2009, http://www.foxnews.com/printer_friendly_story/0,3566, 474925 ,00.html.

13. Ted Johnson and John Glionna, "Postal Supervisor's Shooting Death Baffles Employees," *Los Angeles Times*, July 11, 1995, http://articles.latimes.com/1995-07-11/local/me-22544_1_postal-workers.

14. See Melody Mendoza, "NLC Librarian Sentenced to 25 Years for Murder," *The Ranger*, October 14, 2010, http://www.theranger.oreg/nlc-librarian-sentenced-25-years-for-murder-1,2366019.

15. Rachael Bell, "Workplace Homicide," *TruTv*, undated, http://www.trutv.com/library/crime/notorious_murders/mass/work_homicide/r.html.

16. Rene Lynch, "Man Gets 60 Years for Deadly Shooting Spree," *Los Angeles Times*, September 4, 1993, http://articles.latimes.com/1993-09-04/local/me-31559_1_fairview-center.

17. Greg Bluestein, Associated Press, "Lawyer: Ga. Soldier in Shooting Was on a Strict Diet," *Boston.com*, August 30, 2010, http://www.boston.com/news/nation/articles/2010/08/30/lawyer_ga_soldier_in_shooting_was_on_strict_diet/.

18. Associated Press, "Cops: 2 Killed After Former Employee Opens Fire at Pa. Warehouse," *FoxNews.com*, August 2, 2008, http://www.foxnews.com/printer_friendly-story/0,3566,396464,00.html. Also see "Former Employee Arrested in Deadly Pa. Shooting," *CBS*, August 2, 2008, http://cbs3.com/topstories/shooting.simon.and.2.785808.html; and "Former Employee Kills Two at Bristol Warehouse," *ABC*, August 2, 2008, http://abclocal.go.com/wpvi/story?section=news/local&id=6301504.

19. Ibid.

20. Ibid.

21. Ibid.

22. Patrick G. Lee, Kerry Burke, and Helen Kennedy, "Madman Stalks and Murders Yale Doc," *NY Daily News*, April 27, 2010, p. 7; also see Barry Leibowitz, "Confession in Yale Doctor Vajinder Toor's Murder? Lishan Wang Says He Was There and He's Sorry, Claim Cops," *CBS News*, April 30, 2010, http://www.cbsnews.com/8301-504083_162-20003891-504083.html.

23. See Coleman, *The Copycat Effect*, note 8 *supra* at 155.

24. Doren P. Levin, "Ex-Postal Worker Kills 3 and Wounds 6 in Michigan," *New York Times*, November 15, 1991, http://www.nytimes.com/1991/11/15/us/ex-postal-worker-kills-3-and-wounds-6-in-michigan.html?scp=1&sq=November%2015,%201991%20Royal%20Oak&st=cse.

25. See Baron, note 6 *supra* at 49.

26. Ibid.

27. Doren P. Levin, "Ex-Postal Worker Kills 3 and Wounds 6 in Michigan," *New York Times*, November 15, 1991, http://www.nytimes.com/11991/11/15/us/ex-postal-worker-kills-3-and-wounds-6-in-michigan.

28. Allman v. Dormer Tools, Inc., N.C., Buncombe County Super. Ct., No. 97 CVS 01161, May, 4, 1999. "Counsel Hurdles Workers' Compensation Barrier to Hold Company Liable for Death Caused by Rampaging Employee," *Association of Trial Lawyers of America Law Reporter*, October 1999.

29. Ibid. This in oblique reference to the 1995 bombing of the World Trade Center in New York City, in which a rented Ryder truck was used to transport the explosive material and was traced to the terrorists who perpetrated the act.

30. Charles E. Brown, Eli Sanders, and Christine Clarridge, "Two UW Doctors Killed in Shooting," *Seattle Times*, June 29, 2000, http://university.seattletimes.uwsource.com/archive/?date=20000629&slug=402935.

31. James K. Song, "7 Dead in Nimitz Hwy. Xerox Shooting," *Star Bulletin*, November 2, 1999, http://archives.starbulletin.com/1999/11/02/news/story1.html; also see Rachael Bell, "The Xerox Murders," *TruTV*, no date indicated, http://www.trutv.com/library/crime/notorious_murders/mass/work_homicide/5.html.

32. See *Wikipedia*, s.v. "Xerox murders," http://en.wikipedia.org/wiki/Xerox_murders, p. 2.

33. See Baron, note 6 *supra* at 7–15.

34. Ibid.

35. Ibid.

36. Ibid.

37. Jarrett Murphy, "Six Dead in Mississippi Massacre," *CBS News*, July 9, 2003, http://www.cbsnews.com/stories/2003/07/09/national/main562301.shtml; also see Brian Ross and David Scott, "Lockheed Workplace Murders Targeted Blacks," *ABCNews*, May 12, 2005, http://abcnews.go.com/CleanPrint/cleanprintproxy.aspx?1288639049703, also see Matt Volz, Associated Press, "Gunman Opens Fire at Lockheed Martin Plant in Mississippi; Six Dead including Shooter," *Boston.com*, July 8, 2003, http://www.boston.com/news/daily/08/plant_shooting.htm.

38. Ibid.

39. Ibid.

40. See generally Meryle Secrest, *Frank Lloyd Wright—A Biography* (Knopf, 1992).

41. Ibid., at 217–18.

42. In one case, it should be mentioned, an employer clearly jumped the gun and responded prematurely to what he perceived as a sign that a case of workplace murder was imminent. Denise Coleman, a thirty-something Illinois postal worker, was immediately fired in late 2005 after she underwent psychiatric counseling and revealed to her psychiatrist that she often had dreams in which she murdered her supervisor. The psychiatrist reported the dream to postal authorities, who responded by immediately firing Coleman for having had homicidal *thoughts*. An appellate federal judge later reversed the effect of this ruling, however, and permitted her to proceed with her discrimination lawsuit against the USPS. See *Coleman v. Donahoe*, 667 F.3d 835 (7th Cir. 2012).

43. See Coleman, note 8 *supra* at 155.

44. For the details of the local NAACP and its involvement with the Anthony DeCulit murder/suicide, see www.murderpedia.com, http://murderpedia.org/male.D/d/deculit-anthony.htm, also see "Postal Worker in Milwaukee Shoots 3 and Kills Himself," *New York Times*, December 20, 1997, http://www.nytimes.com/1997/12/20/us/postal-worker-in-milwaukee-shoots-3-kills-himself.html.

45. Charles E. Brown, Eli Sanders, and Christine Clarridge, "Two UW Doctors Killed in Shooting," *Seattle Times*, June 29, 2000, http://university.seattletimes.uwsource.com/archive/?date=20000629&slug=402935.

46. Ibid.

47. See Stephanie Armour and Tom Ankner, "Inside the Minds of Workplace Killers," *USA Today*, July 14, 2004, http://www.usatoday.com/money/workplace/2004-07-14-workplace-killings_x.htm.

48. See "Understanding Supervisor-Targeted Aggression: A Within-Person Between-Jobs Design," *Journal of Applied Psychology* 90, no. 4 (2005), p. 736.

49. Ibid., at 737–38. That the incentive and often the motive to commit extreme violence, including murder, germinates at a toxic workplace is echoed in the psychoanalytic study by Dr. Michael A. Diamond. He concludes that "beyond and including the public sector workplace, violence and aggression at work stem from organizational members experiences of *shame* and *injustice* on the job. The combination of oppressive organizational cultures and persecutory organizational identities may contribute to these experiences and to violence of workers against co-workers and subordinates against supervisors." Emphasis in original. "Administrative Assault: A Contemporary Psychoanalytic View of Violence and Aggression in the Workplace," paper presented by Michael A. Diamond, June 15, 1997, at the 14th annual meeting of the International Society for the Study of Organizations, as part of the ISPSO Library, http://library.ipso.org/library/administrative-assault-contemporary-psychoanalytic-view-violence-and-aggression-workplace; also see *The American Review of Public Administration*, http://arp.sagepub.com/content/27/3/228.abstract.

50. This exchange between Dr. Lector and Agent Starling occurs at approximately 57 minutes into the movie.

51. In this sense, *schmuck*, like its English equivalent, is generally used by males, and with gusto; few impolite words express comparable contempt. However, the word 'putz' is not to be

used as lightly or indiscriminately, or when around women or children. It's much more offensive than *schmuck*, which may be used in a teasing and affectionate way, vulgar though it is. But the word 'putz' has an "obscene, much more pejorative ambience." See Leo Rosten, *The Joys of Yiddish* (McGraw-Hill, 1968), pp. 356–57 and 298.

52. The Peter Principle holds that in every organizational hierarchy, every competent employee will continue to get promoted or elevated higher and higher up the ladder until he or she reaches the position at which he or she is no longer competent, and at some point, every position in the organization will be filled with someone who is incompetent and cannot perform the duties required by the job. Lawrence J. Peter and Raymond Hull, *The Peter Principle—Why Things Always Go Wrong* (Buccaneer Books, 1993).

53. Not much is known or available on the early personality development of most of the workplace murderers. In a handful of cases, however, the publicity surrounding the murders and the criminal trials or other disposition was so massive that it provided substantial biographical information via TV news, interviews, articles, even books. In these instances, there's credible evidence that even as teenagers and young adults the perpetrators always felt like outsiders and couldn't fit in with the rest of the crowd. In this regard, Doonan's *Murder at the Office* (p. 10) sheds invaluable light on the background of Mark Barton, whose early conferences with a psychologist reveal this feeling of always being an outsider.

11. IRONIES, TRENDS, AND TROUBLESOME FACTS

1. See Bruce Barry, *Speechless: the Erosion of Free Expression in the American Workplace* (Barrett-Koehler Publications, Inc., 2007), pp. 26–27.

2. Ibid.

3. See *Brinker Restaurant Corp. v. Superior Court of San Diego*, 40 Cal. 40th 1069 (2012.) Also see http://californiaemploymentlaw.foxrothschild.com/tags/brinker-restaurant-corp-v-supe/.

4. Ibid.

5. See Donna Ballman, "10 Workplace Rights You Think You Have—But Don't," *AOL Jobs*, May 3, 2011, http://jobs.aol.com/articles/2011/05/03-workplace-rights-you-think-you-have-but-don't/.

6. See Anthony Baron, *Violence in the Workplace—A Prevention and Management Guide for Businesses* (Pathfinder, 1993), pp. 7–15.

7. See Emily Bazelon, "Tragedy at the *Virginia Quarterly Review*," *Slate*, September 27, 2010, http://www.slate.com/toolbar.aspx?action=print&id=2268832,

8. See Carolyn Kellogg, "Editor Ted Genoways Will Leave *Virginia Quarterly Review*," *Jacket Copy*, April 4, 2012.

9. Despite the breadth of the general rule, some limitations might apply. If the actions of the boss are actually threatening to the safety of the employees, a complaint to OSHA (or the state equivalent) could be made. It's also illegal to retaliate against an employee for making a safety complaint, whether formally submitted to OSHA or just expressed informally to the employer. Also, if the conduct of the boss includes discriminatory elements, such as racial or sexist comments, or if it's directed only at members of a particular racial, gender, or other protected demographic, the employer might be liable for it as prohibited discrimination.

10. Cloutier's book is entitled *Profits Aren't Everything, They're the Only Thing* (Harper-Collins Publishers, 2009). Cloutier is the founder and CEO of American Management Services, a consulting firm for small and medium-sized businesses, and has been dubbed the Turnaround Ace by *Businessweek*.

11. Cloutier's view that it's crazy and insane for a boss to use "love" as an employee motivator, of course, is a sly reference to the corporate culture espoused by Gary Kelly, chairman and CEO of Southwest Airlines. The fifth-largest airline in the US, Southwest is the only major airline to earn a profit every year since 1973 (39 years!). The company's business culture is an employee-centered view that treats employees first and encourages nonleadership, collaboration, sharing, and civility among its "family" of employees, all of whom share a

corporate "LUV." See Tracy Mueller, "Southwest Airlines CEO Kelly On LUV, Leadership, and Employee and Customer Satisfaction," *McCombs Today*, October 8, 2009, http:// www.today.mccombs.utexas.edu/2009/10/southwest-airlines-ceo-kelly-on-luv-leadership-and-employee-and-customer-satisfaction/. "Cloutier's philosophy couldn't be more different, and his slim book serves as a wake up call for small business owners who have been hit hard by the recession. 'Don't blame the economy,' he writes. "Recession or no recession, if your small business is failing, it's your fault!' Cloutier dishes out tough love in pithy chapters that introduce his 15 profit rules (e.g., 'Love your Business More than Your Family,' 'The Best Family Business Has One Member' and 'Teamwork Is Vastly Overrated'). While Cloutier's provocative pronouncements seem designed for maximum shock value, each rule relies on practical business principles: maintain tight controls, pay for performance and focus on sales at all times. This blunt work will not be for the timid business owner afraid to re-evaluate operations, planning, compensation or family dynamics. For those ready to focus on profits, though, Cloutier's book is loaded with valuable advice on how to get back on track and stay in the black in any economic environment." *Publishers Weekly* 256, no. 25 (June 22, 2009), p. 38.

12. Ibid.

13. See Bearden v. Georgia, 461 US 660 (1983), in which the US Supreme Court ruled that debtors' prisons violated the Equal Protection Clause of the Fourteenth Amendment.

14. Alain Sherter, "Jailed for $280: The Return of Debtors' Prisons," *Yahoo!Finance*, April 23, 2012, http://finance.yahoo.com/news/jailed-for--280--the-return-of-debtors--prisons.html.

15. Ibid.

16. Ibid.

17. Ibid.

18. Ibid.

19. Ibid.

20. Jeffrey Pfeffer, "Lay Off the Layoffs," *Newsweek*, February 5, 2010, http:// www.newsweek.com/id/233131/output/print.

21. Daniel Goleman, *Emotional Intelligence—Why It Can Matter More than IQ* (Bantam Books, 1995).

22. Ibid., pp. 240–41.

23. Brian Vandiver, "Do Employees Have a Statutory Right to 'Pack Heat' at Work?" *Labor & Employment Blog*, Mitchell Williams, September 1, 2011, http://www .mitchellwilliamslaw.com/do-employees-have-a-statutory-right-to-%E2%80%9Cpack-heat%E2%80%9D-at-work.

24. Ibid.

25. Ibid.

26. Ibid.

27. Ibid.

28. Kentucky's workplace protection statute permitting employees to possess guns in their parked vehicles recently withstood a challenge by Oklahoma employers. The state's employers argued, unsuccessfully, that the statute conflicted with their obligations under OSHA regulations to provide a safe work environment, and should therefore be struck down under the Supremacy Clause. The appellate court disagreed with their reading of the OSHA statute. *Ramsey Winch, Inc. v. Henry* 555 F.3d 1199 (10th Cor. 2009).

29. The specific requirements of the policies and guidelines for employees with concealed weapons licenses will vary from state to state. Those selected here were adopted loosely from the list accessed at *MaineBiz*, "My Right Trumps Your Right: Guns in the Workplace," by Rick Dacri, Dacri & Associates, LLC, July 25, 2011. The seven steps are as follows: (1) Periodically assess these policies and guidelines to ensure that they incorporate all the elements contained in the law of the domicile state; (2) Ensure that these policies and guidelines also encompass all those features that are unique to murder and homicide; (3) Ensure that the senior managers and supervisors are sufficiently familiar with the material to explain the basic questions; (4) Train and periodically test all managers and supervisors on their knowledge and practical application of the policies and guidelines; (5) Require every employee with a concealed weapon permit to register both the weapon and the vehicle in which the weapon will be kept; (6) Require every such employee to promptly notify the company of any change in any information on which the

permit was originally based and issued, and the status of the permit, e.g., revocation, date of expiration; and (7) Require every such employee to know the requirements for keeping the weapon out of view while inside the vehicle, and for securing the vehicle while on company property.

30. Rich Schmitt, "How the NRA Pushed the Right to Pack Heat Anywhere," *Freedoms-Phoenix*, November 15, 2011, http://www.freedomphoenix.com/News/107706-2012-03-18-how-the-nra-pushed-the-right-to-pack-heat-anywhere.htm?EdNo=001&From=.

31. Ibid.

32. Bonnie Buck, Jonathan Lloyd, Olsen Ebright, and Thomas Watkins, "SoCal Murder-Suicide Father Awash in Debt," *NBCSouthernCalifornia*, January 28, 2009, http://www.nbclosangeles.com/news/local/BREAKING-NEWS-Bodies-Found-in-Wilmington-Home.html Also see Jennifer Lawinski, "California Dad in Family Killings Left Suicide Note Citing Loss of His, Wife's Jobs," *FoxNews.com*, January 28, 2009, http://www.foxnews.com/printer_friendy_story/0,3566,483645,00.html.

33. Ibid.

34. See *Wikipedia*, s.v. "Charles Whitman," http://en.wikipedia.org/wiki/Charles _Whitman.

35. See Tom Gorman and Richard Serrano, "Postal Employee Kills Wife, Two Co-Workers," *Los Angeles Times*, August 11, 1989, http://articles.latimes.com/1989-08-11/news/mn-207_1_postal-employee. Also see Robert Welkos and Tom Gorman, "Disgruntled Postman Goes on Shooting Spree; 3 Slain Escondido Gunman Is Brain Dead," *Los Angeles Times*, August 10, 1989, http://articles.latimes.com/1989-08-10/news/mn-479_1_brain-dead.

36. See Andrew H. Malcolm, "Deaths On the Iowa Prairie: 4 New Victims of Economy," *New York Times*, December 11, 1985, http://www.nytimes.com/1985/12/11/us/deaths-on-the-iowa-prairie-4-new-victims-of-economy.html. Also see Bruce Brown *The Lone Tree Tragedy: A True Story of Murder in America's Heartland* (Crown Publishing Group, 1989).

37. See Emily Yellin, "Blaze That Led to 3 Killings Was Arson, Investigators Say," *New York Times*, March 10, 2000, http://www.nytimes.com/2000/03/10/us/blaze-that-led-to-3-killings-was-arson-investigators-say.html.

38. See *Wikipedia*, s.v. "John List," http://en.wikipedia.org/wiki/John_List.

39. These cases are to be distinguished from those cases in which the perpetrator's workplace attack was preceded by the murder of a neighbor, a coworker, or someone else who wasn't related by blood. These perpetrators included Jennifer San Marco, Frank Garcia, Giocondo Navek, etc.

40. In other clashes, other CEOs and corporate leaders escaped with just minor injuries. But still others, whether armed or unarmed, were not so lucky. Sid Agrawal, the CEO of SiPort, a digital radio semiconductor developer based in Santa Clara, CA, and Maurice J. Spagnoletti, a Puerto Rican banking CEO who had ordered an audit of a bank suspected of fiscal impropriety, were among those shot and killed. These CEOs were murdered for a host of reasons, and the dead included Andy Hadjicostis, Gagandip Singh, James Po Ho Cheung, Alfred Herrhausen, Tim MacKay, and Federico Bloch.

41. In another tragedy, Joginder Choudhary, an assistant general manager at auto parts manufacturer Allied Nippon (and no relation to Lalit Chaudhary at Graziano) was reportedly eating lunch when he was attacked by hundreds of employees. He and two senior managers had to be hospitalized along with members of the human resources department after workers attacked them, along with members of the board of directors, in Ghaziabad, a suburb of Delhi. The violent workers claimed they were protesting the layoffs of former coworkers; the executives, some of whom were armed, claimed that they had come to negotiate peacefully, and had fired into the air when the attacks started.

42. One early case of American political assassination was that of Louisiana governor Huey Long. On September 8, 1935, Long was at the state capitol attempting to gain passage of a redistricting plan, which would automatically oust a longtime political opponent, Judge Henry Pavey. About an hour before the voting session ended, the son-in-law of Judge Pavey, Dr. Carl Weiss, approached Long, pulled a handgun from his suit, and fired from four feet away. The governor's bodyguards opened fire, hitting Weiss more than thirty times. Weiss died at the

hospital two days later, on September 10, 1935. See *Wikipedia*, s.v. "Huey Long," http://en.wikipedia.org/wiki/Huey_Long.

43. Robert Weissberg, "Deciphering the Occupy Wall Street Movement," *American Thinker*, May 13, 2012, http://www.americanthinker.com/2012/05/deciphering_the_occupy_wall_street_movement.html.

44. Ibid.

45. "Rise in Religious Bias Complaints at Work," *Newsday*, January 24, 2012, http://www.newsday.com/news/nation/rise-in-religious-bias-complaints-at-work-1,3476848 .

46. Ibid.

47. Ibid.

48. See Tina L. Meyers "Claims of Workplace Religious Discrimination on the Rise," *Times-Picayune*, May 26, 2012, http://blog.nola.com/faith/2012/05/claims_of_workplace_religious.htm.

49. Ibid.

50. "Muslim Woman Wins $5 Million in Discrimination Lawsuit against AT&T for 'Harassment from Her Co-workers because of Her Religion,'" *MailOnline*, May 5, 2012, http://www.dailymail.co.uk/news/article-2140252/Muslim-woman-wins-5million-discrimination-lawsuit-AT-T-harassment-workers-religion.html.

51. Ibid.

52. Ibid.

53. Ibid.

12. EMPLOYER RESPONSE, RESPONSIBILITY, AND RESOLVE

1. James Oliver Huberty's massacre at the Ysidro, San Diego, McDonald's restaurant was not included in the study of workplace murder only because—like Colin Ferguson, Ted Kaczynski, and John E. List —he was not employed at the time of the event. His case is referenced here and in the corresponding text solely as an aid in the discussion and assessment of the role played by the McDonald's Food Corporation management and the nature of its response. Also see *Wikipedia*, s.v. "San Ysidro McDonald's massacre," http://en.wikipedia.org/wiki/San_Ysidro_McDonald's_massacre. Huberty's comment to his wife before he shot up the twenty-two folks at the McDonald's in San Diego.

2. Ibid., re: Huberty's second comment, "hunting humans."

3. Ibid.

4. Most of this scenario was loosely paraphrased from a chapter in *McDonald's—Behind the Arches*, by John F. Love (Bantam Books, 1986), pp. 380–82.

5. Ibid

6. Ibid.

7. Ibid.

8. Ibid.

9. Ibid.

10. On the factual particulars of the James Oliver Huberty massacre, see www.murderpedia.com, also see *Wikipedia*, s.v. "San Ysidro McDonald's massacre," http://en.wikipedia.org/wiki/San_Ysidro_McDonald's_masssacre. Also see *McDonald's—Behind the Arches*, note 4 *supra*, pp. 380–82.

11. See Gian Luigi Ferri file; also see http://murderpedia.org/male/F/f/erri-gian-luigi.htm.

12. Ibid.

13. Ibid.

14. Ibid.

15. Ibid.

16. Ibid.

17. Ibid.

18. See Mike France et al., "Office Violence: After the Shooting Stops," *Businessweek*, March 12, 2001, http://www.businessweek.com/print/magazine/content/01_11b3723113

.htm?chan=mz. "Less than two years after [the] gunman's rage left eight people dead in its California Street offices," the article stated, "the bicoastal Pettit & Martin [law firm] is shutting its doors. The decision to dissolve the 120-lawyer firm followed a period marked by difficult fiscal times and the departure of some top attorneys. No mention was made of the [July 1993] attack by Gian Luigi Ferri, a failed businessman who killed eight people and wounded six. Ferri killed himself at the end of the deadly rampage" (see "S.F. Law Firm, Site of 8 Slayings, to Close," *Los Angeles Times*, March 7, 1995, http://articles.latimes.com/1995-03-07/local/me-39795_1_s-f-law-firm).

19. Scores of cases presented facts in which the perpetrator was fired from the job, and in which the facts strongly suggest that at least part of the anger and rage that precipitated the workplace murder was attributable to *how* they were fired. These cases include those of Fernando Ruiz, Louis Darrell Kinyon, and Omar Thornton.

20. Gaining entry to the workplace by former employees has become less of a problem in recent years. Most companies have become far more security-conscious, especially in the wake of multimillion-dollar settlements, and the 9/11 attacks. Also, some cases had such a devastating effect that the affected industries often responded immediately to the catastrophic fallout. As an example, in the weeks following the David Burke suicide/mass murder in which all thirty-eight passengers and the crew of five were destroyed in the crash of Pacific Southwest Airlines Flight 1771, the airline industry quickly changed its procedures and instituted guidelines that required the immediate submission of all airline badges, IDs, and other credentials the instant individuals were no longer employees of the company.

21. A number of lists were considered here, and these points of consideration are a distillation of several articles and an intermittently verbatim adaptation of "How to Survive a School or Workplace Shooting," wikiHow, http://www.wikihow.com/Survive-a-School-or-Workplace-Shooting.

22. See Mike France, note 18 *supra*.

23. Ibid.

24. Ibid.

25. See the EMDR Institute, Inc., http://www.emdr.com/general-information/what-is-emdr.html.

26. See Mike France, note 18 *supra*.

27. Ibid.

28. Ibid.

29. A fairly recent development in this area of the law is the emergence of "negligent security" claims. The doctrine of negligent security allows recovery by injured parties against property owners and property managers for foreseeable criminal attacks by third parties. Under now well-established rules, attacks that occur in certain places—like apartments, hotels and motels, condominiums, bars, college and university dormitories and campuses, shopping centers and malls, private clubs, amusement parks, and other public areas—may give rise to a negligent security claim. Recently, courts and legal commentators have indicated that the doctrine may be extended to cover new types of attacks and associated security risks, including terrorist attacks, identity theft and cyberspace attacks, and Megan's Law failures.

13. GUIDELINES FOR WORKPLACE SAFETY, SECURITY, AND CONTROL

1. Kenneth Kesner, "New UAH Science Lab Thinks Big," *Huntsville Times*, October 14, 2007, http://www.huntsvillealabamausa.com/news/biz_news/2007/101407_uahshelby.html.

2. Ibid.

3. The VLF metal detector (with automatic tuning) sells (at Wal-Mart) for approximately $64.25. Most retail stores offer the Hunter Fan Track IV metal detector with three operating modes, which is listed at discount for 109 dollars, with additional costs for accessories, if desired.

4. See generally Carl V. Nelson, "Metal Detection and Classification Technologies," at http://techdigest.jhuapl-edu/TD/td2501/Nelson.pdf.

5. John Rudolph, "NYPD Testing Long-Distance Gun Detection Device," *HuffPostCrime*, January 18, 2010, http://www.huffingtonpost.com/2012/01/18/nypd-gun-detection-device _n_1213813.html.

6. Ibid.

7. Ibid.

8. On July 24, 1998, a man entered the Capitol building in Washington, D.C., with a .38-caliber handgun concealed under his clothing. A security checkpoint with a portal weapons detection system had been set up at the building entrance. Realizing that his gun would be detected if he went through the portal, the man simply stepped around it. He was immediately confronted by the police officer who was operating the portal. The man drew his gun and killed the officer. When a second officer approached, the man shot and killed the second officer as well. This tragedy highlights the need to detect and respond to weapons, but at a *safe distance*, to allow security guards to deal with the situation. And the limitation of current security-detection portal systems is that they must be near an individual in order to work. The solution is obviously to move the portal farther away from the potential assailant. For a persuasive, well-presented discussion of both the issues and the answers to these questions, see Chris Tillery, deputy director for science and technology at the National Institute of Justice (NIJ), "Detecting Concealed Weapons: Directions for the Future," *NIJ Journal* 258, October 2007.

9. Reference to specific units of weapons detection technology, particularly Sago's ST-150, is not meant or intended as an endorsement of the product, but is presented for informational purposes only, as an example of the technologies and devices that are commercially available.

10. Donna Lieberman being quoted by John Rudolph at note 5 *supra*.

11. Ibid. If effective, Lieberman said, the device could "essentially bring to an end the NYPD's controversial 'stop-and-frisk' campaign, which subjects more than half-a-million New Yorkers per year to largely random search by the police." Police officials, however, have defended the searches as necessary to remove illegal guns from the streets, but civil liberties groups have decried them as a racially biased and unconstitutional invasion of privacy. According to Lieberman, "If the NYPD is moving forward with this, the public needs more information about this technology, how it works and the dangers it presents."

12. Physicist John Federici being quoted at note 5 *supra*.

13. See Associated Press, "Boss Allegedly Kills Worker at Employment Services Building," HighBeam Research, March 18, 1998, http://www.highbeam.com/doc/1P1-19779631.html. Also see "News: Two Killed in Shooting at State Employment Headquarters 3/19/98," *Amarillo Glove*, March 19, 1998, http://amarillo.com/stories/031998/LA 0675.001.shtml.

14. Several cases like these were found in the public sector, but virtually all occurred in the private sector. They included the cases of John Harrison, John Raglund, and Keon Suk Oh, among others.

15. See Richard Esposito et al., "Binghamton Rampage Leaves 14 Dead, Police Don't Know Motive," *ABC News*, April 3, 2009, http://abcnews.go.com/US/story?id=7249853& page=1. Also see Ray Rivera and Nate Schweber, "Before Killings, Hints of Plans and Grievance," *New York Times*, April 4, 2009, http://www.nytimes.com/2009/04/05/nyregion/05suspect.html. Also see www.murderpedia.com.

16. Ibid.

17. Ibid.

18. Ibid.

19. Ibid.

20. Ibid.

21. This list, a distillation of several articles collected on the topic, relies most on the text of the voluminous report published by the New York Police Department and entitled "New York City Police Department, Active Shooter—Recommendations and Analysis for Risk Mitigation," by Police Commissioner Raymond W. Kelly, undated.

22. See Don Tennant, "Workplace Violence: 'One-Third of Americans Go to Work Every Day Afraid,'" *ITBusinessEdge*, February 24, 2012, http://www.itbusinessedge.com/cm/blogs/tennant/2012/02.

23. Lindsay McCrum, *Chicks with Guns* (Vendome Press, 2011).

24. *Publisher's Weekly*, for example, calls the book "absolutely seductive." *Field & Stream* notes the "striking beauty" of the full-page photographs. The *Houston Chronicle* says the book is "gorgeous." And the *New York Times* calls it a "handsome new book of photographs . . . that neither glorify nor vilify their subjects." See the Vendome Press press release at http://www.vendomepress.com/chicks-with-guns/.

25. See note 23 in chapter 11, *supra*.

26. This logic suffers from several assumptions, first, that the person in the audience is an expert shot who will know, within split seconds, what degree of force is required. A person who, in short, is likely an expert like a police officer or a member of a security firm. Had more "amateurs" in the crowd been armed at the Arizona murder spree, about the only guarantee is that even more bloodshed than already occurred would have resulted.

27. See Christopher Intagliata, "Gun-toting Bias to See Guns Toted—A Person Holding a Gun May Be More Likely to Think They See a Weapon Being Carried by Another," *Scientific American*, March 22, 2012, http://www.scientificamerican.com/podcast/episode.cfm?id=gun-toting-increases-bias-to-see-gu-12-03-22.

28. Ibid.

29. Ibid.

30. Ibid.

14. CONCLUSION

1. Michael A. Bellisiles, "Arming America," *New York Times*, Books on the Web, 2000, http://www.nytimes.com/books/first/b/bellesiles-arming.html.

2. Ibid.

3. Ibid.

4. Ibid. (emphasis added).

5. See Patricia Cohen, "Scholar Emerges from Doghouse," *New York Times*, August 3, 2010, http://www.nytimes.com/2010/08/04/books/04bellisles.html.

6. Ibid.

7. Ibid. This characterization was offered by Marc Favreau, Bellesiles's new editor at New Press, a nonprofit publisher which has since published Bellesiles's subsequent historical work.

8. Based on a survey whose results were published in *USACarry*, "Percentage of Firearms Ownership by State," Wyoming has the most at 59.7 percent, and Washington, D.C., has the least, with 3.8 percent. The top dozen states with the highest percentages of gun ownership were as follows: Wyoming at 59.7 percent, Alaska with 57.6 percent, Montana with 57.7 percent, South Dakota with 56.6 percent, West Virginia with 55.4 percent, Mississippi with 55.3 percent, Idaho with 55.3 percent, Arkansas with 55.3 percent, Alabama with 55.3 percent, North Dakota with 50.7 percent, Kentucky with 47.7 percent, and Wisconsin with 44.4 percent. The states with the lowest percentages of gun ownership were as follows: Washington, D.C., with 3.6 percent, Hawaii with 8.7 percent, New Jersey with 12.3 percent, Massachusetts with 12.6 percent, Rhode Island with 12.8 percent, Connecticut with 16.7 percent, New York with 18.0 percent, Illinois with 20.2 percent, Maryland with 21.3 percent, California with 21.3 percent, Florida with 24.5 percent, and Delaware with 25.5 percent. Also see http://www.usacarry.com/forums/general-firearm-discussion/9841-percent-firearms-ownership-state.html.

9. The states that lead the nation in gun deaths are Alaska, Mississippi, Louisiana, Alabama, and Wyoming. According to a survey by Common Dreams, October 24, 2011, a more complete listing of the states that lead the nation in gun death rates (per 100,000) is as follows: Alaska's gun ownership rate is 60.6 percent, its gun death rate is 20.64; Mississippi's gun ownership rate is 54.3 percent, its gun death rate is 19.32; Louisiana's gun ownership rate is

45.6 percent, its gun death rate is 18.47; Alabama's gun ownership rate is 57.2, its gun death rate is 17.53; and Wyoming's gun ownership rate is 62.8, its gun death rate is 17.45. Conversely, the states with the lowest per capita gun death rates (per 100,000) are as follows: Hawaii's gun ownership rate is 9.7 percent, its gun death rate is 3.18; Massachusetts's gun ownership rate is 12.8, its gun death rate is 3.42; Rhode Island's gun ownership rate is 13.3, and its gun death rate is 4.18; New York's gun ownership rate is 18.1, and its gun death rate is 18.1; and New Jersey has a 11.3 gun ownership rate, and a gun death rate of 11.3. See http://www.commondreams.org/newswire/2011/10/24-7.

10. See Nancy Smith, "The 10 Best Places to Retire," *CBS MoneyWatch*, March 8, 2012. The best cities in which to retire, in descending order, are Austin, TX; Clearwater, FL; Fort Collins, CO; Marquette, MI; Pittsburgh, PA; Portland, OR; Santa Fe, NM; Walnut Creek, CA; Washington, DC; and Winston-Salem, NC. Also see http://finance.yahoo.com/news/the-ten-best-places-to-retire.html.

11. See Malika Worrall, "10 Best States in Which to Start a Business," *CNNMoney*, undated. The states are, in descending order, South Dakota, Nevada, Wyoming, Washington, Florida, Michigan, Texas, South Carolina, Virginia, and Alabama. See http://money.cnn.com/galleries/2007/fsb/index.html. The same survey, reported by Parija Kavilanz, *CNNMoney*, listed the best states in which to start a "small" business, as follows: first is Arizona, second Texas, then California, Colorado, Alaska, Missouri, Nevada, Vermont, Idaho, and finally Florida. See http://money.cnn.com/galleries/2012/smallbusiness/1206/gallery.best-places-entrepreneurs/9.html.

12. See Sophie Bushwick, "The Top 10 Cities for Technology," *Scientific American*, August 19, 2011. The top technology-friendly cities: in first place are Seattle/San Francisco Bay area, CA; Los Angeles, CA; Austin, TX; Orlando, FL; Raleigh-Durham, NC; Pittsburgh, PA, New York City, NY; Boston, MA; and Washington, DC. See http://www .scientificamerican.com/article.cfm?id=the-top-10-cities-for-technology.

13. See Lisa Johnson Mandell, "The 10 Best Cities to Find a Job," *AOL Jobs*, March 17, 2011, http://jobs.aol.com/articles/2011/03/17/10-best-cities-to-find-ajob/. The listing, in descending order, is Saint Paul, MN; Austin, TX; Salt Lake City, UT; Boston, MA Milwaukee, WI; Richmond, VA; Albany, NY; Baltimore, MD; Pittsburgh, PA; and Dallas, TX. A Gallup poll, reported by Maxwell Strachen in the *Huffington Post*, "The Top 11 States to Find a Job," is dramatically different, listing the states, in descending order, as North Dakota, Washington, D.C., South Dakota, Alaska, Arkansas, West Virginia, Maryland, Texas, Oklahoma, Iowa, and Pennsylvania.

14. See Sophie Bushwick, "Best of the Best Top 10 Cities: Green Living, Health, Air Quality and Technology," *Scientific American*, August 22, 2011. The cities, in descending order, are San Francisco, CA; Washington, DC; Seattle, WA; Boston, MA; New York City, NY; Minneapolis, MN; Denver, CO; Portland, OR; Los Angeles, CA; and Chicago, IL. Also see http://www.scientificamerican.com/article.cfm?id=best-of-the-best-top-10-cities-green-living-health-air-quality-tech&wt.mc_id=SA_CAT_SP_20110822.

15. According to Francesca Levy, "America's Best Places to Raise a Family," *Forbes.com*, June 7, 2010, the best places in America to raise a family are, in descending order, Des Moines–West Des Moines, IA; Harrisburg-Carlisle, PA; Rochester, NY; Syracuse, NY; Provo-Orem, UT; Odgen-Clearfield, UT; Pittsburgh, PA; Knoxville, TN; Albany-Schenectady-Troy, NY; and Buffalo-Niagara Falls, NY. Also see http://www.forbes.com/2010/06/04/best-places.family-lifestyle-real-estate-cities-kids.html.

16. According to Joel Stonington and Venessa Wong, "Best Places to Raise Your Kids," *Bloomberg Businessweek*, the top half-dozen places to raise your kids, in descending order, are Blacksburg, VA; Arlington, NE; Morton Grove, IL; East San Gabriel, CA; Austin, TX; and Hampton Manor (a suburb of Albany), NY. See http://realestate.msn.com/slideshow.aspx?cp-documentid=27223932. Also see Betsy Schiffman, "The Best Places With the Best Education," *Forbes.com*, February 14, 2003, whose list includes, in descending order, the following areas: Raleigh-Durham-Chapel Hill, NC; Boston, MA; Albany-Schenectady-Troy, NY; Saint Louis, MO-IL; Chicago, IL; Rochester, NY; Austin-San Marco, TX; San Francisco, CA; Washington, DC, and Dayton-Springfield, OH. See http://www.forbes.com/2003/02/14/cx_bs_0214home.html.

17. According to one survey, "America's Best Cities for Foodies," *Sperling's Best Places*, http://www.bestplaces.net/docs/studies/americas_top_foodie.cities.aspx, the top ten places, in descending order, are Santa Resa/Napa, CA; Portland, OR; Burlington, VT; San Francisco, CA; Providence, RI; Boston, MA; Seattle, WA; Santa Fe, NM; and Santa Barbara, CA.

18. See John W. Miller, president of Central Connecticut State University, *CCSU*'s "America's Most Literate Cities—2010," which are, in descending order, as follows: Washington, DC, Seattle, WA; Minneapolis, MN; Atlanta, GA; Pittsburgh, PA; San Francisco, CA; Saint Paul, MN; Denver, CO; Portland, OR; and Saint Louis, MO. See http://www.ccsu.edu/page.cfm?p=8227.

19. See Sophie Bushwick, "The Fittest Cities; The Top 10 Cities for a Healthy Life," *Scientific American*, August 17, 2011. The cities, in descending order, are Minneapolis–Saint Paul, MN; Washington, DC; Boston, MA; Portland, OR; Denver, CO; San Francisco, CA; Hartford, CT; Seattle, WA; Virginia Beach, VA; and Sacramento, CA. See http://www.scientificamerican.com/article.cfm?id=the-top-10-cities-for-a-healthy-life.

20. The top ten most frequently mentioned cities for green living, health, air quality, and technology include New York City, NY; San Francisco, CA; Washington, DC; Seattle, WA; Boston, MA; Minneapolis, MN; Denver, CO; Los Angeles, CA; Chicago, IL; and Miami, FL. See note 19 *supra*. The cities (and states) included on the list of top fifty places in the world for general quality of life are Honolulu, HI (29th); San Francisco, CA (30th); Boston, MA (36th); Chicago, IL (43rd); Washington, DC (43rd); New York City, NY (47th); Seattle, WA (48th); and Pittsburgh, PA (49th). See Mercer Quality Living Survey (2011 rankings), http://www.mercer.com/press-releases/quality-of-living-report-2011#Americas.

21. Alaska ranks second highest among states with the highest percentage of its population owning and registering guns, with 57.6 percent; Idaho comes in at seventh, with 55.3 percent. See note 13 *supra*.

22. Alaska and Idaho also rank high—fifth and ninth, respectively—on a list of the ten best states in which to start a small business. See Parija Kavilanz, at note 16 *supra*.

23. Among the dozen states with the highest percentage of gun ownership, Montana ranks third, with 57.7 percent. See note 13 *supra*.

24. Montana is perhaps the only state in the union where the rule of employment at will has been discarded. This was accomplished, moreover, not by the rule being swallowed by judicially created exceptions, but by an act of the Montana legislature, and the statute effectively overrules the common-law doctrine of employment at will. The statute "is unique in allowing employees to sue for wrongful discharge if an employer does not have 'good cause' for the termination. And 'good cause' means a 'reasonable job-related grounds for dismissal,' such as a failure to perform a job competently, disruption of the business, or some other legitimate business reason." See Bruce Barry, *Speechless—The Erosion of Free Expression in the American Workplace* (Berrett-Koehler, 2007), pp. 58–59.

25. See Jeanine Skowronski, "The Drunkest States in America," *The Street*, January 18, 2012. The states with the highest per capita consumption of alcohol are, in descending order: Wisconsin, then Nebraska, North Dakota, Washington, D.C., Massachusetts, Iowa, Montana, Illinois, Alaska, and in 10th place is Vermont. Also see http://www.thestreet.com/story/11378947/1/thedrunkest-states-in-america.html.

26. See Leah Goldman and Gus Lubin, "The 10 Fattest States in America," *Business Insider*, July 7, 2011, who list the states with the highest percentage of obese residents (per 100,000). In first place is Mississippi, with 34.4 percent of its residents classified as obese; next is Alabama with 32.3 percent; then West Virginia with 32.2 percent; Tennessee with 31.9 percent; Louisiana with 31.6 percent; Kentucky with 31.5 percent; Oklahoma with 31.4 percent; South Carolina with 30.9 percent; Arkansas with 30.6 percent, and in tenth place is Michigan, 30.5 percent of whose residents are obese. See http://www.businessinsider.com/fattest-statesin-america-2011-7#alabama-323-of-people-are-obese-9.

27. See "America's Laziest States—2010," *Bloomberg Businessweek*, November 7, 2010. The laziest states are as follows: the most lazy is Louisiana, the next laziest is Mississippi, next is Arkansas, then North Carolina, Tennessee, Kentucky, West Virginia, South Carolina, Alabama, Delaware, New York, Missouri, and number thirteen is Arizona. See http://images.businessweek.com/ss/10/07/0722_laziest_states/14.htm. Another survey, reported by

Catherine Rampell, the *New York Times*, *Economix*, is essentially the same. See http://economix.blogs.nytimes.com/1210/07/29/americas-laziest-states/.

28.   According to the most recent US Census Bureau polls, the states with the lowest percentage of residents with a BA degree or higher are as follows: lowest is West Virginia, with only 17.1 percent of its residents with a BA degree or higher; then Arkansas with 18.8 percent; next Mississippi with 19.4 percent; Kentucky with 19.7 percent; and then Louisiana with 20.3 percent of its residents with a BA degree or higher. On the other side of the coin, the states with the highest percentage of residents with a BA degree or higher are as follows: the "smartest" state is Washington, D.C., with 48.2 percent of its residents with a BA degree or higher; next highest is Massachusetts with 38.1 percent; then Connecticut with 35.6 percent; Colorado with 35.6 percent; and Maryland with 35.2 percent. See Angie Mohr, "Most and Least Educated States," *Investopedia*, August 31, 2011, http://www.investopedia.com/financial-edge/0811/Most-and-Least-Educaed-States.aspx#axzz1y9j5dPN3.

29.   According to *Forbes.com*, "States with High Smoking Rates," include, in descending order, West Virginia, Indiana, Kentucky, Missouri, Oklahoma, Tennessee, Mississippi, Arkansas, Nevada, and Alabama. See http://www.forbes.com/1210/02/18/smoking-nicotine-addiction-lifestyle-health-lung-cancer-highest_slide_12.html.

30.   According to "The Worst Drivers in America," *USNews*, the ten states that have the highest per capita rate of motor vehicle accidents are as follows: in first place is North Dakota; in second place is Montana; third place is Kentucky; then Louisiana, Oklahoma, Alaska, Missouri, Delaware, Idaho, and then Texas. See http://www.thedailybeast.com/galleries/2010/09/22/the-worst-drivers-in-america.html#slide29.

31.   See "Neighborhood Scout's Top 100 Worst Performing Public Schools in the US," *Neighborhood Scout*, http://www.neighborhoodscout.com/neighborhoods/school-district-ratings-worst100/. Of the hundred schools, just five states contribute more than half (or 53): Michigan leads, with fifteen schools listed; Louisiana has fourteen listed; Arkansas has nine; North Carolina has eight; and Maryland has seven.

32.   See and compare the states listed in note 33 *supra* with the states listed in note 13 *supra*. The comparison shows that the states that lead the nation in gun ownership—West Virginia, Arkansas, Mississippi, and Kentucky—are the same states with the lowest percentage of residents with a BA degree or higher. Mississippi, which is near the top of the lists of states with the highest rates of gun ownership and injury, also ranks at or near the bottom of other lists. According to a recent Gallup poll, while Mississippi residents feel good about their own future, the state "has the lowest percentage of people employed full-time and the lowest median income in the country . . . [Mississippi also] ranks worst in the country in the percentage of the population living below the poverty line and in the percentage of residents who feel like their manager treats them like a partner and not like a boss. Mississippi is also among the worst in several important areas of health. The state had the second-highest rate of obesity and the fifth-highest percentage of smokers. It is also ranked second worst in finding a safe place to exercise and has the lowest percentage of residents who have visited the dentist in the last year." See Michael B. Sauter, Alexander E. M. Hess, Lisa Uible, and Samuel Weigley, "America's Most (and Least) Livable States," *The 24/7 Wall St. Morning Newsletter*, August 18, 2012, http://247walst.com/2012/08/08/the-states-where-people-will-and-wont-want-to-live/5/.

33.   See Ric Burns, "Into the Deep: America, Whaling, and the World," *American Experience*, PBS, 2010, DVD.

34.   Derek Thompson, "The Spectacular Rise and Fall of U.S Whaling: An Innovation Story," *Comment*, February 22, 2012.

35.   Ibid.

36.   Ibid.

37.   Ibid.

38.   Ibid.

39.   Ibid.

40.   For a concise discussion of the origins and growth of rap music and the evolution of hip-hop culture, see Ronald D. Brown, "The Politics of Mo' Money, and the Strange Dialectic of Hip Hop," review of *The Hip Hop Generation and the Crisis in African American Culture* by Bakari Kitwana, *Vanderbilt Journal of Entertainment Law and Practice* 5 (2003), 59, 60.

41. "The History of Rap: Vol 1: The Genesis," *Hip Hop Network.Com*, http://www.hiphop. asp.

42. Ibid.

43. Ibid.

44. Ibid.

45. "These young kids came from poverty and desolation and conquered the world." See *And You Don't Stop: 30 Years of Hip Hop*, episode 1, "Back in the Day," VH1, June 2005, citing Bill Adler, DefJam Records, 1984–1990. Also see "Thug Life: Hip Hop's Curious Relationship with Criminal Justice," January 2009, by andre douglas pond cummings, http:// works.bepress.com/andre_cummings/1.

46. See Dana Williams, "It's Bigger Than Hip Hop," *Tripod*, http://danawilliams2.tripod.com/hiphop.htm.

47. Ibid.

48. See E. Jerry Persaud, "The Signature of Hip Hop: A Sociological Perspective," *International Journal of Criminology and Sociological Theory* 4, no. 1 (June 2011), 626–647, p. 630.

49. See James Vassilopoulos, "A Glimpse at the History of Rap," *GreenLeft*, October 4, 2000.

50. See Henry A. Rhodes, "The Evolution of Rap Music in the United States," *Yale-New Haven Teachers Institute* 4, citing Steven Hager, *Hip Hop: the Illustrated History of Break Dancing, Rap Music and Graffiti* (St. Martins, 1984).

51. "The Ballot or the Bullet" speech is the name given to a public speech delivered by Malcolm X on April 3, 1964, at Cory Methodist Church in Cleveland, Ohio. In the speech, Malcolm X advised blacks to judicially exercise their right to vote, and warned that continued governmental attempts to prevent blacks from exercising their right to vote might make it necessary for them to take up arms instead. The speech has been ranked seventh in the top one hundred American speeches of the twentieth century by 137 leading scholars of American public address.

52. See *Curiosity.com*, "How Did Rap Start?" http://curiosity.discovery.com/question/how-did-rap-start.

53. Ibid.

54. Virtually every history of rap music describes the first wave of rappers and their early struggles in ways that more than justify use of the terms "gifted," "imaginative," "ingenious," "creative," and "industrious," with a do-it-yourself work ethic that led to their later success.

55. See Steven Best and Douglas Hellner, "Rap, Black Rage, and Racial Difference," *Enculturation* 2, no. 2 (Spring 1999), emphasis added.

56. See, e.g., Charles E. Kubrin, "Gangstas, Thugs, and Hustlas: Identity and the Code of the Street," *George Washington University*, 2005, http://www.gwu.edu/~soc/docs/kubin_gangstas.pdf; also see Jennifer Copley, "Does Rap Music Make Young People More Accepting of Crime and Violence?" *Music Psychology: Rap Music*, May 11, 2011, http:// www.metaphoricalplatypus.com/ArticlesPages%20Music/Rap%20Music.html; also see Chuck Philips, "Gangsta Rap: Did Lyrics Inspire Killing of Police?" *Los Angeles Times*, October 17, 1994 (reporting on two teenagers whose defense in a Milwaukee murder trial includes assertion that Tupac Shakur's angry lyrics influenced them in the slaying of a police officer), http:// articles.latimes.com/1994-10-17/entertainment/ca-51308_1_police-officer.

57. See "United States Crime Rates, 1960–2010," Ottawa University, http:// www.disastercenter.com/crime/uscrime.htm.

58. Ibid.

59. In 1975, the murder rate in New York City, per 100,000 inhabitants, was 1,996; a decade later in 1985 it was 1,683; and in the year 2000 it dropped to 952. See "New York Crime Rates 1960–2010," http://www.disastercenter.com/crime/nycrime.htm.

60. Forcible rapes in 1975 numbered 5,099; a decade later in 1985 they rose slightly to 5,706, and then plummeted in 2000 to 3,530. Ibid.

61. Aggravated assaults in 1975 numbered 54,593, in 1985 they numbered 68,270, and in 2000 they dropped again to 60,090. Ibid.

62. Burglaries in 1975 numbered 301,996, they dropped in 1985 to 219,663, and then dropped in 2000 to 87,946. Ibid.

294									*Notes*

63. Larceny-thefts in 1975 numbered 447,740, rose in 1985 to 502,276, and in 2000 dropped to 340,901. Ibid.

64. Vehicular thefts in 1975 numbered 116,274, dropped slightly in 1985 to 106,537, and then dropped by almost 50 percent in 2000 to a mere 54,231. Ibid.

65. Robberies in 1975 numbered 93,499, dropped in 1985 to 89,706, and then dropped by more than 50 percent in 2000 to 40,539. Ibid. Of course, the popularity of gangsta rap music during this period didn't "cause" these dramatic drops in crime. The explanations range from the effect of New York state's extremely harsh Rockefeller drug laws, to New York City mayor Giuliani's "get tough" crime policies, to the ever-shifting demographics throughout the city, to name just a few of several legitimately contributing factors. While no single factor "caused" the drops, they more likely resulted from the cumulative effect of all of the above, and then some. Still, the cited statistics, particularly as they pertain to New York City and the South Bronx, clearly challenge the view that gangsta rap music "causes" crime when the statistics suggest that the widespread growth and popularity of the music might well have had a cathartic effect instead, and just the opposite was true.

66. The general drop in the homicide rate in Los Angeles, the second birthplace of gangsta rap, while less dramatic, was still pronounced. In 1975 homicides in LA numbered 556; a decade later in 1985 they rose to 777, but dropped significantly in 2000 to 542. Ibid.

67. Since the very beginning, making rap music has always been about "making something out of nothing." Former gangsta rapper Ice-T, now an actor in a popular detective series, has recently released a documentary on rap music to explain the music to a new generation of rap fans who may not know the origins of rap and how it slowly evolved over the decades to form the core of a hip-hop culture that now spans the globe. He describes it as a "nonviolent" "youth movement" that was started in a Bronx housing project. The documentary is appropriately titled *The History of Hip-Hop: Making Something out of Nothing. Chanel4News,* "Ice-T and the History of Hip Hop," July 21, 2012, http://www.channel4.com/news/ice-t-and-the-history-of-hip-hop .

68. A highly successful venture capital investor in Silicon Valley, Ben Horowitz has used rap lyrics as instructional tools in his classes, and on one occasion, faced with the stress of an auditing mishap that jeopardized a billion-dollar sale, he gleaned guidance from the lyrics of "Stranger" by popular rap artist Kanye West. See Claire Cain Miller, "Using Rap to Teach Pithy Lessons in Business," *New York Times,* February 19, 2012, http://www.nytimes.com/2012/02/20/technology/blogger-uses-rap-to-teach-pithy-business-lessons.html?pagewanted=all.

69. See Sunny Bindra, "What Google Can Teach Us about Leadership Skills," *Sunwords.com,* May 30, 2011, citing Adam Bryant of the *New York Times*, March 12, 2011, http://www.sunwords.com/2011/05/30/what-google-can-teach-us-about-leadership-skills/.

70. See Adam Bryant's interview of Carol Smith, etc., "No Doubts; Women Are Better Managers," *New York Times*, July 25, 2009, http://www.nytimes.com/2009/07/26/business/26corner.html?pagewanted=all.

71. See Sunny Bindra, note 74 *supra*.

72. See Richard Florida, *The Rise of the Creative Class* (Basic Books, 2002), pp. 223–34.

73. See Fred Smith and Sarah Allen, "Urban Decline (and Success) in the United States," *EH.net*, February 5, 2010, http://eh.net/encyclopedia?article/Smith.Urban-Decline.

74. See note 77 *supra*, at pp. 215–48, or chapters 12 and 13, and 14.

75. See "The World's Oldest Companies—The Business of Survival," *The Economist*, December 16, 2004, http://www.economist.com/node/3490684.

76. Quoting obituarily from the writings of the late Gore Vidal. See Hillel Italie, "The Great, Entitled Gore Vidal," *Columbia Daily Tribune*, August 5, 2012, http://www.columbiatribune.com/news/2012/aug/05/the-great-entitled-gore-vidal/.

77. Ibid. (emphasis added).

78. See Sabir Shah, "China Serves as Classic Example of Effective Gun Control Laws," *News-International*, August 8, 2011, http://www.thenews.com.pk/Todays-News-2-61678-China-serves-as-a-classic-example-of-effective-gun-control-laws.

79. The Wikipedia gun ownership roster lists 178 countries by per capita rates of gun ownership, that is, the number of privately owned small firearms divided by the number of

residents. See *Wikipedia*, s.v. "Number of guns per capita by country," http://en.wikipedia.org/wiki/Number_of_guns_per_capita_by_country.

80. Japan ranks a lowly 164th with only .6 guns per 100 residents; Malaysia ranks 133rd with 1.5 guns per 100 residents; Vietnam ranks 128th with 1.7; China ranks 102nd with 4.9; Philippines ranks 105th with 4.7; Singapore ranks 169th with .5; Indonesia ranks 169th at .5; South Korea ranks 149th at 1.1; Cambodia ranks 109th at 4.3; and Laos ranks 145th at 1.2.

81. The rankings of the various countries differ slightly, but their "average" standing is used throughout the discussion only to facilitate and simplify references to their respective places on the Wikipedia gun ownership list.

82. The twenty hottest growing economies in the world, listed in ascending order, along with their total estimated growth rates, are Niger (13.3%), Bangladesh (13.3%), Cambodia (13.5%), Uzbekistan (13.6%), Kazakhstan (13.7%), Tanzania (13.9%), Ghana (14%), Democratic Republic of the Congo (14%), Nigeria (14.3%), India (14.5%), Haiti (14.5%), Angola (14.7%), Uganda (14.8%), Ethiopia (15.2%), Rwanda (15.5%), Mozambique (15.6%), Laos (15.6%), China (17.7%), and Sierra Leone (19.5%), and the absolute hottest economy is that of Iraq (25.4%). See "Hottest Growing Economies in the World," *SiliconIndia News*, July 26, 2012, http://www.siliconindia.com/news/business/Hottest-Growing-Economies-in-the-World-nid-124610-cid-3.htm.

83. With two exceptions, the twenty "Hottest Growing Economies in the World" also ranked near the bottom of the list of gun countries. Niger was 160th, Bangladesh was 169th, Cambodia was 109th, Uzbekistan was 133rd, Tanzania was 137th, Ghana was very low at 174th, the Democratic Republic of the Congo was 137th, Nigeria was 133rd, India was 110th, Haiti was 164th, Uganda was 137th, Ethiopia was 174th, Rwanda was 164th, Mozambique was 99th, Laos was 145th, China was 102nd, and Sierra Leone was 164th. The two exceptions to this trend are Angola, whose economy is the 9th hottest while it's also a relatively high 34th on the Wikipedia gun ownership list; and Iraq, the most glaring exception, which is near the top of the Wikipedia gun ownership list at 7th, yet is also the absolute "hottest" economy with a sizzling 25.4% estimated growth rate.

84. This list, released by the World Bank, lists the hottest twenty-nine economies and their projected growth rates over the next two years, based on the World Bank's 2013 and 2014 growth estimates. See Matthew Boesler, "Presenting: The Hottest Economies In the World," *BusinessInsider*, June 20, 2012, http://www.businessinsider.com/29-of-the-worlds-fastest-growing-countries-2012-6?op=1.

85. The twenty-five countries, along with their projected growth rates over the next two years, are as follows: Botswana (12.1%), Republic of Congo (12.3%), Tajikistan (12.3%), Guinea (12.9%), Cape Verde (13%), Vietnam (13.2%), Indonesia (13.2%), Niger (13.3%), Bangladesh (13.3%), Cambodia (13.5%), Uzbekistan (13.6%), Kazakhstan (13.7%), Tanzania (13.9%), Ghana (14%), Democratic Republic of Congo (14%), Nigeria (14.3%), India (14.5%), Haiti (14.5%), Uganda (14.8%), Ethiopia (15.2%), Rwanda (15.5%), Mozambique (15.6%), Laos (15.6%), China (17.7%), and Sierra Leone (19.5%). The four countries that ranked high on the Wikipedia gun list but also had very high projected growth rates are Panama (12.6%), Zambia (12.9%), Angola (14.7%), and of course Iraq with the highest projected growth rate of 25.4%. Ibid.

86. Based on this ranking, the ten fastest-growing economies in the world over the next forty years (along with their annual growth rates) are Egypt (6.4%), Sri Lanka (6.6%), Indonesia (6.8%), Mongolia (6.9%), the Philippines (7.3%), Vietnam (7.5%), Bangladesh (7.5%), Iraq (7.7%), India (8.0%), and the country with the highest annual growth rate, Nigeria (8.5%). All but Iraq rank near the bottom of the Wikipedia gun ownership list of 178 countries. On that list, of course, America is 1st, and Tunisia is last at 178th. How do these countries with the world's fastest-growing economies place on the Wikipedia gun ownership list? Egypt is 115th, Sri Lanka is 133rd, Indonesia is 169th, Mongolia is 126th, the Philippines is 105th, Vietnam is 128th, Bangladesh is 169th, India is 110th, and Nigeria is 133rd. Iraq is the only anomaly, as its economy is among the ten fastest growing and it's also near the top of the Wikipedia gun ownership list, at 7th. See Christine Jenkins, "The 10 Fastest Growing Economies of the Next 40 Years," *Business Insider*, March 1, 2011, http://www.businessinsider.com.

87. Ibid.

88. Every weapon is also meticulously registered, however, and their transfer and sale are strictly regulated. This explains why, despite the widespread ownership and possession of assault weapons required by law, there's virtually no Swiss crime.

89. This is a slight embellishment of the observation made in Carol Reed's noir classic, *The Third Man* (1949), in which the Harry Lime character (played by Orson Welles) memorably quips at the end of the tense Ferris wheel scene that in "Italy for 30 years under the Borgias they had warfare, terror, murder, and bloodshed, but they produced Michelangelo, Leonardo da Vinci, and the Renaissance. In Switzerland they had brotherly love—they had 500 years of democracy and peace, and what did that produce? The cuckoo clock."

90. See "The Chinese Restaurant as Ghetto Indicator?" *The Click Heard Around the World*, September 28, 2010, http://www.rikomatic.com/blog/2010/09/the-chinese-restaurant-as-a-ghetto-indicator.html.

91. See Jennifer 8. Lee, *The Fortune Cookie Chronicles—Adventures in the World of Chinese Food* (Grand Central Publishing, 2009). In this work, Lee, a *New York Times* journalist, traces the history of the origins and popularity of Chinese food in America. She also exposes the indentured servitude Chinese restaurant owners expect from illegal immigrant chefs, many of whom are exploited for as long as it takes them to earn enough money to return home. And home is usually the province of Fujian in southern coastal China, "the single largest exporter of Chinese restaurant workers in the world today," and in which a fishing village has sent three-quarters of its population to work in US restaurants, and a school actually teaches youngsters how to speak "restaurant English" before their trip to America. Also see Peter Kwong, *Forbidden Workers—Illegal Chinese Immigrants and American Labor* (New Press, 1997), pp. 1–4.

92. Any doubt in this regard may be dispelled by a simple experiment: walk into any such eating establishment at dinnertime and order any dish that takes longer than ten minutes. During those ten minutes, stand aside and silently count the number of customers and transactions, then "guesstimate" how much cash goes across the counter with each purchase times six to equal one hour. Next, multiply the amount of cash received in that one hour by the number of hours the restaurant stays open every day (usually between ten and fifteen hours a day); next, multiply that amount by 364 days a year (Chinese restaurants don't typically observe Kwanzaa, Ramadan, Martin Luther King Day, Chanukah, Rosh Hashanah, or Yom Kippur, and they're usually open even on Christmas Day and New Year's Eve). Finally, factor in the likelihood that the business overhead is minimal (as they usually own the building and reside above, below, or at the rear of the restaurant), and all the employees are either members of the same family or distant cousins or other relatives who are being exploited and grossly underpaid. Only then may the casual observer begin to fathom how even the tiniest, hole-in-the-wall restaurant may easily gross a half-million dollars a year—all cash.

93. Another factor that may explain why so many of these small, loosely organized restaurants effectively resist greater organizational concentration is the current state of employment law in this area. As the nature of many Chinese restaurants may require that they not hire non-Asians (or hire only Asians), this form of racial discrimination would likely withstand a challenge under civil rights laws that prohibit racial discrimination. The defense would rest on the grounds that the discrimination preserves the ethnic character or desired "atmosphere" of the eating environment, and that the discrimination, far from constituting an act of racial discrimination, is instead a bona fide occupational qualification (a BFOQ) in furtherance of a legitimate business goal. See, e.g., *Ferrill v. the Parker Group, Inc.* 168 F.3d 468 (11th Cir. 1999). (Although the court ruled the facts sufficient to establish a case of racial discrimination, the opinion's discussion of the BFOQ defense is instructive.) Also see William R. Bryant, "Note: Justifiable Discrimination: The Need for a Statutory Bona Fide Occupational Qualification BFOQ Defense for Race Discrimination," 33 *Ga. L. Rev.* 211 (1998).

94. *Asian American Nation*, "Asian American Men: Stereotypes and Reality," 2011–2012, http://www.asianamericannation.com/asian-american-men.htm.

95. See Peter Kwong, note 91 *supra*.

96. Cynthia Estlund, *Working Together: How Workplace Bonds Strengthen a Diverse Democracy* (Oxford University Press, 2004), p. 13.

Selected Bibliography

BOOKS

Adriansen, David. *Workplace Violence Prevention Training*. VDM Verlag, 2008.

Amato, Joseph. *When Father and Son Conspire: A Minnesota Farm Murder*. Iowa State University Press, 1988.

Ames, Mark. *Going Postal—Rage, Murder, and Rebellion, from Reagan's Workplaces to Clinton's Columbine and Beyond*. Soft Skull, 2005.

Baron, S. Anthony. *Violence in the Workplace—A Prevention and Management Guide for Businesses*. Pathfinder, 1993.

Barry, Bruce. *Speechless—The Erosion of Free Expression in the American Workplace*. Berrett-Koehler, 2007.

Bowe, Marisa, ed. *Gig: Americans Talk About Their Jobs*. Crown Publishing Group, 2001.

Braverman, Mark. *Preventing Workplace Violence: A Guide for Employers and Practitioners*. Sage Pubs, 1998.

Brown, Bruce. *The Lone Tree Tragedy: A True Story of Murder in America's Heartland*. Crown Publishers, 1989.

Byron, Christopher. *Testosterone, Inc.—Tales of CEOs Gone Wild*. John Wiley and Sons, Inc., 2004.

Capozzoli, Thomas K., et al. *Managing Violence in the Workplace*. CRC Press, 1996.

Coleman, Loren. *The Copycat Effect: How the Media and Popular Culture Trigger the Mayhem in Tomorrow's Headlines*. Simon and Schuster, 2004.

Doonan, Brent C. *Murder at the Office*. New Horizon, 2006.

Downs, Alan. *Corporate Executions—The Ugly Truth About Layoffs, etc*. Amacon, 1995.

Estlund, Cynthia. *Working Together: How Workplace Bonds Strengthen a Diverse Democracy*. Oxford University Press, 2004.

Evans, Thomas. *The Education of Ronald Reagan: The General Electric Years and the Untold Story of His Conversion to Conservatism*. Columbia University Press, 2008.

Farb, Daniel, et al. *Workplace Violence Guidebook*. University of Health Care, 2005.

Fishman, Charles. *The Wal-Mart Effect*. Penguin, 2006.

Florida, Richard. *The Rise of the Creative Class*. Basic Books, 2002.

Fraser, Jill Andresky. *White-Collar Sweatshop—The Deterioration of Work and Its Rewards in Corporate America*. W. W. Norton and Co., 2001.

Garson, Barbara. *The Electronic Workshop*. Penguin Books, 1989.

Gill, Martin L. *Violence at Work*. Willan Publishing, 2001.

Goleman, Daniel. *Emotional Intelligence—Why It Can Matter More than IQ.* Bantam Books, 1995.

Grossman, Dave. *On Killing: The Psychological Cost of Learning to Kill in War and Society.* Little, Brown, Co., 1995.

Heckscher, Charles. *White-Collar Blues—Management Loyalties in an Age of Corporate Restructuring.* Basic Books, 1995.

Hill, Herbert. *Black Labor and the American Legal System.* University of Wisconsin Press, 1977.

Hochschild, Arlie. *The Time Bind.* McMillan Press, 1997.

Kelleher, Michael, D. *New Arenas for Violence—Homicide in the American Workplace.* Praeger, 1996.

———. *Profiling the Lethal Employee: Case Studies of Violence in the Workplace.* Praeger, 1997.

Kelloway, E. Kevin, ed. *The Handbook of Workplace Violence.* Sage, 2006.

Kerr, Kim. *Workplace Violence: Planning for Prevention and Response.* Elsevier Science, 2010.

Kwong, Peter. *Forbidden Workers— Illegal Chinese Immigrants and American Labor.* New Press, 1997.

Lasseter, Don. *Going Postal.* Kensington Publishers, 1997.

Lee, Jennifer 8. *The Fortune Cookie Chronicles—Adventures in the World of Chinese Food.* Grand Central Publishing, 2009.

Letts, Elizabeth. *Eighty Dollar Champion: Snowman, the Horse that Inspired a Nation.* Random House, 2011.

Lewis, Gerald, et al. *Violence in the Workplace: Myth and Reality.* Taylor and Francis, 1998.

Levine, Daniel. *Disgruntled—The Darker Side of the World of Work.* Berkley Press, 1998.

Liebert, John, and William J. Birnes. *Suicidal Mass Murderers.* CRC Press, 2011.

Lies, Mark. *Preventing and Managing Workplace Violence: Legal and Strategic Guidelines.* American Bar Association, 2008.

London, Sondra. *Guns and Day Trading.* Hyperion Press, 2005.

Love, John F. *McDonald's—Behind the Arches.* Bantam Books, 1996.

Mack, Stephanie Madoff. *The End of Normal.* Blue Rider Press, 2011.

Martin, Christopher R. *Framed: Labor and the Corporate Media.* ILR Press, 2004.

McElhaney, Marc. *Aggression in the Workplace.* AuthorHouse, 2004.

Menninger, Karl A. *Man against Himself.* Harcourt, Brace and World, Inc., 1938.

Newfield, Jack. *Only in America—The Life and Crimes of Don King.* William Morrow and Co., 1995.

O'Boyle, Thomas. *At Any Cost—Jack Welch, General Electric, and the Pursuit of Profit.* Random House, 1999.

Paludi, Michele A., et al. *Understanding Workplace Violence—A Guide for Managers and Employees.* Praeger, 2006.

Peter, Laurance J., et al. *The Peter Principle—Why Things Always Go Wrong.* Buccaneer Books, 1993.

Renekly, Richard G. *Human Resources.* Barrons, 1997.

Richardson, James. *Willie Brown—A Biography.* University of California Press, 1996.

Rosten, Leo. *The Joys of Yiddish.* McGraw-Hill, 1968.

Rubio, Philip. *There's Always Work at the Post Office: African American Postal Workers and the Fight for Jobs, Justice, and Equality.* University of North Carolina Press, 2010.

Rybczynski, Witold. *Waiting for the Weekend.* Viking, 1991.

Salcido, Carmine. *Not Lost Forever—My Story of Survival.* HarperCollins, 2009.

Schell, Bernadette H., and Nellie Lanteigne. *Stalking, Harassment, and Murder in the Workplace.* Quorum Books, 2000.

Schor, Juliet B. *The Overworked American—The Unexpected Decline of Leisure.* Basic Books, 1993.

Secrest, Meryle. *Frank Lloyd Wright: A Biography.* Knopf, 1992.

Sennett, Richard. *The Corrosion of Character—The Personal Consequences of Work in the New Capitalism.* W. W. Norton and Co., Inc, 1998.

Shilts, Randy. *The Mayor of Castro Street—The Life and Times of Harvey Milk*. Saint Martin's Press, 1988.
Southerland, Mittie D. *Workplace Violence: A Continuum from Death to Threat*. Anderson Pub. Co., 1997.
Strasberg, Lee. *A Dream of Passion—The Development of the Method*. Little/Brown, 1987.
Styron, William. *The Confessions of Nat Turner*. Random House, 1967.
Terkel, Studs. *Working—People Talk about What They Do All Day and How They Feel about What They Do*. New Press, 1997.
Thaler, Linda Kaplan, et al. *The Power of Nice: How to Conquer the Business World With Kindness*. Crown Publishers, 2006.
Wilkinson, Carol. *Violence in the Workplace*. Government Institutes, 1998.
Wolf, Michael J. *The Entertainment Economy*. Times Books, 1999.
Wurtzel, Elizabeth. *Bitch—In Praise of Difficult Woman*. Doubleday, 1998.

ARTICLES

Albrecht, Steve. "My Interview of a Double Workplace Murderer." *Psychology Today*, February 21, 2012.
Armour, Stephanie. "Inside the Minds of Workplace Killers." *USA Today*, July 14, 2004.
Barling, Julian. "Understanding Supervisor-Targeted Aggression." *Journal of Applied Psychology* 90, November 2005.
Brown, Ronald. "The Politics of Mo' Money, and the Strange Dialectic of Hip Hop." Review of *The Hip Hop Generation and the Crisis in African American Culture* by Bakari Kitwana. *Vanderbilt Journal of Entertainment Law and Practice* 5 (2003), 59–72. Diamond, Michael, A. "Administrative Assault: A Contemporary Psychoanalytic View of Violence and Aggression in the Workplace." Paper presented at the 14th annual meeting of the International Society for the Study of Organizations as part of ISPSO Library in Philadelphia, Pennsylvania, June 15, 1997.
France, Michael, et al. "Office Violence: After the Shooting Stops." *Businessweek*, March 12, 2001.
Pfeffer, Jeffrey. "Lay off the Layoffs." *Newsweek*, February 13, 2012.
Turse, Nick. "Economic Fallout Has Spurred an Epidemic of Murder and Suicide that Has Gone Largely Unnoticed." *AlterNet*, June 5, 2009.
Weissberg, Robert. "Deciphering the Occupy Wall Street Movement," *American Thinker*, May 3, 2012.
Wong, Alex. "The Asian Suicide Phenomenon." *Hardboiled*, April 30, 2012.

Index

abuse: childhood, 265n9; employee, 11–12, 65, 170, 171, 282n49
African Americans. *See* blacks
aftermath control, 218–221
Agrawal, Sid, 187, 188
akathisia, 163
Alaska gun ownership, 291n21
Albrecht, Steve, 3, 273n53
Alexander, Stuart ("Sausage King"), 75, 104, 271n17
Alito, Samuel A., 153
All-Tech Investment Group, 203–205
Amato, Joseph, 6
Amayo, Mario, 74
American Civil Liberties Union, 180
ancestry and country of origin, religious harassment and, 190–191
Andresky Fraser, Jill, 16
antidepressants, 182
Antilak, Ladislav, 41, 93, 142
Arizona shopping mall shooting, 1–2
Arming America—The Origins of a National Gun Culture (Bellesiles), 225–226
Asian Americans: desexualization of male, 238; education and status of, 126; female perpetrators, 98, 127; as model minority, 238; myth about, 125–127; as perpetrators, 126–127, 216–217; racial factor and, 96–98; suicide among, 133; as victims, 97–98, 126; workplace

murder statistics on, 97, 127
Asian suicides, 125–126, 139, 278n3, 185
assassination, boardroom, 188, 285n42
AT&T, 190–191
Aziz, Khalid, 130

Baker, Debra, 45
Baker, William, 38, 159
Bambaataa, Afrika, 231
Barling, Julian, 65, 170, 171
Barnes, Ron, 154
barricades, how to handle, 202
Barton, Mark, 72, 91, 94, 267n27, 150, 172
Bashir, Susan, 190–191
Bath massacre, 42, 82–83, 150, 186
Baxter, Clifford, 105, 106, 153
Beck, Matthew, 142, 278n14
Beckwith, Holmes, 9, 253n19
Benitez, Ruben Orlando, 104, 109
Big Trouble (Lukas), 23
billionaire CEOs, 188
Bishop, Amy, 9, 33–35, 40, 87; academic achievements, 34; arrest and charges, 56; disclosures on past of, 56–57, 58; as disliked, 172; EEOC filing by, 64; faculty review of, 261n32; handgun acquisition, 57; hiring of, 51, 55, 58; intensity and focus, 77; letter-bomb probe, 57; racial factor, 58, 98; resume of, 55; San Marco and, 67; students and colleagues on, 63; tenure denied, 34,

301

About the Author

Ronald D. Brown was born and raised in Newark, New Jersey, and graduated from Arts High School. After living and studying in Italy, France, and Libya, he received a BA in political science from Rutgers College in 1973 and earned a JD from Rutgers University School of Law in 1976. After a clerkship for Justice Mark A. Sullivan of the New Jersey Supreme Court, he served four years as an assistant U.S. attorney with the U.S. Department of Justice. After his tenure as a federal prosecutor, he spent the next decade in private law practice in Newark, during which he settled a $1 million medical malpractice suit, successfully argued a precedent-setting corporate case before the state's highest court, and tried more than one hundred criminal jury trials, including a dozen homicides. He studied labor law and alternative dispute resolution at New York University Law School and also studied labor and employment law at Columbia Law School, from which he earned an LLM in 2004. He has taught criminal law and lectured extensively on issues of criminal law and labor and employment law. He has served as a labor law advisor to the U.S. army and as a labor and employee specialist for the U.S. Department of Agriculture in Washington, D.C. His previously published scholarship includes "Book Review: *Only One Place of Redress: African Americans, Labor Unions, and the Courts from Reconstruction to the New Deal*," *Journal of Labor Research* 24, no. 1 (Winter 2003) and "The Politics of Mo' Money, Mo' Money, and the Strange Dialectic of Hip Hop," review/ essay/comment on *The Hip Hop Generation—Young Blacks and the Crisis in African American Culture* by Bakari Kitwana, *Vanderbilt Journal of Entertainment Law and Practice* 5 (2003), 59–72. He currently commutes between New York City and Washington, D.C.